THE CONTEMPORARY
ATLAS
OF
CHINA

THE CONTEMPORARY
ATLAS
OF
CHINA

EDITORIAL BOARD

PROFESSOR NATHAN SIVIN
FRANCES WOOD
PENNY BROOKE
COLIN RONAN

COLLINS
PUBLISHERS
AUSTRALIA

A Marshall Edition
Conceived, edited and designed by
Marshall Editions Ltd.
170 Piccadilly,
London W1V 9DD

Copyright © 1988 by Marshall Editions Limited

COLLINS PUBLISHERS AUSTRALIA

First published in Australasia in 1989 by
William Collins Pty Ltd,
55 Clarence Street, Sydney NSW 2000

National Library of Australia
Cataloguing-in-Publication data:

The Contemporary atlas of China.

Includes indexes.
ISBN 0 7322 0053 9.

1. China – Maps. I. Sivin, Nathan. II. Wood, Frances. III. Ronan, Colin A. (Colin Alistair), 1920–

912' . 51

Maps pages 12–35
Copyright © Cartographic Publishing House, China and Esselte Map Service AB, Sweden

EDITOR **Jinny Johnson**
TEXT EDITOR **Anne Kilborn**
AMERICAN EDITOR **Liz Duvall**
ASSISTANT EDITOR **Shelley Turner**
MANAGING EDITOR **Ruth Binney**

ART DIRECTOR **John Bigg**
ART EDITOR **Peter Bridgewater**
DESIGNER **Linda Henley**
PICTURE EDITOR **Zilda Tandy**
PRODUCTION **Barry Baker**
Janice Storr

ARTWORK **Jane Lanaway**

Typeset by Servis Filmsetting Limited, Manchester, UK

Originated by Reprocolor Llovet SA, Barcelona, Spain

Printed and bound in Belgium by Usines Brepols SA

1 2 3 4 5 93 92 91 90 89

CONTENTS

A SENSE
OF PLACE IN A LAND
OF CHANGE

It is only natural for people who have lived their lives in one community to find others strange. Few in our society ever work with, or even encounter, people from China, and we are used to thinking of that country as distant, bursting with people and, above all, exotic.

Stereotypes are an obvious recourse for thinking about what one does not know. I was told as I was growing up that Chinese are evasive and inscrutable—propositions that since I knew none, I could not test. Years later, reading reports by Chinese diplomats of the 1840s, I found them assuring their superiors in Beijing that foreigners are unpredictable in their judgments, and that one can never tell by their faces what they are thinking and feeling. This suggested to me that the label of exoticism, like other stereotypes, is more revealing about our fantasies than about the people we attach it to.

As over the past decades I have been able to live and work among Chinese and other Asians, I find most of them, like people everywhere else, striving to find or maintain a habitable niche in an uncertain world. Far from being exotic, they seem to cope as sensibly as they can with their obligations and yearnings. Their horizons may be limited by public irrationalities, past and present, but so are ours. Much that seems picturesque to the casual visitor is due to poverty—poverty that limits opportunity, slows change, and keeps people using the old even while they aspire to the new.

Whether China is exotic or not, it is without doubt full of wonders. Gardens of mosses growing out of ancient glazed roof tiles in the old imperial palace; the spreading forest of needle-like limestone pinnacles, ten to fifteen feet tall, rising straight out of the soil at Shilin near Kunming; hundreds of troupes of Tianjin farmers after the harvest performing pantomime opera in full costume on six-foot stilts; a calligrapher in Guilin with a brush in each hand simultaneously writing two columns of characters, each graph as balanced as an abstract painting; archaeological workmen meticulously resurrecting thousands of lifesize clay warriors, each with individual features, from the earth that has covered them for more than two thousand years: these capture the imagination of people who see them daily just as they fascinate travellers who pass by only once.

There may once have been a time when busy people could ignore the wonders, predicaments and tragedies of the rest of the world without obvious detriment to themselves. That is no longer the case. Foreign travel for business and pleasure has become the norm because politics, trade and culture are now thoroughly international. Lobbying over customs tariffs may pit a Japanese corporation that employs thousands of American workers against an American company that fabricates its products abroad. A Cornish potter may draw as deeply on Oriental as on European traditions. Missiles sold by China to earn foreign exchange for modernization may prolong a war in the Arabian Gulf and thus affect elections in Europe. Information about the rest of the world is essential, and understanding may be the best protection against— if the reader will pardon a technical term—mutual assured destruction.

Being informed about one of the most rapidly changing countries in a ceaselessly changing world is not at all easy. This volume, it seems to me, offers an excellent start. It is organized as an atlas, and in that capacity has drawn on the resources of Chinese experts as well as Western cartographers. It is meant to help readers form the sense of place that is essential in thinking about a land nearly as large, and at least as diverse, as all of Europe.

In addition to its maps, which reveal many dimensions not only of topography but of human activity, *The Contemporary Atlas of China* is richly furnished with photographs that convey the look of places, people and artefacts. Much of its space is devoted to essays on every aspect of China, past, present, and even future—the latter not so much to predict as to point out the problems that thoughtful people will want to keep in mind. All these components make this a volume in which readers who have become curious about China are apt to find the information they are hoping for.

NATHAN SIVIN

Professor of Chinese Culture and of the History
of Science, University of Pennsylvania;
Visiting Associate Director of the Needham Research Institute,
Cambridge, England

A CHRONOLOGY OF CHINA

This chronology picks out key events in Chinese history over the centuries. It gives an idea of the relationship between them and when they occurred in comparison with developments in the rest of the world. Most of the major political and dynastic changes have been included, as well as significant cultural developments. But the selected entries represent only a fraction of the possible list of important events in ancient and modern China. Wherever possible, entries have been chosen to tie in with the text of the Atlas, in order to provide a framework in which China's historical development can be more clearly understood.

PREHISTORY	3000 BC	2500 BC	2000 BC	1500 BC	1000 BC	500 BC	0	100 AD

600,000 BC
Lantian Man, the earliest known Palaeolithic human living in China. (Remains found in Shaanxi Province.)

400,000 BC
Peking Man, Palaeolithic cave dweller who uses stone tools and fire, living near present-day Beijing.

?3000 BC
Yangshao or Painted Pottery Neolithic culture, typified by Banpo village in Shaanxi Province.

2737 BC
Shen Nong, traditional "inventor" of Chinese agriculture.

?2000 BC
Longshan Black Pottery culture with settled agriculture, a precursor of the Shang dynasty.

1818 BC
"Xia dynasty", traditionally the first Chinese dynasty. (It has been linked to the Yangshao or Longshan cultures.)

?1480 (or earlier)
Shang dynasty centred on the capital at Anyang in Henan Province. Bronze culture in Yellow River valley produces impressive ritual vessels.

1122 BC
Wu, King of Zhou, defeats last Shang emperor.

c. 479 BC
Death of Confucius.

453–221 BC
Final collapse of Zhou rule as small kingdoms vie for power.

c. 300 BC
First "Great Walls" built by Warring States.

246 BC
Cheng becomes king of Qin state, one of Warring States.

230–221 BC
Qin state gradually overpowers other Warring States.

221 BC
Cheng becomes first emperor of China as Qin Shi Huangdi.

210 BC
Death of first emperor.

206 BC
Qin dynasty overthrown.

202 BC
Liu Bang first emperor of Han under reign name of Gaozu.

200 BC
Chang'an becomes Han capital. (It was on the site of present day Xi'an and was planned as a rectangular grid.)

141 BC
Emperor Wudi ascends throne. Period of Chinese expansion, especially southward.

90 BC
Death of Sima Qian, historian who produced the prototype dynastic history, the *Shi Ji.*

87 BC
Death of Emperor Wudi.

AD 9
Wang Mang interregnum "Xin dynasty", when Wang usurps the Han throne and attempts to introduce reforms.

25
Eastern Han begins under Liu Xiu after Red Eyebrow Rebellion—a peasant revolt against Wang Mang.

65
Buddhism first recorded in China.

79
Five Classics of Confucianism assembled.

82
Han History published official dynastic histor modelled on *Shi Ji.*

100
Chinese translation Buddhist text from India recorded.

17
Confucian classic engraved on stone a a symbol of thei permanence

18
Yellow Turba Rebellion inspired b popular Taoism lead to downfall of Ha dynast

1
Cao Cao in control much of northe China. His family late found the W dynasty, forcing th abdication of the la Han emperc

SHANG DYNASTY (?1480–1122 BC)

ZHOU DYNASTY (1122–221 BC)

WARRING STATES PERIOD (453–221 BC)

QIN DYNASTY (221–206 BC)

SPRING AND AUTUMN PERIOD (772–481 BC)   **HAN DYNASTY 206 BC–220 AD**

REST OF THE WORLD

2 million BC
Early man in Africa, *Homo erectus.*
500,000 BC
Java Man.
100,000 BC
Homo sapiens (Neanderthal Man).

3000–1560 BC
The first pharaohs.
2700 BC
Great Pyramid built.
2500–1500 BC
Indus Valley Civilization.

1600–1200 BC
Mycenaean Civilization in Greece.
1347–1338 BC
Tutenkhamun— Egyptian pharaoh.

1280–1250 BC
Moses and the flight from Egypt.

c. 563–c. 483 BC
Gautama, the Buddha.
428 BC
Birth of Plato, Greek philosopher.
59–44 BC
Julius Caesar, Consul and Dictator of Rome.

c. 36
Crucifixion of Jesus Christ.

117
Roman Empire a its greatest exter

200	300	400	500	600	700	800	900	1000	1100	1200

440
Taoism becomes the official religion of the Northern Wei dynasty.

490
Buddhist caves begun in Yungang and Luoyang.

496
Shaolin monastery founded—later becomes a major centre of Chan (Zen) Buddhism.

585
Great Wall and Grand Canal construction begins.

605
Luoyang rebuilt as the eastern capital of the Sui dynasty.

629
Xuanzang (Tripitaka), a Buddhist monk, travels to India. (His historical journey later fictionalized in *Journey to the West* or *Monkey*.)

630
Tang dynasty extends its power into Central Asia.

684–705
Empress Wu, an autocratic ruler and patron of Buddhism, on the throne.

712
Tang Xuanzong Emperor presides over the golden age of Tang culture and a period of border consolidation against Turkish and Tibetan incursions.

755
Rebellion led by An Lushan rebels devastates northern China and leads to the execution of Yang Guifei, the emperor's favourite concubine.

762
Death of the poet Li Bai (Li Po).

770
Death of the poet Du Fu.

868
First woodblock-printed book.

907
Five Dynasties (North China) and Ten Kingdoms (South China) period. China divided.

1012
Introduction of early ripening rice helps agricultural and commercial expansion.

1038
Xixia (Tangut) dynasty founded in northwestern China by Tibetan tribes.

1040
Printing with movable type begins.

1068
Wang Anshi, a government minister, attempts to revive the Song economy through financial and political reforms.

1084
Comprehensive Mirror for Aid in Government published, a history written by Sima Guang, a conservative opposed to Wang Anshi's reforms.

1115
Jin Empire founded in north by Jurchen nomads from Manchuria.

1126
Khitan nomads from Manchuria and Mongolia capture Song capital of Kaifeng.

1127
"Temporary" capital for Southern Song established in Hangzhou.

1196
Zhu Xi synthesizes and reinterprets Confucian classics. (This "Neo-Confucianism" emphasized the Four Books—*Analects, Mencius, Great Learning, Doctrine of the Mean*—and became the orthodox interpretation of Confucianism.)

1206
Chinggis (Genghis) Khan rises to power in Mongolia.

1215
Chinggis (Genghis) Khan conquers large parts of northern China.

1233
Mongols take Kaifeng, Henan Province.

1260
Khubilai, grandson of Chinggis (Genghis), becomes Great Khan of the Mongol Empire.

1271
Yuan dynasty formally founded.

1275
Marco Polo in China.

SUI DYNASTY (581–618)

NORTHERN AND SOUTHERN DYNASTIES (420–581)

THREE KINGDOMS PERIOD (220–280)

TANG DYNASTY (618–906)

SONG DYNASTY NORTHERN SONG PERIOD (960–1126)

FIVE DYNASTIES AND TEN KINGDOMS PERIOD (907–959)

SOUTHERN SONG PERIOD (1126–1279)

227
Sassanid Empire in Persia.

330
Founding of the Byzantine Empire.

445
End of the Roman Empire. Sack of Rome by the Vandals.

622
Flight of Muhammed and followers from Mecca to Medina.

768–814
Charlemagne—Charles the Great, King of the Franks.

890
Viking invaders control much of northern and central England.

900
Death of King Alfred the Great.

1066
Norman Conquest of England by William the Conqueror.

1215
Magna Carta, Charter of English political and civil liberties, granted by King John.

1250–1533
Inca Empire in Peru.

A CHRONOLOGY OF CHINA/2

| 1300 | 1400 | 1500 | 1600 | 1700 | 1800 | 1820 | 1840 | 1860 | 1880 |

1520
Cannons brought from Portugal used by Ming troops.

1570
Journey to the West (Monkey) published.

1582
Jesuit missionary Matteo Ricci arrives in China. Goes to Beijing in 1601.

1405–33
Maritime expeditions of Zheng He, court eunuch.

1403–35
Ming Great Walls built in defence against Mongols.

1421
Capital moved from Nanjing to Beijing to strengthen Chinese power in the face of the Mongol threat.

c. 1619
Jinpingmei (Golden Lotus), a novel of merchant society, noted for its unusually explicit erotic passages.

1620
The Dutch establish a trading base in Taiwan.

1351
Red Turbans in revolt against Mongols.

1363
Zhu Yuanzhang takes control of rebellion.

1368
Zhu Yuanzhang becomes first Ming emperor.

1644
Rebellion led by Li Zicheng against the Ming dynasty, followed by Manchu invasion of China.

1650
Catholic church established in Beijing.

1662–1722
Kangxi Emperor.

1673
Anti-Qing rebellion by Wu Sangui and others in south and southwest China.

1720
Qing forces impose a ruler on Tibet.

1735–95
Qianlong Emperor.

1745
The Scholars, a novel by Wu Jingzi, published.

1751
Qing forces occupy Tibet and make it a protectorate.

1763
Death of Cao Xueqin, author of *Dream of the Red Chamber*.

1793
Macartney Embassy arrives from Britain to request trade and diplomatic relations.

1795
White Lotus Rebellion in northern China led by Buddhist-influenced secret society attempts to restore Ming dynasty.

1813
Eight Trigrams Rebellion revives White Lotus ideas, imperial court attacked.

1820
Opium being imported by British.

1839
First Opium War between Britain and China over Chinese efforts to stop opium trade.

1842
Treaty of Nanjing ends Opium War; Hong Kong ceded to Britain. Treaty Ports opened.

1850
Taiping Rebellion led by quasi-Christian group establishes independent Heavenly Kingdom of Great Peace in southern China.

1852–68
Nian rebellions in northern China.

1853–55
Small Sword (Triad) uprising in Shanghai region.

1856
Arrow or Second Opium War between Britain and China.

1856–75
Muslim rebellions in northwest and southwest China.

1860
Convention of Beijing after Second Opium War. When signing the Convention the Chinese accept the right of foreign diplomats to reside in the capital.

1860s
Self-strengthening movement attempts to resist foreign encroachment and the collapse of Qing power.

1870
Tianjin Incident—anti-Christian riots and murders.

1875
Empress Dowager Cixi ruling through infant Guangxu Emperor.

1883
Sino-French War lea to loss of Qing contr over Vietnam.

1894–9
Sino-Japanese Wa leads to loss of Qin control over Korea

1899–19
Boxer Rebellic against Qir misgovernment an foreign encroachmer

YUAN DYNASTY (1271–1368)

MING DYNASTY (1368–1644)

QING DYNASTY (1644–1911)

1325–1521
Aztec Empire in Mexico.

1455
Gutenberg Bible, early European example of printing from movable type, published in Germany.

1492
Columbus discovers Bahamas.

1577–80
Voyages of Sir Francis Drake, English admiral and navigator.

1645–60
Oliver Cromwell and the English Revolution.

1775–83
War of American Independence.

1789
French Revolution.

1809
Charles Darwin born.

1818
Karl Marx born.

1861–65
American Civil War.

1899–19
Boer War

900 **1920** **1940** **1960** **1980**

1912
Abdication of Puyi, last Qing emperor.

Yuan Shikai, Qing loyalist, becomes first President after Sun Yat-sen resigns in his favour.

1916
Warlord period begins after death of Yuan Shikai.

1919
May 4th Movement. Student demonstrations against Japanese takeover of German concessions in Shandong Province lead to a radical New Culture Movement.

1921
Chinese Communist Party founded.

1925
Death of Sun Yat-sen.

1926
Northern Expedition led by Chiang Kai-shek to defeat the northern warlords and unify China.

1927
Communist-led risings in Shanghai, Guangzhou (Canton), and elsewhere crushed.

1928
Nanjing government established by Chiang Kai-shek.

1928
Mao Zedong establishes guerrilla base in Jinggangshan, Jiangxi Province.

1931
Jiangxi Soviet, major communist base, established.

1931
Japan invades Manchuria.

1934
Long March begins in Jiangxi Province.

1935
Zunyi Conference on Long March confirms Mao as leader of the Chinese Communist Party.

1936
Xi'an Incident. Chiang Kai-shek kidnapped by officers demanding an anti-Japanese United Front with the Communists.

1937
Japan invades China after the Marco Polo Bridge Incident.

1937–45
War of Resistance against Japan.

1937–47
Yan'an Soviet government established at the end of the Long March.

1938
Chiang Kai-shek moves capital to Chongqing in southwestern China.

1946–49
Civil War between Nationalists and Communists.

1947–52
Land Reform in liberated areas brings about widespread redistribution and the collapse of landlord power in the countryside.

1949
The People's Republic is proclaimed.

1950
People's Liberation Army marches into Tibet.

1953
First Five Year Plan for the national economy.

1953
Agricultural cooperatives started.

1956
Hundred Flowers Movement briefly encourages artistic and political debate.

1957
Anti-Rightist Movement attacks critics of the Communist party who emerged in the Hundred Flowers period.

1958
Great Leap Forward— an attempt to rush industrialization.

1958
People's Communes formed.

1960
USSR withdraws economic support for China—the beginning of a bitter Sino–Soviet dispute.

1962
Sino–Indian War over border dispute.

1966
Cultural Revolution launched by Mao Zedong.

1969
Ninth Communist Party Congress ends most violent phase of Cultural Revolution.

1971
Death of Lin Biao in air crash after failed coup attempt against Mao.

1972
President Nixon's visit to China marks beginning of normalization of diplomatic relations with rest of the world.

1972
People's Republic takes seat in United Nations.

1973
Tenth Congress of Chinese Communist Party. Gang of Four radicals in compromise Central Committee with Deng Xiaoping.

1976
Death of Zhou Enlai and Mao Zedong. Hua Guofeng briefly succeeds Mao as Chairman. Gang of Four arrested.

1977
Deng Xiaoping becomes Deputy Chairman of Chinese Communist Party and Vice-Premier.

1978
Four Modernizations become national policy. Responsibility system in countryside replaces communes.

1986
Visit of HM Queen Elizabeth II to China.

1987
China invades Vietnam.

1987
Zhao Ziyang becomes General Secretary of Communist Chinese Party at 13th Communist Party Congress which decides on political restructuring, reduction in party control and greater economic reform.

1988
The controversial Enterprise Law is passed by the 7th National People's Congress held in March.

1905
Tongmenghui (United League) founded by Sun Yat-sen in Japan.

1911
Republican rising in Wuchang over railway nationalization plans leads to series of anti-Qing riots.

PEOPLE'S REPUBLIC OF CHINA (1949–)

REPUBLIC OF CHINA (1912–1949)

1905
Russian Revolution.

1914–18
First World War.

1917
October Revolution in Russia.

1939
Germany invades Poland.

1939–45
Second World War.

1941
Pearl Harbor.

1945
Hiroshima and Nagasaki A-bombed.

1953
Death of Stalin.

1956
Suez invasion.

1963
President Kennedy assassinated in Dallas.

1979
USSR invades Afghanistan.

1988
The 1987 INF (Intermediate Nuclear Forces) agreement ratified at Reagan/Gorbachev Moscow Summit in May.

THE MAPS OF CHINA

The People's Republic of China—the third largest country in the world after the USSR and Canada—covers a total area of approximately 9.6 million sq km (3.7 million sq mi). It is the world's most populous country; it is estimated that there are 1.08 billion Chinese, nearly a quarter of the population of the world.

China is situated on the eastern part of the continent of Asia. Its territory extends from longitude 73°E in the west to longitude 135°E in the east, a distance of some 5,200 km (3,230 mi). From north to south it spans a distance of 5,500 km (3,400 mi) from latitude 53°N in the north to the Nansha Islands in the South China Sea in the south (latitude 4°N).

Environmental conditions vary considerably over this great land-mass. Climate zones range from cool-temperate in the north to tropical in the south. Topographically it includes vast deserts, the highest plateau and the highest peak on earth. About a third of China is mountainous.

The maps on the following pages show this huge and extraordinarily varied land in detail. The legend here explains the conventions used for denoting features such as boundaries, cities and rivers, and different terrains, such as desert, mountain and grassland.

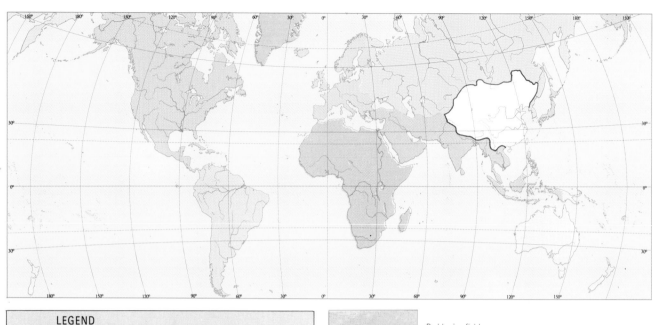

LEGEND

★	Capital	⌐⌐⌐⌐	Great Wall
◎	Capital of Province, Autonomous Region, or Municipality, under the Central Government	▲	Peak
◎	City with Municipal Government	✕	Pass
—	Seat of Autonomous Prefecture / Seat of League or Prefecture	∼∼	Perennial river, Seasonal river
⊙	County seat	—⊢—⊢—	Canal
○	Town or village	◯	Perennial lake
	International boundary / Undefined international boundary		Seasonal lake
—·—·—	Boundary of Province, Autonomous Region, or Municipality, under the Central Government		Reservoir
—··—··—	Boundary of Autonomous Prefecture or League		Flood storage area
— — —	Regional boundary	•	Well or spring
·······	Ceasefire line		Dry watercourse
——————	Railway		Swamp
— —	Highway, track		Forest preserve
— — — —	Shipping route		Coral reefs

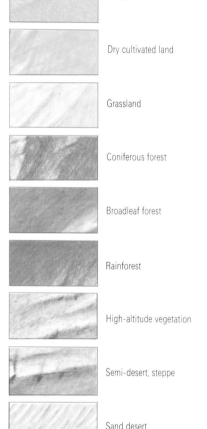

	Paddy rice field
	Dry cultivated land
	Grassland
	Coniferous forest
	Broadleaf forest
	Rainforest
	High-altitude vegetation
	Semi-desert, steppe
	Sand desert
	Rock desert
	Barren mountains and high mountain desert
	Glacier and permanent snow

The key layout (right) shows the way in which the map of China is sectioned over pages 14 to 35. It has been divided according to cartographic conventions and the individual maps do not necessarily correspond to provincial boundaries within China. All the map sections overlap slightly for ease of reference.

China's South Sea territory is shown to a smaller scale than the mainland maps on a separate page.

The national boundaries of China on this map are drawn after the *"Map of the People's Republic of China"*, published by the Cartographic Publishing House, China, in 1980
Equal-area Conical Projection

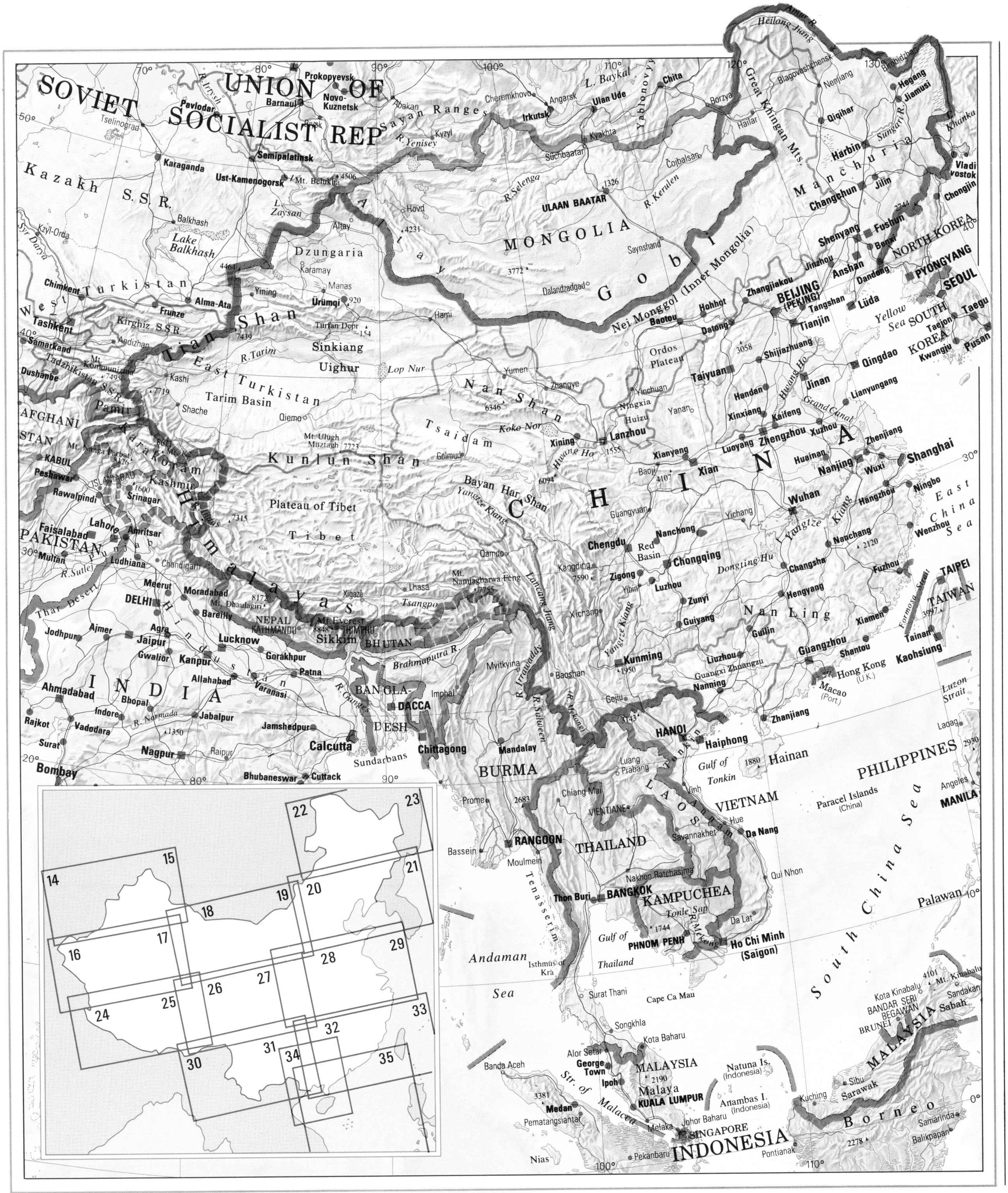

UNION OF
SOVIET
SOCIALIST REP
Kazakh S.S.R.
Kirghiz S.S.R.
Tadzhikistan S.S.R.
West Turkistan
Prokopyevsk
Barnaul
Novo-Kuznetsk
Pavlodar
Tselinograd
Semipalatinsk
Karaganda
Ust-Kamenogorsk
Mt. Belukha
4506
Balkhash
Lake Balkhash
L. Zaysan
Kzyl-Orda
Syr Darya
Chimkent
Tashkent
Samarkand
Dushanbe
Frunze
Alma-Ata
Andizhan
Mt. Kommunizma
7495
Sayan Ranges
R. Yenisey
Abakan
Biysk
Kyzyl
Cheremkhovo
Irkutsk
Angarsk
L. Baykal
Ulan Ude
Chita
Yablonovyy
Kyakhta
Sühbaatar
Čojbalsan
Borzya
Hailar
Heilong Jiang
Amur R.
Great Khingan Mts.
Blagoveshchensk
Nenjiang
Qiqihar
Harbin
Hegang
Jiamusi
Birobidzhan
Sungari R.
Khanka
Vladivostok
Manchuria
Changchun
Jilin
Chongjin
2744
Shenyang
Fushun
Benxi
Anshan
Dandong
Jinzhou
NORTH KOREA
PYONGYANG
SEOUL
SOUTH KOREA
Taegu
Pusan
Kwangju
Yellow Sea
MONGOLIA
ULAAN BAATAR
1326
R. Selenga
R. Kerulen
Saynshand
Dalandzadgad
3772
Gobi
Hovd
4231
Altay
Altay
Dzungaria
Karamay
Manas
Ürümqi
920
Yining
4464
Turkistan
Tian Shan
7439
Turfan Depr.
154
Hami
Sinkiang
Uighur
Lop Nur
R. Tarim
East Turkistan
Kashi
7719
Tarim Basin
Shache
Qiemo
Pamir
AFGHANISTAN
KABUL
Peshawar
Mt. Nanga Parbat
8126
ISLAMABAD
Rawalpindi
Karakoram
8611
Kashmir
Srinagar
1600
Lahore
Amritsar
Faisalabad
PAKISTAN
Multan
Punjab
R. Sutlej
Thar Desert
Ludhiana
Chandigarh
Meerut
DELHI
Moradabad
Bareilly
Jodhpur
Ajmer
Jaipur
Agra
Gwalior
Kanpur
Lucknow
Gorakhpur
Allahabad
Varanasi
Patna
Ahmadabad
INDIA
Indore
Bhopal
R. Narmada
Jabalpur
1350
Rajkot
Vadodara
Surat
Nagpur
Raipur
Jamshedpur
Calcutta
Bombay
Bhubaneswar
Cuttack
Hindustan
R. Indus
7315
Himalayas
Mt. Dhaulagiri
8172
NEPAL
KATHMANDU
Mt. Everest
8848
THIMPHU
Sikkim
BHUTAN
Brahmaputra R.
R. Ganges
BANGLADESH
DACCA
Chittagong
Sundarbans
Imphal
Kunlun Shan
Mt. Ulugh Muztagh 7723
Plateau of Tibet
Tibet
Tsaidam
Golmud
Nan Shan
6346
Koko Nor
Yumen
Zhangye
Xining
Lanzhou
1555
Huang He
Ningxia Huizu
Yinchuan
Ordos Plateau
Bayan Har Shan
6094
Yangtze Kiang
Qamdo
Xigazê
Lhasa
Tsangpo
Mt. Namjagbarwa Feng
7755
Lancang Jiang
Nei Monggol (Inner Mongolia)
Baotou
Hohhot
Datong
Zhangjiakou
BEIJING (PEKING)
Tangshan
Tianjin
Lüda
Qingdao
3058
Shijiazhuang
Taiyuan
Yanan
Handan
Jinan
Lianyungang
Xinxiang
Kaifeng
Grand Canal
Luoyang
Zhengzhou
Xuzhou
Xianyang
Xian
Baoji
4107
Huainan
Nanjing
Zhenjiang
Wuxi
Shanghai
CHINA
Guangyuan
Wuhan
Hangzhou
Ningbo
East China Sea
Yichang
Nanchong
Chengdu
Red Basin
Chongqing
Nanchang
2120
Wenzhou
Kangding
7590
Zigong
Yibin
Luzhou
Dongting Hu
Changsha
Fuzhou
TAIPEI
TAIWAN
3997
Formosa Strait
Zunyi
Hengyang
Xiamen
Xichang
Guiyang
Nan Ling
Guilin
Tainan
Kaohsiung
Kunming
1950
Liuzhou
Guangzhou
Shantou
Hong Kong (U.K.)
Macao (Port.)
Guangxi Zhuangzu
Nanning
Zhanjiang
Baoshan
Myitkyina
R. Irrawaddy
R. Salween
R. Mekong
Gejiu
3143
HANOI
Haiphong
Gulf of Tonkin
1880
Hainan
BURMA
Mandalay
Prome
2683
Bassein
RANGOON
Moulmein
Tenasserim
Luang Prabang
Chiang Mai
VIENTIANE
LAOS
Annam
Vinh
Hue
VIETNAM
Da Nang
Savannakhet
THAILAND
Nakhon Ratchasima
Qui Nhon
Thon Buri
BANGKOK
KAMPUCHEA
Tonle Sap
1744
PHNOM PENH
Da Lat
Ho Chi Minh (Saigon)
Gulf of Thailand
Andaman Sea
Isthmus of Kra
Surat Thani
Cape Ca Mau
Songkhla
Kota Baharu
Alor Setar
George Town
Ipoh
MALAYSIA
Malaya
2190
KUALA LUMPUR
Banda Aceh
3381
Medan
Pematangsiantar
Str. of Malacca
Melaka
Johor Baharu
SINGAPORE
Natuna Is. (Indonesia)
Anambas I. (Indonesia)
Nias
Pekanbaru
INDONESIA
Pontianak
Kuching
Sarawak
Sibu
Borneo
MALAYSIA
Sabah
BRUNEI
BANDAR SERI BEGAWAN
Kota Kinabalu
Mt. Kinabalu
4101
Sandakan
Samarinda
Balikpapan
2278
South China Sea
Paracel Islands (China)
PHILIPPINES
Luzon Strait
Laoag
2930
Angeles
MANILA
Palawan
50°
40°
30°
20°
10°
0°
70°
80°
90°
100°
110°
120°
130°
22
23
15
14
21
19
20
18
17
16
29
28
27
26
25
24
33
32
31
34
35
30

Scale 比例尺 1:25 000 000

KILOMETERS 0 500 1000
STATUTE MILES 0 200 400 600

NORTHERN XINJIANG

Most of this area is taken up by the vast Junggar Pendi (Basin) on the northwestern periphery of China. The basin is virtually surrounded by mountain ranges; the Altay range, to the northeast, forms the frontier between the Mongolian People's Republic and China.

While rainfall is sufficient to maintain some forest on the lower mountain slopes, most of the low-lying land is at best only capable of providing grazing. The region is sparsely inhabited and most people are dependent on animal herding for their livelihood.

There is some agricultural land around the Xinjiang capital of Urumqi, where rivers flowing north from the Tian Shan range provide some irrigation.

Scale 比例尺 1:4 000 000

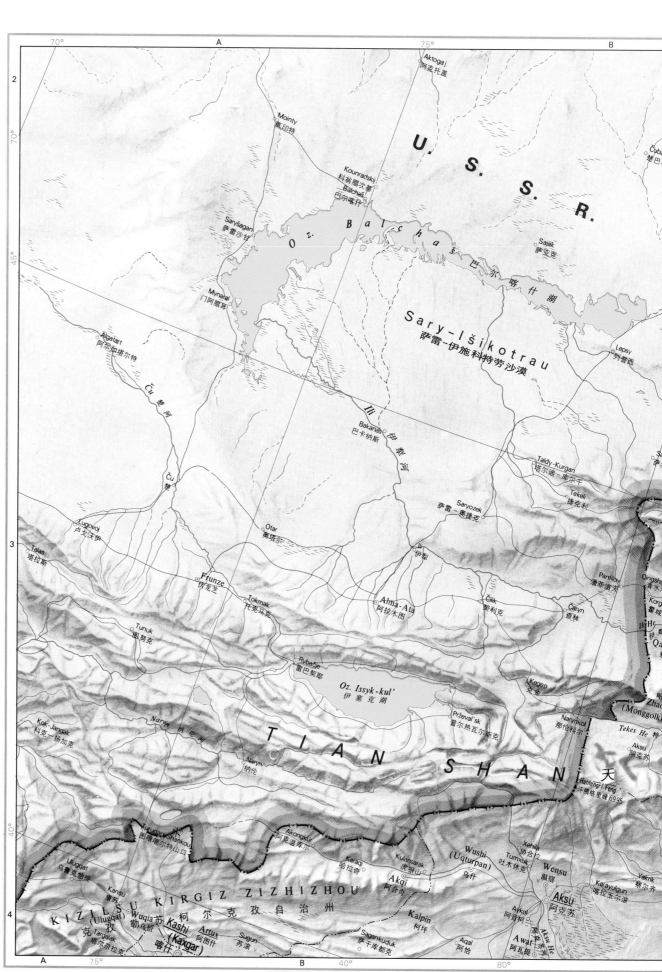

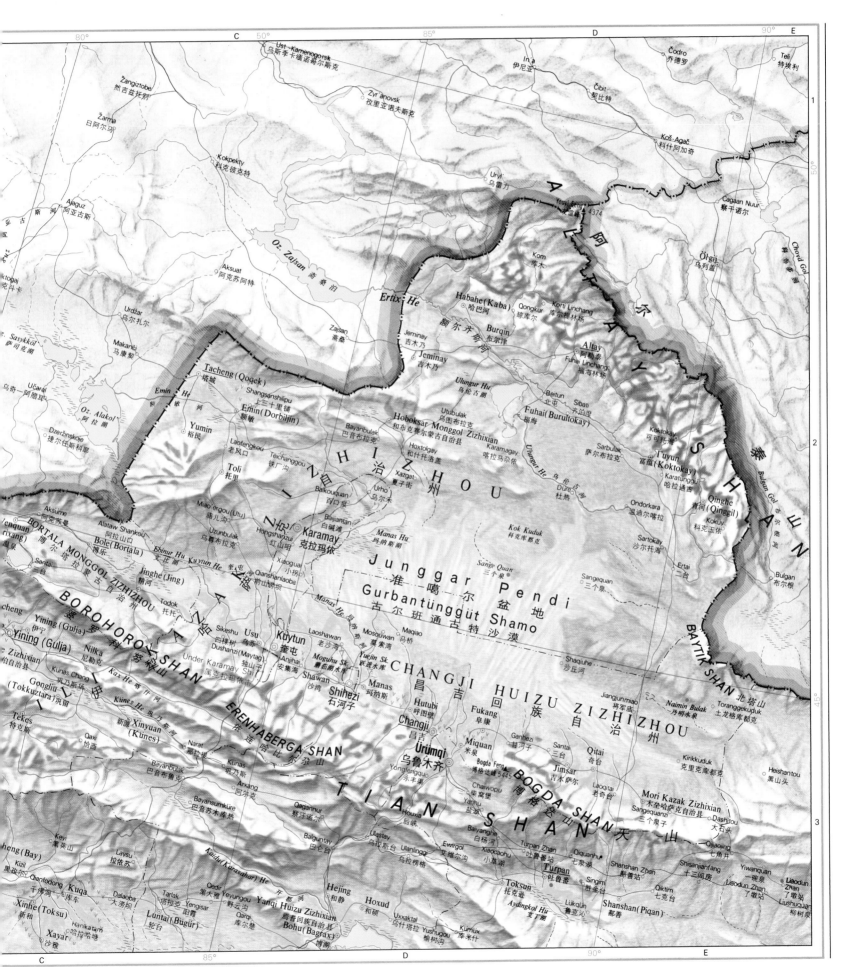

Ust'-Kamenogorsk
乌斯季卡缅诺哥尔斯克

In a
伊尼亚

Čodro
乔德罗

Teli
特埃利

Žangiztobe
然吉兹托别

Zyr anovsk
孜里亚诺夫斯克

Čibit
契比特

Koš-Agač
科什阿加奇

Žarma
日阿尔马

Kokpekty
科克彼克特

Cagaan Nuur
蔡干诺尔

Alaguz
阿亚古斯

Uryl'
乌雷力

Youyi Feng 4374
友谊峰

Ölgij
乌列盖

Chovd Gol
布尔根

Ertix He
额尔齐斯河

Habahe (Kaba)
哈巴河

Qongkur
琼库尔

Korti Linchang
库尔齐林场

Urdžar
乌尔扎尔

Jeminay
吉米乃

Burqin
布尔津

Oz. Zajsan
斋桑泊

Zajsan
斋桑

Jeminay
吉木乃

Altay
阿勒泰

Fuhai Linchang
福海林场

Aksuat
阿克苏阿特

Koktokay
可可托海

Makanči
马康契

Tacheng (Qoqek)
塔城

Shangsanshilipu
上三十里铺

Ullungur Hu
乌伦古湖

Beitun
北屯

Sibati
齐泊度

Tuyun
富蕴 (Koktokay)

Sasykköl
萨司克湖

Utubulak
乌图布拉克

Karamagay
喀拉玛盖

Fuhai (Burultokay)
福海

Yumin
裕民

Emin He
额敏河

Emin (Dorbiljin)
额敏

Hoboksar Monggol Zizhixian
和布克赛尔蒙古自治县

Sarbulak
萨尔布拉克

Qinghe (Qinggil)
青河

Oz. Alakol
阿拉湖

Laofengkou
老风口

Bayanbulak
巴音布拉克

Hoxtolgay
和什托洛盖

Ondorkara
温迪尔喀拉

Koktokay
可可托海

Dzeržinskoje
捷尔任斯科耶

Toli
托里

Teichanggou
铁厂沟

Xazgat
夏子街

U;lungur He
乌伦古河

Dure
杜热

Ulungur He
乌伦古河

Sartokay
沙尔托海

Balkouquan
百口泉

Urho
乌尔禾

Ertai
二台

Bulgan
布尔根

BORTALA MONGGOL ZIZHIXIAN
博尔塔拉蒙古自治州

Alataw Shankou
阿拉山口

Miao ergou (Utu)
庙儿沟

Baijiantan
白碱滩

Kok Kuduk
柯克库都克

Bole (Bortala)
博乐

Uzunbulak
乌尊布拉克

Hongshanzui
红山嘴

Karamay
克拉玛依

Manas Hu
玛纳斯湖

Sange Quan
三个泉

Sangequan
三个泉

Jinghe (Jing)
精河

Bhnur Hu
艾比湖

Kuytun He
奎屯河

Xiaoguai
小拐

Junggar Pendi
准噶尔盆地

Todok
托托

Qianshanlaoba
前山涝坝

Manas He
玛纳斯河

Gurbantünggüt Shamo
古尔班通古特沙漠

Yining (Gulja)
伊宁

Nilka
尼勒克

Dushanzi (Maytag)
独山子

Anjihai
安集海

Mosouwan
莫索湾

Maqiao
马桥

Shaqiuhe
沙丘河

BAYTIK SHAN
北塔山

Nalmin Bulak
乃明水泉

Toranggekuduk
土龙格库都克

Yining (Gulja)
伊宁

BOROHORO SHAN
博罗科努山

Kunas Chang
坤乃斯场

Kax He
喀什河

Moguhu Sk.
墨湖水库

Shawan
沙湾

Manas
玛纳斯

Hutubi
呼图壁

Fukang
阜康

Ganhezi
甘河子

Jianglunmiao
将军庙

Gongliu
巩留

Xinyuan (Künes)
新源

Künes He
巩乃斯河

Shihezi
石河子

Changji
昌吉

CHANGJI HUIZU ZIZHIZHOU
昌吉回族自治州

Jimsar
吉木萨尔

Santai
三台

Qitai
奇台

Kirikkuduk
克里克库都克

Tekes
特克斯

Narat
那拉提

Künas
巩乃斯

Ürümqi
乌鲁木齐

Miquan
米泉

Heishantou
黑山头

ERENHABERGA SHAN
依连哈比尔尕山

Bayanbulak
巴音布鲁克

Arxang
阿尔先

Yongfengguo
永丰渠

Bogda Feng 5445
博格达峰

Laoqitai
老奇台

Mori Kazak Zizhixian
木垒哈萨克自治县

Dashitou
大石头

Qaxi
恰西

Bayansumküre
巴音苏木库热

Chaiwopu
柴窝堡

Yanhu
盐湖

Sangequan
三个泉子

Sangequan
三个泉子

Qijiaojing
七角井

Qagannur
察汗诺尔

TIAN SHAN
天山

BOGDA SHAN
博格达山

Keyi
塞英山

Houxia
后峡

Baiyanghe
白杨河

Turpan Zhan
吐鲁番站

Qiquanhu
七泉湖

Shanshan Zhan
鄯善站

Shisanjianfang
十三间房

Yiwanquan
一碗泉

Balguntay
巴仑台

Ulastay
乌拉斯台

Ulanlinggi
乌兰林格

Ewirgol
艾维尔沟

Xiaocaohu
小草湖

Turpan Zhan
吐鲁番站

Qiktim
七克台

Liaodun Zhan
了墩站

Kaidu (Karaxahar) He
开都河

Qedir
策大雅

Yeyungou
野云沟

Hejing
和静

Hoxud
和硕

Uxxaktal
乌什塔拉

Singim
胜金台

Shanshan (Piqan)
鄯善

Liushuquan
柳树泉

Cheng (Bay)
拜城

Kizil
克孜尔

Laysu
拉依苏

Tarlak
塔拉克

Yengisar
英吉沙

Qargi
库尔勒

Yushugou
榆树沟

Lükqin
鲁克沁

Kumux
库米什

Qanfedong
千佛洞

Kuqa
库车

Dalaoba
大涝坝

Yanqi Huizu Zizhixian
焉耆回族自治县

Toksun
托克逊

Aydingkol Hu
艾丁湖

Xinhe (Toksu)
新和

Hanikatam
哈尼喀坦

Luntai (Bügür)
轮台

Bohu (Bagrax)
博湖

Bagrax Hu
博斯腾湖

Xayar
沙雅

Copyright © Cartographic Publishing House, China and Esselte Map Service, Sweden

SOUTHERN XINJIANG

The Tian Shan range divides Xinjiang, the huge northwestern region of China, into two. The map shows the southern half which is warmer and drier than the Junggar region to the north.

A vast, deep basin (the Tarim Pendi), most of which is desert, occupies much of the region. To the south of the basin lies the Kunlun mountain range and the ranges of Tibet. To the west beyond Kashi (Kaxgar) are further ranges of high mountains belonging to the Tadzik and Kirgiz Soviet Republics. The peoples of these border regions speak Turkic languages akin to that of the Uygur people of Xinjiang.

Meltwater from the mountains supplies irrigation for limited agriculture, but herding is the traditional occupation of southern Xinjiang.

Scale 比例尺 1:4 000 000

Baicheng (Bay) 拜城
Kizil 黑孜尔
Qiantodong 千佛洞
Kuqa 库车
Laysu 拉依苏
Xinhe (Toksu) 新和
Xayar 沙雅
Hanikatam 哈拉哈塘
Dalaoba 大涝坝
Tarlak 塔拉克
Yengisar 央塔克
Luntai (Bügür) 轮台
Qedir 第尔大雅
Yevungou 野云沟
Qarqi 阔什
Yanqi Huizu Zizhixian 焉耆回族自治县
Bohu (Bagrax) 博湖
Kaidu (Karaxahar) He 开都河
Hejing 和静
Ulanlingqi 乌拉楞格
Hoxud 和硕
Uxxaktal 乌什塔拉
Yushugou 榆树沟
Kumux 库米什
Toksun 托克逊
Turpan 吐鲁番
Ulanlinggi 乌拉楞格
Qiquanhu 七泉湖
Shanshan Zhan 鄯善站
Singim 胜金台
Shisanjianfang 十三间房
Qijiaojing 七角井
Yiwanquan 一碗泉
Qiktim 七克台
Shanshan (Piqan) 鄯善
Lükqun 鲁克沁
Aydingkol Hu 艾丁湖

mankol 蒙库勒
Tarim He 塔里木河
Tarim 塔里木
Hadadong 哈达墩
Caohu 草湖
Korla 库尔勒
Mirsali 米尔沙里
Yuli (Lopnur) 尉犁
Süget 苏盖提
Qongkol 群克
Xingdi 兴地
Kongi He 孔雀河
Bosten (Bagrax) Hu 博斯腾湖
Wutonggou 梧桐沟
Biratar Bulak 必尔阿塔尔布拉克

KURUKTAG
库鲁克塔格

维 吾 尔 自 治 区
UYGUR ZIZHIQU
木 Pendi 盆地
kan Shamo
玛 干 沙 漠
BAYINGOLIN 巴音郭楞 MONGGOL ZIZHIZHOU 蒙古自治州

Lop Nur 罗布泊
Argan 阿尔干
Kox Kuduk 科奇库都克
Kum Kuduk 库木库都克

Aralqi 阿拉勒其
Luobuzhuang 罗布庄
Ruoqiang (Qarklik) 若羌
Miran 米兰
Dongluk 墩力克
Baxkorgan 巴什库尔干

Qarqan He 车尔臣河
Tatrang 塔他浪
Tatlikbulak 塔特勒克布拉克
Waxxari 瓦石峡
Yandakkak 央大什格克
Xorkol 索尔库里
Honggouzi 红沟子
Niubiziliang 牛鼻梁
Obo Liang 俄博梁

Katma 开特奚
Qiemo (Qarqan) 且末
Ruoqiang He 若羌河

ALTUN SHAN 阿尔金山
HAIXI MONGGOLZU ZANGZU 海西蒙古族藏族
KAZAKZU ZIZHIZHOU 哈萨克族自治州

Qingqillik 青格力克
Hadilik 哈迪勒克
Andirlangar 安迪尔兰干
Yawatongguzlangar 牙通古孜兰干
Atqan 阿羌
Koramlik 库拉木勒克
Tura 吐拉
Korgan 库尔干
Atgan 阿尔干
Karamiran He 喀拉米兰河

Mangnai Zhen 茫崖镇
Tomorlog 铁木里克
Youshashan 油沙山
Aral 阿拉尔
Gas Hu 格孜库里
Changweiliang 长尾梁
Dawusi 大乌斯
Shuizhan 水站
Youdunzi 油墩子
Mangnai 茫崖
Yilping 一里平
Xi Tatjnar Hu 西台吉乃尔湖

Bostan 博斯坦
Karasay 喀拉萨依
eyik
Karamiran 喀拉米兰

Patkaglik 帕特喀格里克
Ayakkum Hu 阿牙格库木湖
Aqqikkol Hu 阿其克库勒湖

KUNLUN SHAN 昆仑山

QIMANTAG 其曼塔格
Akkokesay 阿克库楚克赛
Behleg 伯喀里克
Tulagi Ar Gol 楚拉克阿拉干河
Gang 甘森
Tart 塔尔丁
Urt Moron 乌图美仁

Muztag 木孜塔格 7723
Karamiran-Shankou 喀拉米兰山口
ARKATAG SHAN 阿尔喀塔格山
昆 仑 山
Bukadaban Feng 布喀达坂峰 6860
Nur Turu 奴土勒
Boluntay 布伦台

HOH XIL SHAN
Margai Caka 玛尔盖茶卡
Rola Co 若拉错
可可西里山
Hoh Xil Hu 可可西里湖
Xijir Ulan Hu 西金乌兰湖
Unuli Horog 埃塔里开尔戈
Huiten Nur 雷通湖
Hoh Sai Hu 霍赛湖
Kunlun Shankou 昆仑山口
Qumar Heyan 楚玛尔河沿
Wudaoliang 五道梁
Qumar He 楚玛尔河

Chagdo Kangri 查多岗日
Gangmar Co 冈玛错
Gomo Co 戈木错
Dogai Coring 多格错仁
Ring Co 令错
Ulan Ul Hu 乌兰乌拉湖
Elsen Nur 艾森诺尔

THE NORTHERN STEPPES

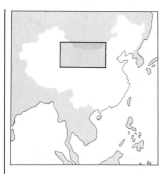

The Inner Mongolia (Nei Mongol) Autonomous Region occupies much of the area covered by this map. The northern section, beyond the Chinese frontier, is part of the Mongolian People's Republic (Outer Mongolia). The Great Wall, built to protect Chinese farmers from incursions by nomadic Mongolian herdsmen, follows a winding course from the east through the middle of the map and ends close to Yumen. The latter was the beginning of the old Silk Road to western Asia.

The whole vast region may be thought of as a corridor, lying between the Tibetan mountain ranges to the southwest and the deserts (Shamo) of Mongolia. The province of Gansu, at the centre of the map, represents the historic extension of Chinese imperial rule in a northwesterly direction.

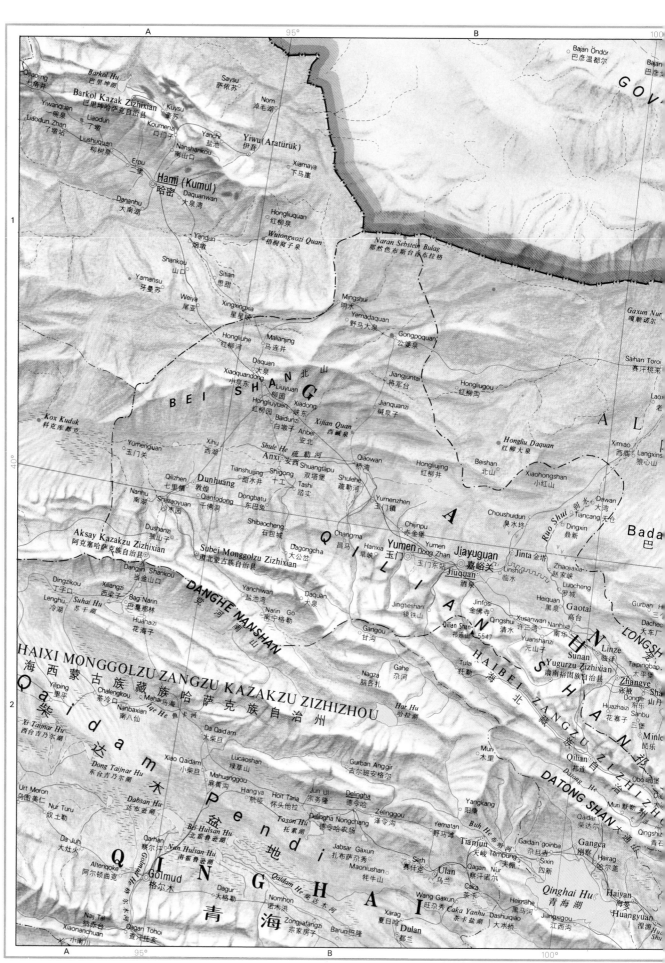

Scale 比例尺 1:4 000 000

KILOMETERS
STATUTE MILES

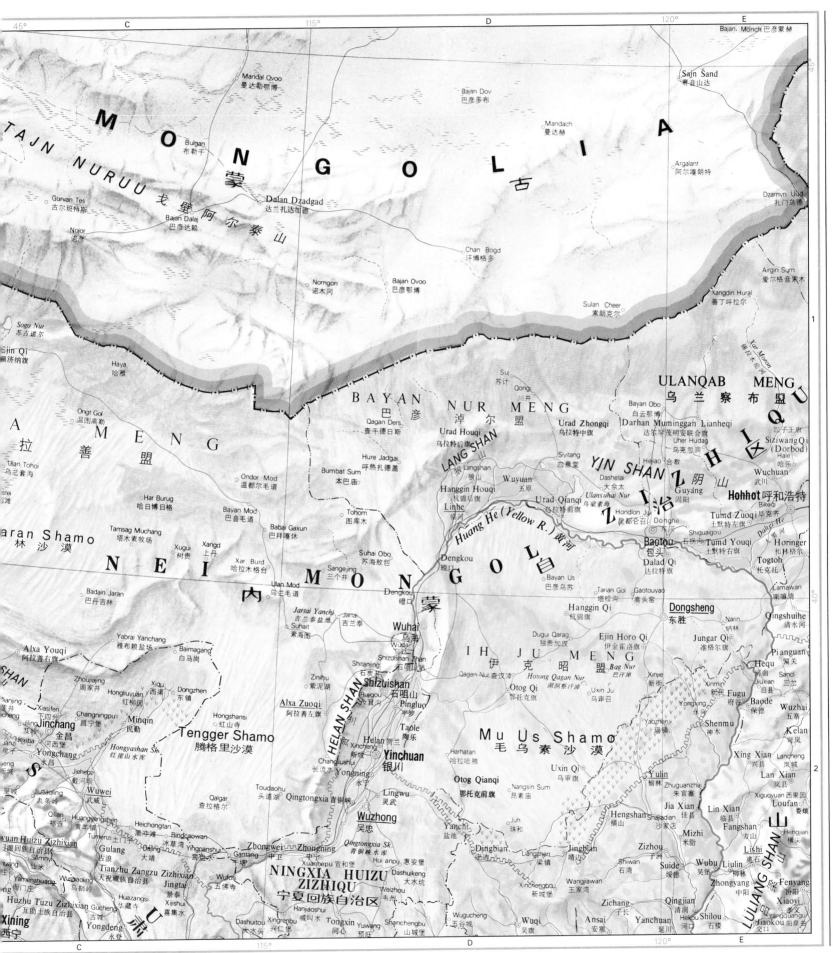

LIAONING, HEBEI, BEIJING AND TIANJIN

The most developed territory in northern China is shown on this map, centred on Beijing and its neighbour Tianjin. The province of Liaoning is the southern, most industrialized section of the northeast; its capital Shenyang is the fourth largest city in China.

The industrial installations founded by the Japanese during their occupation of the northeast have been greatly developed since 1949. As a result industry in both Beijing and Tianjin has been stimulated. Oil is being extracted along the coast of the Bohai Sea, and Shanxi, in the west, is China's principal coal producer. Many other cities, such as Shijiazhuang in the south, and Fushun and Benxi in the north, have shared in this industrial expansion.

However, most people in this area still depend on agriculture for their livelihood; wheat, millet and cotton are major crops.

Scale 比例尺 1:4 000 000

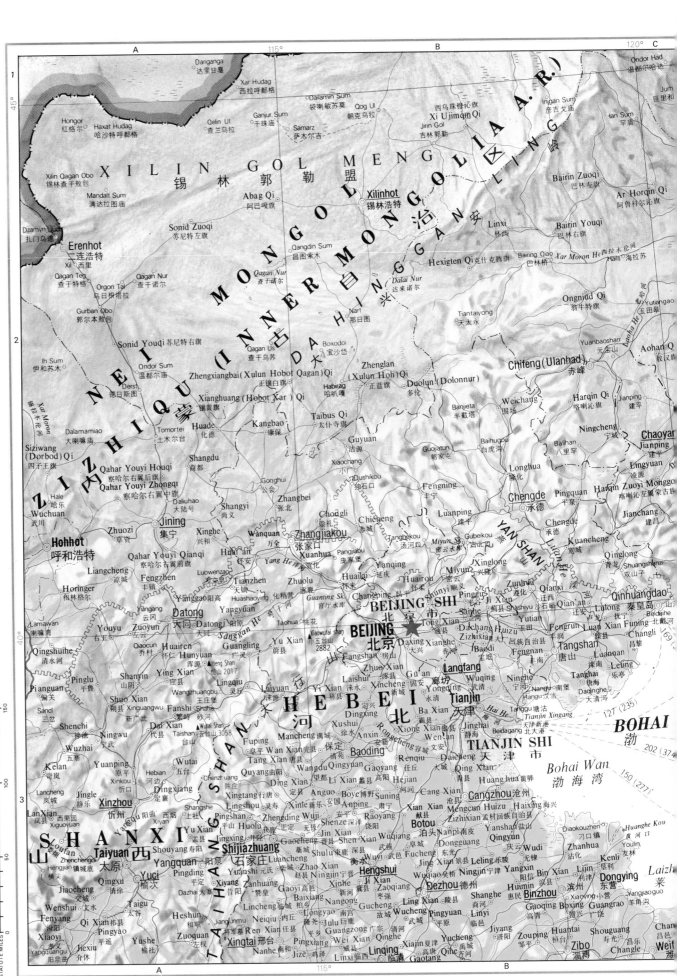

125° D 130° E

Golin Baixing 高力板 Tongyu 通榆 Lanzijing 兰字井 Bianzhao 边昭 Haxat 哈什坨 Halahai 哈拉海 Dehui 德惠 Shulan 舒兰 Dongjingcheng 东京城 Ningpo Hu 宁坡湖 Jingbo 镜泊 Liaozigou 罗子沟 Chunhua 春化

Dongminzhutun 东民主屯 Taipingchuan 太平川 Taipingshan 太平山 Changling 长岭 Nong'an 农安 Jiutai 九台 Halaha 哈拉哈 Fengguang 凤光 Lafa 拉法 Qianjin 前进 Huangnihe 黄泥河 Tianqiaoling 天桥岭 Wangqing 汪清

Golin Qi Bayan Qagan 白音嘎查 Ih Tal 伊和塔 Jargalang 吉尔嘎郎 Maolin 茂林 Huaidezhen 怀德镇 Yitong Yantongshan 烟筒山 Changchun 长春 Dafengman 大丰满 Jiaohe 蛟河 Naizishan 奶子山 Antu 安图 Yanji 延吉 Tumen 图们 Hunchun 珲春

Horqin Zuoyi Zhongqi 科尔沁左翼中旗 Qianguo 前郭 Jilin 吉林 Yongji 永吉 CHAOXIANZU ZIZHIZHOU 朝鲜族自治州 Namwang 南阳

Kailu 开鲁 Xinkai He 新开河 Xiliao He 西辽河 Shuangyang 双阳 Chaluhe 岔路河 Yongji 永吉 Songhua Hu 松花湖 Dunhua 敦化 YANBIAN 延边 Longing 龙井 Kaishantun 开山屯

Tongliao 通辽 Shuangliao 双辽 Lishu 梨树 Erlongshan Sk 龙山水库 Huade 华德 Yingchengzi 营城子 Panshan 磐石 Hongshi 红石 Jiapigou 夹皮沟 Songjiang 松江 Helong 和龙 Musan 茂山

Baixingt 八仙筒 Sanjiangkou 三江口 Bamiancheng 八面城 Siping 四平 Pinggang 平岗 Xifeng 西丰 Huinan 辉南 Namhong 那尔轰 Baishan 白山 Lushuhe 露水河 Baitoushan Tian Chi 白头山天池 Myonggan 明川

Horqin Zuoyi Houqi 科尔沁左翼后旗 Baolizhen 宝力镇 Changtu 昌图 Donliao 东辽 Fuyuan 富源 Hailong 海龙 Shansonggang 杉松岗 Jingyu 靖宇 CHANGBAI SHAN 长白山

Naiman Qi 奈曼旗 Hure Qi 库伦旗 Kangping 康平 Tongjiangkou 通江口 Qingyuan 清原 Liuhe 柳河 Songshuzhen 松树镇 Songjianghe 松江河 Fusong 抚松 Chongjin 清津

Jiumiao 旧庙 Hartao 哈拉套 Zhangwu 彰武 Daqing 大青 Tieta 铁法 Kaiyuan 开原 Nanzamu 南杂木 Sanyuanpu 三源浦 Hunjiang 浑江 Changbai 长白 Chaoxianzu Zizhixian 长白朝鲜族自治县 Kilju 吉州

Fuxin Monggolzu Zizhixian 阜新蒙古族自治县 Faku 法库 Tieling 铁岭 Fushuncheng 抚顺城 Yongling 永陵 Xinbin 新宾 Tonghua 通化 Dalizi 大栗子 Hyesan 惠山 Kapsan 甲山

Beipiao 北票 Fuxin 阜新 Heishan 黑山 Xinmin 新民 Shenyang 沈阳 Fushun 抚顺 Qingyuancheng 清原城 Laoling 老岭 Ji'an Manpo 满浦 RANGRIM-SANJULGI Kanggye 江界

Jinlingsi 金岭寺 Yi Xian 义县 Beizhen 北镇 Dahushan 大虎山 Hun He 浑河 Dengta 灯塔 Erhulai 二户来 Huanren 桓仁 Tianshifu 田师付 Shanyanzi 山羊子 Wiwon 渭原 Kanggye 江界 2522

Liaozhong 辽中 Liaoyang 辽阳 Benxi 本溪 Changjin-ho 长津湖 Puksubaek-san Pukchong 北青

Jinzhou 锦州 Jin Xian 锦县 Tai'an 台安 Benxi 本溪 Liaoyang 辽阳 Kuandian 宽甸 Changjin 长津 Hamhung 咸兴

xian Nanpiao 南票 Tashan 塔山 Panshan 盘山 Dawa 大洼 Haicheng 海城 Niuzhuang 牛庄 Qingchengzi 青城子 Tongyuanpu 通远堡 Yalu Jiang 鸭绿江 Supung 水丰 Huichon 熙川

Jinxi 锦西 Jinxi 塔山 Anshan 鞍山 Guanshui 灌水 Fengcheng 凤城 Shanghekou 上河口 Hungnam 兴南

nousuo 沙后所 Yingkou 营口 Yingkou 营口 Xiuyan 岫岩 Kuandian 宽甸 QIAN SHAN 千山 Sinuiju 新义州 Dandong 丹东 Kaechon 价川 Hamhung 咸兴

Liaodong Wan 辽东湾 Suizhong 绥中 Gai Xian 盖县 Xiongyuecheng 熊岳城 Wezi 苇子 Gushan 孤山 Donggou 东沟 Chongju 定州 Kowon 高原 Wonsan 元山 Tong-choson-man 东朝鲜湾

haiguan Huatong 华铜 Laohutun 老虎屯 Fu Xian 复县 Zhuanghe 庄河 Dagushan Yalujiang Kou 鸭绿江口 Sunchon 顺川 Yangdok 阳德 Sinpyong 新坪

249 (419) 226 (419) Fuzhou 复州 Chengzitan 城子坦 Shicheng Dao 石城岛 Kumgang-san 金刚山 1638

168 (311) Wudao 五岛 Xinjin 新金 Pikou 皮口 Changhai 长海 159 (294) So-choson-man 西朝鲜湾 Pyongsong 平城 Pyongyang 平壤 Kumgang-san 金刚山

Jin Xian 金县 Changshan Qundao 长山群岛 Xinangzhen 新港镇 180 (330) PYONGYANG 平壤 Taedong 大同 KOREA 朝鲜 TAEBAEK-SANJULGI 太白山

Lushun 旅顺 Dalian 大连 Nampo 南浦 Sariwon 沙里院 Wonsan Sokcho 束草 Kangrung 江陵

218 (403) 220 (410) Chunchon 春川 Kangrung 江陵

Bohai Haixia 渤海海峡 To Shidao 至石岛 93 (172) Changyon 长渊 Haeju 海州 Kaesong 开城 Seoul 汉城 Uljin 蔚珍

Miaodao Qundao 庙岛群岛 150 (278) Cholwon 铁原 Wonju 原州 Samchok 三陟

117 (217) 89 (165) Haeju 海州 Onggin 瓮津 Kanghwa-man 江华湾 Seoul 汉城 Inchon 仁川 Chunchon 忠州

Changdao 长岛 Huang Xian 黄县 Yantai 烟台 Muping 牟平 Jiurongcheng 旧荣城 Rongcheng Wan 荣城湾 Chongju 清州 Wonju 原州

Longkou 龙口 Penglai 蓬莱 Qixia 栖霞 Yaocun 姚村 Wendeng 文登 Rongcheng 荣成 Chonan 天安 Andong 安东 Yongdok 盈德

Zhaoyuan 招远 Ye Xian 掖县 Chedao 车道 To Dalian 至大连 272 (504) Chongju 清州 Taejon 大田

河 Laixi 莱西 Rushan 乳山 Shidao 石岛 To Yantai 至烟台 238 (441) Ryongsin (Kunhung) 龙新里 (近兴) Pohang 浦项

Pingdu 平度 Jianglabao 姜家坡 Haiyang 海阳 Taegu 大邱 Kyongju 庆州

SEA OF JAPAN 日本海

LIAONING 辽宁 JILIN 吉林 JILIN HADA LING 吉林哈达岭 LAOYE LING 老爷岭 HAMGYONG-SANJULGI 咸镜

JIREN MENG 吉林盟

120° C 125° D 130°

NORTHEASTERN CHINA

The northern section of the northeast of China, once known as Manchuria, is shown on this map. It comprises a vast undulating plain confined by two mountain ranges, the Da Hinggan to the west and Xiao Hinggan to the east. Beyond the mountains to the west, lies part of Inner Mongolia. The area is generally extremely cold and, in the northernmost part, has only the briefest of summers.

The original Manchu population of the plain has been increasingly assimilated with the Han Chinese. But the northeast has only been open to Han settlement for about a hundred years, and between 1933 and 1945 was effectively ruled by Japan. Since 1945 the area has experienced great influxes of Chinese settlers and rapid industrial development. China's principal oilfield is at Daqing near the centre of the plain.

Scale 比例尺 1:4 000 000

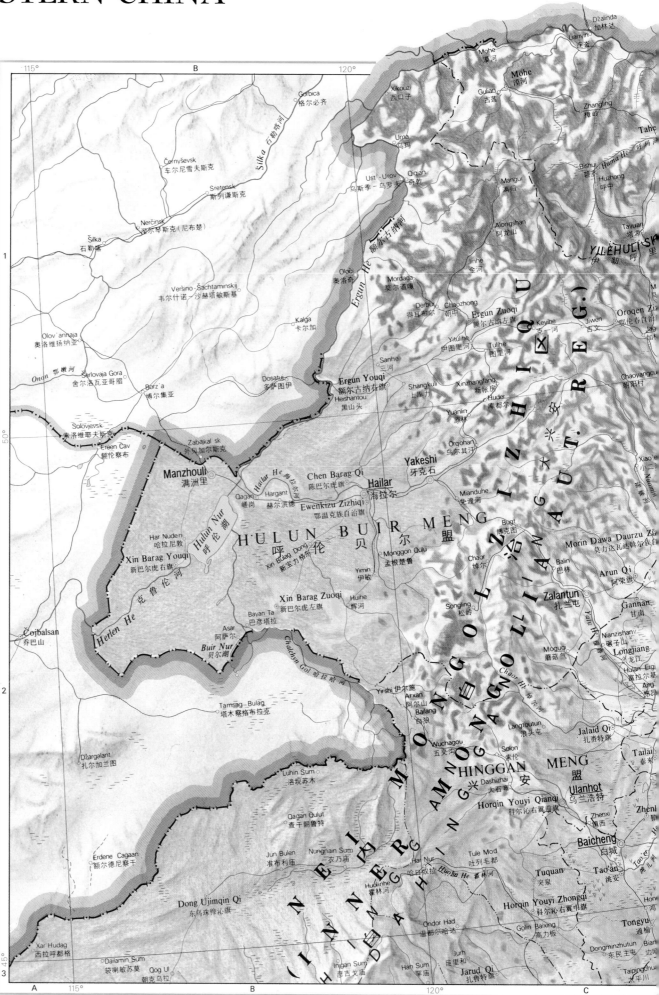

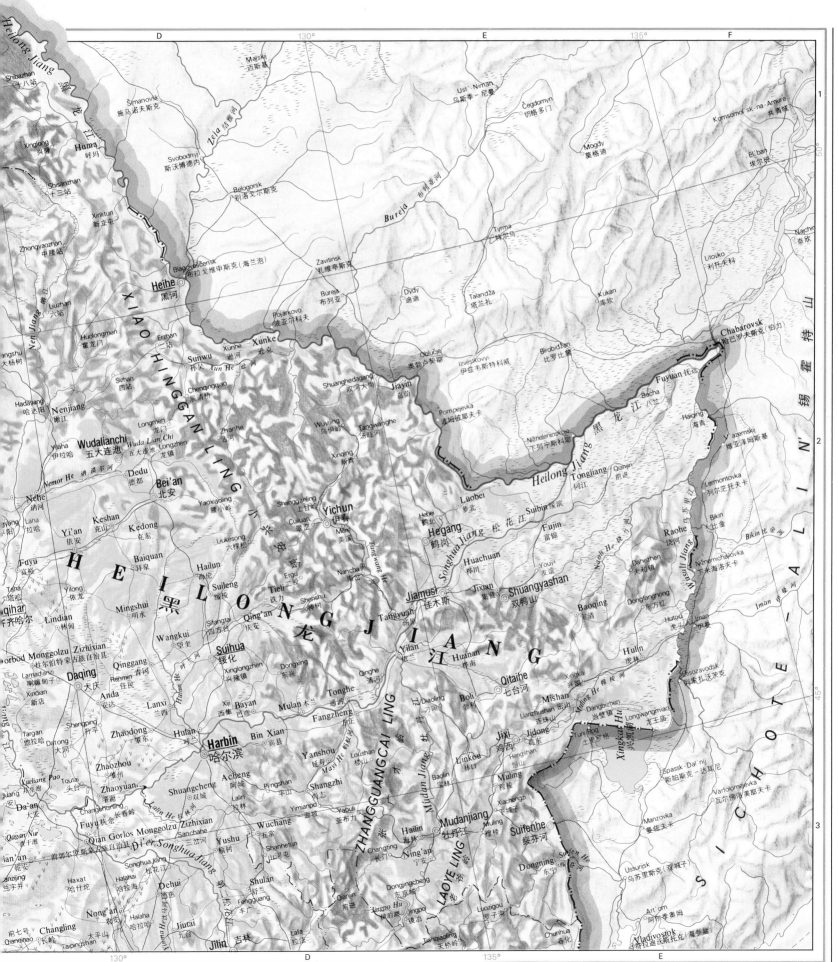

TIBET

The Tibetan massif—the so-called 'roof of the world'—is shown on this map. Along its southern border lie the mighty Himalayas, and beyond them the plains of India. The general elevation of the Tibetan region is around 4,000 to 6,000 m (13,000 to 20,000 ft) above sea level. But many ranges and individual peaks are higher than this—Qomolangma (Mount Everest) is 8,848 m (29,028 ft).

The climate of Tibet is extremely severe, with fewer than 50 frost-free days a year, except in the milder gorges of the southwest. Much of the area is uninhabited rocky desert and the population density for the whole region is only two people per sq km (five per sq mi).

Scale 比例尺 1:4 000 000

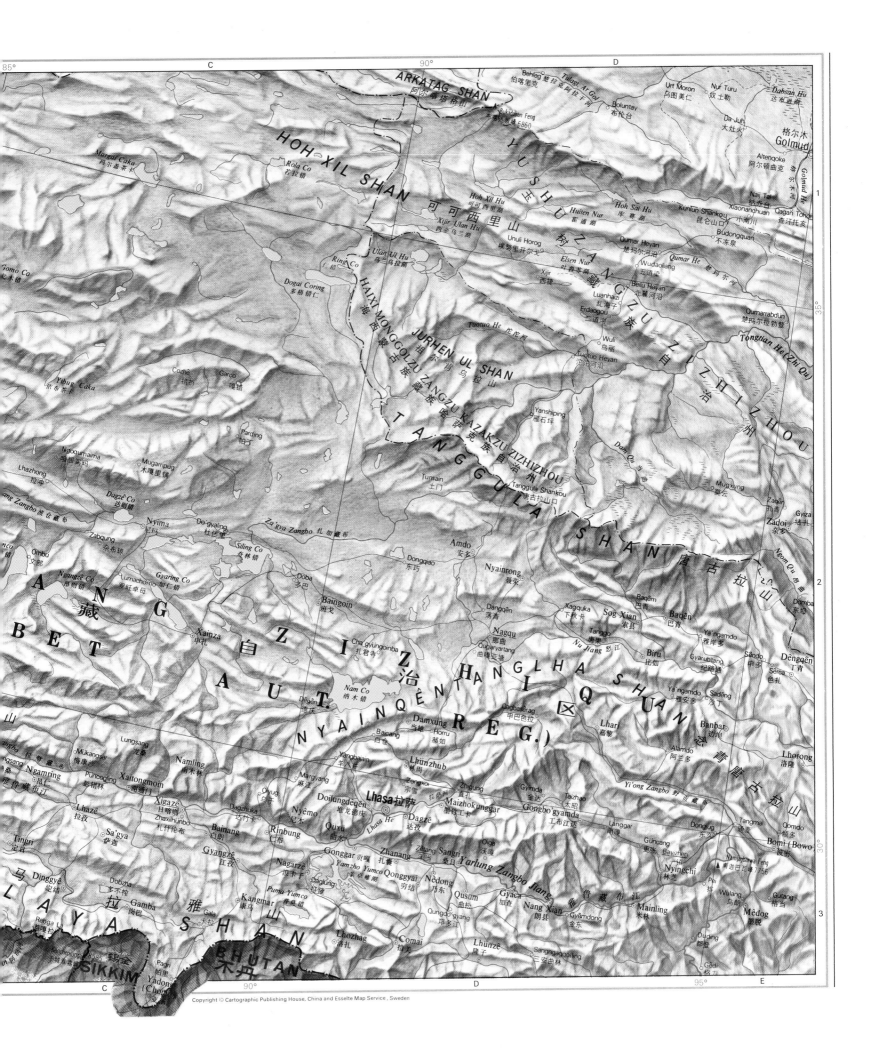

ARKATAG SHAN
阿尔喀塔格山

HOH XIL SHAN

YUSHU ZANGZU ZIZHIZHOU
玉树藏族自治州

Bukadaban Feng
布喀达坂峰 6860

Behleg 楚拉克阿拉干河
Tulagt Ar Gol

Boluntay 布伦台

Urt Moron 乌图美仁
Nur Turu 奴土勒

Dabsan Hu 达布逊湖

Da Juh 大灶火

Golmud 格尔木
Golmud He

Altenqoke 阿尔顿曲克

HOH XIL SHAN
可可西里山

Hoh Xil Hu 可可西里湖

Unuli Horog 埃兹里乌尔戈

Huiten Nur 董通湖

Hoh Sai Hu 库赛湖

Kunlun Shankou 昆仑山口

Xiaonanghuan 小南川

Naij Tal 纳赤台

Qagan Tohoi 查汗托亥

Budongquan 不冻泉

Margai Caka 玛尔盖茶卡

Rola Co 若拉错

Xijir Ulan Hu 西金乌兰湖

Ulan Ul Hu 乌兰乌拉湖

Ring Co 仁错

Qumar Heyan 楚玛尔河沿

Qumar He 楚玛尔河

Wudaoliang 五道梁

Elsen Nur 吐鲁莽湖

Xijir 西捷

Beilu Heyan 北麓河沿

Luanhaizi 乱海子

Erdaogou 二道沟

Qumarrabdun 楚玛尔拉勃登

Gomo Co 芘木错

Dogai Coring 多格错仁

HAIXI MONGOLZU ZANGZU ZIZHIZHOU 海西蒙古族

JURHEN UL SHAN
祖尔肯乌拉山

Tuotuo He 沱沱河

Yanshiping 雁石坪

Wuli 乌丽

Tuotuo Heyan 沱沱河沿

Tongtian He (Zhi Qu) 治

Yibug Caka 茶布茶卡

Cozhê 措折

Garco 嘎错

Parding 帕丁

KAZAKZU ZANGZU 哈萨克族 ZIZHIZHOU 自治州

Tumain 土门

Tanggula Shankou 唐古拉山口

Dam Qu 当曲

Mugxung 姿云

Zagên 咂根

Gyiza 结仁

Zadoi 宗多

Lhazhong 拉冲

Ngoqumaima 嘎居麦玛

Mugarripug 木嘎里铺

Dagzê Co 达则错

TANGGULA SHAN 唐古拉山

Ngom Qu 鲁曲

Ang Zangbo 波仓藏布

Nyima 尼玛

Do'gyaling 杜佳里

Za'gya Zangbo 扎加藏布

Amdo 安多

Ngangzê Co 昂则错

Zabqung 余布琼

Siling Co 奇林错

Dongqiao 东巧

Nyainrong 聂荣

Xagquka 下秋卡

Bagên 巴青

Baqên 巴青

Domba 东坝

Ombu 文部

Lumachomo 路玛机错母

Gyaring Co 加林错

Doba 多巴

Dangqên 荡青

Nagqu 那曲

Sog Xian 索县

Tanggo 唐果

Ya'ngamdo 雅安多

Sadêng 沙丁

Sândo 申多

Dêngqên 丁青

Sêrca 色扎

ANG 藏 G
TIBET

Xainza 申扎

Cha'gyungoinba 扎君寺

Qugaryartang 曲嘎迁塘

Nu Jiang 怒江

Biru 比如

Gyarubtang 纪路塘

BET AUT.

Nam Co 纳木错

HANGLHA I SHAN QU 青尼古拉山

Banbar 边坝

Lhari 嘉黎

Lhorong 洛隆

NYAINQÊN T (REG.)

Damxung 当雄

Qagbasêrag 甲巴色拉

Alamdo 阿兰多

Bab 山

Degên 德庆

Baicang 白仓

Horru 郝如

Lhünzhub 林周

Yangbajain 羊八井

Gyimda 金达

Taizhao 太昭

Langgar 浪嘎

Lungsang 元藏

Mükangsar 梅康萨

Namling 南木林

Margyang 麻江

Oiyug 尼庆

Zhigung 直贡

Yi'ong Zangbo 野贡藏布

Tangmai 通麦

Lhasa 拉萨
Lhasa He 拉萨河

Dongjug 东久

Guncang 贡藏

Püncogling 彭措林

Xaitongmoin 谢通门

Ngamring 昂仁

Doilungdêqên 堆龙德庆

Maizhokunggar 墨竹工卡

Gongbo'gyamda 工布江达

Nyingchi 林芝

Baizhên 巴贞

Xigazê 日喀则

Nyêmo 尼木

Dagzê 达孜

Olga 沃卡

Namjagbarwa Feng 南迦巴瓦峰 7756

Bomi (Bowo) 波密

Lhazê 拉孜

Zhaxilhünbo 扎什伦布

Dazhuka 达竹卡

Quxü 曲水

Tingri 定日

Sa'gya 萨迦

Rinbung 仁布

Quxü 曲水

Zhanang 扎囊

Zêtang 泽当

Sangri 桑日

Yarlung Zangbo Jiang 雅鲁藏布江

Mainling 米林

Gyamdong 金东

Wulang 乌朗

Dinggyê 定结

Dobzha 多不辖

Gonggar 贡嘎

Nagarze 浪卡子

Nêdong 乃东

Qusum 曲松

Gyaca 加查

Nang Xian 朗县

Mêdog 墨脱

Gutang 格当

Gamba 岗巴

Gyangzê 江孜

Daglung 打隆

Bainang 白朗

Yamzho Yumco 羊卓雍错

Qonggyai 穷结

Nang Xian 朗县

Duding 都登

Gêdoi 格定

Kangmar 康马

Puma Yumco 普莫雍错

Qundo'gyang 邛多江

Lhozhag 洛扎

Comai 措美

Lhünzê 隆子

Sangngaggoiling 三安曲林

LAYA SHAN 雅鲁山

SIKKIM 锡金

BHUTAN 不丹

Pagri 帕里

Yadong (Chomo) 亚东

SICHUAN

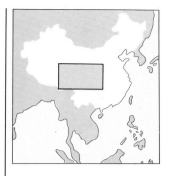

The most distinctive and important of the contrasting areas on this map is the basin of Sichuan Province. This basin, surrounded on all sides by mountain ranges and high plateaus, is a vast enclosed agricultural area and is the most densely populated of all the earth's isolated regions.

To the west of Sichuan lies the edge of the Tibetan massif, with its high mountains and deep gorges, which extends over much of the province of Qinghai. To the north are the southern parts of Gansu and Ningxia and, beyond the Qin Ling escarpment, the southern edge of the North China Plain. Qinghai, Gansu and Ningxia are all sparsely populated and among the poorest regions of China.

Scale 比例尺 1:4 000 000

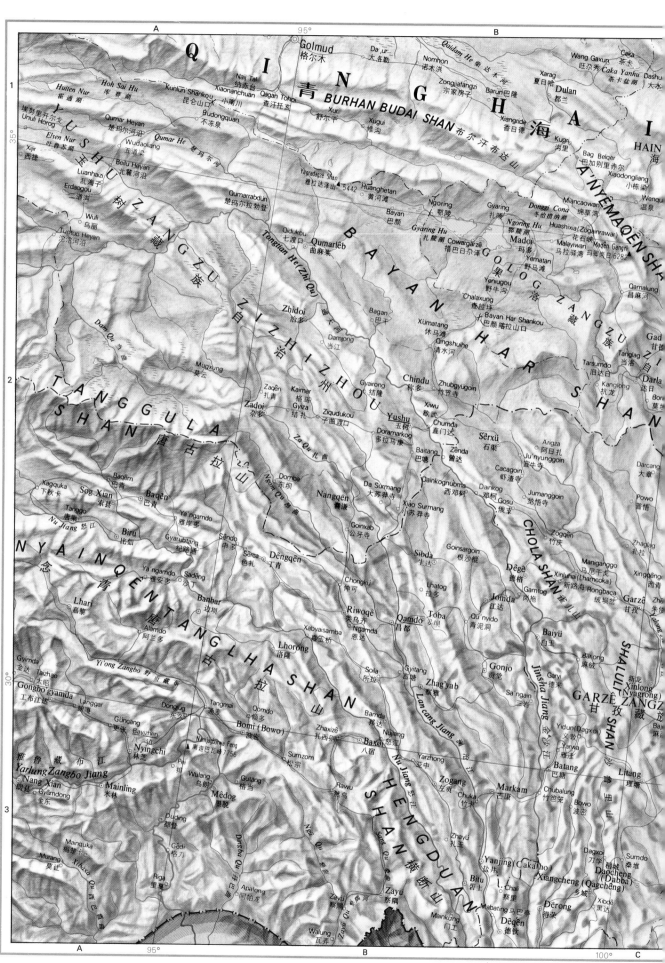

100°   C   105°   D   110°

Qinghai Hu Haiyan Xinzhuang Yamenzhuang Datong Wushaoling Tianzhu Zangzu Zizhixian Wufosi 五佛寺 Weizhou 韦州 Xin Xiangbu 新城堡 Wangjiawan 王家湾

青海湖 Heima 黑马河 Xiahe 夏河 Qili 乞儿庄 Wulingzi 乌鞘岭 大坂族族自治县 Jingtai 景泰 NINGXIA HUIZU ZIZHIQU Zichang 子长

Hehai Jiangxigou Datong 大通 Huzhu Tuzu Zizhixian Huazangsi 华藏寺 Xijishui 喜集水 宁夏回族自治区 Ansai 安塞

Huangyuan 互助土族自治县 古城 Yongdeng 永登 Baiyin 白银 Dashuitou Xingrenbu Tongxin Yuwang Shanchengbu 山城堡 Wuqi 吴旗

涅源 *Huang Shui* Ledu 乐都 Gucheng Hongchengzi 靖远 Haiyuan Yan'an

Xining 西宁 Ping'an 平安 Minhe 民和 Yaojie Hongchengzi 红城子 Dijiatai 同心 预旺 Hongde 洪德 Jinding 金鼎 Danbazhai 杨家岭

Gonghe 共和 Guide 贵德 Jainca Hualong Huizu Zizhixian 盐锅峡水库 Yuzhong 榆中 Chankou 巅口 Qiying 七营 Maojing 毛井 Huan Xian 环县 Huachi 华池 延安

ZANGZU ZIZHIZHOU Xunhua/Salarzu Zizixian 化隆回族自治县 Lanzhou 兰州 Chankou 界石铺 Shenjiahe SK. Donghuachi 甘泉 Nanniwan

藏族自治州 Xinghai 兴海 Bacang Xinjie 新街 Dongxiangzu Zizhixian Gangouyi Xiji 西吉 将 Jiangtaibu 泾原 Guyuan Pengyang Zhiluo 直罗 Qingyang 庆阳 Fu Xian 富县

HUANGNAN Tongren 同仁 LINXIA HUIZU ZIZHIZHOU 临夏 Linxia Dongxiangzu Zizhixian 会宁 Huining Jieshipu Longde 隆德 固原 Liupan Shan Zhengning 镇原 Qingyang Luochuan 洛川 Huangling

ZANGZU Zêkog 泽库 Hezheng 和政 东乡 自治县 Guanghe 广河 Dingxi 定西 Jingning 静宁 **Pingliang** 平凉 Jingchuan 泾川 Ningxian 宁县

黄南 藏族 Kangle 康乐 Linxia 临夏 Lintao 临洮 Mazhen Huajialing Longde Chongxin 崇信 Changwu 长武 Yijun 宜君

Ra gyagoinba Guinan Ponggartang 和政 临河 Weiyuan 渭源 Tongwei 通渭 Zhuanglang 庄浪 Huating 华亭 Lingtai 灵台 Binxian 彬县 Chengcheng 澄城

XIQING SHAN Xiahe 夏河 Gyagartang Hezuozhen 合作镇 Longxi 陇西 Zhangjiachuan Huizu Zizhixian Longxian 陇县 Qianyang 千阳 Qianxian 乾县

玛曲 Maqên Luqu 碌曲 Lintan 临潭 Zhang Xian 漳县 Long Xian Qingshui 清水 Baishui 白水

GANNAN ZANGZU ZIZHIZHOU Jonê Min Xian 岷县 Wushan 武山 **Tianshui** 天水 Fenggeling Baoji 宝鸡 **SHAANXI** 陕

Xingxiaoinba Waxu 尕海 Diebu 迭部 Lintan Luomen Gangu Qianyang Baoji 宝鸡 Qishan 岐山 Fufeng Qian Xian Gaoling 高陵

Hu ang He (Yellow R.) Maqu 玛曲 Tewo 迭部 Dangchang 宕昌 Li Xian 礼县 Mayan Liangdang 两当 Hui Xian 徽县 Mei Xian 眉县 Lintong 临潼 **Xi'an** 西安

黄河 Dagcanglhamo (Langmusi) Shimen Zhugqu 舟曲 Xihe 西和 Jiangluozhen Cheng Xian 成县 Taibai 太白 Hu Xian Chang'an 长安 Lantian

MIN SHAN Bailong (Hadapu) Wudu 武都 Kang Xian 康县 Lueyang 略阳 **QIN LING** 秦

Zoige 若尔盖 Baxi Razisi 然子寺 Nahping 南坪 Zhongzhai 中寨 Linjiang 临江 Mian Xian 勉县 **Hanzhong** 汉中 Foping 佛坪 Ningshan 宁陕 Shang Xian 商县

颜 喀 拉 山 Baima 班玛 Zêmdasam Wagên Huangshengguan 黄胜关 Wen Xian 文县 Bikou SK. Qingchuan 青川 Nanzheng 南郑 Xixiang 西乡 Shiquan 石泉 Zhashui 柞水 Shanyang

ABA (NGAWA) ZANGZU ZIZHIZHOU Hongyuan 红原 Songpan (Sungqu) 松潘 Shuijing 水晶 Pingwu 平武 Ningqiang 宁强 Zhenba 镇巴 Ziyang 紫阳 Zhen'an 镇安

阿坝藏族 自治州 Zamtang Mewa Maoergai Zhenjiangguan **Jialing Jiang** Baishui Guangyuan 广元 Nanjiang 南江 碑坝 Ankang 安康

Sêrtar 色达 Barkam 马尔康 Heishui 黑水 Beichuan 北川 Jiange 剑阁 Wangcang 旺苍 **DABA SHAN** Langao Zhuxi 竹溪

Luhuo (Zhaggo) Jinchuan (Quqên) 金川 Maowen Qiangzu Zizhixian Jiangyou 江油 Cangxi 苍溪 Bazhong 巴中 Tongjiang 通江 Wanyuan 万源 Baisha Zhenping 镇坪

Dawu 道孚 Xiaojin (Zainlha) 小金 Li Xian 理县 An Xian 安县 **Mianyang** 绵阳 Zitong 梓潼 Langzhong 阆中 Pingchang 平昌 Chengkou 城口 Daoshiping

QIONGLAI SHAN Danba (Rongzhag) Wenchuan 汶川 Mianzhu 绵竹 Yanting 盐亭 Nanbu 南部 Yilong 仪陇 Xuanhan 宣汉 Wuxi 巫溪

DAXUE SHAN Dujiangyan 都江堰 **Shifang** 什邡 **Deyang** 德阳 Zhongjiang 中江 Xichong 西充 Peng'an 蓬安 Yingshan 营山 **Daxian** 达县 Kaijiang 开江 Wushan 巫山

Kangding (Dardo) 康定 Pi Xian 郫县 Peng Xian Guanghan 广汉 Shehong 射洪 Pengxi 蓬溪 **Nanchong** 南充 Dazhu 大竹 Fengjie 奉节

Chengdu 成都 Xindu 新都 Jintang 金堂 Suining 遂宁 Qu Xian 渠县 Wanxian 万县 Yunyang 云阳

SICHUAN 四川 Dayi 大邑 Chongqing 崇庆 Shuangliu 双流 Jianyang 简阳 Lezhi 乐至 Pengxi Yuechi 岳池 Guang'an 广安 Linshui 邻水 Liangping 梁平 Wan Xian

Baoxing 宝兴 Qionglai 邛崃 Pujiang 蒲江 Pengshan 彭山 Ziyang 资阳 Tongnan 潼南 Hechuan 合川 **Yangtze R.** 长江

Ya'an 雅安 Mingshan 名山 Meishan 眉山 Renshou 仁寿 Anyue 安岳 Wusheng 武胜 Fengdu 丰都 **Chang Jiang** **EXI TUJIAZU**

Luding (Jagsamka) 泸定 Hongya 洪雅 Danleng 丹棱 Qingshen 青神 合川 Shizhu Tujiazu Zizhixian Lichuan 利川 **Enshi** 恩施

Gongga Shan 7556 Yingjing 荥经 Jiajiang 夹江 Jingyan 井研 Zizhong 资中 Tongliang 铜梁 Changshou 长寿 Fengdu **MIAOZU ZIZHIZHOU**

贡嘎山 Emei 峨眉 **Leshan** 乐山 Weiyuan 威远 Dazu 大足 Bishan 壁山 Jiangbei 江北 Fuling 涪陵 Xuan'en 宣恩 Hefeng 鹤峰

Hanyuan 汉源 Emei Shan 3099 Rong Xian 荣县 Neijiang 内江 Rongchang 荣昌 **Chongqing** 重庆 Qianjiang Tujiazu Miaozu Zizhixian Xianfeng 咸丰

Shimian 石棉 Jinkouhe 金口河 Qianwei 犍为 Zigong 自贡 Longchang 隆昌 Ba Xian 巴县 Wulong Pengshui Miaozu Tujiazu Zizhixian Laifeng 来凤

DALIANG SHAN 大凉山 Muchuan 沐川 Nanxi 南溪 Fushun 富顺 Jiangjin 江津 Nanchuan 南川 Youyang Tujiazu Miaozu Zizhixian

Ebian Qianwei 峨边 **Yibin** 宜宾 **Luzhou** 泸州 Lu Xian 泸县 Qijiang 綦江 Wanshe Daozhen 道真 Yongshun 永顺

35° 1

2

30° 3

HENAN, ANHUI, JIANGSU, ZHEJIANG AND SHANGHAI

The most densely populated and economically important region of China is shown on this map. The combined population of the areas shown is around 330 million, almost a third of China's total.

Most of the region is part of the vast North China Plain, dominated by the Yellow River in its middle course. The southern quarter of the map shows much more varied country, with many lakes, through which the Yangtze River winds an often mountainous course before flowing out to sea near Shanghai.

The conventional ''boundary'' between north China (dry, cold in winter, with wheat and millet as staple grains) and south China (wet, warm in winter, with rice as staple grain) lies along the line of the Huai River and the Qin Ling escarpment.

Scale 比例尺 1:4 000 000

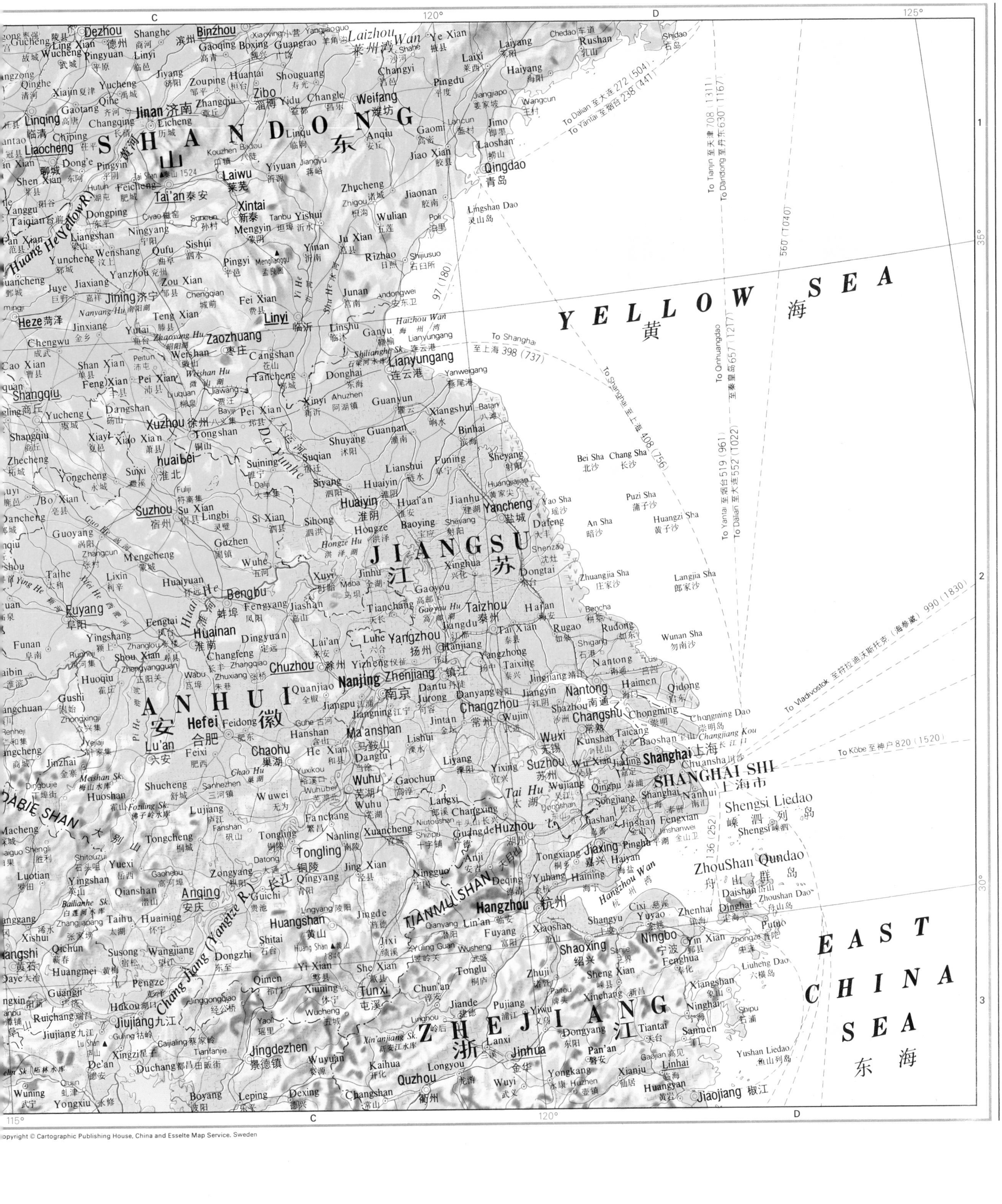

SHANDONG 山东

JIANGSU 江苏

ANHUI 安徽

ZHEJIANG 浙江

YELLOW SEA 黄海

EAST CHINA SEA 东海

Jinan 济南
Qingdao 青岛
Nanjing 南京
Shanghai 上海
SHANGHAI SHI 上海市
Hefei 合肥
Hangzhou 杭州
Ningbo 宁波
Wuhu 芜湖
Tunxi 屯溪

Laizhou Wan 莱州湾
Haizhou Wan

Chang Jiang (Yangtze) R.
Huang He (Yellow R.)

Tai Hu 太湖
Hongze Hu 洪泽湖
Chaohu 巢湖
Gaoyou Hu
Boyang

Shengsi Liedao 嵊泗列岛
ZhouShan Qundao 舟山群岛
Zhoushan Dao
Yushan Liedao

Lingshan Dao 灵山岛

TIANMUSHAN 天目山
DABIE SHAN

YUNNAN AND GUIZHOU

Yunnan Province in the southwest of China shares the rugged topography of southeastern Tibet and the fringes of the Himalayas. Its landscape is extremely varied, ranging from snow-capped mountains to subtropical gorges. Guizhou to the east is mainly high plateau country, with striking limestone scenery, which extends south into neighbouring Guangxi.

In both Yunnan and Guizhou the high temperatures usually associated with a subtropical situation are tempered by high altitude, producing a climate often described as "eternal spring". Inhabitants of the two provinces include many from minority nationality groups such as the Miao, Yi, Zhuang and Yao. There are people of 22 different minorities in Yunnan, more than in any other province.

Scale 比例尺 1:4 000 000

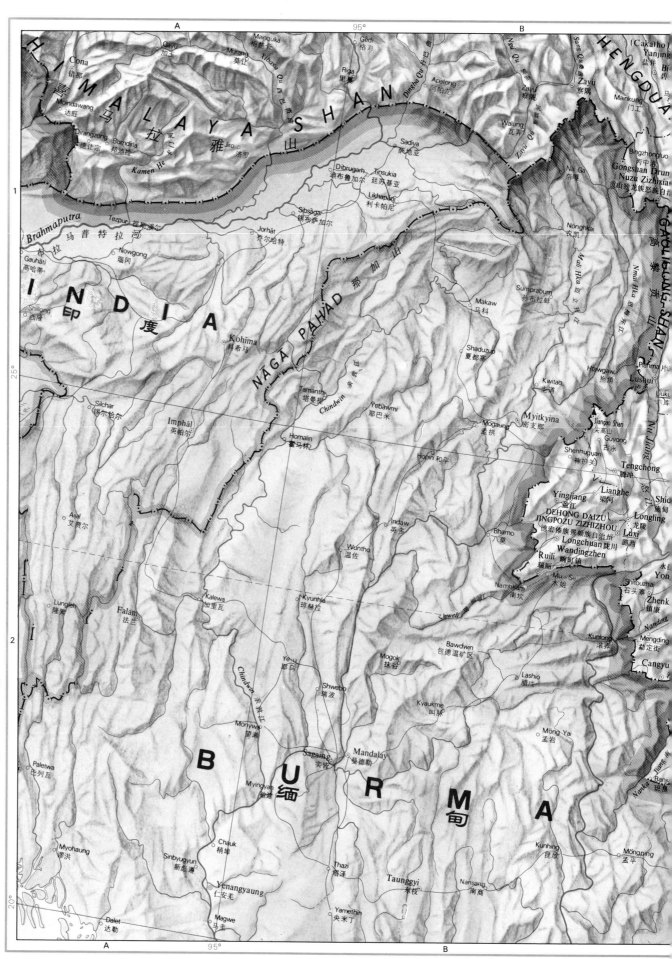

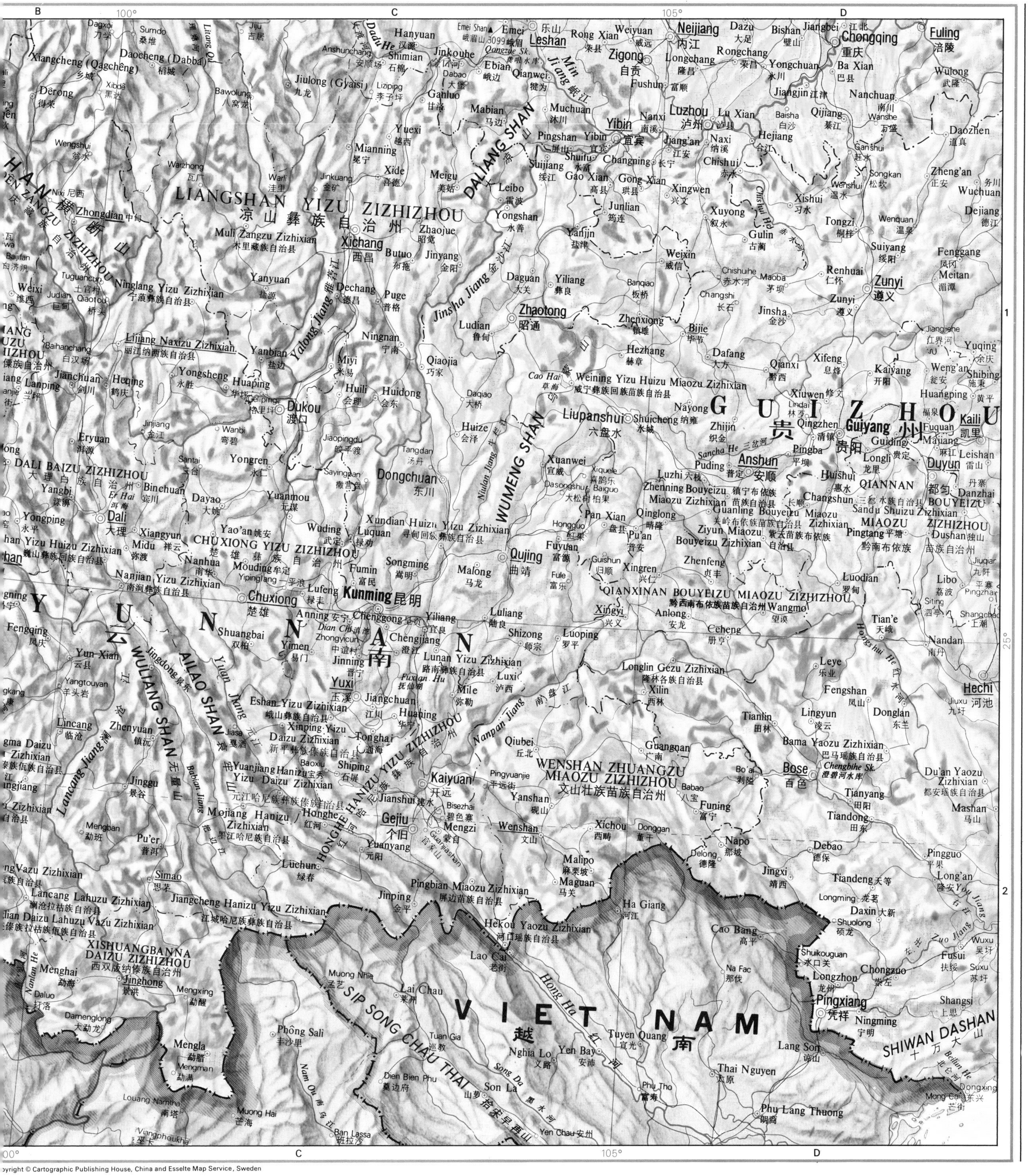

LIANGSHAN YIZU ZIZHIZHOU
凉山彝族自治州

DALIANG SHAN

HENGDUAN ZANGZU ZIZHIZHOU

WUMENG SHAN

GUIZHOU 贵州

DALI BAIZU ZIZHIZHOU
大理白族自治州

CHUXIONG YIZU ZIZHIZHOU

YUNNAN 云南

AILAO SHAN

WULIANG SHAN

HONGHE HANIZU YIZU ZIZHIZHOU

QIANXINAN BOUYEIZU MIAOZU ZIZHIZHOU
黔西南布依族苗族自治州

QIANNAN BOUYEIZU MIAOZU ZIZHIZHOU
黔南布依族苗族自治州

MIAOZU ZIZHIZHOU

WENSHAN ZHUANGZU MIAOZU ZIZHIZHOU
文山壮族苗族自治州

XISHUANGBANNA DAIZU ZIZHIZHOU
西双版纳傣族自治州

SIP SONG CHAU THAI

VIET NAM 越南

SHIWAN DASHAN 十万大山

Chongqing 重庆   Fuling 涪陵
Neijiang 内江   Zigong 自贡
Leshan 乐山   Emei 峨眉
Yibin 宜宾   Luzhou 泸州
Zunyi 遵义   Guiyang 贵阳
Anshun 安顺   Kaili 凯里   Duyun 都匀
Kunming 昆明   Qujing 曲靖
Dukou 渡口   Dali 大理   Chuxiong 楚雄
Yuxi 玉溪   Gejiu 个旧   Mengzi 蒙自
Wenshan 文山   Xingyi 兴义
Bose 百色   Hechi 河池
Pingxiang 凭祥

Xichang 西昌   Zhaotong 昭通
Liupanshui 六盘水   Bijie 毕节

Jinsha Jiang 金沙江   Lancang Jiang 澜沧江
Yuan Jiang 元江   Nanpan Jiang 南盘江
Hong Ha 红河   Hongshui He 红水河

THE SOUTHEASTERN PROVINCES

The landscapes of the southeastern provinces are exceptionally complex and diverse, with varied mountain masses separating innumerable valleys and small plains. The rocky coastline is indented with many bays and inlets and fishing is an important economic activity. The climate is subtropical and very humid, and the area is subject to typhoons in autumn.

The south coast looks out to Southeast Asia and the world beyond. Most Chinese who emigrate overseas originate from provinces of the south coast. It is important in overseas trade and all the original Special Economic Zones—Xiamen, Shantou, Shenzhen and Zhuhai—are along this coast. Hong Kong and Macao, both occupied by foreign powers but due to be returned to China, are also in this area. So too is Taiwan, which since 1949 has been ruled as an independent republic.

The inland provinces on the map, Jiangxi and Hunan, look north, toward the Yangtze River.

Scale 比例尺 1:4 000 000

GUANGXI AND HAINAN ISLAND

Guangxi is bordered to the east by the highly developed Guangdong Province and to the west by the much poorer, isolated and mountainous Yunnan. It represents the transition between the two. Guangxi is peopled by many minority nationalities and is an Autonomous Region for the Zhuang people, China's largest minority group.

The tropical island of Hainan is becoming an important and productive area and is scheduled for accelerated development. Hitherto part of Guangdong Province it is due to be established as a separate province in the late 1980s.

Scale 比例尺 1:4 000 000

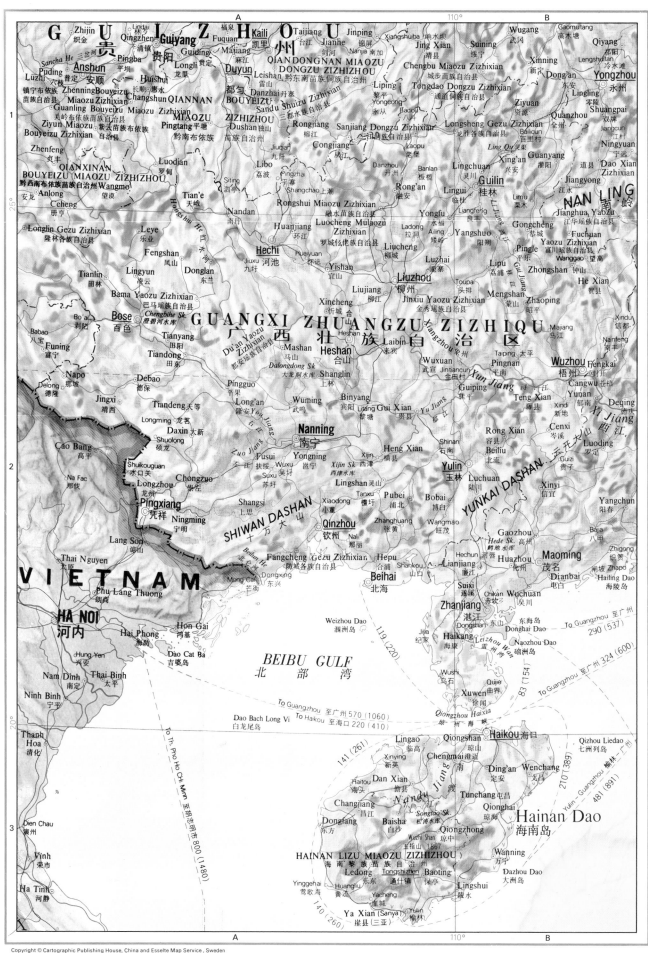

THE SOUTH CHINA SEA ISLANDS

The South China Sea Islands come under the administration of Guangdong Province. There are more than 200 coral islands and reefs, not all inhabited, in three groups—east, west and south. It is thought that there may be rich undersea oil reserves in the area.

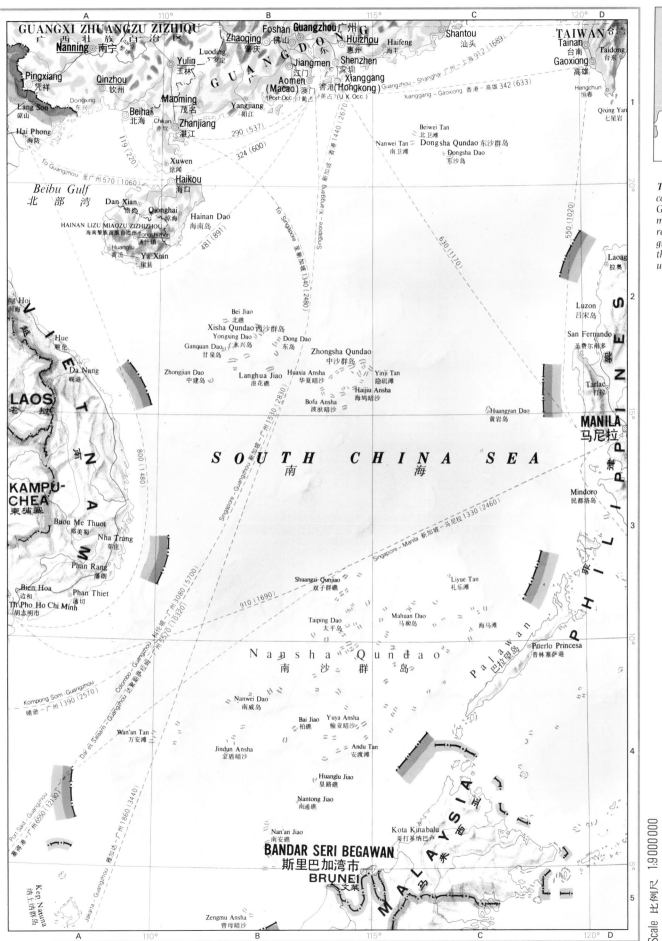

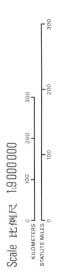

Scale 比例尺 1:9 000 000

CHINA: FACT FILE

CAPITAL

Beijing

POPULATION

1982 Census:
1,003,913,927

1987 estimate:
1,080,000,000

1987 birth rate: 21.04 per thousand

Average life expectancy: 69 years

CURRENCY

Renminbi or RMB
Basic monetary unit: the yuan. At 1988 exchange rate, 3.72 yuan = US $1.00

LANDMASS

China, situated on the eastern part of the continent of Asia, has a total area of about 9,600,000 sq km (3,700,000 sq mi), some 7 percent of the world's land-mass. Around 5,000 offshore islands, with a total area of 80,000 sq km (31,000 sq mi) are also part of China. It is the third largest country in the world after the USSR and Canada.

TOPOGRAPHY

China's 9.6 million sq km (3.7 million sq mi) is divided as follows:

Mountains	33 percent
Plateaus	26 percent
Basins	19 percent
Plains	12 percent
Hills	10 percent

COASTLINE

China's coastline is 18,000 km (11,185 mi) long from the mouth of the Yalu River on the Chinese/Korean border in the north, to the mouth of the Bicang River on the Chinese/Vietnamese border in the south. The coast is flanked by the Bohai, Yellow, East and South China Seas.

RIVERS

There are more than 50,000 rivers in China. The longest, the Yangtze (Chang Jiang) is the third longest river in the world.

MAJOR RIVERS
Yangtze River (Chang Jiang) 6,300 km (3,915 mi)
Yellow River (Huang He) 5,464 km (3,395 mi)
Heilong River (Heilong Jiang) 3,101 km (1,927 mi) (in Chinese territory)
Pearl River (Zhu Jiang) 2,210 km (1,373 mi)
Liao River (Liao He) 1,390 km (864 mi)
Hai River (Hai He) 1,090 km (677 mi)

LAKES

China has more than 2,800 lakes with an area exceeding 1 sq km (0.3 sq mi). More than 130 exceed 100 sq km (40 sq mi).

FRESHWATER LAKES
Lake Poyang, Jiangxi 3,583 sq km (1,383 sq mi)
Lake Dongting, Hunan 2,820 sq km (1,090 sq mi)
Lake Taihu, Jiangsu 2,425 sq km (936 sq mi)
SALTWATER LAKES
Lake Qinghai, Qinghai 4,583 sq km (1,770 sq mi)
Lake Nam Co, Tibet 1,940 sq km (750 sq mi)

MOUNTAIN RANGES

A third of China's landmass is mountainous. Of the 14 mountains in the world that are over 8,000 m (26,000 ft) above sea level, 9 are in China or on its borders. The world's highest peak (Mount Everest) is on the border of Tibet and Nepal. (*Shan* is the Chinese for mountain.)

MAJOR MOUNTAIN RANGES	
Himalayas, highest peak (Mt Everest/ Qomolangma):	8,848 m (29,028 ft)
Karakorum Mountains, highest peak:	8,611 m (28,251 ft)
Hengduan Mountains, highest peak:	7,556 m (24,790 ft)
Tianshan Mountains, highest peak:	7,435 m (24,393 ft)
Nyainqentanglha Mountains, highest peak:	7,111 m (23,330 ft)
Gangdise Mountains, highest peak:	7,095 m (23,277 ft)
Tanggula Mountains, highest peak:	6,137 m (20,134 ft)
Qilian Mountains, highest peak:	5,826 m (19,114 ft)
Altay Mountains, highest peak:	4,374 m (14,350 ft)

ADMINISTRATIVE REGIONS

Provinces

Autonomous Regions

Municipalities

China is divided into 21 provinces, 5 Autonomous Regions and 3 municipalities. Autonomous Regions were created for the largest minority nationalities in those areas where they are concentrated. The name of each Autonomous Region incorporates that of the principal national minority among its inhabitants.

Towns and cities are administered by their province or Autonomous Region. The three municipalities, however, report directly to central government.

PROVINCES		
Anhui	Henan	Qinghai
Fujian	Hubei	Shaanxi
Gansu	Hunan	Shandong
Guangdong	Jiangsu	Shanxi
Guizhou	Jiangxi	Sichuan
Hebei	Jilin	Yunnan
Heilongjiang	Liaoning	Zhejiang

AUTONOMOUS REGIONS

Guangxi Zhuang	Tibet
Inner Mongolia	Xinjiang Uygur
Ningxia Hui	

MUNICIPALITIES

Beijing	Shanghai	Tianjin

CLIMATE

Climate zones in China range from cold-temperate to tropical, but the greater part of the country falls in the temperate and subtropical zones.

● **Rainfall**
Southeastern China has generally adequate rainfall, with more than 800 mm (31 in) annually. Northern China receives well under 800 mm (31 in) a year and much of the Central Asian half of the country is very dry with under 200 mm (8 in) of rain a year. Part of this area is desert with under 25 mm (1 in) of rain a year.

Most of China's rainfall is in the summer months. But in areas with less rainfall, particularly north China, it is unreliable and drought is not uncommon. Floods are more common in southern China. However, both the north and south of the country occasionally experience either drought or flood.

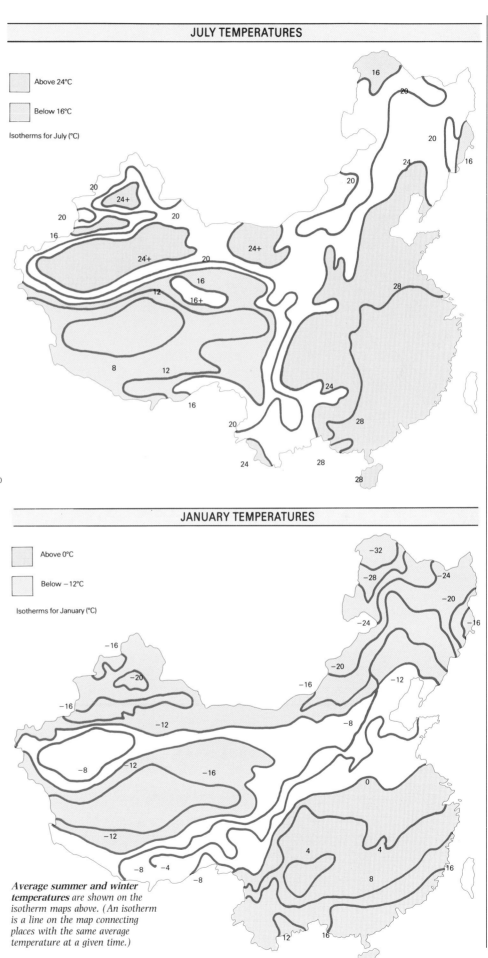

JULY TEMPERATURES

Above 24°C

Below 16°C

Isotherms for July (°C)

JANUARY TEMPERATURES

Above 0°C

Below −12°C

Isotherms for January (°C)

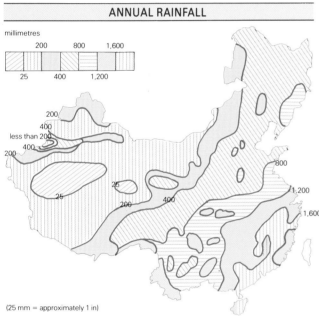

ANNUAL RAINFALL

millimetres
200 800 1,600
25 400 1,200

(25 mm = approximately 1 in)

The average annual rainfall for China is shown here. Only the southeast of the country has an adequate supply, while much of western China is desert with under 25 mm (1 in) of rain a year.

● **Summer temperatures**
In the eastern China lowlands summer temperatures are generally high, above 24°C (75°F). The northeast and mountain peripheries are cooler—16° to 20°C (61°–68°F). Inland, the low-lying desert basins of the northwest (Xinjiang) are hot, 20° to 24°C (68°–75°F), but the high mountain ranges and plateaus of Tibet are always relatively cold (below 16°C/61°F).

Summer temperatures in China are fairly reliable—much more so than the rainfall. The weather is generally hot and humid; the prevailing winds come from the seas to the south and southwest.

● **Winter temperatures**
China is cold (for its latitudes) everywhere in winter, due to north winds from the Siberian anticyclones. The mean isotherm of freezing—0°C (32°F)—divides north from south. The south is cool, but on the south coast average temperatures rise to 16°C (61°F). North China and Tibet become extremely cold with temperatures below −12°C (10°F); in the northeast average temperatures fall as low as −32°C (−26°F) or lower.

Winter temperatures are generally reliable; the weather is usually dry and often sunny, with little rain or snow.

Average summer and winter temperatures are shown on the isotherm maps above. (An isotherm is a line on the map connecting places with the same average temperature at a given time.)

NORTHEAST CHINA

The Northeast is an area of harsh climate but considerable economic importance, and comprises three provinces: Heilongjiang, Jilin and Liaoning. The fertile Northeast Plain that occupies much of the region is surrounded by a broken "horseshoe" of mountainous terrain, much of which is densely forested; here are China's richest and most accessible timber reserves.

Winters in this region are long and bitterly cold; temperatures fall to $-19°C$ ($-2°F$) in the north of Heilongjiang. Summers are short but hot, with average temperatures of $20°$ to $24°C$ ($68°$ to $75°F$). Average annual rainfall for the area is around 600 mm (23.6 in), falling mostly in the summer months.

Previously known as Manchuria, the Northeast was occupied by the Japanese from 1931 to 1945. Attracted by its rich resources of coal and iron, they established a heavy industry base in the area which was still of great importance in the early years of the People's Republic. In China's first Five Year Plan (1953–57), which sought to strengthen the nation's industry by building on existing foundations, no centre was of greater importance than the iron and steel works at Anshan in Liaoning. Still China's largest iron and steel complex, it produces over 20 percent of national output.

Industrial and agricultural development in the Northeast have been helped by its having the most extensive rail network in the country, supplemented by good road, river and air communications. Port facilities, too, are being modernized, particularly at Dalian in Liaoning, to cope with the increasing volume of primary products from the region.

Heilongjiang is the most northerly province of China. Forested mountain ranges dominate the north, while much of the south is fertile plain turning to swamp land in the east. The province is rich in natural resources, possessing extensive coal, iron ore, gold and oil deposits. With the discovery of the huge oil reserves at Daqing, it became the leading oil producer in the country. Heilongjiang is also China's main source of timber, but in May 1987 a month-long forest fire, the worst in the history of modern China, devastated over a million hectares (two and a half million acres) of virgin forest.

Despite the severe winter weather and the short growing season, crops thrive on the fertile plains during the warm summer months. Wheat, maize, millet and sunflowers (for seed oil) are important crops, and Heilongjiang is the biggest producer of soy beans in China.

Harbin, the provincial capital, is a centre for rail and road communication in the Northeast. An industrial city, it is a major producer of machines and machine tools.

The province of **Jilin** includes forested upland areas as well as part of the Northeast Plain. Its resources include coal, iron ore, gold, copper and timber. More unusual products from the Changbai mountain area

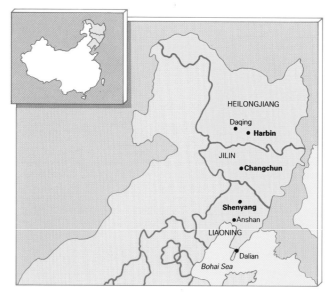

POPULATION	
Liaoning	36,860,000
Heilongjiang	33,110,000
Jilin	22,980,000

Parts of Northeast China are heavily industrialized, but forest-clad mountains and vast wilderness areas still remain. The region is noted for its nature reserves as well as for its iron and steel plants.

in Jilin are sable fur and ginseng. Ginseng root has been cultivated here for more than 1,600 years, and is prized for its medicinal and restorative powers.

Maize is the most important crop in Jilin; soy beans, sugar beet, rice and millet are also grown.

China's first modern automobile plant was built at Changchun, the provincial capital, in the fifties. The province still produces more motor vehicles than any other—97,000 in 1985. With a population of well over a million, the city's manufacturing industries include machine building, chemicals and electrical appliances as well as motor vehicles.

Thanks to its rich mineral resources, **Liaoning**, the most southerly of the three provinces, has become one of China's most important industrial areas. A leading producer of pig iron, steel and coke, it ranked third of all provinces in industrial output in 1985. The giant iron and steel complex at Anshan is founded on local iron ore and coal, together with local supplies of manganese and limestone. Rich deposits of copper, lead, zinc and magnesium supply Liaoning's machine building industry. The presence of Anshan has encouraged the growth of other industries in the province, including metallurgy, coal mining and chemicals, while textiles and paper making are important light industries.

Crops grown on the province's fertile Liao Plain include maize, sorghum, millet and some rice. Cotton and fruit are also important, and Liaoning is second only to Shandong in apple production.

Shenyang, the provincial capital, is the largest city in the region, with a population of more than three million. A major industrial centre specializing in the production of machine tools and mining equipment, it is at the hub of the densest rail network in China.

NORTH CHINA

Important both for its agriculture and industry, the North China region is one of the most densely populated areas of the country. It includes the provinces of Hebei, Shandong, Henan, Shaanxi and Shanxi, and two municipalities, Beijing and Tianjin. The municipalities report directly to central government and are not under the jurisdiction of any province. (Because of its importance, Beijing, the capital, is described separately on pages 54 to 55.)

Much of **Hebei** Province is occupied by part of the fertile North China Plain, bordered by mountains to the west and north. Cotton is an important crop, and the province is China's second largest producer. Wheat, maize and potatoes are also grown in abundance. Fruit crops, particularly pears, are important; they, as well as apples, grapes and dates, grow on the plains and hills. More mountainous areas yield crops of apricots, persimmons, chestnuts and walnuts.

Shandong is a coastal province with a major port and naval base at Qingdao, extensive fishing grounds famed for their giant prawns, and numerous salt fields. Much of the interior of the province is hill country, and at its heart is one of China's Sacred Mountains: Mount Tai. The mountain is 1,500 m (4,921 ft) above sea level, and visitors can climb some 7,000 granite steps cut into its side to admire the ancient temples and the view from its summit.

A leading province both industrially and agriculturally, Shandong was second only to Jiangsu in total output in 1985. It is the top producer of maize, cotton and apples and is second only to Henan in wheat production. Tobacco, tussore silk, sweet potatoes and temperate fruits are other farm products, and the breeding of livestock for meat is also important.

Agricultural land predominates in **Henan** Province, China's leading producer of wheat and tobacco. The latter is particularly important since the Chinese produce, and smoke, more cigarettes than any other nation in the world. Most of the province lies to the south of the Yellow River (Huang He). Schemes to conserve water and control the periodic flooding of this mighty river, known as "China's Sorrow" (for the devastation it inflicts when in flood), are crucial to agricultural production.

The northern part of **Shaanxi** Province is dominated by the loess plateau, where, with irrigation, farming, livestock breeding and forestry thrive. To the south of the plateau wheat and maize are the major crops on the densely populated Weihe Plain while farther south still, sugar cane, tea, and temperate fruits are grown.

Industries at Xi'an, the provincial capital, include a steel plant, textiles, fertilizers and machine tools, principally for the manufacture of irrigation equipment. Xi'an also boasts one of China's main tourist attractions: the army of terracotta soldiers guarding the tomb of the first emperor, Qin Shi Huangdi.

Most of **Shanxi** is more than 1,000 m (3,280 ft)

POPULATION	
Henan	77,130,000
Shandong	76,950,000
Hebei	55,480,000
Shaanxi	30,020,000
Shanxi	26,270,000
Beijing municipality	9,600,000
Tianjin municipality	8,080,000

The loess or yellow earth plateau covers some 1,550,000 sq km (600,000 sq mi) of the North China region. Over the centuries this fine earth has been blown down from the deserts of Mongolia and deposited to depths of 100 m (328 ft) or more in places. Sparse wild vegetation has allowed streams and rain to carve dramatic gulleys in the plateau; but the loess is fertile and, with irrigation, crops thrive.

above sea level and the province includes the eastern edge of the loess plateau. The fertile valley of the Fen River runs more or less north to south through the mountains and hill country before meeting the Yellow River. Shanxi has long fought the problems created by the flooding and silting up of the Yellow River. Successful irrigation and drainage projects, and hillside terracing, have brought great improvements and agriculture, livestock breeding and forestry have all benefited. Wheat, maize and sorghum are major crops.

The capital Taiyuan uses locally mined coal and iron ore to support its iron and steel industry. Machine building, chemicals, electricity and textiles are also important. The province has the largest chemical fertilizer factory in China.

The municipality of **Tianjin** is the third largest urban centre in China. It occupies an area of 11,000 sq km (4,247 sq mi) and has a population of more than eight million, including rural residents. Handling up to fifteen million tonnes of cargo a year, it is North China's principal industrial port and nationally is second only to Shanghai. Its impressive list of industries includes iron and steel, machine building, chemicals, motor vehicles, electronic products, textiles—particularly carpets—and a variety of consumer goods, notably sewing machines and bicycles.

Despite its industrial status, Tianjin is also a city of great charm, and still preserves much distinctive nineteenth-century colonial architecture.

NORTH-NORTHWEST CHINA

A landscape of rugged mountains, vast plateaus and desert, the Northwest includes the province of Gansu and the three Autonomous Regions of Nei Mongol (Inner Mongolia), Ningxia Hui and Xinjiang Uygur. The name of each Autonomous Region incorporates that of the principal national minority among its inhabitants. Together the four present an unbroken rampart of territory separating, and protecting, China's heartland from her northern and western neighbours—the USSR, Mongolia, Afghanistan, Pakistan and India.

Much of **Inner Mongolia** consists of wild plateau land or steppe, at some 1,000 m (3,280 ft) above sea level, which becomes more and more arid toward the west. A mountain range divides the steppe from the more fertile area around the Yellow River to the south of the region. The climate is severe, with long cold winters, low rainfall and frequent droughts.

Of the total population of more than 20 million, only some 2.7 million are Mongols. Many Chinese have settled in the region since the 1960s and, although it is still economically backward, Inner Mongolia is far from being the poorest part of China. On the northern grasslands or steppe the traditional activities of the Mongols still prevail—the breeding of sheep, cattle, camels and horses. The livestock herds provide wool and leather as well as meat and dairy products. Inner Mongolia is the largest producer of sheep wool, goat wool and cashmere in China.

The Inner Mongolian capital of Hohhot, which in the late 1940s boasted only one bus, by the late 1980s had become a modern city of high-rise blocks and 790,000 inhabitants. Its industries include textiles, chemicals and sugar refining. Baotou is the major industrial city of the region and has one of the biggest iron and steel complexes in the country.

Ningxia lies between the province of Gansu and Inner Mongolia, and is divided from the latter by a mountain range. The Yellow River passes through the centre of Ningxia and there are yet more desolate mountains to the south. The irrigated valleys of the Yellow River provide the main farming areas of the region, where wheat, rice and millet are grown.

The long narrow province of **Gansu** stretches from the edge of the Gobi Desert in the northwest to the loess plateau on the borders of Shaanxi in the southeast. Wheat is the main crop, and, thanks to successful irrigation, fruits, particularly melon, are important in the southeast and in oases elsewhere in the province. Like its neighbours Gansu has a low industrial output, but it has potential hydroelectric power from the Yellow River and rich oil reserves.

Lanzhou, the capital, is the major city of the Northwest. Situated on the banks of the Yellow River, it is an industrial centre and notorious for its pollution. Its major industry is petrochemicals and its petroleum equipment plant is the largest in Asia. It is also the major centre for atomic and other military research in China.

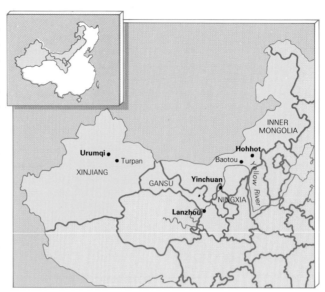

POPULATION	
Gansu	20,410,000
Inner Mongolia	20,070,000
Xinjiang	13,610,000
Ningxia	4,150,000

Vast sand dunes of the Gobi Desert loom over this oasis alongside an irrigation ditch in Gansu. Such oases can stretch for 80 km (50 mi) or more and produce a wide variety of crops, the most important being cotton. Willow and poplar trees provide bursts of colour in autumn.

The largest of all the provinces and Autonomous Regions of China, **Xinjiang** occupies one-sixth of the country. Its population, however, is only 13 million—about 1.3 percent of the total. Although many minority nationalities inhabit the region, the Uygurs, with a population of some 5.9 million, form the largest group.

Xinjiang is virtually surrounded by mountains and is crossed by the Tian mountain range which divides the Tarim Basin in the south from the Dzungarian Basin area in the north. Most of the mountains are over 4,000 m (13,120 ft) high and snow-topped, creating scenery of breathtaking beauty.

Because of its low annual rainfall and extreme temperatures, Xinjiang's agriculture depends on successful irrigation. Water is brought down from the mountains to the low-lying basins via underground channels—thus preventing evaporation by the hot sun—and turns these potential deserts into fertile land. The Turpan (Turfan) Basin, for example, which lies 160 m (525 ft) below sea level and where temperatures can reach 48°C (118°F) has been transformed into a thriving fruit-growing area by successful irrigation. Turpan melons and grapes are famed country wide. Other major crops in Xinjiang are wheat, maize, millet, apples and pears.

This vast province is rich in mineral resources such as nickel, lead, copper and manganese and its three large basins all have oil deposits. However, these resources are still to be fully exploited. Urumqi is the capital of Xinjiang and has a population of about a million people. Its industries include petroleum, iron and steel, sugar refining and textiles.

CENTRAL CHINA

The region of Central China, which is endowed with such natural advantages as a temperate to subtropical climate, many waterways and plenty of fertile land, is the most economically advanced in the whole country. It includes the municipality of Shanghai, the largest city in China, and six provinces. North of the Yangtze are Jiangsu, Anhui and Hubei; south of the river are Zhejiang, Jiangxi and Hunan (described on pages 46 to 47).

Although the great Yangtze, China's principal artery of inland navigation, bisects this region of plains to the north and hill country to the south, it also lends it a geographical unity. Indeed, water is a characteristic of Central China. Many other rivers and canals criss-cross the plains, and the region is scattered with numerous large lakes.

Jiangsu, a coastal province situated on the lower reaches of the Yangtze, is low lying. It is the most densely populated province in China and the most productive. In 1985 it ranked second overall in both agricultural and industrial productivity. Fertile soil, plenty of water sources and a temperate climate make conditions excellent for agriculture, and Jiangsu produces 10 percent of China's total output of both rice and wheat. Maize, tubers, oilseed rape and silkworm cocoons are other farm products. Raising livestock, particularly pigs, is another important source of income for Jiangsu as are both freshwater and ocean fishing.

Jiangsu is a heavily industrialized province and its key industry is textiles. It is a leading producer of cloth and yarn and second only to Zhejiang in silk production. Other light industries, such as paper making, woollen goods and cigarettes, are of considerable importance. Heavy industry, such as iron and steel, motor vehicles and machinery, is concentrated in the cities of Wuxi and Nanjing, the provincial capital.

To the west of Jiangsu lies **Anhui**. This province is divided into three distinct regions by its major rivers: Huaibei, north of the Huai River; Huainan, between the Huai and Yangtze Rivers; and Wannan to the south of the Yangtze. Huaibei is part of the North China Plain and is situated less than 50 km (164 ft) above sea level. Successful irrigation has made it possible to grow rice in what was traditionally a wheat-growing area, thus maximizing productivity. Cotton and soy beans are other major crops.

Between the Huai and the Yangtze in Huainan, hill country predominates, broken by valleys, plains and many lakes. Rice, tea and bamboo all thrive here, particularly in the fertile Yangtze valley area. Wannan, in the south of Anhui, has more rugged terrain, at about 600 to 900 m (2,000–3,000 ft) above sea level, and is renowned for its beauty. There is little agricultural land here, but tea is grown on the hillsides and lush forests yield timber.

Coal is Anhui's most important resource, the main reserves being in Huainan at the centre of the

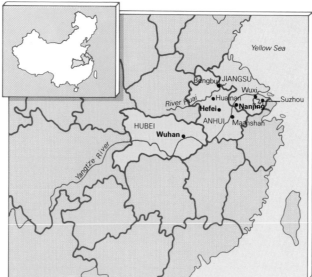

POPULATION	
Jiangsu	62,130,000
Anhui	51,560,000
Hubei	49,310,000

The Grand Canal is at the hub of a complex waterway network in this region of lakes, rivers and canals. Pictured here at Suzhou, it is still a vital and much used transport route, and an important factor in the area's prosperity.

province. Iron ore deposits at Maanshan on the Yangtze supply a steel plant there as well as steel and machine building industries in Wuhu, Bengbu and Hefei. Light industries in Anhui include textiles, cigarette manufacture and food and tea processing.

Hefei, the provincial capital and main economic and cultural centre of the province, has expanded rapidly since the 1950s and, by the late 1980s, had a population of over half a million. Major industries include iron and steel, machine building, chemicals and electronics.

Hubei (meaning "north of the lake") takes its name from its location north of Dongting Lake. With an area of 2,820 sq km (1,090 sq mi) this is the second largest freshwater lake in China and a major landmark in the province. Western Hubei is mountainous, averaging 1,000 m (3,280 ft) above sea level, while much of the east of the province is made up of the Yangtze–Hanshui plain.

Mild winters, hot summers and abundant rainfall—the summer average is 1,000 mm (39 in)—make Hubei ideal for rice cultivation, and it is one of the top four provinces in output. Cotton is another important crop, and wheat, maize and tubers are also grown in some quantity. Tea is cultivated in hilly regions. The many lakes in the province are ideal for fish breeding and freshwater fish and shellfish are in plentiful supply.

Hubei's major mineral resources are copper, limestone and anthracite. Industry is centred around Wuhan, the provincial capital and fifth largest city in China with a total population of nearly three and a half million. Its location on the north-south rail link between Beijing and Guangzhou has contributed to the success of this Yangtze River port.

CENTRAL CHINA/2

The three southern provinces of the Central China region are Zhejiang, Jiangxi and Hunan. These run roughly east to west, south of the Yangtze River. Also just south of the river is the municipality of Shanghai, China's largest city.

Coastal **Zhejiang** is China's smallest mainland province and is renowned for its scenic beauty. In the north of the province is a flat plain, part of the Yangtze valley. This area is crossed with many waterways, rivers and manmade canals, including the Grand Canal which ends at Hangzhou, the provincial capital.

To the south of the plain is mountainous land in the east and lower-lying, agricultural land to the west. The coastline is heavily indented, with many offshore islands, and there are major fishing grounds all along the coast. Zhejiang is a leading provider of both ocean and freshwater fish and shellfish.

The most densely populated and intensively farmed area lies to the north of the province, which, like southern Jiangsu, is part of the Taihu Plain. Rice is the province's major crop; rapeseed and silkworm cocoons are other important farm products. The hills and mountains of Zhejiang yield bamboo and tea, and the province heads the national production tables in both items. Southeastern Zhejiang is also a leading producer of citrus fruits.

Light industries, such as textiles, particularly silk, paper making, cigarettes and soft drinks, account for most of Zhejiang's industrial output. There are several hydroelectric plants, one of which supplies Shanghai.

Hangzhou, the capital, has a population of more than a million. Often referred to as "silk city", its factories manufacture silk, satins, brocades, silk parasols and other handicraft items. Other industries include iron and steel, oil refining, electronics and machine building.

Jiangxi Province, southwest of Zhejiang, is bordered to the north by the Yangtze. A rim of mountainous land fringes the province to the east, south and west, gradually descending to Lake Poyang in the north. Poyang, China's largest freshwater lake, is some 3,583 sq km (1,383 sq mi) in area and rich in fish and other aquatic resources. The plains surrounding Poyang form the main farming area in the province; rice is the major crop. In the more mountainous regions forestry, livestock raising and fruit growing are the main economic activities.

Coal is Jiangxi's major resource, and much of it goes to supply the iron and steel industry at Wuhan in neighbouring Hubei. Porcelain has, for centuries, been Jiangxi's most important product and the town of Jingdezhen is known as China's "porcelain capital". Major industries are concentrated in and around the provincial capital of Nanchang. These include machine building, cotton textiles, food processing—particularly rice milling and oil processing—and insecticides.

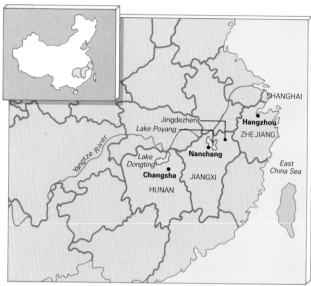

POPULATION	
Hunan	56,220,000
Zhejiang	40,300,000
Jiangxi	34,600,000
Shanghai municipality	12,170,0000

Fertile lowlands criss-crossed by many rivers make Jiangxi Province "a land of fish and rice" Like most of Central China, the area is intensively cultivated and densely populated. Rice is the main crop, grown on low terraces, while tea is cultivated on the gentle hills. The rivers and lakes are rich in fish.

Hunan lies south of Lake Dongting, the second largest freshwater lake in China. Mountains to the east, south and west of the province gradually give way to plains around Dongting in the north.

Rice and tea are the major crops. In 1985 Hunan was China's leading rice producer, accounting for about 14 percent of total output. Oil-bearing crops such as rape and sesame, sugar cane and tobacco are other cash crops. Where agriculture is impossible, forested hillsides yield some important products, particularly, tea oil seed and tong oil seed. (Tea oil is an edible oil, while tong oil is used in paints and varnishes.)

Hunan has large deposits of coal, lead, zinc and antimony in addition to some manganese, tungsten and tin. Provincial industries of note include machine building, particularly mining machinery, generators and machine tools, textiles, paper milling and food processing. There is also a thriving handicraft industry, producing such items as embroidery and multi-coloured umbrellas.

Shanghai is one of China's three municipalities and has the largest population of any city in the country. A major port and trading centre, it is also the great commercial and industrial city of China and leads the country in industrial output. Among its vast number of heavy industries are iron and steel, crude-oil processing and ship building. Light industries include textiles, electronics and the manufacture of items such as bicycles, radios, and TV sets.

The port of Shanghai handles more than one-third of China's annual cargo and ships travel from it to more than 300 ports worldwide.

SOUTH CHINA

Lush green hills and highlands typify the South China region, much of which lies in tropical or subtropical zones. It includes the provinces of Guangdong—the fourth most populous in the country—Fujian, and the Guangxi Zhuang Autonomous Region. Geographically, but not historically, Taiwan, Hong Kong and Macao also fall within this area.

The climate of the south is humid, with long, warm, wet summers, which allow double and sometimes even triple cropping, and mild, mainly dry winters. Summer monsoons water the rice fields as well as a variety of fruits and vegetables, sugar cane, rubber, and oil palms. But the region is also in the path of summer typhoons which regularly wreak havoc with floods and wind damage. The coastline of South China is heavily indented with bays and inlets and there are numerous offshore islands; fishing is thus a traditional activity.

Economically thriving, **Guangdong** is one of the top six provinces in terms of productivity. The Pearl River delta, at its heart, is one of the richest agricultural areas in China, producing rice, tubers, sugar cane and fruits. Guangdong is not only a leading producer of rice but also accounts for nearly half of China's sugar cane crop. The large variety of fruits grown in the province include lychees, tangerines, pineapples and bananas. Tropical crops such as coconuts and coffee are also grown on the beautiful island of Hainan. At present part of Guangdong, Hainan has applied for provincial status.

Rubber trees thrive in the humid climate and produce the bulk of China's output. Silkworm raising and fish breeding are other important money earners. With its extensive coastline, Guangdong has long reaped a rich harvest from the sea and is a leading provider of fish and shellfish in China.

Guangzhou (Canton), the capital of Guangdong, is the most important city in South China. A busy industrial centre, Guangzhou has iron and steel, shipbuilding and chemical industries as well as a variety of light industries, producing aluminium goods, silk, paper, bicycles, sugar, and so on. A city with a history of more than two thousand years, it attracts many tourists who come to admire its ancient temples and other sights, as well as its parks luxuriant with tropical plants.

Three of China's four Special Economic Zones—cities where industrialists and exporters are given special privileges and foreign investors protected from bureaucratic frustrations—are in Guangdong. The three, Shenzhen, Shantou and Zhuhai, have helped to boost the economy of the province.

The coastal province of **Fujian** is predominantly mountainous and hilly, with scant flat arable land. Despite this, rice is a major crop in the narrow river valleys and on terraced hillsides; sugar cane, root vegetables, fruits and tea also flourish in the mild, humid climate. Forested hills yield rubber, oils and

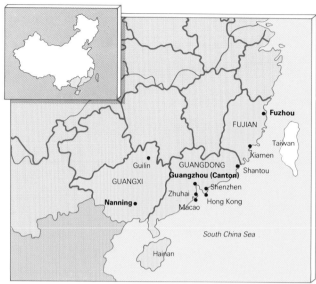

POPULATION	
Guangdong	62,530,000
Guangxi	38,730,000
Fujian	27,130,000

The limestone peaks of Guilin are Guangxi's most famous landmark. The mist-shrouded spires, that soar straight up from the flat terrain on either side of the bamboo-fringed Xi River, have inspired poets and artists for centuries.

resins as well as timber. Scarcity of land suitable for farming has forced many to turn to the coast for their livelihood, and catches of many varieties of fish, shellfish and seaweed are an important source of income for this province as they are for Guangdong.

Fuzhou, the provincial capital, is the industrial centre of Fujian and a busy port. Its industries include machine building, chemicals, electronics, sugar refining and textiles. It is also noted for its handicrafts, particularly its fine lacquerware. The city of Xiamen is the fourth of the Special Economic Zones and Fujian's second commercial and industrial centre.

Guangxi was made an Autonomous Region for the Zhuang people in 1958. The Zhuang, China's largest national minority, account for 35 to 40 percent of the population in the region.

Much of Guangxi is mountainous but there is a central region of gentler limestone hills and plains. Although only 10 percent of the land is suitable for agriculture, most of the population is dependent on farming for a livelihood. Consequently agricultural incomes are well below the national average. Rice, sugar cane and fruits are the main crops. A forestry industry has developed, producing, as in Fujian, wood oils and pine resin as well as timber.

The mineral resources of Guangxi—significant deposits of manganese as well as tin and coal—have yet to be fully exploited. Guangxi's hydroelectric potential is to be developed both for export to neighbouring Guangdong and as a base for its own industrial expansion.

The regional capital Nanning is also a centre for light industry; food processing, sugar refining and machine building are among its major activities. Liuzhou is the other industrial centre of the province.

SOUTHWEST CHINA

The three provinces of Southwest China, Sichuan, Guizhou and Yunnan, have a combined population of well over 160 million. Sichuan, the most populous province in China, already has more than 100 million—if it were a separate nation it would rank eighth in the world. All three provinces are landlocked; only Yunnan shares international boundaries, with Burma, Laos and Vietnam.

Much of the region is ruggedly beautiful, a mixture of high plateaus, basins and narrow valleys, with a lush plain in the red soil of Sichuan. Many of the rivers are vigorous headwaters and a great potential source of hydroelectric power, which is yet to be fully exploited. More than 50 percent of the nation's hydroelectric capacity is concentrated in the Southwest. In addition, there are considerable mineral deposits: coal, oil, natural gas, iron ore, copper, bauxite, tin, gold, potassium and mercury.

The climate ranges from temperate in the north to tropical in the far south of the region, other than at high altitudes. In Sichuan, for example, rainfall averages about 1,000 mm (39 in) a year, falling mostly in the summer months. Summers are hot, with temperatures often well above 30°C (86°F), and winters mild, with average temperatures remaining above 1°C (34°F). Hence this part of China has a particularly abundant flora and crops thrive.

Much of the eastern part of **Sichuan** Province is occupied by the Red Basin, which lies less than 500 m (1,640 ft) above sea level. This attractive area of fertile plains and hills is crossed in the south by the Yangtze River and circled by mountainous country, most of which is more than 1,000 m (3,280 ft) high. The Red Basin, and particularly the Chengdu Plain near its western borders, is an exceptionally productive agricultural area. The main food crop is rice, grown both on the plain and on the terraced hillsides of the Red Basin. Wheat, maize, sugar cane and broad beans are also grown. Oilseed rape, fruit and tea are the major cash crops.

Sichuan developed slowly in the past, in part because its mountain ranges blocked access to the rest of China except by river. New rail and highway networks have encouraged industrial growth, particularly in paper manufacture and textiles. Sichuan is one of China's leading silk producers.

Chengdu is the capital of Sichuan Province, but Chongqing is its largest industrial city and the biggest urban centre in the Southwest. There are over 2,300 factories there, with industries including iron and steel, machine building, chemicals, paper making and textiles.

The provinces of Yunnan and Guizhou together occupy a vast plateau, dissected by canyons and scattered with mountains. **Guizhou's** isolation keeps it one of the poorest provinces in China. It accounts for less than one percent of the country's industrial output and the average income is only half the national average. More than 87 percent of the land is

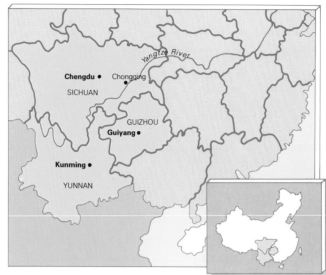

POPULATION	
Sichuan	101,880,000
Yunnan	34,060,000
Guizhou	29,680,000

Sichuan is the most populous province in China and one of the most fertile. In its temperate climate, rice, wheat and vegetable crops thrive on a patchwork of intensively cultivated land.

mountainous, and poor communications leave many villages isolated. Rice, maize and potatoes are grown for food, while oilseed rape and tobacco are the main cash crops.

Despite its present poverty and economic backwardness, Guizhou has potential. It possesses rich mineral deposits of coal, iron ore, phosphorous, manganese, aluminium and mercury. There are plans in hand to exploit these natural assets and the province may have a much brighter future. At present machine building and chemical industries are being developed and textiles and cigarette manufacture are important.

A land of plateaus and mountain ranges, **Yunnan** extends south of the Tropic of Cancer. As many as twenty-three minority nationalities live in the province, more than in any other. Although not as poor as Guizhou, Yunnan is also backward economically and its productivity is comparatively low. Agricultural crops include rice, maize, wheat and sugar cane; in tropical areas, coffee, coconuts, bananas, tea and even rubber can also be grown. Cotton and tobacco are important cash crops—Yunnan has the second highest tobacco production in China.

Reserves of coal, iron ore and tin have helped the development of iron and steel, machine building and chemical industries in the province. Kunming, the capital, is known as the City of Eternal Spring because of its pleasant climate. Although close to the tropics, it is some 1,900 m (6,230 ft) above sea level. The capital is also the industrial centre of the province and is noted for the production of machine tools and optical instruments. Air links to northern and to coastal China have encouraged the city's development since the late 1970s.

TIBET AND QINGHAI

Known as the "roof of the world", the Qinghai-Tibet plateau is a sparsely populated mountain wilderness. The plateau itself lies at an average of 4,000 m (13,120 ft) above sea level but is dominated on its southwestern border by the mighty Himalaya range, which isolates it from the Indian subcontinent. The plateau is now divided into two administrative units: the Tibetan or Xizang Autonomous Region, and the province of Qinghai.

Tibet covers an area roughly twice that of Texas, and has a population of less than two million, the lowest of any of China's regions or provinces. Population density is only two people per square kilometre. In northern Tibet the land averages some 5,000 m (16,000 ft) above sea level. The climate is cold and dry, with biting winds and rarefied air. Although the growing season lasts only three months, the strong summer sun enables crops such as barley and vegetables to be grown, and sheep, goats and horses are raised on the rich pastures. The yak is the main draught animal, and its meat, milk, hide and hair are all used. The staple Tibetan diet is ground and roasted barley, tea and yak butter.

In southern Tibet, however, the valleys of the Yarlung Zangbo River have a milder climate and an annual rainfall of more than 500 mm (19.7 in). Here the growing season is at least six months and there may be double cropping. Main crops are highland barley, winter wheat, rye and buckwheat. Stock raising is important, too, as it is everywhere in Tibet; there are more than twenty-two million head of livestock in the region. Life for the Tibetan herdsmen has changed little over the centuries.

Tibet is reputed to have rich mineral deposits—as yet unexploited—and important hydroelectric and solar energy potential. Industries introduced by the Chinese include thermal and hydroelectric power stations, iron smelting, farm machinery works and processing plants for primary produce. Tibet is the only part of China without rail connections but a modernized highway network has improved communications. Heavy-duty trucks now take only two weeks to travel the Sichuan-Tibet highway from Chengdu to Lhasa. Before the improvements, the journey had to be made by yak and took three months. Moreover the road was only open three months of the year.

Tourism is Tibet's newest industry. In 1986 nearly thirty thousand tourists visited Tibet, a third of them from the United States. Its Himalayan peaks are a major attraction, and more than twenty of them, including Mount Everest (Qomolangma) are now open to visiting mountaineers.

The capital of Tibet is Lhasa, situated at 3,540 m (11,610 ft) above sea level. Dominating the city from its rocky perch is the Potala Palace, traditional home of the Dalai Lama. Before the 1954 treaty which reasserted China's claim to sovereignty over Tibet, the Dalai Lama ruled the land. For Tibetans he

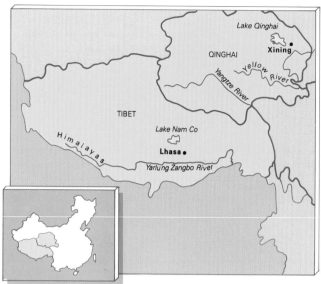

POPULATION	
Qinghai	4,070,000
Tibet	1,990,000

Its mountainous, inhospitable terrain makes Tibet the least populated of all China's regions. Gyangze (right), a settlement clustered around a temple, is one of the few sizable towns.

represented at once deity, patriarch and temporal ruler. The present Dalai Lama fled from Tibet in 1959, during a period of considerable political and economic upheaval, to live in exile over the border in India.

Mountains and vast areas of grassland dominate neighbouring **Qinghai** Province, where China's two greatest rivers, the Yangtze and the Yellow River, rise. To the south of the province lies the Qinghai Plateau, at an average height of 4,000 m (13,120 ft) above sea level; in the northeast is the Qinghai or Kokonor Basin, and in the northwest, the Qaidam Basin, which is part desert, part salt marsh. Conditions in this arid, inhospitable province are hard and Qinghai is one of the three poorest areas in China. Winters are long and cold and rainfall low—only 25 mm (1 in) a year over much of the area. Irrigation is essential to farming, which is concentrated in the east of the province. Spring wheat, highland barley and potatoes are the main crops.

The Qaidam Basin may hold the key to any prospect of improvement in Qinghai's future. Some 240,000 sq km (92,660 sq mi) in area, it possesses reserves of oil, coal, iron ore, non-ferrous metals and non-metallic minerals, including asbestos, potassium and salt. Already, Qaidam Basin, which used to be sparsely populated, supports more than 290,000 people; and more than a dozen industries, including chemicals, asbestos and petroleum, have been established in the area.

Xining, in the east, is the administrative and industrial capital of the province. Present industries include iron and steel and coal; and a magnesium processing plant is under construction. Near Xining is the Taer Monastery or Kumbum, one of the most important monasteries of Tibetan Buddhists.

BEIJING

The national capital, Beijing is situated near China's east coast on the northernmost edge of the great North China Plain. The city itself lies on the plain at only 44 m (144 ft) above sea level, but it is flanked to the north and west by mountain ranges. Beijing is a municipality under direct control of central government and occupies an area of some 16,800 sq km (6,500 sq mi). Its total population, including that of counties under its administration, is 9,600,000.

Winters in Beijing are cold and dry with average temperatures as low as −4°C (24.8°F) in January. Summers are hot and humid. July is the hottest month with average temperatures of 25.8°C (78.4°F) and most of the annual rainfall occurs in July and August. Spring and autumn are probably the most pleasant times of the year, with moderate temperatures and little rain.

Beijing is an ancient city. The earliest recorded evidence of settlement on or near the present site dates from 3000 to 2000 BC. And fragments of the skull of what is termed "Peking Man", found near the city, provide evidence of human settlement there some 500,000 years ago.

Under many different names the city has served intermittently as the capital of China since the fourteenth century. The name Beijing, or northern capital, was first applied to today's city by the third Ming emperor in 1421. The splendid buildings of the Imperial Palace, once the residence of the imperial court, date from this period. The Palace is also known as the Forbidden City because, in imperial times, ordinary people were forbidden to enter it.

The visitor to Beijing is inevitably drawn to the great buildings of the past—The Temple of Heaven and Hall of Prayer for Good Harvests, the Summer Palace, the fifteenth-century gate, Qian Men. But these are jostled by monuments to the present. Outside the Imperial Palace is Tiananmen Square which celebrates the People's Republic of China. Covering about 40 hectares (99 acres), it is one of the largest squares in the world and contains the Monument to the People's Heroes, the Great Hall of the People, the Museums of Chinese History and the Chinese Revolution and the Chairman Mao Memorial.

Beijing is one of China's leading industrial centres as well as its administrative capital. Besides heavy industries that include iron and steel, machine building, chemicals and power equipment, it supports a range of light industries, such as textiles, handicrafts, electrical and electronic goods.

The high concentration of industry contributes to one of Beijing's major problems: air pollution. In 1988 China's first survey of industrial pollution revealed that Beijing has become one of the world's most polluted cities, with air sixteen times as contaminated as that of Tokyo. Another cause of the pollution is the use of solid fuel for heating and cooking. In an effort to reduce this problem residents

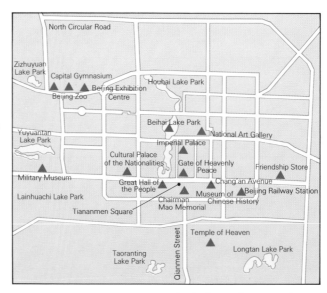

POPULATION	
Beijing	9,600,000

At the heart of Beijing is the magnificent Imperial Palace. This view looks over the rooftops of its many halls, toward Tiananmen Square.

are to be supplied with better quality coal to cut soot levels. Long-term plans aim to replace coal with gas. Motor vehicles are the third form of pollutant and, as a result of the survey, will be required to be fitted with pollution control devices.

Although agriculture is not normally associated with cities, some 424,000 hectares (1,047,715 acres) of land are under cultivation in rural areas of Beijing. In 1985 the municipality produced 2,197,000 tonnes of grain, mostly maize and wheat. Fruit crops, particularly apples, pears and grapes, are also important.

In 1983 a plan for Beijing's future development was ratified. It covers the years up to 2000 by when it is hoped that Beijing will have been transformed into a modern city which nevertheless mirrors its proud history, traditions and culture. A major objective is to alleviate the chronic housing problem by gradually rehousing some city dwellers in new estates in the inner suburbs. These are to be provided with their own services, shopping and cultural facilities. In addition, three new satellite towns are to be developed in the outer suburbs.

Despite overcrowding, inadequate facilities, poor housing, and air and noise pollution, Beijing, as the historic and cultural capital of China, is a major tourist attraction. In 1985 it received some 739,600 overseas visitors, and the figure is on the increase. But many tourists have complained of the poor services and conditions in the city. In response, the Beijing Tourism Bureau has issued regulations for hotel staff and tourist guides, and drawn up a list of the hotels and restaurants which qualify for use by foreign visitors. Although Beijing boasts many superb scenic spots and historic monuments, amenities will need to be expanded if the rapid growth of the tourist industry is to be sustained.

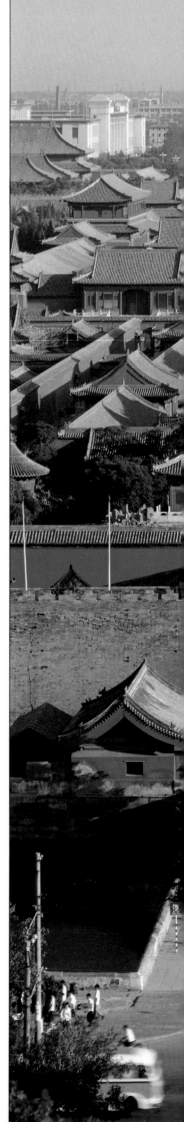

PLANT LIFE

An estimated 30,000 species of flowering plants occur in China, and new ones are being discovered and described almost daily. Many are unique to China, particularly those found in the mountains of the west and southwest. The exceptionally rich flora can be attributed to this huge country's widely varied habitats in a great range of climates, soils and elevations.

China can be divided into two main categories of habitat. In the north and west, covering about half the landmass, grasslands and deserts predominate; in the east and south forests are most characteristic. The grasslands and semi-deserts are mainly grazed, and there is some cultivation of arable grasses where irrigation permits. Drainage is mostly internal with few rivers flowing away from these areas.

In the wooded regions, with their plains and fertile river valleys, much of the land has been cultivated. A number of major rivers drain eastward across terrain interrupted by low hills and mountain ranges. In both main areas, many gradations are to be found from one habitat type to another.

Nowhere in China can the richness of the flora be better demonstrated than in the province of Yunnan, in the country's extreme southwest. In the southern part of the province, close to the border with Burma, is dense tropical and subtropical rainforest typical of that widespread in Southeast Asia. Farther north, and throughout much of central and east Yunnan, evergreen broad-leaved forests of oak, schima and laurel with large areas of secondary pine dominate.

These give way in the northwest of the province, where the altitude increases, to mixed deciduous and coniferous woodland. Montane coniferous woodland of larch, fir and spruce takes over on the great mountain ridges dissecting the region. Above the treeline, at about 4,000 m (13,000 ft), scrub (often of rhododendrons), scattered meadows and open rocky areas support a rich variety of alpine flowers.

About 8,000 years ago an almost unbroken expanse of forest would have stretched from the south of China northward on the eastern side of the country. This would have been a gradation from tropical rainforest through broad-leaved evergreen and broad-leaved deciduous forests to the northern boreal coniferous forests. However, as in other countries, man's influence on China's natural vegetation has been dramatic. Much forest has been cut to increase agricultural land, and to provide fuel, so that the forests are now only a vestige of their former glory.

The magnificent areas that still survive are now less at risk than before, thanks to the efforts of the country's growing number of conservationists. The importance of woodland and forest, with their rich variety of trees, and the value of a prodigious range of herbs and smaller plants for medicinal, culinary or decorative purposes, has long been recognized by the Chinese. Today measures are being taken to preserve

Magnolia delavayi (top left) *This small evergreen tree reaches a height of about 10 m (33 ft) and produces large deliciously scented blooms. It grows on mountain slopes in Yunnan Province.*

Primula bulleyana (top right) *One of a number of so-called bog primulas that thrive along the banks of streams and marshy places on lower mountain slopes in southwestern China.*

Meconopsis delavayi (middle left) *The genus Meconopsis includes the striking blue poppies that hail from the Himalayas and southwestern regions of China. This particular species, which is 8 to 15 cm (3–6 in) tall, is known only from the Lichiang Snow Range in northwest Yunnan Province.*

Tofieldia yunnanensis (middle right) *The genus Tofieldia occurs right across the northern hemisphere, where most species inhabit mountain regions. The species shown here, only 6 to 8 cm (2–3 in) tall, grows in parts of southwestern China.*

Iris delavayi (left) *This beautiful wild iris grows along the banks of streams and on boggy mountainsides in southwestern China.*

and protect the fragments of natural and unspoilt flora that remain.

Since the late 1960s the Chinese have been engaged in a systematic, province by province, analysis of their flora: the *Flora Sinica*. The work is unlikely to be completed, however, until the first or second decade of the twenty-first century.

The great plant collectors of the nineteenth and early twentieth centuries (most of whom were Irish, British or French and, later, American) were well aware that China was a treasure trove of species. Botanists such as the Abbé Delavay, Reginald Farrar, George Forrest, Robert Fortune, Augustine Henry, Frank Kingdon Ward and Ernest Henry Wilson systematically searched the country, particularly the provinces of Gansu, Sichuan, Yunnan and south-eastern Tibet, for specimens. Many of the species they brought back and introduced in the West proved hardy, and some of the most familiar plants in Western gardens today originated from China.

Among the trees are several species of maple, cherry and plum as well as the handkerchief tree, *Davidia involucrata*; the foxglove tree, *Paulownia tomentosa*; the maidenhair tree, *Gingko biloba*; the dawn redwood, *Metasequoia glyptostroboides* and the Chinese plum-yew, *Cephalotaxus fortunei*. Familiar shrubs include many species of rhododendron, azalea and camellia, as well as species of deutzia and philadelphus, daphne, cotoneaster, forsythia, clematis, rose, and many more. The richest sources of plant introductions were probably the herbaceous and alpine species, including many varieties now long established in the West of iris, saxifrage, gentian and primula (primrose).

Rhododendron yunnanensis *This sweetly scented species was one of the many rhododendrons collected in China by plant hunters in the 19th century and taken back to Western gardens. It is an open shrub, growing to 3 m (almost 10 ft), with flowers ranging from white to deep pink.*

Rhododendrons grow in great profusion in the mountains of Sichuan and neighbouring Yunnan, particularly between altitudes of 2,500 and 3,500 m (8,000 to 12,000 ft).

ANIMAL LIFE

With its great size and remarkable diversity of habitats—ranging from flat, grassy plains to the world's highest mountains, from deserts to tropical forests, as well as huge rivers and lakes—China has more species of vertebrate wildlife than any other single country. There are 450 species of mammals (13.5 percent of the world total); 1,195 species of birds (11.2 percent of the world total); 460 species of reptiles and amphibians, and around 2,000 species of fish. Research on invertebrate species in China has barely begun and it will be some years yet before there is any indication of numbers.

Although some creatures have become relatively scarce in much of China, due to environmental abuse and unlawful hunting and trapping, the country has certain areas which abound with wildlife. Outstanding among these is Xishuangbanna, in the southernmost part of Yunnan Province, where some 253 species of mammals—more than half China's total— are found in the tropical forests. They include leopards, Bengal tigers, the Indian elephant, gibbons and monkeys. Among the 400 species of bird recorded in the area are some of China's most beautiful, such as the Asian fairy bluebird, the long-tailed broadbill and Mrs Gould's sunbird.

In northeastern China, where temperatures can plummet to −50°C (−58°F), there exist areas undisturbed by man. The Northeast China tiger survives in forests which are also home to the brown bear, sable, red deer and European lynx. The scaly-sided merganser duck breeds beside fast-flowing rivers, and huge marshes are the summer haunts of red-crowned and white-naped cranes.

China's most famous native animal is the giant panda, now found only in Sichuan, Gansu and Shaanxi Provinces, where it feeds mainly on bamboo. Its ancestors were far more widely distributed and less specialized in diet, like the smaller omnivorous red panda which ranges from southwestern China to Qinghai Province.

Of China's three races of tiger the rarest—and the only race endemic to China—is the South China tiger. The forty to sixty animals remaining may be doomed by deforestation and illegal hunting. Both the Northeast China tiger (also rare) and the Bengal tiger are protected in nature reserves.

Other endemic rarities include the golden monkey, found in mountain forests from Gansu Province south to Guizhou Province; the black muntjac, a tiny deer living in the forests of the middle and lower Yangtze Valley; the Yangtze River dolphin of which only about 300 remain; and the single-humped Bactrian camel, some 200 of which are known to exist in the deserts of Xinjiang in western China.

Eight of the world's fourteen species of crane breed, winter or spend all year within China's borders. The red-crowned crane—used in painting and other Chinese arts as a symbol of long life—breeds in the northeastern wetlands. More than half the total

The golden or snub-nosed monkey, Pygathrix roxellana (top), *inhabits the mountain forests of southern China. The monkeys live in troops and feed on fruit, buds, leaves and bamboo shoots.*

Cranes (above) *are among the 150 species of birds to be seen at the large Zhalong nature reserve near Qiqihar in Heilongjiang Province.*

The red panda, Ailurus fulgens (below), *lives in bamboo forest but its diet is less specialized than that of its giant relative. It feeds on grass, fruit, nuts and even on mice and small birds.*

world population of 1,400 red-crowned cranes winter at the marshes of the eastern coasts. More than 90 percent of the world's known population of Siberian cranes, some 1,600 birds, were counted wintering at the Lake Poyang Nature Reserve in Central China in 1988.

Nineteen of the world's fifty-six pheasant species occur wholly or largely within China. Several are highly ornate—such as Reeve's pheasant, with a tail five times its body length; and the male golden pheasant with crimson underside and yellow crest. Most are forest birds, with at least eight species now rare and facing possible extinction.

China is an important destination for migratory birds. Great numbers fly to the south of the country in winter to avoid the harsh climate of eastern Russia and northern China. Others arrive in spring to breed, while still more are transient, passing through the country each spring and autumn *en route* to and from their winter refuges farther south. Notable among the latter are shorebirds, several of which winter in southern Australia and breed in the far north of Siberia. They gather in huge flocks at coastal estuaries, which are of immense importance as "refuelling stations" along the migration routes.

Reptiles include the Chinese alligator, found only along the Yangtze River, mainly in Anhui Province. A small species at 1.2 to 1.8 m (4 to 6 ft) in length, it is related to the North American Mississippi alligator. In 1976, with only 100 known in the wild, it appeared near extinction, but more thorough surveys and effective conservation measures increased the number of the wild population to around 500 by 1987. Still more are being reared in captivity at an alligator breeding centre.

There are some 800 species of freshwater fish in China, at least half of which occur only there. One, the Chinese sturgeon, a fierce predator found in the Yangtze River, is the largest freshwater fish in the world, at up to 4 m (13 ft) in length.

The giant panda is now an endangered species. Once these creatures ranged over much of eastern China, but, with the destruction of large areas of bamboo forest, on which they depend for their food, they have become increasingly rare. In order to protect the remaining wild population, which by 1988 had dwindled to only 800 animals, the government has established 12 panda reserves. The largest is the 2,000-sq km (770-sq mi) Wolong reserve in Sichuan.

In this picture a young giant panda, Ailuropoda melanoleuca, is feeding on bamboo—its principal food—in a forest in Sichuan. Its forepaws are specialized for grasping the bamboo stems: each has an elongated wristbone that is effectively a sixth digit, against which the first and second digits can be flexed.

The golden pheasant, Chrysolophus pictus (below), is a native of China that has been introduced into Europe. The female bird is much plainer than the gorgeously plumaged male.

CONSERVATION

The luxuriant tropical forests of Xishuangbanna in southernmost Yunnan are exceptionally rich in plants and wildlife. Endangered species such as the Bengal tiger, the green peafowl, the grey peacock pheasant and the rufous-necked hornbill occur there, as well as the more common gibbons, wild boar, slow loris and many other creatures.

Five areas of the forest, which covers some 25,000 sq km (9,600 sq mi), are already protected, and a National Park is being established there with the aid of the World Wide Fund for Nature. This will allow better access to the forest for visitors and should promote interest in conservation among the local people. There is already a Tropical Plant Institute deep in the heart of the forest.

Although the arts and literature in China express a deep feeling for nature, the relationship between man and his environment has often been far from harmonious. The most consistent threats to many species of both plants and wildlife have been loss of habitat, mainly through deforestation and pollution, and unlawful hunting and trapping. The Chinese are now more conservation-conscious than in the past but, as elsewhere in the world, there are long-term difficulties to solve.

Deforestation has long been a major problem: north China was largely deforested by 1225. If it continues at the 1987 rate, it has been projected that the country will lose three-quarters of its forests by the year 2000. In the late 1980s only about one-third of China's forests produced usable timber, so trees were being felled in areas rich in wildlife. It is likely that by around 1995, the Elliot's pheasant (already an endangered species) will be extinct in Jiangxi, one of the few provinces where it is still found, if the forests it inhabits there are destroyed. Logging is scheduled to begin in an area of virgin forest in Guangdong Province, while a nearby area of secondary forest has, ironically, been designated as a nature reserve as it is of no economic value.

Conservation in modern China is still suffering the impact of the period following the establishment of the People's Republic in 1949. Then, deforestation accelerated as fuel was sought for a million backyard smelting pots, built when Mao urged the peasants to produce their own pig iron. The "grain first" policy, which emphasized the importance of grain production in the struggle to keep the nation fed, also led to deforestation, and to erosion and desertification, as attempts were made to grow wheat in unsuitable areas. Even in the 1980s heavy demand for wood as fuel, particularly in rural areas, continues.

A campaign aimed at combating pests proved ecologically unsound. "Four Evils" (sparrows, rats, flies and bugs) were selected for mass extermination. Vegetation was cleared to remove insect breeding sites; and in the non-selective war against the sparrow, millions of other birds died—up to 800,000 were killed in three days in Beijing alone. Mao was eventually persuaded that the mosquito should replace the sparrow in the campaign.

Hunting and trapping for financial gain is always difficult to control. During the 1987 season, some US $135,000 worth of skins—including those of ten state-protected species such as tigers, leopards and even pandas—were reputedly traded each day at a market in Jiangxi Province. People have even been caught attempting to smuggle giant panda skins into Hong Kong. The collection of living things for use as medicines also has its effect on the environment. Some part of almost every wild plant, fungus and creature is judged to have a beneficial effect on some ailment.

Industry has generally developed with little regard for the environment, leading to serious pollution. Anti-pollution measures, such as controlling the emissions from smokestacks and reducing discharge into rivers, have worked well in several areas, but are expensive. The effects of acid rain are already evident and could become worse since China relies on coal to provide much of its power. (Emissions from burning coal are among the major pollutants that cause acid rain.)

On the positive side, since 1976 legislation has been introduced to protect China's environment and wildlife. The media increasingly carry features on natural history, which have proved extremely popular, and the numbers of conservationists are growing. By 1987 there were 333 nature reserves covering 19.33 million hectares (47 million acres)—roughly 2 percent of the land area. Some, such as the Changbai Mountain Reserve in Jilin Province and the subtropical forest reserve of Dinghushan in Guangdong Province, are intended to protect outstanding ecosystems; others were established for the benefit of rare plants and animals.

Reserves exist for threatened mammals such as the golden monkey, the Northeast China tiger and the Chinese river dolphin (the world's only surviving freshwater dolphin, found in the Yangtze and referred to as the "panda in the water"). Twelve reserves exist to protect the giant panda; the principal one at Wolong in northern Sichuan is home to at least seventy of these creatures.

The World Wide Fund for Nature (which has a panda as its emblem) has provided for a panda research centre at Wolong and is establishing a National Park in the species-rich tropical forests of Xishuangbanna, Yunnan Province.

Another international organization playing an important conservation role in China is the International Crane Foundation, which is devoted to research on and protection of these birds. The most notable of China's fourteen crane reserves is Lake Poyang in Jiangxi Province. Here in winter some 1,600 Siberian and 2,000 white-naped cranes, 50,000 swan geese and roughly a quarter of a million other waterfowl gather to make what one ornithologist described as "the greatest bird spectacle in Asia".

Other conservation initiatives in China range from providing nestboxes and feeding stations to entice birds into a Beijing park (the city has remarkably few wild birds) to the "Great Green Wall". The latter is a highly ambitious reafforestation scheme aimed at preventing the southward spread of the Gobi Desert by planting a 7,000-km (5,600-mi) belt of trees.

China clearly has good intentions for the future, but its conservation policies are threatened by the growth of an already huge population, with attendant demands on land use. Protecting the environment and wildlife while China develops will be extremely challenging.

Badly polluted air forces this cyclist in Guangzhou to wear a protective mask. Traffic is the main source of pollution in Guangzhou which has more cars than any other city in the country. A 1988 survey revealed, however, that 60 Chinese cities suffer unacceptably high levels of pollution, caused by industry and by the burning of solid fuel for cooking and heating as well as by traffic.

THE GREAT WALL

The *wanli changcheng*, or Great Wall of Ten Thousand Li, stretches some 2,400 km (1,500 mi), from Shanhaiguan on the Bohai Gulf to the east of Beijing, across into Chinese Central Asia. To the Chinese it is one of the most important symbols of their nation's greatness and the longevity of its culture. It is unthinkable that a distinguished visitor to China should leave without climbing part of the wall, and it has become a regular destination for tourists, both foreign and Chinese. Indeed, the Chinese have a saying which, roughly translated, means, "You're nobody till you've seen the Great Wall," and thousands of Chinese visitors have scrawled their names on it—much to official disapproval.

The wall's origins can be traced back to the turbulent period of Chinese history known as the Warring States (453–221 BC). At this time various kingdoms were struggling for supremacy after the disintegration of the Zhou Empire. As well as battling with each other, the most northerly states—Qin, Zhao and Yan—were concerned with protecting their communities, which were mainly agricultural, from incursions by the nomadic cattle-raising Xiongnu. These people, possibly related to the Huns who invaded the Roman Empire, lived in the steppes to the north. Qin and the other northern kingdoms built border fortifications of dykes and earthworks to defend themselves against the Xiongnu, and some states also constructed their own defensive walls as protection from neighbours.

In 221 BC the king of Qin subdued all the rival Warring States and united China, proclaiming himself Shi Huangdi, "first emperor" of the Qin dynasty. He then ordered the consolidation and extension of the existing walls, and the foundations of the Great Wall as it is today were laid. The rulers of the Han dynasty (206 BC–AD 220) continued to maintain and lengthen the wall as part of their policy of containing the Xiongnu and of extending Chinese control westward. Subsequent governments did the same, particularly that of the Sui dynasty in the sixth century.

Most of the structure of the wall visible today is much later than this. It dates from the Ming period (1368–1644), after Chinese forces had driven the Mongols back to the steppes. The Mongols, who as nomadic invaders were in many ways the successors to the Xiongnu, had occupied China since the thirteenth century. The Ming wall, built in the early fifteenth century, followed the lines of the old walls only roughly; more up-to-date construction methods were introduced and the wall proved useful in repelling the Mongol attacks of 1438–49. During and after this attempted invasion an inner wall was built, and in some places there are double and even triple walls.

Parts of the wall, notably those dating from the Ming period, are in relatively good repair, but in northwestern China there are many derelict remains of earlier walls. Even sections of the Ming wall near Beijing have been depleted by farmers looking for good-quality stone to repair their pigsties.

The wall by itself was never a physical barrier to invasion; it always depended for its effectiveness on adequate garrisons, as well as on sophisticated military organization and effective communication between the watchtowers.

In addition to being a military boundary, the wall has for centuries marked one of the most fundamental cultural divisions in continental East Asia— between the northern, stock-breeding nomads and the settled agrarian populations who were concentrated to its south. This division was by no means absolute; "frontier" society on both sides of the wall became a fascinating and complex mixture of economies, cultures, languages and ways of life which played a vital part over the centuries in defining the nature of "Chineseness".

The western extremity of the Ming period Great Wall lies in arid landscape near the town of Jiayuguan in Gansu Province. The watchtower overlooks a vast panorama of barren desert that is in stark contrast to the lush hills surrounding the eastern end of the wall on the other side of China.

This flat desert land lies between mountain ranges to the north and south, and the Jiayu Pass at the end of the wall has always been of great strategic importance.

Like a great dragon snaking its way across the mountains, the Great Wall is the only manmade structure visible from the moon.

This section near the village of Badaling, visible in the right of the picture, is only 64 km (40 mi) from Beijing and is consequently the most visited part of the wall. Badaling village reaps a considerable income from the tourist trade.

The wall varies in height and width along its length but this section is about 6–7 m (20–23 ft) high and about 6.5 m (21 ft) wide at the base. Some of the pathway along the wall is stepped and visitors are often surprised at its steepness (above).

THE GREAT WALL/2

THE GREAT WALL

▪▪▪▪▪▪ Ming Great Wall (15th century)

▨▨▨▨▨▨ Manchurian defence line (17th century)

The Manchurian defence line, *which extended the Great Wall,* *was developed to counter the threat* *from the Manchus to the north.*

On its journey from the east coast of China to the northwestern province of Gansu some 2,400 km (1,500 mi) away, the Great Wall snakes over mountains and through valleys, and crosses the Yellow River in several places.

The average height of the wall is 8 m (26 ft) and the average width at the top 6 m (20 ft). Watchtowers and fortresses are stationed at strategic points along its length. Offshoots from the main wall follow the lines of earlier fortifications.

BUILDING THE WALL

Local materials had to be used to build the wall since transport of other materials over long distances was both impractical and expensive. In the west, the wall was mainly of earth and unfired brick, but farther east, construction techniques were more advanced, with greater use of brick and stone.

The earliest sections were basically defensive ditches with walls of earth built up by pounding the soil into wooden frames.

The wall built by Emperor Qin Shi Huangdi was more sophisticated. It is thought that the watchtowers were built first, and that the linking walls used the rammed-earth technique, but on a foundation of rubble and stone. The walls were then faced with brick and topped with a brick road surface.

Most of the Ming-period reconstruction of the Great Wall was in stone.

BUILDERS OF THE WALL

No one volunteered to go to the frontiers of civilization to build the wall. The earliest builders were conscript soldiers or slaves, who toiled under atrocious conditions, in the reign of the autocratic Qin Emperor.

During the Han dynasty, soldiers were accompanied by slaves, who were freed on condition that they went to the border, and by convict work gangs. Other labourers were peasants who had lost their livelihoods.

The community that grew up around the wall acquired a character of its own, part agricultural, part military. It is a generally difficult area to farm, since the soil is poor and rocky, so complete self-sufficiency was not possible. In the less authoritarian Ming dynasty, governments offered inducements, such as licences to participate in the salt trade, to attract people to the frontier life.

The Hongwu Emperor in the first Ming reign (1368–98) made his older sons responsible for garrisoning the wall, and a system known as merchant colonization developed. Traders from the Shanxi and Shaanxi areas in northern China, as well as from the more prosperous south, were given licences to participate in the lucrative salt trade based in the Yangtze region, which was a government monopoly. This was on condition that they would transport grain to the frontier regions—not in itself a profitable enterprise.

In parallel with this merchant colonization policy was the military colonization programme; in this, soldiers and their families combined garrison duties with working the land they had been allocated. Assignment to these military colonies was hereditary, so generations of soldier-farmer families lived out their lives on the wall.

EARLIER GREAT WALLS

••••••• Walls earlier than Qin

━ ━ ━ ━ Qin Wall (2nd century BC)

The first defence line across *China was the Qin-dynasty wall* *that consolidated earlier structures.*

DIMENSIONS OF THE WALL AND ITS TOWERS

2.7 m

76 cm

4 m

Tower

Wall

11-12 m

Stone
1.5 m

Stone
1.5 m

Rubble

Stone base
1.2-1.5 m

Stone

12 m

(1 m = 3 ft 3 in)

Most watchtowers were up to
12 m (40 ft) tall and about 12 m
(40 ft) square at the base. The
base was usually constructed of
stone and the wall itself of rubble

or earth, faced with brick or stone.
The dimensions of the wall and
tower (above) are typical of much
of the 15th-century section of the
Great Wall.

*Garrisons stationed in
watchtowers* at strategic intervals
along the wall ensured its
effectiveness as a defence. From

these towers, which housed troops
and the supplies and weapons they
needed, the surrounding
countryside could be defended.

LIFE ON THE WALL

Stand today on a
watchtower on a cool
autumn evening,
feeling the beginning
of a winter wind
whistling down from
the Gobi Desert, and it
is easy to imagine
what life must have
been like for a soldier
on garrison duty.
Archaeologists have
found letters from
officers of the Han
period stationed at the
wall, complaining of
their remoteness from
civilization, low pay,
low status and
wretched conditions.

For ordinary Han-
dynasty conscript
soldiers the journey to
the frontier might
mean a march of 6 to
8 weeks from their
villages in central
China. Having
travelled through
difficult terrain they
found themselves in an
inhospitable climate,
living among border
people whose
language, dress and
culture were alien to
their own.

Here, their duties
would include
manning the
watchtowers and
defending them with
cross-bows against
mounted invaders;
using flag, fire and
smoke signals to
communicate with
neighbouring
garrisons; and
providing official
messenger services. In
addition, the towers,
walls and living
accommodation had to
be maintained and
extended, and many
men were employed in
growing such
vegetables and grain
as could be coaxed out
of the meagre soil.

POETS AND THE WALL

Conditions on the frontier
are a constant theme in
Chinese literature. *Fighting
South of the Ramparts*, an
anonymous Han-dynasty
poem from about the first
century AD, begins:

"They fought south of the
ramparts
They died north of the wall.
They died in the moors and
were not buried.
Their flesh was the food of
crows."

Seven centuries later, one of
China's greatest poets, Li Bai
(Li Po), wrote a poem with
the same title and rhythm.
In it he commemorated the
Chinese armies far from
home and growing old
fighting the Xiongnu (Huns):

"The Huns have no trade
but battle and carnage,
They have no fields or
ploughlands,
But only wastes where

white bones lie among
yellow sand
Where the House of Qin
built the Great Wall that
was to keep away the
Tartars,
There, in its turn the House
of Han lit beacons of
war.
The beacons are always
alight, fighting and
marching never stop."

Li He, a near-contemporary
of Li Bai, gave a chilling
evocation of the atmosphere
of a Great Wall garrison in
his poem *On the Frontier*. He
described a Xiongnu horn
calling up the north wind,
roads disappearing into the
sky, and a thousand miles of
moonlight on the wall. For Li
He the Great Wall also
meant damp flags, the chill
clang of metal marking the
watches of a cold night, and
perpetual danger lurking in
the surrounding sands.

FOUNDER OF THE WALL

Consolidating the Great Wall
was only one of the
achievements of the first
emperor, Qin Shi Huangdi.
He conquered the other
Warring States from his
kingdom of Qin, and in 221
BC set up a unified empire
and established a pattern of
imperial rule that lasted
nearly 2,000 years.

His chancellor, Li Si,
waged an ideological battle
against scholars whose ideas
conflicted with the
authoritarian Legalist school
of philosophy that he
espoused. He is said to have
ordered the burning of books
he considered unorthodox
and had many academics
executed.

HISTORIC PLACES ON THE WALL

● **Shanhaiguan**—meaning
"the pass between the
mountains and the sea"—is
at the eastern limit of the
Great Wall where it meets
the Bohai Gulf. It was an
access route from
Manchuria, in the Northeast,
into China and an important
strategic point in the Ming
defence against the
Manchus. In 1644, when
the Manchus did invade, this
was their point of entry.

● **Badaling**, only some 64 km
(40 mi) from Beijing, is the
part of the wall most
accessible from the capital,
and therefore the most
visited. This section of the
wall dates from the 15th

century. A long stretch of it
has been restored, although
unrestored sections are
visible from the watchtowers.

● **Jiayuguan** was the last
Ming outpost on the wall
and the effective limit of
Chinese influence in Central
Asia in that dynasty. Lying
about 400 km (250 mi)
north of Lanzhou, it is today
an industrial town. The early
Ming fort, dating from 1372,
has been restored and is the
most westerly landmark still
standing on the wall.

The Han-period wall ran
much farther west than
Jiayuguan, but derelict earth
walls are all that remain of
it today.

THE EMPERORS

The origins of imperial rule in China lie in the mists and myths of prehistory. Although the names are known of quasi-divine rulers such as Shennong, who is credited with introducing agricultural techniques, the Yellow Emperor, Huangdi, and Yao and Shun who are regarded as exemplary monarchs, there is as yet no real evidence that any of them existed. More certainty surrounds the kings of the Shang dynasty (c. 1480–1122 BC). Their names are recorded in inscriptions found on bones used for divination, which date back to before the twelfth century BC. Tradition also tells of two heroic kings of the Zhou period in the twelfth century BC—Wen and his son Wu—who were later taken as models of how an emperor should rule.

The emperor tradition has complex roots in which the political and the religious are intertwined. Authority to rule is conferred by *Tian* (Heaven), partly nature personified, partly the seat of Shang Ti, highest of the gods. The emperor was known as the Son of Heaven, and he worshipped this Heaven in the same way that his subjects worshipped their own mortal ancestors who had become spirits after death. He was able to rule because he had the "mandate of Heaven"—a divine right to the throne. Were he overthrown, either by a rebellion or a palace coup, his successors would claim that this mandate had been withdrawn because of his wickedness, and Heaven had approved his successor.

The first emperor of a united China was Qin Shi Huangdi. Although his reign (221–210 BC) was brief, it set the pattern by which China was ruled until 1911. The emperors passed the imperial "dragon" throne to their successors, usually to the eldest son. As long as the succession remained in one family, that dynasty ruled. Rebellions sometimes overthrew dynasties, when failing administration led to both peasant unrest and waning support from the elite. Some dynasties, such as the Qin, were short-lived; the last dynasty, known as the Qing or Manchu, lasted 267 years. (A table of the most important dynasties appears overleaf.)

Dynasties could also be overthrown by invasion from the northern steppes. The Han Empire was able to keep out the barbaric Xiongnu, but Song China was taken over by nomads and incorporated into the Mongol Empire. This empire ruled China as the Yuan dynasty until a Chinese rebellion brought the Ming to power. This dynasty in turn was overthrown by Manchu invaders from the Northeast who set up their own Qing dynasty.

Underlying the pattern of rebellion, invasion and dynastic change there was a basic continuity in imperial rule. This continuity was possible because government depended not just on the personal rule of the emperor but on a sophisticated civil service, both in the capital and the regions. This first took shape in the Han period and was refined over the centuries until it developed into one of the most literate and

The lavish scale and rigid formality of court life are portrayed in almost photographic detail in this Qing-dynasty painting. It is typical of many such works depicting the minutiae of imperial life and ceremonies.

A carpet leads the eye across the middle of the painting, to where the emperor is seated in the raised hall, looking down on kneeling officials. Members of the court taking part in this imperial ceremony are positioned according to a strict hierarchy. Their uniforms denote their rank, and many of them carry banners or pennants.

complex bureaucracies the world has ever known (see also pages 70 to 71).

The ideology of the bureaucracy was Confucianism, which provided both a moral and a practical guide to government. The system, based on the teachings of the philosopher Confucius (551–479 BC), set out a hierarchical structure, which stretched from the emperor down through his officials to the family unit. It affirmed that the emperor by ritual and example could inspire correct behaviour in his subjects, the official could set the example for commoners, and the father could guide his family, to make a perfect society. Authority implied the responsibility to love and support those below. Confucius saw laws and punishments as counter-

This glorious tiled conical roof (below) is in the Hall of Prayer for Good Harvests, part of the splendid Temple of Heaven complex in Beijing. Here the emperor came early in the Lunar New Year to offer a prayer for a successful harvest.

First built in 1420, the Hall had to be reconstructed in 1890–96 after being struck by lightning and burned down. The entire structure is said to be of wood, with all wooden joinery—no metal has been used, even for nails. The interior of the Hall is brightly painted with motifs such as the dragon and phoenix, which represent the emperor and empress.

productive and unnecessary, but the state relied on them. This conventional ethical code, which claimed to be Confucian, strongly backed imperial rule.

Emperors governed through their ministers and officials, but they also had important rituals to perform, normally connected with seasonal festivals. For example, in December the Qing ruler would traditionally offer ceremonial prayers at the Temple of Heaven in Beijing, having been carried with a retinue of thousands to the Altar of Heaven there. At the Spring Festival (Chinese New Year) they returned to pray in the beautiful Hall of Prayer for Good Harvests. This ritual was believed to ensure abundant crops throughout the empire. It also emphasized the supernatural aspect of the emperor's position.

THE EMPERORS/2

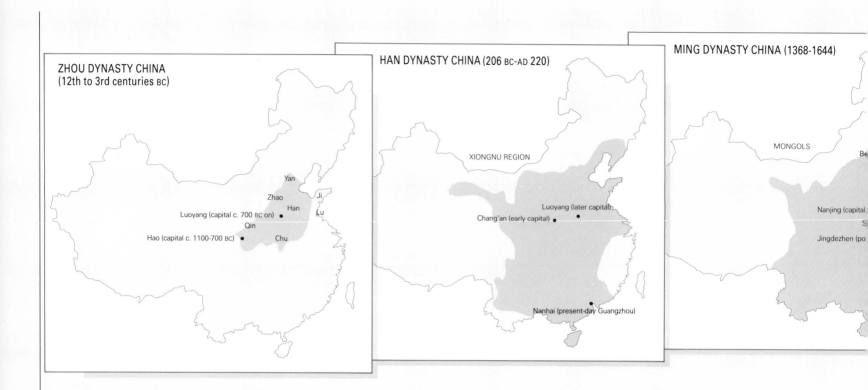

ZHOU DYNASTY CHINA
(12th to 3rd centuries BC)

Yan
Zhao
Ji
Han
Lu
Luoyang (capital c. 700 BC on)
Qin
Hao (capital c. 1100-700 BC)
Chu

HAN DYNASTY CHINA (206 BC-AD 220)

XIONGNU REGION
Luoyang (later capital)
Chang'an (early capital)
Nanhai (present-day Guangzhou)

MING DYNASTY CHINA (1368-1644)

MONGOLS
B
Nanjing (capital
S
Jingdezhen (po

DYNASTIES AND IMPERIAL NAMES

An emperor was often known by several different names. He normally took a reign name when he came to the throne. But, up until the Ming dynasty in the late 14th century, he might change this from time to time if his horoscope indicated that this would be auspicious.

After their deaths, emperors were given honorific temple names by which they were known to posterity.

Thus, the rebel Zhu

Yuanzhang, whose armies finally established him as the first Ming emperor after the defeat of the Mongols in 1368, took the reign title of Hongwu ("Vast military success"). After his death he was known as Taizu ("Grand ancestor"), a title often given to the founding emperor of a new dynasty.

Dynastic names often give a clue to the qualities to which the ruling house aspired, or to their regional or ethnic origins. The Han dynasty was founded by Liu

Bang, a king of the state of Han. Over the centuries, the word Han has come to be used to describe the ethnic Chinese as a whole (in contrast to non-Chinese minorities, such as Tibetans). Today, both the spoken Chinese language and written characters are known as Han.

The name Ming was chosen for the dynasty that liberated China from Mongol rule. It means "brightness" or "radiance" and suggests emergence from a dark age.

THE IMPERIAL COURT

Emperors ruled through a complex bureaucracy of court officials who might or might not be members of the imperial family.

During the Ming dynasty (1368–1644), memorials (formal letters from officials to the emperor reporting on events or suggesting policy changes) and imperial edicts outlining policy were processed by a group of Grand Secretaries.

This Grand Secretariat had considerable power and was in charge of the Ministries of

Finance, Civil Appointments, Rituals, War and Works. It functioned as a kind of cabinet, but Grand Secretaries could act only with the approval of the emperor.

During the Manchu Qing dynasty (1644–1911), the emperors tightened their control even further by appointing Grand Councillors to superintend the Grand Secretaries. Manchu nobles were brought in over the ethnic Chinese to fill the most senior posts.

MAJOR CHINESE DYNASTIES AND PERIODS

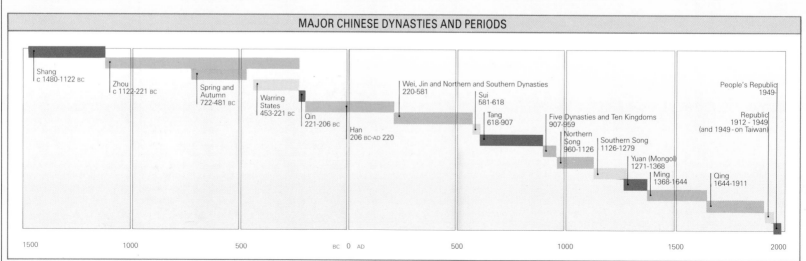

Shang
c 1480-1122 BC

Zhou
c 1122-221 BC

Spring and
Autumn
722-481 BC

Warring
States
453-221 BC

Qin
221-206 BC

Han
206 BC-AD 220

Wei, Jin and Northern and Southern Dynasties
220-581

Sui
581-618

Tang
618-907

Five Dynasties and Ten Kingdoms
907-959

Northern
Song
960-1126

Southern Song
1126-1279

Yuan (Mongol)
1271-1368

Ming
1368-1644

Qing
1644-1911

People's Republic
1949-

Republic
1912 - 1949
(and 1949 - on Taiwan)

1500   1000   500   BC 0 AD   500   1000   1500   2000

Dates for the earliest dynasties are still approximate. The traditional date for the Shang, for example, is 1480 BC, but the dynasty may well have begun as early as the 17th century BC.

QING DYNASTY CHINA (1644-1911)

OUTER MONGOLIA
(1697 under Qing rule)

INNER MONGOLIA
(1635 under Qing rule)

Beijing

XINJIANG
(1724-1866, 1878 under Qing rule)

Qingdao

QINGHAI
(1724 under Qing rule)

Yangzhou

Shanghai

TIBET
(1720 under Qing rule)

Ningbo

Xianggang (Hong Kong)

The changing boundaries of an expanding China are shown at selected periods. The Qing-dynasty *map includes the dates on which areas such as Tibet formally came under China's administration.*

EUNUCHS

In the Ming period, the Imperial Palace in Beijing was divided into 2 areas. Government officials worked in the front part while the emperor lived with his wives and concubines in the palaces and courtyards at the back. This area was off-limits to adult males. Menial tasks were dealt with by servant women. Administrative and other roles were undertaken by eunuchs, who had their own complex bureaucracy.

Boys intended as palace eunuchs were commoners, selected and castrated at an early age. A family considered it a great honour if their son was chosen.

Some eunuchs became extremely powerful in the palace, and could even influence imperial decisions. Others were sent to the regions as military commanders or special commissioners to ensure the supply of luxuries, such as porcelain, to the palace. As descendants of commoners, with no offspring of their own to favour, eunuchs could usually be relied upon to be loyal to the emperor.

Eunuchs played a significant role in court politics as early as the Han dynasty (206 BC–AD 220), but their power and corruption became notorious under the Ming when the number in service at any one time may have reached 20,000. In the 15th century they ran a secret service and a eunuch clique controlled the infant Zhengtong Emperor (1435–49).

In the early 17th century, the infamous eunuch Wei Zhongxian operated a spy network, using it to control the capital and much of the country.

When the Qing dynasty came to power in 1644, steps were taken to reduce the eunuchs' power. Subsequently, although they continued their original roles in the palace, eunuchs never again dominated political life.

IMPERIAL REIGNS

● QIN SHI HUANGDI (reigned 221–210 BC) During his reign Qin Shi Huangdi, first emperor of China, turned China into a strongly centralized state. Weights, measures and coinage were standardized to regulate and control trade. And a single form of written Chinese was adopted for use by a burgeoning bureaucracy.

The Qin dynasty survived his own reign by only 3 years, but it gave the Han dynasty that followed a firm foundation on which to build. He is best known today for the extraordinary army of thousands of lifesize terracotta horses and soldiers found in huge pits near his tomb.

● HAN WUDI (reigned 141–87 BC) Wudi, the fifth emperor of the Han dynasty, ruled at a time when the empire was expanding to the south and west from the cradle of Chinese civilization in the Yellow River area. His officials began a major programme of canal building to facilitate transportation of grain from the fertile south to the northern cities.

Wudi was a contradictory personality. Although Confucian thought developed during his reign, and he was interested in mystical Taoism, he was also a despot. He earned the condemnation of generations of scholars for ordering the castration of the great historian Sima Qian because he dared to speak in defence of a general who was not in favour at the time.

● TANG TAIZONG (reigned 626–649) The second son of the Tang dynasty's founding emperor, Li Shimin won early fame as a military commander. Having organized a palace coup,

in which he forced his father to abdicate, he then became emperor under the name of Tang Taizong.

Tang was a positive ruler, deeply involved in the machinery of government. His reign was distinguished by military victories over Tibetans and Turks in the west, and the establishment of diplomatic relations with central and western Asiatic states.

● KHUBILAI KHAN (reigned 1260–1294) Khubilai was the grandson of Chinggis (Genghis) Khan, who founded the Mongol Empire.

In 1260 Khubilai became Great Khan of the Mongol Empire, and ruled concurrently as emperor of China. He moved the imperial court south from the Mongolian heartland to Beijing—then known as Dadu (Great Capital)—for the winter months. From there his armies completed the conquest of southern China.

The young Khubilai had come under the influence of Chinese advisers, and as Khan he ruled through Chinese institutions and protected Confucianism. In 1271 he took the Chinese dynastic title Yuan ("beginning") for the Mongol rule of China.

● THE WANLI EMPEROR (reigned 1572–1620) The reign of the Wanli Emperor was the longest in the Ming dynasty. The early part of it was noted for its prosperity and reforms, largely due to the influence of the Grand Secretary Zhang Juzheng.

When Zhang died, the emperor withdrew from affairs of state. The civil service weakened, while increased court expenditure and military adventures led to factional crises from which the Ming dynasty was never to recover.

● THE KANGXI EMPEROR (reigned 1662–1722) Kangxi, third son of the Manchu Qing dynasty's founding emperor, was an intelligent, energetic and conscientious ruler.

He realized that China, as an agricultural society, had to be ruled through its Confucian bureaucracy, and could not just be subdued by Manchu cavalry as his predecessors had thought. He strengthened the nation's defences and suppressed a major revolt, but is best known for his sponsorship of the arts, his scholarship and his administration.

● THE EMPRESS DOWAGER, CIXI (1835–1908) Toward the end of the Qing dynasty, China was ruled officially by the Tongzhi Emperor (1862–1874) and the Guangxu Emperor (1875–1908). Both took the throne as children, and were, in fact, puppets of Cixi, a former concubine of the Xianfeng Emperor (1850–1861).

By manipulating the succession and the court for her own ends, Cixi became the effective ruler of China and resisted all attempts at modernization.

SEE ALSO PAGES
70–73, 80–81, 82–83

SOCIETY IN IMPERIAL CHINA

Chinese society has always been predominantly agricultural. Even today some 80 percent of the population works on the land, and in the past that proportion was still higher. For nearly two thousand years, until the early years of the present century, this agricultural society was dominated by the ideas of Confucius (c. 551–479 BC), the Chinese philosopher, who had very definite views about how society was and should be organized.

According to the Confucian view of the world, there were only four social groups worth considering. At the top were the educated scholar-gentry comprising landowners and state officials in central or local government. Immediately below them came the peasants. They were given this relatively high status, in spite of their poverty and lack of power, because Confucianism saw agriculture as a central and morally most desirable economic activity. Third came the artisans and craftsmen. At the bottom of the social scale were the merchants.

This was always something of an idealized picture. And, as China evolved over the centuries, undergoing dynastic crises, rebellion, foreign invasion, and finally contact with the expanding Western empires, the ideal became increasingly removed from reality. However, China's administrators and thinkers had all been educated in a system which saw this as the *only* way society could function, so they had difficulty in understanding the real transformations that were taking place in the social order.

One of the most remarkable features of the Chinese imperial administration was the selection of civil servants by examinations taken at several different levels. This system began during the Han dynasty around the second century BC and was progressively refined. Eventually it became so successful that even conquerors, such as the Mongols and Manchus, adapted it to their own use.

To succeed in these examinations (from which women were excluded), students required a thorough knowledge of the major Confucian classics—the *Analects*, *Mencius*, the *Great Learning* and the *Doctrine of the Mean* (the Four Books).

In theory, the examinations were open to all, so that officials could be selected purely on merit. In practice, the time needed for preparation meant that only those young men whose families could support them while they studied could enter. Candidates were thus drawn mainly from the landowning classes. Examinations were taken at three levels—district, provincial and national. Those who passed the final examination received the *jinshi* (presented scholar) degree. So important was the date on which they were awarded their *jinshi*, that it would be recorded in their official biographies, along with their dates of birth and death.

Until the middle of the Northern Song dynasty (approximately AD 1000), Chinese society could be compared to the feudal societies of Europe, with large estates owned and run by aristocratic families. Economic and social changes in the Song dynasty freed China from some of the restrictions imposed by aristocratic rule, and allowed it to become more productive, more commercialized and more urbanized. There was also a significant increase in population. This commercial revolution was followed by another in the sixteenth century. By this time the power of the merchants had increased and many of the landlords and scholar-gentry were in debt to them. The Confucian ideal of scholar-gentry at the top of the social ladder with mere traders at the bottom was often reversed in practice.

The four-class system also failed to take account of whole groups of people who did not fit into the idealized Confucian structure. This despite the important roles they had always played in Chinese history. Soldiers, for example, were not included, although every dynasty relied heavily on military might for conquest and control. And thousands of "marginal" people—boatmen, innkeepers, pedlars, actors, "singing girls"—were also officially ignored by the system. But all of them would have been known to the Confucian scholars who maintained it, as would the bandits and rebels who often occasioned the downfall of dynasties.

Dynastic change and foreign invasions frequently brought about major alterations in the structure of society. When the nomadic Manchus invaded China in 1644 and set up the Qing dynasty they brought with them their own highly developed social structure. Their aristocrats were absorbed into the scholar-gentry class and were given preference over native Chinese in many senior posts as part of a policy to dilute Chinese scholar-gentry power. Thus for much of the Manchu Qing dynasty, up to the present century, society was divided on ethnic as well as social lines.

The hard-working life of the Chinese peasant is depicted in this Yuan-dynasty painting of a rice harvest (above). Workers, both men and women, are busy stripping and winnowing their crop and loading the grain into baskets to take away for storage. One woman, in the centre of the painting, has paused to feed her baby, not even taking the time to leave her post.

Rice was the most important crop in southern China. Then, as now, agriculture was the basis of the Chinese economy.

Civil servants for the imperial administration were selected by a three-tier examination system which dated back to the 2nd century BC. This Qing-dynasty painting (right) shows candidates at the lowest level examination.

Examinations demanded not only a thorough knowledge of the major Confucian classics, but also an ability to interpret them according to current orthodoxy and in an acceptable literary style. This took years to accomplish, but successful candidates would be rewarded with great prestige and privilege.

By the later years of the Qing dynasty the examination system had become so stylized and rigid that it effectively stifled creative thought. Although some people realized that the system was outmoded, and hindering China's development, the court blocked any attempts at reform. Because the examinations were the only route to advancement, people continued to sit them until they were finally abandoned in 1905.

召試縣令

SOCIETY IN IMPERIAL CHINA/2

URBAN SOCIETY

Towns and cities existed in China from as early as the Shang (c. 1480–1122 BC) and Zhou (c. 1122–221 BC) dynasties, when they were the power bases for kings. Some towns grew as regional capitals or administrative centres (always under central control) and others as markets, the latter especially after the commercial revolution that began in about AD 1000.

Towns developed in a variety of ways. Every county had an administrative centre where the local magistrate, whose powers were governmental as well as legal, had his office. The county town was invariably walled, and the life of the townspeople was strictly supervised by the officials.

There were also commercial and industrial towns such as Jingdezhen which specialized in the production of pottery and porcelain, Suzhou which made silk and cotton, and Foshan near Guangzhou (Canton) which was an important iron and pottery manufacturing centre.

Towns developed a culture of their own, different from the traditional ways of the countryside. In the south, where absentee landlordism was more common, the wealthy landowners often preferred to spend most of the year away from their estates. In towns such as Hangzhou and Suzhou they could find elegant and sophisticated company.

In the 18th century the town of Yangzhou, where there were many wealthy salt merchants, was notorious for the ostentatious way of life of its inhabitants. But at the same time these people were great sponsors of the arts and scholarship.

Indeed, urban life had a profound influence on the development of the novel, short stories and drama. These all found a ready audience in the leisured classes of southern Chinese towns from the Yuan period onward.

LIFE IN THE COUNTRYSIDE

The pattern of landholding in the countryside of imperial China varied over the centuries. In general, though, there were always more peasant owner-occupiers in the north where land is more difficult to farm. The fertile south traditionally had a far higher proportion of large estates with many absentee landlords.

Country life was always governed by the seasons and the farming calendar, unless outside agencies, such as invasion or rebellion, intervened.

Family and extended family ties were extremely important and, particularly in southern China, whole villages often consisted of families linked to one another by lineage bonds.

The focal point of a village would be the ancestral temple or hall, where tablets commemorating their forebears were kept as reminders of the ties that bound families together.

Although rural life could be peaceful and prosperous, the peasants were often victims of drought, flood and other natural disasters that ruined the harvest. But whatever the harvest they had to pay a grain tax exacted by the state as well as their rent. A high tax demand combined with a poor harvest often led to rebellion. And peasant revolts frequently led to the downfall of dynasties: the Han and Ming dynasties, for example, were established after such uprisings.

THE ROLE OF WOMEN

With few exceptions women had no status or power outside the family. A girl could expect less food and poorer care than a boy while a child at home. And she would look forward with some trepidation to the time when she was betrothed, usually while still very young.

Marriages were transactions between parents, rather than arrangements between individuals. So, a girl's wedding marked the day she ceased to be the daughter of her own parents and moved to her husband's family home, as daughter-in-law.

There she would have many menial and onerous duties to perform for her husband's mother who ruled the home. In time she would become a mother-in-law herself, and only then would she be able to exercise some control over her family and her life.

For women on farms, life was especially arduous, with the dual burden of farm and family. But even high-born women, whose daily life was made easier by servants, faced major restrictions. In Shen Fu's autobiographical *Scenes from a Floating Life* he tells how his wife, desperate to escape from the purdah of her upper-class household, went in disguise with her husband and a friend to see what life in the outside world was like.

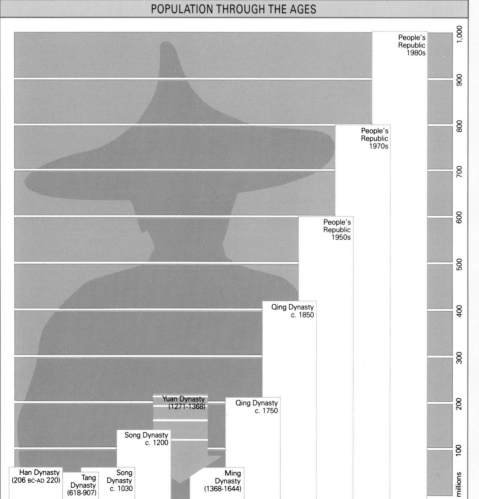

POPULATION THROUGH THE AGES

People's Republic 1980s

People's Republic 1970s

People's Republic 1950s

Qing Dynasty c. 1850

Yuan Dynasty (1271-1368)

Qing Dynasty c. 1750

Song Dynasty c. 1200

Han Dynasty (206 BC-AD 220)

Tang Dynasty (618-907)

Song Dynasty c. 1030

Ming Dynasty (1368-1644)

1,000 900 800 700 600 500 400 300 200 100 millions

Pre-20th-century statistics, usually collected for tax purposes, are unreliable but give an approximate guide to the growth of China's population. There are no accurate figures for the dramatic decline in population known to have occurred during the 13th-century Mongol conquest.

FOOTBINDING

The most obvious indicators of the social position of a woman in traditional Chinese society were her feet. The custom of binding feet was started by the upper classes during the Song dynasty.

At the age of 5, girls had their feet bent over and tightly bandaged until the bones of the arch were broken and the toes turned underneath. As a result, the adult foot was about half normal size and regarded as highly erotic.

Tiny "lily" feet restricted movement, making the woman economically useless, but more of a commodity in the marriage market. Large feet made marriage prospects poor. It was a measure of a family's status that it could afford to bind the feet of its women.

The practice of footbinding continued into the 20th century, despite attempts to stop it, and was only finally made illegal by the Communists in 1949.

THE GRAND CANAL

⊢──┤ Grand Canal

The longest manmade waterway in the world, the Grand Canal extends about 1,794 km (1,115 mi), making a vital link between north and south China.

TRAVEL AND COMMUNICATIONS

Throughout the history of the Chinese Empire communications have been a great problem. In the north, overland travel was on foot, on horseback or, if loads were to be carried long distances, by camel. Horses and carts are still a common sight in the rural outskirts of Beijing.

In southern China, road building was hampered by mountainous terrain. But an abundance of rivers and lakes allowed a complex system of water transport to be developed. Raw materials and manufactured products were all moved by boat, and many people lived on houseboats.

The main rivers—the Yellow River (Huang He) and the Yangtze (Chang Jiang)—run roughly west-east. This did not help communication between the rice-rich south and the capital, which was almost always located in the north.

After coastal grain shipments were abandoned, because of pirates and typhoons, the problem was solved by the extension of the Grand Canal around 1300. It connected the fertile

Officials, travelling in style in a horsedrawn carriage, are depicted on a rubbing from the design on a Han-dynasty tomb brick.

Huai valley in the south with the Yuan capital on the site of present-day Beijing, and was the main north-south artery in China until the rail network took over in the 20th century.

ASSOCIATIONS AND SECRET SOCIETIES

Many important developments in Chinese life occurred outside the ordered traditional framework of loyalty to family, officialdom and the emperor. Associations of many kinds were formed to support people in their work, or while they were away from their homes and families.

Craftsmen, for example, had their own trade guilds. Travelling merchants could always find a place to stay, and obtain advice on local conditions, from mutual aid associations in the main towns. These organizations were open and usually officially tolerated, since they posed no threat to the imperial order.

China also had a long tradition of secret societies which did threaten and sometimes helped to overthrow, the state.

Many such societies had a religious basis, such as the White Lotus Society which can be traced directly back to 12th-century Buddhist sects and, indirectly, to the 4th century. Members of this sect rebelled in the late 18th century with the aim of overthrowing the alien Manchu Qing dynasty. And, although the rising was suppressed, White Lotus ideas were adopted by the Boxer rebels of 1899–1901.

One of the most significant threats to imperial order in the 19th century was the Taiping Rebellion (1850–64). This originated in 2 secret societies—the Heaven and Earth (part of the Triads) and the quasi-Christian God Worshippers.

THE TRIAD SOCIETIES

The best known, but least understood, group of secret societies are the Triads. They began in 1644 in the underground resistance movement which remained loyal to the Ming dynasty after it was overthrown by the Manchu Qing. They were strong in southern China, and played a part in both the Taiping Rebellion and the 1911 Republican Revolution.

Triads, such as the Elder Brother Society, fought with the Red Army in the 1920s and 1930s. Others gradually drifted into the criminal activities in which they are still involved in Hong Kong.

The Green Gang, a society outside the Triad group but which had also taken part in the 1911 revolution, became the mafia of Shanghai in the 1920s. It was used by Chiang Kai-shek to attack communist and trade union organizations in his 1927 anti-revolutionary thrust.

THE HISTORY OF SCIENCE AND TECHNOLOGY

A stone chart of the sky, discovered in 1987 in Jiangsu Province, demonstrates just how ancient is the history of science in China. Prepared some 5,000 years ago, this chart is, as far as is known, the first of its kind in any civilization. It is carved on a huge stone mound and includes the Milky Way, some positions of the sun and moon, and a carefully inscribed north-south line. Other Chinese astronomical observations from as early as the second millennium BC can be reliably dated, and precise details recorded in later centuries of the appearance of new stars, comets, sunspots, eclipses and auroras are of use to astronomers today.

In China as elsewhere science developed alongside magical beliefs. By the first century AD the Chinese recognized that shaped lodestones pointed north or south and by the third that magnetized needles had the same property. By the eleventh they knew of magnetic declination—the difference between magnetic north and geographic north—and needles may have been used in navigation at this time. These discoveries seem to have been stimulated by the magical practices of geomancers, who were the first to use magnetic needles to help them site buildings and tombs in harmony with the earth's vital energy (see pages 148 to 149).

The Chinese, like the peoples of Mesopotamia, Egypt, Greece, Rome and Arabia, built great civilizations on the foundations of technical skills and a knowledge of the natural world. Inventions and discoveries flowed East and West in both directions from the New Stone Age on. After the collapse, and during the slow regrowth of European culture between about the fourth and fourteenth centuries AD, this flow was primarily from East to West, since science and technology continued to grow steadily in China despite interludes of political turmoil.

For the last two millennia China has been managed by a vast bureaucracy, conservative but able, when emperors willed it, to support ambitious projects. A famous example was the construction of the Grand Canal which extends more than 1,770 km (1,100 mi). It was begun in the fourth century BC, but extended and systematized in the sixth, seventh and thirteenth centuries AD. Another was the measurement, in the eighth century AD, of an "arc of the meridian", or north-south line, more than 2,500 km (1,550 mi) long; this provided essential knowledge for the making of accurate maps. Such challenging tasks, involving the cooperation of many people, were clearly beyond the scope of a single feudal lord.

There were some notable differences between the scientific cultures of China and the West. For instance, in China, Korea and Japan, the appearances of "new stars", though not recognized in the West, were recorded and are now of great value to astronomers. On the other hand, though they thought of the universe as infinite with the celestial bodies floating in it, the Chinese never developed a mathematical

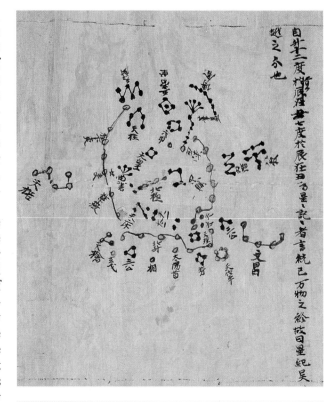

This section of the Dunhuang star chart—painted on silk in about 940—shows the stars around the north celestial pole. The stars of each constellation are joined by lines—a technique invented by the Chinese. Constellations shown include one of the two recognized by both China and the West, the dipper or plough, visible near the bottom of the chart.

The other sections of the chart, showing the curved sky on a flat surface, are an early form of Mercator projection, more than 600 years before it was re-invented by Gerardus Mercator, the famous Flemish cartographer.

The loud clang of a bronze ball falling from the jaws of a dragon into the mouth of a toad alerted rulers to remote earthquakes. Following the direction in which the dragon's head was pointing, they could trace the site and take appropriate action. This ingenious device, invented in AD 132 by the astronomer Zhang Heng, was clearly of immense importance when reports of distant disasters could take weeks to reach the authorities.

The picture shows a bronze reconstruction of this early seismoscope. An explanation of how it worked is given on page 77.

scheme of planetary motions as did the Greeks. It was also in the West that a planetary system centred on the sun was first adopted. However, in "chemistry" Chinese and Islamic alchemists were far more curious about the important question of the fixed proportions in which substances combine chemically than were their Indian and European counterparts.

Because educated men in imperial China all aimed to become government officials, it was they who made many of the advances in understanding the natural world. Even emperors contributed; in the Ming, Zhu Gao-Zhi (reigned 1424–25) made paintings of atmospheric effects observed around the sun. During the Qing dynasty the Kangxi Emperor (reigned 1661–1722) worked with his best scholars on traditional and European mathematics, sponsored books, and himself wrote on natural history.

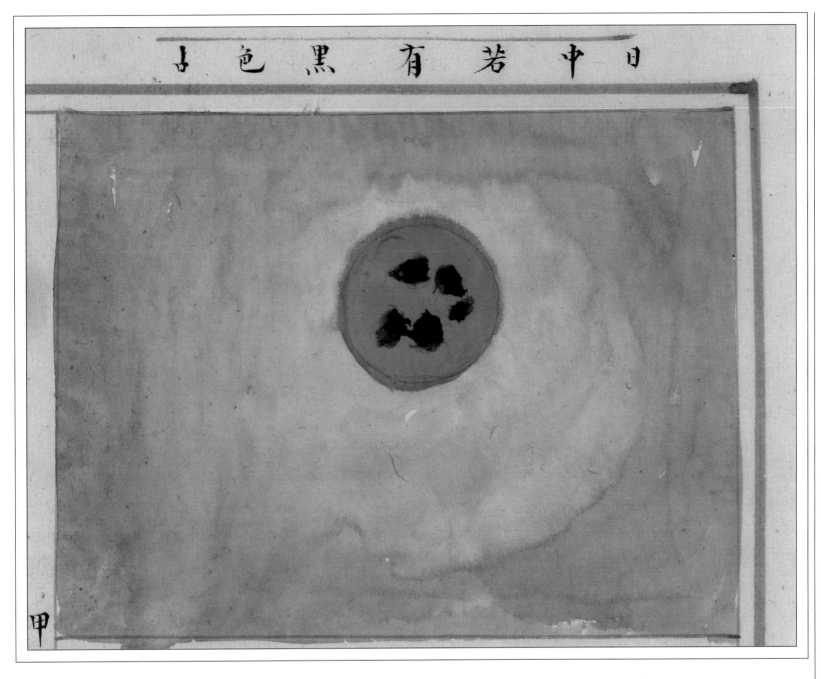

日 中 若 有 黑 色 古

In China science and technology evolved slowly, and after 1300 became increasingly concerned with minor improvements to established methods. In the West, from the fourteenth century onward, the culture shock due to the Renaissance, the Reformation, voyages of discovery and an expansion of trade all caused Europeans to question existing knowledge. This led ultimately to what is sometimes described as the "Scientific Revolution" which, in the sixteenth and seventeenth centuries, ushered in modern science.

When this modern science was brought to the Chinese by Jesuit missionaries in the seventeenth and eighteenth centuries, they welcomed it. Consequently a scientific revolution began there about 1650, but it was of smaller dimensions than that in the West. This was partly because the Jesuits were forbidden to reveal some of the latest knowledge, and partly because in some fields, such as medicine, their doctrines were obsolete and offered few items of interest. Another reason was that the Chinese used what they learned to uphold traditional views of science.

Modern science was to have negligible social consequences for the next 200 years. But work done by the Chinese prior to this remained of great value to the world. Chinese science had already produced such inventions as paper and printing, the magnetic compass and gunpowder, which have affected the lives of all mankind. Today modern science, technology and medicine have become part of Chinese culture. Thus the Chinese have every reason to look forward to new achievements—perhaps even some as great as those in past centuries.

Atmospheric effects around the sun were the subject of paintings by 15th-century Ming Emperor Zhu Gao-Zhi. This example dating from 1425 depicts sunspots, the existence of which the Chinese first recognized in the 4th century BC. Modern observations show the emperor's paintings to be scientifically accurate.

THE HISTORY OF SCIENCE AND TECHNOLOGY/2

GUNPOWDER, PAPER AND PRINTING

A number of world-changing inventions were devised by the Chinese, centuries before their appearance in the West. The 3 for which they are best known are gunpowder, paper and printing.

● **Gunpowder**—The date of the discovery of gunpowder—a mixture of saltpetre, sulphur and carbon—is unknown. It was first mentioned in AD 850, and certainly used for rock-blasting in the 10th century, if not earlier. Fireworks seem to have originated between 850 and 1050.

Gunpowder's first use in war was in 919 in flamethrowers, and in hand-guns a century later. This was 300 years before its similar use in Europe.

● **Paper**—Samples of paper made from hemp, rags and miscellaneous fibres have been found in tombs dating from the 2nd century BC. In AD 105 the court official Cai Lun drew the emperor's attention to the invention. Thereafter the use of the bark of certain shrubs such as paper mulberry made possible smooth durable paper of fine quality.

● **Printing** using carved wooden blocks began to be used in the 7th century. Cast bronze plates were used for printing paper money for the first time in the 11th century; in the same century movable type with characters cast in ceramic was invented.

CIVIL ENGINEERING

● **Canal lock gates** in their first true form were in use in China by the 9th century. Sequences of gates, allowing boats to move up or down a canal in stages, from one level to another, had been built as early as the 3rd century BC. This was 1,400 years earlier than such a design was known in Europe.

● **Cable suspension bridges**, using cables of bamboo, were built to span canals and natural gorges in China by the 1st century BC.

In 580 an iron chain suspension bridge was made over the Yangtze River in Yunnan Province. These two types of bridge were not built in Europe until 1220 and 1745 respectively.

● **The segmental arch bridge** reached a peak of efficiency and beauty in China that was not matched in the West until some 700 years later. The most famous example is the Zhaozhou Bridge in Hebei, which was built in 610 and is still in use.

AGRICULTURE

In China agriculture was affected by developments in metallurgy and mechanical inventions. During the 5th century BC the cast iron used for ploughs and other tools received a heat treatment to produce a malleable, less brittle iron. This allowed deep ploughing, and in the 1st century BC led to the important invention of the mouldboard—a curved iron plate above the ploughshare, which lifts and turns the soil. This arrived in Europe in the 11th century.

● **The wheelbarrow** was in use in China as early as the 2nd century AD. But 100 years later the large Chinese wheelbarrow (*left*) had been developed, a design that has never been surpassed. Because the single wheel is set in the centre, the person pushing does not have to bear the weight and can thus push very heavy loads.

● **The rotary fan winnowing machine** used a spinning wooden fan for separating grain from chaff. It is thought to have been invented in China in the 1st century BC and took 1,400 years to reach the West. A later version, using a crank handle, was developed in the 8th century.

● **The square-pallet chain pump** (or "dragon backbone machine") made efficient irrigation possible using human or animal power.

● **A breast-strap harness** for draught horses was perfected by the 2nd century BC in China, but the first experiments with breast-straps were some 200 years earlier. The breast-strap took at least 800 years to find its way to the West, where the use of a throat harness had strictly limited the weight that could be pulled before the animal began to choke.

By the 5th century AD, the Chinese had invented the horse collar, some 400 years before its use in Europe.

The square-pallet chain pump operates by means of a circulating "chain" made of square pieces of wood (pallets) which hold water. These fit closely in a square trough.

As the chain is moved along the trough by the treadle action of the operators, the wooden pallets carry water from a lower to a higher level.

TEXTILES

● **Large mechanical reeling machines** designed for winding silk from cocoons, made their appearance in the 12th century. A milestone in mechanical engineering, they turned reciprocating (back and forth) motion from a treadle into rotatory motion. This allowed the operator's foot to move up and down, and yet cause a shaft to rotate and drive a machine.

The belt drive used in this invention was a flat belt connecting one rotating shaft with another, thus causing the second also to rotate. This allowed more than one operation to take place at the same time.

● **The draw loom** for weaving intricately figured fabrics was designed and used in China no later than the 1st century BC—400 years earlier than in Europe.

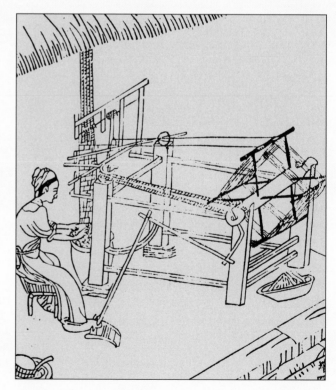

This late 11th-century silk-reeling machine is operated by a treadle which turns a large reel on which the silk is wound. The treadle also operates a belt running from the spindle of the wheel to a pulley; this moves a "ramping arm" to and fro so that the silk is wound evenly across the large reel. The illustration dates from 1843.

MECHANICAL ENGINEERING

● **Double-acting piston bellows**, giving a continuous stream of air, were the most efficient type of air pump before the advent of modern machinery. Widely used in metalwork, they may have been devised as early as the 4th century BC and were thoroughly in evidence by the 1st century AD. Europe had nothing similar until the 16th century.

● **Bellows for metallurgical furnaces** came into use in the 1st century AD. The large machines, driven by a water-wheel, used a crank linkage to push a huge air-flap to and fro. This was an early example of transforming rotary into reciprocating (back and forth) motion.

● **The deep borehole drill** was first used in Sichuan Province during Han times in the 1st and 2nd centuries AD to bring up brine for salt making. The depths of wells reached 100 m (328 ft) by the 4th century, and 250 m (820 ft) by the 7th to 10th centuries.

Even by the Han dynasty (206 BC–AD 220), Chinese methods used derricks, with heavy iron cutting-bits suspended from them by bamboo-skin straps pressed into long, pliable bands. When this supporting technique became known in the West in 1823, it caused a sensation.

The Chinese also used bamboo pipelines to carry away the brine. During the salt making process the brine was often heated by natural gas, also obtained from the deep boreholes.

SCIENTIFIC INSTRUMENTS

● **The seismoscope**, invented in Luoyang in 132 by the astronomer Zhang Heng, detected distant earthquakes. Apparently it contained a heavy pendulum and trigger mechanism to help record the direction from which the earthquake shocks arrived. Soon lost in China, it was not reinvented until 1703 in France.

Inside the seismoscope (see pp. 74–5) was a metal bar so heavy that only earth tremors would shift it. When a tremor occurred the bar swung in its direction. A locking mechanism held the bar still and a ball was released from the dragon pointing toward the tremor. The ball dropped into the mouth of the appropriate toad.

This clock tower, built in Kaifeng by Su Song in 1090, was 9 m (30 ft) high and incorporated the clock escapement invented by Yi Xing in the 8th century. The escapement was operated by a wheel, a detail of which is shown below. The tower was the finest example of the use of this clock escapement in China at the time.

● **The equatorial mounting** was invented in China about 1270 and was adopted by Western astronomers in the 17th century.

It enables astronomical instruments to follow the apparent motion of the stars, caused by the earth's rotation, by one movement instead of two.

● **The clock escapement**, basic to all mechanical timepieces, was the invention of Yi Xing in the 8th century. The mechanism allows the clock to tick away moment by moment and so record the passing of time.

This device lay at the heart of the huge "clock tower" built by Su Song at Kaifeng in 1090. It rotated astronomical instruments on the tower automatically, and displayed the time, shown by figures holding placards as they passed windows in the tower—rather in the style of European clocks of the late Middle Ages.

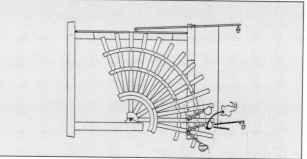

To turn the escapement wheel a water-clock fills one of the "buckets". When full, the bucket moves down, tripping two wooden bars which also move down. A chain from the second pulls two arms (top right) upward. The second of these releases one tooth of the wheel enabling it to turn and record the passing of time.

JOSEPH NEEDHAM

The Chinese kept many records of their enterprise in science, technology and medicine. Though known in general outline by Chinese and Japanese scholars of the 1940s, they were usually ignored outside Asia until the appearance of *Science and Civilization in China* by Joseph Needham (born 1900). The many volumes in this series have been appearing since 1954.

Originally a biochemist, Needham was elected a Fellow of the Royal Society in 1941 for his research.

But already in 1937, when supervising Chinese postgraduate students, he was led to question how such excellent scientists could come from a culture which had not itself developed modern science.

He determined to learn Chinese and find out why. When invited to go to China during World War II, he discussed the question with many Chinese and gathered together a unique collection of Chinese books on scientific subjects.

After that war, he served for a time at UNESCO as Science Director; but on his return to Cambridge University, he entered upon his life's work, writing on the achievements of traditional Chinese science, technology and medicine. In the course of this he came to some conclusions about why modern science had not developed in the East.

Still active in the late 1980s, Needham directs the Needham Research Institute in Cambridge, England.

INTERNATIONAL CONTACTS

Although China has a long coastline with many ports, most international trade and diplomatic contact in the past was westward and overland. The capital city for many of the early dynasties was Chang'an (present-day Xi'an) in the northern heartland. And it was to the Asian continent that China looked both for trade and for trouble, for threats of invasion came frequently from the Central Asian steppes.

The most famous early link between China and the West was the Silk Road (or Route), along which precious Chinese commodities were transported across Central Asia as far as the Roman Empire. But there were other routes to the south, linking China

with India and the Arab and Iranian Empires. Along these trade routes flowed ideas and influences, including Buddhism, which had a profound effect on Chinese thought and society. Buddhism first arrived during the Han dynasty, perhaps between 50 BC and AD 50, and grew in importance up to the eighth century. A steady stream of pilgrims and missionaries travelled back and forth between China and India.

Tang-dynasty Chang'an was one of the major cities of the world and it attracted traders from far away. Both Chang'an and the subsidiary capital Luoyang had settled communities of Iranians, Arabs, Turks and Jews who had come by way of the great Asian trade routes. These Westerners made every aspect of

A camel caravan retracing the old Silk Road, makes its way through the desolate landscape of Xinjiang in northwestern China. Camels have largely been replaced by trucks today but once they were the major form of transport for traders on the Silk Road, much of which passed through desert.

This region of China is inhabited by Uygurs—a Muslim people whose language is akin to Turkish and whose customs are closer to those of Central Asia and Afghanistan than China.

China was invaded from Central Asia and incorporated into the Mongol Empire.

After this, China's contacts with other cultures were again primarily overland, the way the great Italian traveller Marco Polo came. Naval power was used in the Southern Song-period resistance to the Mongols, and in the Mongols' attempted invasion of Japan. These were, however, insignificant compared with the trade, diplomatic missions and military movements across the Asian land mass.

Until the Ming dynasty (1368–1644) the nation's only maritime connections were with the great Arab and Persian merchant seafarers. These traders had dominated ocean trade with China since the Tang period, and left their economic and cultural mark on port cities such as Quanzhou, just as their cousins trading overland had influenced Chang'an.

In the fifteenth century the remarkable voyages of the Ming court eunuch Zheng He to as far away as East Africa created another opportunity for Chinese maritime expansion. Arab influence on the high seas was declining, and for a time it seemed that a Ming merchant fleet might control the eastern oceans. But this was not to be, and the expanding seafaring empires of Portugal, and later Holland, came to dominate trade with East Asia. Ming China retreated from the seafaring challenge.

In 1644 China was invaded by another nomadic steppe people, the Manchus. Once again it became locked into continental Asia and turned its back on what was to be the most serious threat ever to its existence—the dramatic rise of European naval and commercial power.

Upturned eaves add an echo of Chinese style to this mosque in Linxia, Gansu Province in the northwest of China.

New ideas and beliefs as well as goods were brought to China by traders from elsewhere in Asia. During the Tang dynasty (618–907), Arab and Persian settlers founded the first Muslim communities in China. These became particularly well established in the northwest and southwest where there are still many mosques.

Tang life increasingly cosmopolitan. Arab and Persian styles of music, dance and decorative arts became fashionable; the use of Islamic motifs on porcelain persisted at least until the Ming dynasty; and the poems of Li Bai (Li Po), one of the Tang period's greatest poets, contain many exotic echoes of his Central Asian origins.

By the Song dynasty (960–1279), advanced Chinese nautical technology enabled the junks of the Yangtze estuary to sail the high seas. They had crews who knew how to use the compass—a Chinese invention—and who had the necessary navigational skills. A great maritime expansion seemed likely, but this was curtailed when, in the thirteenth century,

INTERNATIONAL CONTACTS/2

THE SILK ROAD

Silk and other luxury goods were traded between China and the Middle East before the Han dynasty (206 BC–AD 220). Indeed, Chinese silk had reached India as early as the 4th century BC. But it was in the Han period that regular trade developed along what became known as the Silk Road.

The road began in the Chinese capital of Chang'an (Xi'an) in northern China. It led northwest via Jade Gate (Yumen) into Turkestan and via Kashi (Kaxgar) into Afghanistan, and finally through Persia to the Mediterranean—a distance of some 11,265 km (7,000 mi).

Essentially it was a series of short caravan routes connecting oases and trading towns, along which camels, yaks or pack mules were used for transport. The cost of moving goods over such a long distance was high, so only items of great value were carried. Westward, silk was the most important commodity; gold, silver and gems moved eastward in exchange.

There is no record of any one merchant having made the journey along the whole of the Silk Road until the time of Marco Polo. Rather, traders took their goods from their home base to the next stage along the route—returning with silk or precious metals.

ROUTES ACROSS ASIA

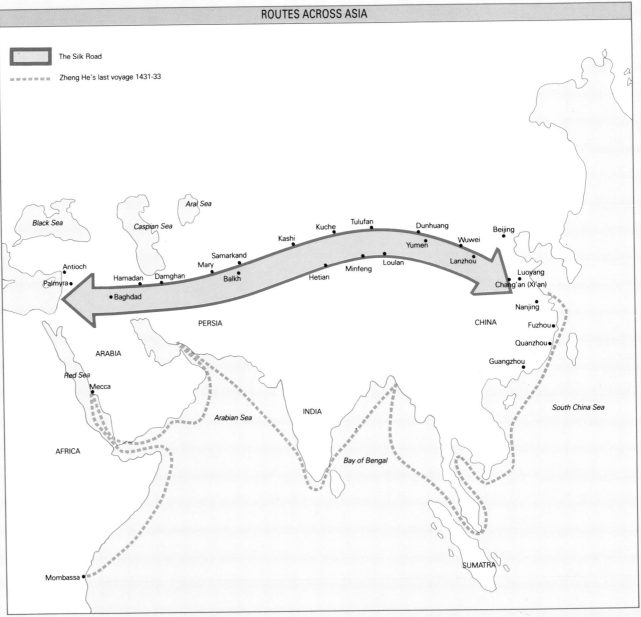

The Silk Road

- - - - - Zheng He's last voyage 1431-33

China's main trading link with the West was overland via the Silk Road, through Central Asia to the Mediterranean. The Chinese also undertook some maritime ventures to the West, the most notable being the seven voyages led by Zheng He in the early 15th century.

LINKS WITH JAPAN

Chinese culture was dominant in East Asia for centuries. It exported to its neighbours techniques, such as the manufacture of porcelain; ideas, such as the Confucian ethical system; and its written language.

The culture of Japan came under considerable Chinese influence in the Tang dynasty (618–907). A Japanese system of writing was developed using Chinese characters; laws were formulated using Chinese law as a model. The cities of Nara and Kyoto (both in their time capitals of Japan) were planned on the same lines as the Tang capital Chang'an.

Japanese Buddhism, including Zen, originated in China. And Confucianism, combined with Japanese feudalism, was part of the framework for rule in Japan from the 17th to the 19th centuries.

QUANZHOU—A MAJOR PORT

Throughout the Song and Yuan periods, the small town of Quanzhou on the southeast coast was China's major port. It was known to its large Arab community as Zaiton.

The Qingzhen Mosque is a monument to Quanzhou's special position in China's history. One of the oldest mosques in the country—it dates back to 1010 and was rebuilt in 1310—it has a gate said to be an exact copy of one in Damascus. In the town's cemetery are stone memorials, bearing Arabic script, to Islamic traders who died in Quanzhou.

Quanzhou was visited and described by both the Arab traveller Ibn Battuta, who crossed Asia between 1325 and 1355, and Marco Polo, who praised it as "a great resort of ships and merchandise from India". He marvelled at the volume of trade, declaring Quanzhou one of the 2 greatest ports in the world at the time. (The other was Alexandria.)

It was from Quanzhou that the Ming navigator Zheng He embarked on his fifth voyage, and a tablet there commemorates an incense-burning ceremony that took place before he set sail.

In 1974, a Song-dynasty (960–1279) sea-going junk was excavated in the bay. It is now on display in Quanzhou, complete with the remains of its cargo of spices and rare timbers—a symbol of the city's glorious maritime and trading past.

GUANGZHOU (CANTON)

In the 17th and 18th centuries, Guangzhou expanded as a port, outstripping its rival Quanzhou. It was opened to Western traders in the 1600s, and in 1757 became the only port legally open to foreign trade as the Qing court struggled to control Western commercial pressure.

All business had to be conducted through a small group of officially approved merchants known as the Cohong, a restriction that was greatly resented by Western traders.

MARCO POLO

Born into a family of Venetian merchants, Marco Polo first travelled to China in 1271 with his father and uncle. Travelling on the old Silk Road, they reached Shangdu, the summer capital of Khubilai Khan in 1275, and then went on to Beijing.

Here Marco gained the trust of the Great Khan, then ruler of China. He served him for 17 years in various capacities, including the governorship of the trading centre Yangzhou. His success was due in large part to his linguistic abilities: he was fluent in Persian, the language used on the caravan routes, and also spoke Chinese.

Marco Polo left China in 1292 from the port of Quanzhou. He arrived back in Venice in 1295 but was taken prisoner in 1298, in the war between Venice and neighbouring Genoa.

While incarcerated, he told tales of his travels to the other inmates. One of them, a professional scribe, recorded his stories which have come down to us as *A Description of the World* or *The Travels of Marco Polo*.

His fellow Venetians, who believed the Mediterranean lands to be the centre of civilization, found Marco Polo's account of the greatness of China improbable. However, time has vindicated many of Marco's claims.

THE VOYAGES OF ZHENG HE

The ocean voyages of the flotilla commanded by the eunuch admiral Zheng He in the early 15th century were remarkable, not only in terms of Chinese navigation, but also in international seafaring history.

Zheng He was a Muslim from Yunnan in southwestern China. At the age of about 10 he was castrated and entered the service of the Ming Yongle Emperor. He trained in the army, saw action against the Mongols at the Great Wall, and became a trusted servant of the emperor.

He was then put in command of a unique series of maritime expeditions that took his ships throughout Southeast Asia and across the Indian Ocean to southern India, the Persian Gulf, the Red Sea and the east coast of Africa.

In the voyage of 1405–7, 62 Chinese ships reached India via Java, Sumatra and Ceylon. Further expeditions in 1407–9 and 1409–11 are marked by stone tablets declaring the kingdoms of South Asia to be vassals of the Ming emperor.

The fourth voyage of 1413–15 took part of the fleet to the Persian Gulf, and on to Aden and East Africa. This was repeated in 1417–19 and 1421–22. On the seventh and final expedition in 1431–33 part of the fleet sailed up the Red Sea to Jeddah and some of the crew visited Mecca.

Zheng He's maritime expeditions were an outstanding achievement on many levels. His ships were ahead of those of established seafaring nations such as Spain and Portugal in their transoceanic voyages. And his missions extended diplomatic contact between the Ming Empire and the Middle East.

It is not clear why they suddenly began—whether the motives behind them were military, expansionist politics, or the search for exotic treasures for the imperial court. Neither is it clear why they stopped abruptly after the seventh voyage. It is known, however, that there was growing concern about their cost, and the regular civil service was unhappy about the prestige eunuchs were gaining at the time.

The government did not follow up the expeditions with commercial contracts. That would have gone against the Confucian ethic. But Zheng He's voyages strengthened the network of maritime trade, and private Chinese merchants were able to exploit this throughout the remainder of the Ming dynasty.

● Zheng He's Ships

The construction of these ships incorporated all the ingenuity of Chinese shipbuilders and was in many respects in advance of Western design. Innovations included a more streamlined hull than was used in the West for another 400 years; the axial rudder; watertight compartments; and multiple masts staggered alternately to port and starboard for better thrust.

The ships were also equipped with another Chinese invention—the magnetic compass.

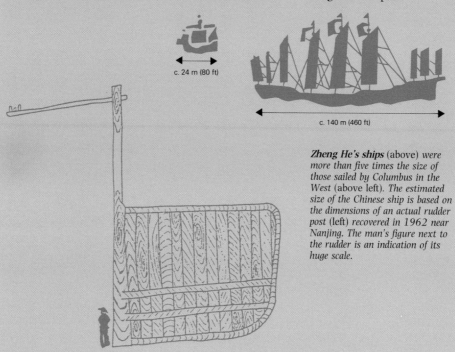

c. 24 m (80 ft)

c. 140 m (460 ft)

Zheng He's ships (above) *were more than five times the size of those sailed by Columbus in the West* (above left). *The estimated size of the Chinese ship is based on the dimensions of an actual rudder post* (left) *recovered in 1962 near Nanjing. The man's figure next to the rudder is an indication of its huge scale.*

THE TRIBUTE SYSTEM

Trade was anathema to orthodox Confucianism, which assigned merchants to the lowest rank of society. It was therefore officially unthinkable that the imperial government should engage in trade with other countries.

Nonetheless, a great deal of trade went on between China and the smaller nations of South and Southeast Asia, particularly during the Ming period. Some of this was private and strictly illegal, but trade also took place between governments. This was represented as tribute from minor vassal states to their overlord—the empire of the great Ming—and gifts in return.

It was by the tribute system that the Chinese Empire acquired many valuable commodities such as horses, from the Mongols, and, from Southeast Asia, the blue pigment for painting porcelain that it could not produce in sufficient quantities at home.

In the late 18th century, when Westerners started to press China for trading rights, it was assumed that they too would fit into the tribute system. Bitter conflict ensued when they did not.

PORTUGUESE AND DUTCH TRADERS

The first Europeans to be seriously involved in trade with China were the Portuguese. In the early 16th century they gradually came to dominate the old Arab trade routes, and established bases in Malacca and in Macao which they eventually colonized. (Macao was formally ceded to Portugal in 1887.)

Dutch merchants, under their East India Company formed in 1602, challenged the Portuguese and finally took over the Eastern trade from them. They were thus the most important traders in the region until Britain and other Western countries became involved in the Guangzhou (Canton) trade in the 18th century.

WESTERN INTRUSION

China's protracted isolation from the rest of the world came to an end in the middle of the nineteenth century when the increasing encroachment of Western nations ushered in an era of revolutionary change. Goods, ideas and people had journeyed between China and Europe over the previous two thousand years as regularly as peace in the intervening lands had allowed, but the Chinese government discouraged foreign contacts from the fifteenth century on. It did not want goods from abroad, and sharply limited trade while in the West empires were being built on it. The Europeans' endless pressure for commercial relations only confirmed the Chinese view that they were barbarians. The Opium Wars of 1839–42 and 1856–60, easily won by the British with their superior weapons, began the "opening up" of China.

Since the mid-1700s Chinese foreign relations had revolved round Guangzhou (Canton), the only port open to Western traders. Here merchants came to buy silks, rhubarb, lacquer, porcelain and, above all, tea. The Chinese considered trade to be a privilege, and not a right, for foreigners. Lord Macartney, a special ambassador sent to China in 1792 by King George III of England to request an extension of trade and diplomatic exchange, was told by Emperor Qianlong: "We possess all things. I set no value on objects strange or ingenious, and have no use for your country's manufactures."

The balance of trade during the eighteenth century was very much in China's favour, but after about 1826 it began to tip the other way. This reversal was caused by the large-scale smuggling of opium by British merchants from India into China. Due to the rapid spread of the addiction the trade grew at an alarming rate—from about three thousand chests of opium in the year 1817 to more than twenty thousand in 1833. This caused the Chinese great concern, and turned their trade surplus to a deficit.

In 1839 Lin Zexu, a special commissioner, was sent to Guangzhou to suppress the opium traffic. His efforts culminated in his holding most of the foreign community hostage and destroying some twenty thousand chests of opium. When the British retaliated by sending an expeditionary force, the first Opium War began.

In 1842 a defeated China signed the Treaty of Nanjing, ceding Hong Kong to Britain and granting her foreign trading rights in five so-called Treaty Ports along the eastern coast: Guangzhou, Shanghai, Ningbo, Amoy (Xiamen) and Fuzhou. Besides promising direct contact between foreign powers and the Chinese government, the treaty also protected missionaries in certain Chinese cities.

After more than a decade of further hostilities between China and the intruding Western powers, the second Opium War began in 1856 when Britain and France bombarded Guangzhou. Toward the end

A Chinese junk is entirely destroyed by cannon fire from a British warship in one of the many sea battles of the Opium Wars. This dramatic painting shows the British ship Nemesis attacking a fleet of junks in January 1841.
The small, ill-equipped wooden junks were no match for the much larger, iron-plated British steamers, armed with powerful cannon. The superior naval strength of the British soon forced the Chinese emperor to negotiate. The result was, for China, an unequal treaty with the West, namely the Treaty of Nanjing in 1842.

of this war, the British forces ordered the burning of the emperor's Summer Palace near Beijing, and drove him into exile. In 1860 China was forced to agree to a second round of "unequal" treaties, which extended the privileges of the European traders and missionaries in China, increased the number of ports open to foreigners and allowed an even wider sale of opium.

While consolidating their commercial, religious and cultural footholds in China itself, the intruders

The great powers of Britain, Germany, Russia, France and Japan are depicted ruthlessly carving up "the cake" of China in a French political cartoon of 1898.

France, personified as a beautiful young woman, is leaning on Russia—an allusion to the dual alliance between the two countries at that time.

The scramble of foreign powers to establish what were termed "spheres of influence" in China reduced the country to a state of semi-colonialism. It also led to the vehement anti-foreign feeling which played a large part in the Boxer Rebellion of 1900.

were also penetrating areas on the borders of China. After brief hostilities in 1883–85, the French took control of Vietnam. Following Europe's lead, Russia gained large tracts of Siberia and Central Asia, while the Japanese took Korea, as well as Taiwan and other Chinese territories.

The European powers in China drew up a series of agreements among themselves by which they recognized each others' privileges and the frontiers of their respective spheres of influence. The spoils shared out in the scramble included leased territories, and railway and mining concessions.

By the first decade of the twentieth century, more than 80 percent of shipping, 30 percent of cotton-yarn spinning, 90 percent of the rail network, and 100 percent of iron production in China was under foreign control. Such was the degree of Western domination that China at this time has been described as "semi-colonial", a state from which it was not freed until after World War II.

WESTERN INTRUSION/2

TREATY PORTS

In the years that followed the Opium Wars of 1839–42 and 1856–60, the intruding foreigners strengthened their position by establishing settlements or concessions in the so-called Treaty Ports.

By 1860 there were 14 of these privileged enclaves where foreigners could live, own property and engage in business under the jurisdiction of their own consuls. Local law and administration (police, roads, sanitation, and so on) were also in their hands. Four more such ports were opened in 1876. Other areas were taken totally under foreign control. The island of Hong Kong, for example, was ceded to the British in the Treaty of Nanjing in 1842 as part of the spoils of war.

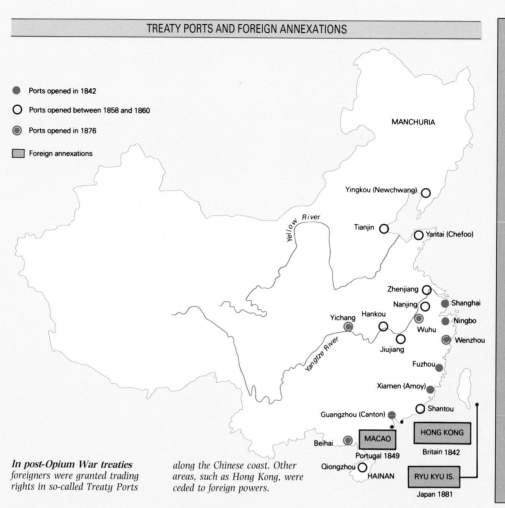

TREATY PORTS AND FOREIGN ANNEXATIONS

- ● Ports opened in 1842
- ○ Ports opened between 1858 and 1860
- ◉ Ports opened in 1876
- ▢ Foreign annexations

MANCHURIA

Yingkou (Newchwang)
Yellow River
Tianjin
Yantai (Chefoo)
Zhenjiang
Nanjing
Shanghai
Yichang
Hankou
Ningbo
Wuhu
Wenzhou
Yangtze River
Jiujiang
Fuzhou
Xiamen (Amoy)
Guangzhou (Canton)
Shantou
MACAO
HONG KONG
Beihai
Portugal 1849
Britain 1842
Qiongzhou
HAINAN
RYU KYU IS.
Japan 1881

In post-Opium War treaties foreigners were granted trading rights in so-called Treaty Ports along the Chinese coast. Other areas, such as Hong Kong, were ceded to foreign powers.

"THE EAST IS RED"

After the People's Republic was founded in 1949, the architectural symbols of rampant commercialism and foreign imperialism, above all in Shanghai, offended Chinese Communists who had spent the war in China's most rugged hinterland.

At the start of the Cultural Revolution the Westminster chimes of the clock on the old Maritime Customs building on the Shanghai waterfront were replaced by the tune of "The East is Red".

THE OPIUM TRADE

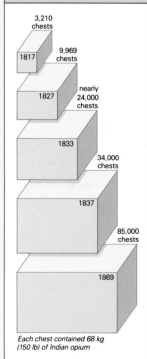

3,210 chests
1817

9,969 chests
1827

nearly 24,000 chests
1833

34,000 chests
1837

85,000 chests
1869

Each chest contained 68 kg (150 lb) of Indian opium

Increasing quantities of opium smuggled into China by the British led to the Opium Wars.

SHANGHAI—A COSMOPOLITAN CITY

The supreme Treaty Port was Shanghai. Its International Settlement (with British and American enclaves), and its French concession, were virtually self-governing.

The International Settlement was run by the British. As one visitor noted in 1938, "A stranger arriving at Shanghai by the P & O would scarcely realize that he was not in a British territory." The streets were named after British imperial outposts such as Simla and Benares. Buildings—notably the clubs and offices along the celebrated Bund, or waterfront—were in Anglo-Indian or French style.

The most infamous symbol of foreign imperialism in Shanghai was perhaps the park laid out at the end of the Bund: not only was a Scottish gardener brought out to reproduce as closely as possible the lawns, rose beds and hedges of an English garden, but one of the regulations posted at the entrance forbade admission to the Chinese; another barred dogs.

As a city dedicated to the making of money, Shanghai attracted tycoons, gangsters and drifters, and was referred to variously as "The Paradise of Adventurers", "The Paris of the East", and "The Whore of Asia". With its communities of Japanese, White Russians, Europeans and Jews, and its visitors from all over the world, it was easily the most cosmopolitan city in Asia.

Shanghai was also a city of cruel contrasts: the glittering life of the foreign businessmen and their rich Chinese associates or compradores existed alongside the misery and poverty of the factory workers and vagrants.

SHANGHAI, 1853

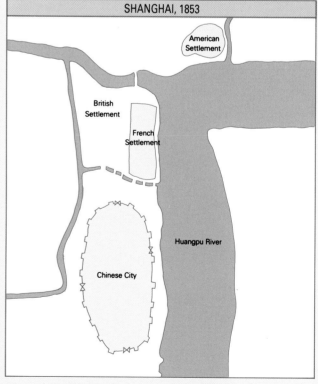

American Settlement

British Settlement

French Settlement

Huangpu River

Chinese City

The non-Chinese population of Shanghai increased rapidly between 1844 and 1930. Foreigners were attracted by the colonial ambiance of the city and the chance to make a fortune in trade.

THE MARITIME CUSTOMS OF SHANGHAI

In 1853, at a time when central government's control over Treaty Ports was in disarray, an offshoot of the Triad secret society called the Small Sword Society seized and occupied the Chinese walled city in Shanghai. Its action was spurred by the Taiping uprising against the imperial throne in the Nanjing area.

In the bloody fighting that followed the Society's occupation and attempt to seize control, the customs officials were driven out of the walled city. So that duties could still be collected for the Chinese government from Western merchant ships entering the port of Shanghai, the British consul and American commissioner set up a provisional inspectorate of customs.

This was the beginning of foreign control of the Imperial Maritime Customs, which one day would be denounced as a means of "draining away the blood of the working Chinese people". But its famous inspector general Robert Hart said of it: "The service which I direct is called the customs service, but its scope is wide and its aim is to do good work for China in every possible direction."

ROBERT HART

In 1863 Robert Hart succeeded the first inspector general, Horatio Nelson Lay. An able, hardworking, Chinese-speaking Irishman, Hart built up the customs service, which by 1875 employed 252 Britons and 156 other Westerners.

By 1898 the customs service was producing a third of the entire revenue of the Chinese government, and it ran the Chinese Imperial Post Office. Hart became a trusted adviser to the Qing court, and was probably the most influential Westerner in China.

Hart did not, however, underestimate the Chinese hostility toward foreigners. He foresaw the day when, "The Chinese will take back from foreigners everything foreigners have taken from China, will pay off old grudges with interest, and will carry the Chinese flag and Chinese arms into many a place that even fancy will not suggest today, thus preparing for the future upheavals and disasters never even dreamed of."

FOREIGNERS IN SHANGHAI

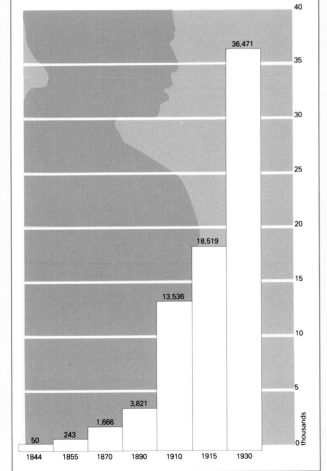

Year	Number
1844	50
1855	243
1870	1,666
1890	3,821
1910	13,536
1915	18,519
1930	36,471

In 19th-century Shanghai, British, American and French settlers lived in privileged zones.

These "mini-colonies" were on land leased outside the original walled Chinese city.

WESTERN MISSIONARIES IN CHINA

The advance of Western business interests in China was paralleled by the efforts of Western missionaries. They were convinced that through the vehicles of Western medicine and Western education, Chinese souls might yet be saved and China itself converted to Christian civilization.

In an apt, if unfortunate, phrase, the Protestant missionaries once described their activities as the "Christian occupation of China". Enjoying the protection conferred by the treaties after the Opium Wars, missionaries penetrated almost every corner of the country. Today, one of the most startling experiences for a Western tourist in China is to find in some remote backwater a cathedral which looks as if it has been physically transplanted there from Europe. One such cathedral is to be found on the road to Mount Wutai from Taiyuan.

The typical missionary settlement was a walled compound enclosing a church, missionary home, school, and hospital or dispensary. It was marked by a British or American flag.

Many missionaries spoke the local dialect, and, so as not to be handicapped by their "foreignness", adopted Chinese dress and even the pigtail or queue. The Bible was translated into both classical written language and the vernacular.

The spreading of Western-style education and medicine was part of the missionaries' work in China, as was involvement in the various reform movements— education for women, public health and hygiene, campaigns against footbinding and opium addiction. Many missionaries were also doctors or teachers, and their efforts resulted in the establishment of large numbers of mission schools, hospitals, and the famous Christian colleges of China, located in Shanghai, Beijing, Hangzhou and elsewhere.

Although it succeeded in promoting Western education, the missionary effort in China failed in its aims of conversion. Indeed, it provoked many anti-Christian riots, which were expressions of both resentment of foreigners and anti-Christian feeling.

THE BOXER REBELLION

Growing anti-foreign feeling, increasing governmental paralysis, and economic depression during the late 1890s in China culminated in the Boxer Rebellion of 1900. Missionaries were among the prime targets of this peasant protest movement whose armies eventually reached Beijing. Here they attacked Chinese Christian converts and besieged foreign legations.

Western powers sent in relief forces, and China found itself at war with all the major European powers, as well as America and Japan. The ensuing treaties further limited China's autonomy.

HARMONIOUS FISTS

The Boxer uprising received its name from the secret society that led this protest movement. The members of the society practised a form of Chinese boxing, a martial arts exercise that sought to prepare the mind and body for combat. A loose translation of the society's name, *Yi He Tuan*, was "Harmonious Fists", which led Westerners to refer to its followers as the "Boxers".

SEE ALSO PAGES 104–5, 184–85

DOWNFALL OF THE EMPIRE

Under the impact of intrusion from Western countries, the pace of change quickened in China during the nineteenth century. In the 1850s and 60s a series of rebellions wracked the country, causing disorder almost everywhere. This combination of internal strife and foreign incursions weakened central power still further. The two-thousand-year-old Confucian system of government was slow to counter these crises and became itself a cause of their aggravation. Although reform movements were initiated in attempts to adapt the ancient order to new challenges, no real modernization, such as was undertaken in Japan at this time, took place in China.

Between the 1860s and 1908 the court was dominated by the Empress Dowager Cixi. A concubine of the Xianfeng Emperor, she had borne him a son, while the empress, his wife, remained childless. After the emperor's death in 1861, this son, aged five, took the throne, with his mother as one of his regents. Although powerful, the Empress Dowager was a wilful and ignorant woman who concentrated her energies on ridding herself of rivals, instead of on ruling wisely.

During this period, a deepening economic crisis speeded the collapse of a dynasty weakened by misrule. And a steep growth in population for which no new land was available led to still more discontent. The Qing court was finally shaken into action, and in the 1890s made some attempts at reform and modernization in an effort to hold onto power. But the Empire was already in its last throes, riddled with opposing factions and corruption. The Empress Dowager's grand-nephew, the three-year-old Puyi, whom she put on the throne just before she died in 1908, was to be the last emperor of China.

Meanwhile, nationalist and anti-Manchu forces were already working to topple the outworn monarchy. Dr Sun Yat-sen, a Cantonese educated in Honolulu and Hong Kong, had already won strong support in his campaign against imperial rule among fellow southerners, Chinese students in Japan, and the overseas Chinese communities in Southeast Asia and America. In 1905 a political party, the United League (Tongmenghui), was founded in Tokyo under his leadership. Its aims were to unite the nationalist forces and overthrow Manchu rule. The party took as its basic doctrine Sun Yat-sen's Three People's Principles (*sanminzhuyi*): nationalism, democracy and socialism, or "the people's livelihood". Termed "the mother of the Chinese revolution", the United League evolved into the Guomindang, or Nationalist party.

In an atmosphere of increasing popular revolt against imperialism and government misrule, a rebellion broke out among army officers in Wuchang on October 10, 1911. Known as the Double Tenth rising because it happened on the tenth day of the tenth month, this is traditionally taken to be the start of the Republican Revolution. Starting in the south,

Puyi, China's last emperor, is shown here standing next to his father (who acted as regent) and his younger brother. Installing her three-year-old grand-nephew on the throne was the last act of the Empress Dowager before her death in 1908. He was the successor to the Guangxu Emperor, whose death mysteriously preceded hers by a day.

But Puyi's reign was short. It came to an end in 1912 when China was declared a republic. His abdication agreement allowed Puyi to continue living a privileged life in the Imperial Palace but he was finally ousted in 1924 by warlord troops.

the provinces one after another repudiated the authority of Beijing. Four months later, in February 1912, the child emperor Puyi abdicated, and a Chinese Republic was declared with Sun Yat-sen as its temporary president.

Later that year, Dr Sun surrendered the presidency to Yuan Shikai, the commander of the most powerful army in China, when the latter came over to the revolution. While the idealistic Sun had envisioned building a democratic government on the ancient foundations of imperial autocracy, Yuan Shikai saw himself as standing in the line of the emperors. After murdering or exiling his various opponents he tried unsuccessfully to enthrone himself and found a new dynasty, just before his death in 1916.

In the period of confusion which followed Yuan Shikai's death, China dissolved into a number of virtually independent provinces governed by greedy and despotic military leaders—the so-called warlords. Hundreds of these men ruled their regions by force and bloodshed, and shifting coalitions in turn controlled the impotent central government. The warlord era, a decade of internal dissent, weakness and intensified foreign rapacity, had begun.

Former concubine of the Xianfeng Emperor (1850–61), Empress Dowager Cixi (left) ruled China unofficially from 1862 to 1908. Officially her role was that of regent, first to her son, the Tongzhi Emperor (reigned 1862–74) and then to her nephew, the Guangxu Emperor (1875–1908), both of whom came to the throne as young children.

The Empress Dowager dominated the two young emperors and held the reins of power in China. But she did not rule wisely, and is remembered as a narrow-minded woman who blocked all attempts at reform and modernization. The marble boat at the entrance to her sumptuously ornate Summer Palace has become a symbol of her misrule. Both it and the palace were built with funds originally allocated to the modernization of the Chinese Navy.

Such behaviour was one of the factors that led to the eventual downfall of imperial rule.

Entrenched and corrupt officialdom, personified here in the "gentleman bureaucrat" (above), came under attack in the late 19th century. Peasants rebelled against the ruling classes, who were perceived as hindering progress by opposing reform.

Dressed in a lavishly embroidered robe, this official is pictured living in great comfort, with his elegant furniture and precious items of porcelain at his side. In his hand is a ruyi sceptre, a symbol of power generally received as a gift from the emperor. The mandarin "button" on top of his hat denotes his rank; those of the highest officials were made of silver or gold.

THE RISE OF THE COMMUNIST PARTY

THE MAY 4TH MOVEMENT

When World War I came to an end, China's hopes of recovering the leased territories it had been forced to yield to Germany were dashed. The Japanese succeeded in persuading Western powers to transfer German rights, for example in Shandong, to them as part of the Versailles Treaty.

This betrayal was a bitter blow to Chinese pride. China had supported the Allies and contributed to the war effort and had expected better treatment.

From May 4, 1919 a period of severe unrest and protest began, both against the foreign encroachment, and, even more importantly, against the officials who had allowed it to happen. Waves of student demonstrations, starting at Beijing University, workers' strikes and anti-Japanese boycotts swept through China. The May 4th Movement, as it came to be known, is now seen as a landmark in the evolution of Chinese nationalism and a harbinger of the communist revolution.

The movement had no precedent in significance or scale. Merchants closed their doors and factory workers struck. Sympathizers even included beggars, thieves, singsong girls and prostitutes who went on strike alongside workers and students. No Beijing street or park was without its student speakers. They stood on boxes, brandished white flags—white is the colour of mourning in China—and lectured their audiences in tears. Mass arrests only provoked more protests, and spread the movement.

AIMS OF MAY 4TH MOVEMENT

The thrust of the movement was to break with tradition and to create an altogether new, modern way of thinking by which China might be revitalized. This entailed the rejection of tradition and the adoption of fresh values. Rather than worship Confucius one writer said, people should worship Darwin and Ibsen.

"Save the country" became the most popular slogan of the time, and saving the country meant the creation of a New China. To achieve this, many intellectuals realized, the Chinese had to take the fate of their country into their own hands.

PUBLICATIONS

This era saw a rapid proliferation of new periodicals with such names as *New Tide*, *Emancipation and Reconstruction*, *The Dawn*, *New Society*, *The New Women* and *Awakening*. Most important was one called *New Youth*, founded in 1915 by Chen Duxiu, a political activist. He later founded certain Marxist groups in Shanghai that were forerunners of the Chinese Communist Party.

Articles in *New Youth* made vehement attacks on China's traditional culture and the magazine soon became the most influential of its time.

Since classical written Chinese was one of the traditions under attack, some of these publications used the vernacular instead of the classical written language. This prompted a literary revolution with many works inspired by Western models. *New Youth* published its first short story in the vernacular in 1918.

FOUNDING THE COMMUNIST PARTY

● First converts

Disillusionment with the West, combined with the success of the 1917 Bolshevik Revolution in Russia, drew Chinese intellectuals to Marxist ideology.

Heading the list of original converts were Li Dazhao, a librarian at the University of Beijing, and Chen Duxiu, editor of *New Youth*.

● The Shanghai Meeting

The party was founded in July 1921 at a secret meeting at a girls' school in Shanghai's French concession. A branch of the party was also established in Paris, where a number of Chinese students—among them such future leaders as Zhou Enlai and Deng Xiaoping—were studying or working.

The meeting in Shanghai was attended by 12 delegates, including the young Mao Zedong. Neither Li nor Chen was present, but a couple of Soviet Communist International (Comintern) agents were.

The group had uncertain convictions and widely divergent interests. Two of those taking part even became traitors during World War II, collaborating with the Japanese. The new party represented by the dozen delegates comprised a mere 57 members. It took 4 years to increase the numbers to 1,000.

● Early days of the CCP

For its first 6 years the Chinese Communist Party saw itself as the party of the working class. It advanced the revolution by enlisting the support of the proletariat and seized chances to build up a labour movement.

In the May 30 Incident of 1925, 11 demonstrators were killed by foreign police in Shanghai. This set off an anti-British boycott and waves of strikes against Western enterprises swept southern China. Party membership leapt. By spring of 1928, it reached 58,000.

THE FIRST UNITED FRONT

At a time when the Soviet Union's Comintern was trying to help Asian countries to form Communist parties, they approached Dr Sun Yat-sen. His Nationalist party (Guomindang) was weak and disunited, and he had failed to interest Western powers in his cause.

The Comintern convinced him that China's best hope of achieving a national revolution lay in an alliance. The Guomindang was reorganized into a Soviet-style party, and the Chinese Communist Party became an organized bloc within it. It was an uneasy coalition.

CHIANG KAI-SHEK'S NORTHERN EXPEDITION

The Guomindang became established in the south, and conditions were ripe for a military challenge to the warlords who still dominated China farther north.

In 1926 the celebrated Northern Expedition began, led by the young Chiang Kai-shek. The campaign was a resounding success. Chiang Kai-shek's forces swept up the Yangtze valley from their Guangdong base toward Shanghai, conquering vast areas from the warlords.

However, Sun Yat-sen had died in March 1925 before the Expedition began. Without his guiding hand the nationalist-communist coalition began to split. The non-communist members of the Guomindang, mostly from well-to-do landlord class families, had little in common with the Communists. And as the Guomindang became more powerful and acquired more land the difference in ideology became more apparent.

While the Communists set up peasant associations and led strikes for better wages in the newly acquired areas, the Nationalists saw this as an attack on their own class. Moreover, the Communists grew increasingly opposed to Chiang Kai-shek himself.

Chiang Kai-shek, at the height of his political powers in the 1920s, pictured with his wife,

Soong Mei-ling. In 1928 he became head of the nationalist government established in Nanjing.

THE NORTHERN EXPEDITION

Route of Chiang Kai-shek's Nationalist armies

HEILONGJIANG

JILIN

INNER MONGOLIA

LIAONING

XINJIANG

BEIJING
TIANJIN

HEBEI

SHANXI
SHANDONG

NINGXIA

QINGHAI

GANSU

SHAANXI

HENAN

JIANGSU

SHANGHAI

ANHUI

HUBEI
ZHEJIANG

TIBET

SICHUAN

JIANGXI

FUJIAN

HUNAN

GUIZHOU

GUANGDONG

YUNNAN
GUANGXI

*The aim of the Nationalists'
Northern Expedition led by
Chiang Kai-shek was to suppress
the warlords who still held power
in many parts of the country.*

CHIANG KAI-SHEK

During the 22 years from 1927 to 1949 the chief figure in Chinese politics was Chiang Kai-shek. This frail-looking soldier's entire career revolved around force, intrigue and violence.

Chiang Kai-shek was born in 1887 the son of a salt merchant at Fenghua near Ningbo (in the province of Zhejiang). He received his military training at the Chinese Military Academy at Baoding, and at the Japanese Military Academy in Tokyo. Later he headed the famous Whampoa Military Academy near Guangzhou, with the assistance of Soviet advisers.

When Sun Yat-sen died in 1925 Chiang succeeded to the leadership of the Guomindang party. He converted to Methodism and thereby secured the support of the missionaries; and he married Soong Mei-ling, the American-educated daughter of a rich and powerful Chinese who had been brought up a Southern Methodist in the United States. Her sister, Soong Ching-ling, had married Sun Yat-sen.

The greater part of Chiang Kai-shek's career was spent fighting two foes: the Japanese Imperial Army, and the Communist Red Army. "The Japanese are a disease of the skin, the Communists are a disease of the heart," was how he characterized them.

In the latter part of his nationalist Nanjing government (1928–36) the Japanese were encroaching further into Chinese territory. But Chiang was more concerned with his battle against the Communists. His power was further reduced by the warlords who still dominated many areas, particularly in the north of the country

Though during World War II he was acknowledged as a leader of a world power, as the People's Republic subsequently grew in strength and international standing his role diminished. He died in 1975 as the ruler of Taiwan, the island exile to which he led the defeated Nationalists in 1949.

In China Chiang's historical role has lately been reassessed, and his birthplace in Zhejiang Province has been made into a tourist attraction.

THE BREAK OF APRIL 12, 1927

In Shanghai the Communists in the General Labour Union had staged a massive strike, defeated the local warlord, and seized control of the city from within to welcome the arrival of Chiang Kai-shek's forces.

At Moscow's instigation, the Communists had decided to let the Guomindang armies enter the cities unopposed. What the Communists did not know was that Chiang had already rallied the support of Shanghai's bankers and businessmen. He used the underworld Green Gang for a surprise attack on the unions. In the early hours of the morning of April 12, 1927, a bloody massacre of communist pickets occurred. A widespread reign of terror against Communists followed.

This ended the orthodox phase of the Chinese Communist Party. Chiang Kai-shek governed from Nanjing, and the Communists went underground. After a radical reshuffling of the party leadership, the Communists staged one abortive urban uprising after another in an attempt to regain some support.

Meanwhile, Mao Zedong was organizing the peasant movement in his native province of Hunan. Over the next 10 years, the Chinese Communist Party was to develop from a workers' party into a party of agrarian revolution.

SEE ALSO PAGES 90–93

THE LONG MARCH

The now legendary retreat in 1934 of Chinese Communists from their base in southern China to Shaanxi Province thousands of miles to the north is known as the Long March. By any standards it was an epic—a defeat turned into triumph.

In 1927 Stalin had ordered the Russian-trained leaders of the Chinese Communist Party to lead an urban uprising, but there was no organized working class available even to strike. Driven to the countryside by this failure, the less doctrinaire leaders, notably Mao, concentrated on organizing peasants and won local support in an isolated mountainous area between provinces. They named their government, and the area under their control, the "Jiangxi Soviet", after collectives set up in Russia in the 1917 revolution.

In this huge area of southern China as many as nine million people may have come under communist control. This gave the Communists valuable experience in developing party and government organizations, and in winning peasant support with extensive land-reform policies. However, the base was under constant attack from the Guomindang nationalist forces of Chiang Kai-shek who officially governed China from Nanjing.

Four of these attacks—known as "encirclement campaigns"—were repelled by the Communists between 1930 and 1933. A fifth, launched in October 1933, was so ferocious that the Communists were forced to abandon their Jiangxi Soviet base. They began a trek that led them far away from the nationalist forces and into the northwest of China. Nearly one hundred thousand people evacuated the base in October 1934. Most were men, but some of the marching units had large contingents of women.

The main body of marchers struck out west through wild areas of the provinces of Guizhou and Yunnan. Here they were constantly harassed by nationalist forces and hostile local people, before turning north toward the final destination, Yan'an in Shaanxi Province. Privations and battles cost many lives, and others dropped out *en route*. Only about ten thousand of the original evacuees finally reached Yan'an where a new base was established. They arrived between September 1935 and October 1936, after covering on foot more than 9,600 km (6,000 mi) of some of the most inhospitable terrain in China.

The march began as a military retreat, but in terms of the Communists' overall political strategy it can be seen as a tactical withdrawal. It removed the party's leaders, and its military forces, from an area where they were constantly vulnerable to nationalist attack to a relatively secure base. From this base they were also in a position to play a leading role in the resistance to the Japanese invasion of China from Manchuria. This was imminent during the march and became a reality in 1937.

Before the Long March, Mao Zedong was only one among several important communist leaders—but

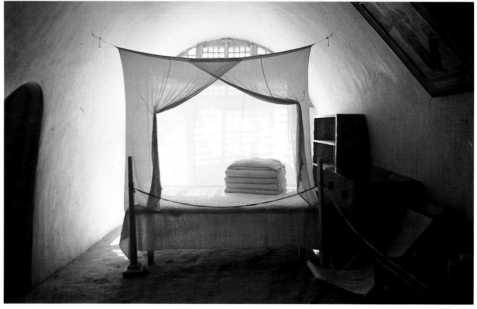

Mao's smiling followers, in heroic mood, bear aloft his portrait as they forge on in the Long March. This painting, now in the Museum of the Long March in Yan'an, does not tell the whole story, however. Only some 10,000 of the original 100,000 communist forces survived the arduous trek, on foot, from their base in Jiangxi to Yan'an in Shaanxi Province—9,600 km (6,000 mi) away.

Mao himself always spoke of the Long March in heroic terms. He wrote: "The Long March is a manifesto. It has proclaimed to the world that the Red Army is an army of heroes . . . The Long March is also a propaganda force. It has announced to some 200 million people in 11 provinces that the road of the Red Army is their only road to liberation."

A hastily constructed pontoon bridge saved the Red Army from their nationalist pursuers at Daoxian in Hunan. Other escape routes were cut off and their only path lay across the river. By lashing together a line of floats or barges and covering them with a pathway of wooden planks, the Communists crossed safely and continued their Long March.

The bridge would have been similar to the one shown (above left), built in the same place in one hour for the photograph.

Mao's simple bedroom (left) at Yan'an is now part of a museum. The Communists made this village their base at the end of the Long March. They lived in the cave dwellings dug out of the loess plateau that are typical of the area.

one with an unorthodox approach to revolution. During the internal party debates over revolutionary strategy that took place during the march, Mao gradually emerged as the Communist party's *de facto* leader. When the various groups arrived in Yan'an at the end of the march, there was no doubt who was in control.

There are countless stories of personal heroism, victories over the enemy and the elements, and tragic losses during the Long March, which has in itself assumed mythical proportions. After 1949, party officials who had taken part in it automatically acquired seniority, prestige and a certain mystique.

As well as Mao himself, Deng Xiaoping, Zhu De (who was one of the founders of the Red Army), and many others who became senior leaders were veterans of the march. In fact, the Long March generation of leaders remained dominant right up until the leadership changes of 1987. The image of the march

as a symbol of revolution-through-suffering remained potent decades after the Liberation and the declaration of the People's Republic in 1949.

The Yan'an base area where the Long March ended has acquired an aura of its own, and the town was a magnet for Chinese and foreign radicals in the 1960s and 70s. The Yan'an period was certainly formative for the policies put into practice by the Communist party after 1949—such as the "mass line" which was designed to reconcile party policies with public opinion. (In theory, the party formulated) its policies in such a way that they would appeal to the "masses". Party officials were supposed to try policies out on the "masses" and suggest adjustments before the party finally adopted them.)

Party policy which demanded that literature and culture became tools to gain popular support for socialism was also defined in Mao's speeches and writings in Yan'an.

THE LIFE OF MAO ZEDONG

CHILDHOOD AND YOUTH

Mao was born in a village in Hunan. This province in south-central China is noted for its spicy cuisine as well as the number of rebels and revolutionaries it has produced.

Mao's father was a farmer who began his working life in debt, but enriched himself by dealing in grain and land and was eventually able to employ 1 or 2 workers. From the age of 6 Mao helped on the farm.

In his own account of his childhood, Mao recalled constant conflict with his father who accused him of laziness and tried to persuade him to follow a career in the rice trade.

Mao's strictly traditional primary school education, from the age of 8 to 13, meant rote learning of the Confucian classics. In his spare time he read such novels of adventure and rebellion as *Water Margin* and the *Romance of the Three Kingdoms*. He was finally allowed to attend a more modern school where he was introduced to Western and reformist ideas, although his classical Chinese education continued.

In the revolutionary year of 1911, Mao enrolled at a secondary school in the provincial capital of Changsha, spent some time in a republican army unit, and then enrolled in a teachers' training college. There he became influenced more and more by the republican and revolutionary ideas in the periodicals that proliferated in the early years of this century—particularly *New Youth*, which became the foremost Marxist journal in China in 1920 as a result of the Russian October Revolution of 1917.

The face of Chairman Mao used to be displayed in every public building, school, factory and home. His portrait is still in Beijing's Tiananmen Square but elsewhere is less in evidence. In the late 1980s acknowledgment of his achievements is tempered by the recognition of his mistakes.

MAO, MARXISM AND THE CHINESE COMMUNIST PARTY

Like many young Chinese at the time, Mao was deeply affected by the student demonstrations of the 1919 May 4th Movement in Beijing (where he worked for a time in the university library), and the intellectual ferment of the New Culture Movement that followed it. He became a trade union organizer in his home province of Hunan, and was one of the founder-members of the Chinese Communist Party at the historic Shanghai meeting in 1921.

Mao was profoundly influenced in these early years by his time at the Peasant Movement Training Institute in Guangzhou. This had been established by Peng Pai, and was directed by Mao in 1926. Through his work there, he became convinced that revolution could occur only in the countryside, not, as the dominant Leninists insisted, among the urban proletariat, which was only just emerging in China.

With his party colleagues, Mao suffered the defeats of the 1927 uprisings and the vicissitudes of the Long March. It was during the march, at the Zunyi Conference in 1935, that he became the undisputed leader of the Communist party, emerging as chairman of the Chinese People's Soviet Republic formed around the Yan'an base at the end of the epic trek.

In Yan'an Mao began to formulate the views and policies that he put into practice when China came under his control in 1949.

MAO'S WIVES

In the traditional Chinese manner, Mao was betrothed to a girl when he was only 13 and she 19. He rejected this arranged marriage and it was never consummated.

His first wife of his own choosing was Yang Kaihui, the daughter of the Professor of Ethics at Beijing University, whom he married in 1920. She bore him 2 sons, one of whom died in combat in the Korean War. She was executed by the Nationalists in 1930.

Although he was married twice more, Mao seems to have been deeply affected by Yang Kaihui, often alluding to her in his poetry. In 1957, for example, he wrote "The Immortals" in response to a poem sent to him by a widow of the revolutionary wars of the 1930s. She had been a close friend of his first wife, who is remembered in this, possibly his most moving poem.

He Zizhen, Mao's second wife, accompanied him on the Long March, during which she gave birth to one of their 5 children. In 1937, while she was away in the Soviet Union having medical treatment, a film actress from Shanghai (then calling herself Lan Ping) arrived in Yan'an. Mao soon divorced He Zizhen to marry the glamorous newcomer who then took the name Jiang Qing.

Mao's party colleagues disapproved of the match and Jiang Qing was not permitted to take part in politics for many years. When she did enter the political arena, catastrophe ensued. As one of the leading radicals of the Cultural Revolution she was later reviled as part of the Gang of Four and blamed for that decade of terror and chaos. She was arrested, tried and imprisoned for conspiracy.

Jiang Qing's name was later linked with such other infamous powerful women in Chinese history as Empress Wu of the Tang dynasty and the Empress Dowager Cixi of the late 19th-century Qing dynasty.

THE LIFE OF MAO ZEDONG	
1893	Born in village of Shaoshan in Hunan Province.
1911	Studied in Changsha and served in republican army unit.
1918	Worked as assistant librarian in Beijing. Influenced by Marxist study groups.
1919	May 4th Movement – Mao organized student protests in Hunan.
1920	Mao organized communist and trade union groups in Hunan. Married Yang Kaihui.
1921	Attended Communist Party 1st Congress in Shanghai and became Hunan Province Party Secretary.
1923	Elected to Chinese Communist Party Central Committee.
1926	Headed Guomindang (Nationalist) Peasant Movement Institute while member of Guomindang in short-lived period of cooperation between Nationalists and Communists.
1927	Wrote *Report on an Investigation into the Peasant Movement in Hunan*. Led section of Autumn Harvest Uprising in Changsha. Retreated to Jingganshan. Lost party posts after failure of uprising.
1928	Mao and Zhu De's Red Army units combined in Jingganshan. Mao living with He Zizhen.
1929	Mao and Zhu set up Soviet base in Jiangxi Province.
1930	Yang Kaihui executed by Guomindang.
1931	Mao proclaimed Chairman of Chinese Soviet Republic in Jiangxi.
1934	Long March began.
1935	CCP conference at Zunyi gave Mao control over party. Mao and Long March armies arrived in Yan'an.
1937	Japan invaded China. Mao and Guomindang in second uneasy alliance. He Zizhen in hospital in USSR.
1938/9	Mao married to Lan Ping (Jiang Qing).
1942	Rectification campaign in Yan'an to implement Mao's policies on party organization, literary and cultural work.
1949	Mao proclaimed formation of People's Republic. Visited Moscow to meet Stalin.
1955	Mao's speech *On the Question of Agricultural Cooperation* stimulated rural collectivization.
1956	Hundred Flowers movement proposed by Mao to stimulate intellectual and political debate brought forth unexpected criticism of the CCP and socialism.
1957	Mao's speech *On the Correct Handling of Contradictions among the People* set limits to criticism of the party.
1958	Mao backed the Great Leap Forward and People's Communes.
1959	Mao clashed with Defence Minister Peng Dehuai who was in favour of modernization of the armed forces and opposed to the Great Leap Forward.
1964	First edition of *Quotations from Chairman Mao* appeared.
1966	Mao launched Cultural Revolution and personally backed Red Guards.
1971	Lin Biao (Mao's chosen successor) apparently killed in air crash after failed coup attempt against Mao.
1972	Mao met US President Nixon on his visit to China.
1973	Mao chaired 10th CCP Congress, his last.
1976	Mao died September 9th.
1987	94th anniversary of his birth marked by 25,000 visitors to Chairman Mao Zedong Memorial Hall in Beijing.

MAO, THE MAN

Mao Zedong was a colossal historical figure—one of the main authors of China's communist revolution and the man who inherited the mantle of emperors and presidents. His fascinating and complex personality combined classical scholarship, sympathy for heroic rebels and bandit outsiders from China's past, peasant shrewdness and coarseness, and great personal wit and charm.

At least in his early years in the Jiangxi and Yan'an Soviets, Mao seemed to be at home with the simple life and rustic humour of the farmers he mixed with. At the same time he was a scholar—an omnivorous reader steeped in philosophy and literature, and a practising poet of some merit. Perhaps he was never completely at ease in either world.

Official Chinese assessments of the part Mao played in the revolution are ambivalent—and constantly changing. He is praised as the founder of the People's Republic, and for his first decade as chairman—the years of reconstruction. But he will not be easily forgiven for the turmoil of the Cultural Revolution that he unleashed in the 1960s.

Calligraphy reveals much about the personality of its creator. Mao was praised for his calligraphy which was vigorous and powerful but idiosyncratic. The example (above) is of the first lines of his poem entitled Mount Liupan, written in 1935.
"The skies are high and the clouds are fleecy,
We watch the flying geese breaking away to the south."

RULER OF CHINA

While contemporary Chinese history has many important figures—Zhou Enlai, the diplomat and statesman; Liu Shaoqi, the manager of the Communist party machine—there is no doubt that Mao towered over them all. He was not a dictator; he never inspired the fear that Stalin did in the Soviet Union, and he was not always able to get his own way.

From 1949, when the People's Republic was founded, until 1959, Mao was head of both the state and the Communist party, and his authority was virtually unchallenged. In 1959, after major policy disagreements over the outcome of the Great Leap Forward and the development of the communes, he relinquished the state chairmanship to Liu Shaoqi, who was to be his arch rival in the coming Cultural Revolution of 1966 to 1976.

In the early 1960s there were serious conflicts between Mao, who was trying to keep to the revolutionary orthodoxy of the Yan'an period, and other party leaders. They were more willing to modify policies to fit in with the need for modernization. These conflicts came to a head in the Cultural Revolution and continued until Mao's death in September 1976.

MAO, THE POET

For a revolutionary, Mao was a most traditional poet. He wrote within the highly formalized structures of classical Chinese verse and, like generations of earlier poets, used the old forms to express contemporary concerns.

The subject matter of his published verse was most often the revolutionary struggle, and military images predominated; but his poetry also revealed his private thoughts.

Literary critics are divided on the merits of Mao's poetry. It was overpraised in the 1960s and 70s, but it is undoubtedly vigorous and its heroic and revolutionary sentiments are genuine.

SEE ALSO PAGES
88–89, 90–91, 94–95

THE CULTURAL REVOLUTION

The traumatic events that shook Chinese society to its foundations in the decade before Mao's death in 1976 were launched in the summer of 1966 as the Great Proletarian Cultural Revolution. What followed was not a revolution, was inimical to both traditional and modern high culture and was hardly proletarian. No one in China today would describe the period as great; it is commonly referred to as the "decade of disaster".

The Cultural Revolution and its aftermath affected every province of China and touched everyone directly or indirectly. Even today, the remnants of slogans from the period can be seen in the remotest villages. However, the most serious disruption was in the cities, particularly major cities such as Beijing, Shanghai and Guangzhou (Canton), and in the provincial capitals where radicals seized power from the existing party committees.

In the years after the failure of the radical Great Leap Forward in 1958, when Mao had tried to drag China out of its backwardness overnight, he had come increasingly into conflict with other senior Communist party and government officials who wanted a more gradual approach. Mao believed that the revolutionary impetus of the Long March, and of the wars against Japan and the Nationalists, was dying down—that Chinese society was becoming ossified and bureaucratic, following the path taken by the USSR. Chinese leaders saw this as state capitalism, a revolution betrayed.

Unable to convince his colleagues that they should adopt a more radical approach, Mao attacked the Communist party establishment. His tactics were at first oblique, then more direct using political and cultural connections that his wife, Jiang Qing, had built up in Shanghai.

The Cultural Revolution was put forward by Mao as an opportunity to assail bourgeois and bureaucratic attitudes in the party. His call was heeded only too readily by frustrated young factory workers and students. Tired of hearing how heroic their parents' generation had been before Liberation in 1949, they were searching for a way to overcome their own powerlessness and lack of control over their own lives and futures.

These young people were formed into Red Guard units, formally approved by Mao at a mass rally in Beijing's Tiananmen Square. They were then set loose to overthrow the existing party and government structure throughout the country in cities, towns, communes, colleges and factories. Most Red Guards were educated children and teenagers from the cities although some came originally from small towns and rural areas.

From the summer of 1966 onward Red Guards were "seizing power" from existing party and government organizations at all levels. For example, a city party committee would be overthrown and replaced by a new, more radical organization. Some

Red Guards with a portrait of their hero, Chairman Mao, show their support at a rally to launch the Cultural Revolution. Many such mass rallies—attended in all by some 10 million young people from all over the country—were held in Beijing's vast Tiananmen Square in the course of 1966 and 1967.

Supporters of the Cultural Revolution, all wearing red arm bands bearing the characters for Red Guard, thronged to the rallies. They came to see their leaders, including Mao himself, and to listen to their speeches urging them to action.

Charged with emotion, these huge crowds sang, chanted slogans and waved flags. Many people became hysterical whenever Mao appeared. The young Red Guards would leave the rallies fired with enthusiasm for the cause and spurred on by their leaders' exhortations to carry out Mao's avowed aim of destroying the old ideology.

party committees then used their own Red Guard supporters to help them get back into control. The intense feuding accompanying this led in many regions to a power vacuum that the army was brought in to fill. Senior party officials—including the state chairman Liu Shaoqi, Deng Xiaoping and the veteran army commander Zhu De—were criticized, humiliated and stripped of their posts. Similar treatment was meted out to provincial officials, managers, college principals and even ordinary teachers—anyone who could possibly be what Mao called a "stinking intellectual", and anyone with the slightest foreign association or possession, past or present.

Army intervention stabilized regional government, often by dominating the Revolutionary Committees which replaced existing political and management structures right down to factory floor level. The most violent and chaotic phase of the Cultural Revolution came to an end in April 1969 when the Ninth Congress of the Communist party was held with Mao and his designated successor Lin Biao in command. However, the pursuit of radical policies did not abate. Maoist ideology was given primacy over economics, diplomacy and all else until Mao died in September 1976.

After Mao's death his wife, Jiang Qing, and her Shanghai-based supporters (later vilified as the Gang of Four) briefly attempted to continue the policies of the Cultural Revolution. But they were arrested, tried and imprisoned for attempting to overthrow the state. After a brief interregnum, the modernizing regime of Deng Xiaoping came to power. As the Cultural Revolution was wound down, the Red Guard units were broken up and their members dispersed.

It is difficult to say precisely how and why the Cultural Revolution happened or what it was really about. There is no doubt that it was partly a factional struggle within the Communist party. It was also an attack on bureaucracy by Mao, and an attempt by him to infuse the party with a new revolutionary spirit. But it is not yet possible to conclude whether this was from genuine political conviction or was just a means of mobilizing the masses against his political foes.

What is certain is that for the majority of Chinese people 1966 to 1976 was a wasted decade. The economy was in chaos and the cities ground to a halt. Teaching was at a standstill, and there is still a lost generation of bitter middle-aged Chinese who missed their chance of higher education or even secondary schooling. Intellectuals and artists suffered particularly badly, and creativity was stifled. Tens of thousands of people died, were injured, persecuted, lost their jobs or were wrongfully imprisoned. Whatever political direction China takes in future, there is a deep determination that there should never be another Cultural Revolution.

MODERN GOVERNMENT/DENG XIAOPING

THE GOVERNING STRUCTURE

Although formally separate, party and state in China overlap in their personnel, functions and authority to such an extent that they are often thought of as forming a single governmental structure.

In fact, party and state form parallel structures. Each administrative or economic unit in the government bureaucracy has an equivalent unit in the party. At the top level, an inner core of individuals exerts power in both domains.

In the late 1980s the clear separation of authority between party and state has become a matter of immense concern to the leadership, and one of the tasks in the overall reform of Chinese society. It will take a long time to build up a new generation of public servants with greater professional expertise who will be able to streamline the unwieldy bureaucracy.

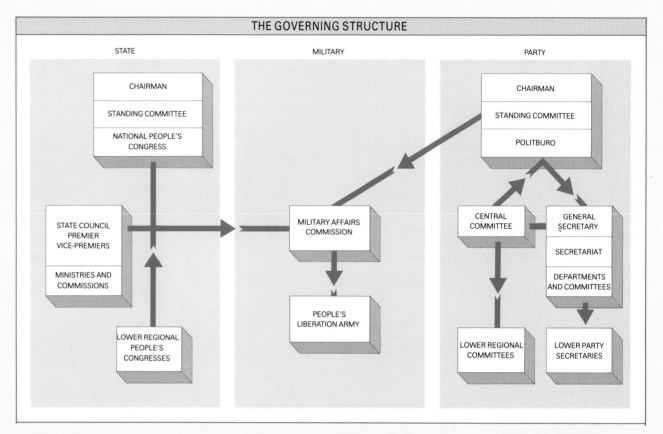

THE GOVERNING STRUCTURE

STATE — MILITARY — PARTY

The relationship between the three arms of the national political structure—state, military and party—is shown in the diagram above. The most influential bodies of all in the governing structure are the party's Politburo and its Standing Committee. At present there is considerable overlap between party and state but reformers want to see a greater separation in future.

THE PARTY

The structure of the party is like a pyramid. At the apex, with supreme power, is the Politburo Standing Committee which governs the Politburo. The Politburo and its Standing Committee are the 2 most influential decision-making bodies in China. But personal prestige is so important that Deng Xiaoping (not a member of either in 1988) is still the ultimate source of all major decisions.

Next in line from the Politburo is the Central Committee which comprises all the top leaders of the party. Little is known about how it arrives at decisions, or to what extent it influences policy.

The Central Committee is served by the Secretariat, the chief of which, the all-powerful General Secretary, is the head of the entire party apparatus. Zhao Ziyang was appointed General Secretary at the 1987 13th Party Congress.

The lower echelons of party organization exist at every level of local government but also throughout society—for example, in factories and schools. Thus, the party is able to exercise direct control over every aspect of Chinese life. But reformers want the party to step back from this role to become the arbiter of policy though not of day-to-day administration.

In a country as vast as China, policies decided upon by central government can work only with the cooperation of local authorities. But local government is not always responsive to central directives and regional bureaucrats and party cadres can sometimes thwart government policies.

THE STATE

The National People's Congress is at the centre of the state structure. A large representational body, it consists of deputies elected by provincial-level congresses, the armed forces, and by overseas Chinese. It meets in full session for a few weeks each year and formally elects the government, amends the constitution and passes new laws.

The Congress in early 1988 was a more lively occasion than usual. The vigorous debates were widely reported and votes were recorded against as well as for candidates for government posts.

The chief administrative organ of the state and true centre of power is the State Council, successively headed, since 1954, by the late Premier Zhou Enlai, Hua Guofeng, Zhao Ziyang and Li Peng. All ministers and heads of Commissions serve on the Council.

Politically, the State Council is subordinate to the party leadership but as the translator of the party's decisions into state action, it is powerful.

Other bodies making up the central government framework include the Supreme People's Court (the highest judicial body), and the Supreme People's Procuracy (public prosecutor). Since 1982 attempts have been made to restructure the state administration, to deal with corruption in its ranks, and to reduce the number of civil servants (roughly 28 million at the time of Mao Zedong's death in 1976).

THE MILITARY

The third major arm of the national political structure is the People's Liberation Army (PLA). Mao used a memorable image when defining the supreme role of the party in military affairs: "Political power grows out of the barrel of a gun. Our principle is that the party commands the gun, and the gun must never be allowed to command the party."

At the head of the PLA is the party's Military Affairs Commission and the state's Central Military Commission. These bodies exercise external direction over the state's Ministry of National Defence.

The Commission is of central importance, and has been under the control of Mao Zedong, Lin Biao, and Deng Xiaoping. It formulates military police under the direction of the Politburo, and appoints a political commissar to work alongside the commanding officer of every army headquarters or unit.

FACTIONALISM

The Chinese Empire always had one ruler, the Son of Heaven. The sharing of power by a collective leadership is new to the Chinese, and the political structure can be overridden by personal charisma.

During the Cultural Revolution, Mao stood above the party, ruling by personal decree. When Deng Xiaoping came to power in 1978, his personal prestige was such that he became the ultimate decision-maker.

The power of personality in Chinese political life makes factionalism inevitable. A top politician in Beijing is like a patron or sponsor, with his loyal following of protégés and supporters, many of whom are also patrons in their turn. As the beneficiaries of their chief's power and prestige, they have an interest in ensuring that no other leader expands his authority at the expense of their sponsor.

Thus Chinese officials work in a mesh of personal favours and political ties, mutual obligations, nepotism and rivalry; one faction is pitted against another, divided by differences of background, experience and ideology. They become expert at assessing how their patrons are faring in the power struggle at the top, adroitly switching sides if need be.

Since the late 1970s the main split in Chinese politics has been between the so-called reformists (represented by Hu Yaobang and Zhao Ziyang) and the conservatives (represented by Chen Yun and Peng Zhen). In the most general terms, Deng Xiaoping can be seen as someone in whom the 2 sides come together—being at once an advocate of reform, and an upholder of strict party control.

Deng Xiaoping has been the most powerful man in China since 1978. Although at the 1987 Party Congress he stepped down from most of his posts, he remains highly influential.

DENG'S EARLY CAREER

Deng Xiaoping was born in 1904 in Guang'an, Sichuan Province. From 1920 to 1926 he studied in France under the auspices of the Work-Study Scheme (a Chinese programme aimed at producing the educated men the country needed). There he worked in a steel factory, met Zhou Enlai, and joined the Communist party.

After a brief period at the Sun Yat-sen University in Moscow, Deng returned to China to work for the then left-leaning warlord, Feng Yuxiang. Feng later sided with Chiang Kai-shek against the Communists and from 1927 to 1931 Deng worked for the underground communist movement in Wuhan, Shanghai and Guangxi, where he organized strikes and staged rebellions against the nationalist government.

In the revolutionary base in Jiangxi, he was attached to the political department of the Red Army. By 1934, when he embarked on the Long March, he had already acquired considerable political and military expertise. Later, as a political commissar in the army Deng had a distinguished war record. He played a leading part in campaigns against the Japanese and in the civil war, culminating in the capture of Nanjing, the Guomindang's capital, in 1949.

DENG'S POLITICAL CAREER

What chiefly distinguished Deng Xiaoping's career was his ability to bounce back after each of several political "falls".
• The first of his famous "comebacks" was in 1934, a year after he had been stripped of all his posts and disgraced. Ironically, he had been purged for supporting Mao's ideas on agrarian reform and guerrilla tactics against those of the Politburo.
• Deng's second political eclipse was prompted by the Cultural Revolution, when his name was coupled with that of Liu Shaoqi as a "top party person taking the capitalist road".

Banished from the political stage, he worked as a mechanic and grew vegetables in rural Jiangxi. He was brought back to Beijing in 1973 by the ailing Zhou Enlai, who, before he died, determined to set China on a path toward the Four Modernizations. Deng seemed Zhou's obvious successor.
• The third of Deng's political setbacks was then engineered in 1976 by Jiang Qing (Mao's widow) and the rest of the Gang of Four. He was accused of failing to understand the Marxist creed, and of representing capitalist trends within the party.

The fall of the Gang a few months later signalled the rise of Deng. In 1978 he was invested with the power to overturn Maoism, and set China on what he termed its "second revolution".

THE NEW LEADERSHIP

The 13th Party Congress in late 1987 saw the retirement of several of China's oldest leaders from both the Politburo and the Central Committee, and the rise of a new generation.

Deng Xiaoping stepped down from all his posts, but kept his control of the army as chairman of the Military Commission. Considerable limelight was turned on Zhao Ziyang, who became not only Party General Secretary, but also Deng's deputy on the Military Commission. The premier's job he vacated went to Li Peng, the adopted son of Zhou Enlai.

The appointment of Li and other new men indicates an advance toward Deng's goal of rejuvenating the top leadership.

With Li Peng and Zhao Ziyang on the Politburo Standing Committee are Qiao Shi, Hu Qili and Yao Yilin. Yao Yilin is one of three Vice-Premiers as well as holding a major portfolio as Minister in Charge of the State Planning Commission. Hu Qili and Qiao Shi have long party careers behind them, and take care of ideology and party discipline.

NEW DIRECTIONS

Those pushing for a further liberalization of China's economic and political system have been accused of betraying Marx. And their inability to justify the reforms ideologically has made their position awkward.

With the much publicized announcement at the 1987 Party Congress that China was still at "an initial stage of socialism", and that it had a long way to go in the achievement of full socialism, Zhao Ziyang hoped to end the argument over whether or not his economic reforms were Marxist.

Also announced at the congress were administrative reforms, aimed at reducing political and government interference in the management of the economy. Admittedly these reforms loosened the party's grip only a little, but any voluntary limitation of powers is an unusual act for a Communist party.

POPULATION AND MINORITY NATIONALITIES

Although China is the third largest country in the world, covering more than 9,600,000 sq km (3,700,000 sq mi), the population must feed, clothe and house itself from only a small proportion of its vast landmass. Deserts, mountains and eroded plains not fit for habitation or for crop growing cover some two-thirds of the country; the remainder has to support more than a billion people.

When a Chinese demographer in the 1950s dared to protest about the baby boom that had followed the end of civil war and Japanese occupation, the national press vilified him as a counter-revolutionary and pessimist. The official view was that the government could keep subsistence ahead of population growth. From the mid-1950s to mid-1970s there were periodic but unsustained attempts to limit the population. But before the dawn of the 1980s, economists and planners saw that Ma Yinchu had been right. China's population—having doubled since the communist takeover—was using up land, food and resources faster even than the revitalized economy could produce them. It would require drastic action for China to avoid a disastrous level of overpopulation by the year 2000.

Since 1984 government policy has imposed a limit of one child per couple in urban areas, and two in the countryside after attempts to restrict people to one had failed. The limit has generally been observed in the towns where higher standards of education and severe housing shortages combine to persuade most people of the sense of small families.

But it is in the villages that the battle to control China's population will be won or lost. The peasants inhabit a world in which beliefs and values have been passed down from one generation to the next. Their view of childbearing and family life is based upon traditional ideas of fertility and the importance of producing sons to please one's ancestors, and as an assurance of care and protection in old age; daughters leave home on marriage. They also have a keen awareness of the material wealth represented by an extra pair of hands in an economy which encourages farmers to get rich but forbids them to hire help.

Fines are levied on couples who defy the authorities' injunctions to limit their families. Despite this, enough people are determined to have more children that in some provinces the birth rate is as high as 25 per thousand. In 1987 a sample survey showed a growth rate of 1.48 percent, a substantial rise on the 1985 figure of 1.1 percent.

Exceptions to the one-child rule are the minority peoples (those belonging to ethnic groups other than Han Chinese) who make up some 7 percent of China's population. These people, such as Mongolians, Tibetans and Uygurs, are allowed to have larger families than the rest of the population. One reason for this is that most minority groups inhabit sparsely populated border areas where some increase in numbers is beneficial.

Huge crowds spilling onto the road are an everyday occurrence in this Shanghai shopping street. Bicycles are banned from such areas and the heavy congestion makes it hard even for buses to move.

It is in the densely populated cities such as Shanghai that the burden of China's huge population is most evident. Restricting babies to one or two per couple may achieve too little, too late. The population seems set to break the 1.2 billion barrier by the year 2000.

People of the 55 minority nationalities in China total some 67 million, or about 7 percent of the population. They have their own languages and traditions and most differ in appearance from the Han Chinese.

The Uygurs (top left) are a Muslim people concentrated in the Xinjiang area of northwestern China. The women wear a version of Islamic dress but cover their head with scarves rather than veils.

The Mongols (top right) are traditionally nomadic herding people. They live in Inner Mongolia, the Autonomous Region created for them, and in neighbouring provinces.

The Zhuang people (bottom left) are the largest of the minority nationalities with a population of more than 13 million. Most live in Guangxi, Yunnan and Guizhou in southwestern China and their culture and language are linked to those of the neighbouring Burmese.

The Kazaks (bottom right) are Muslims who lead a nomadic life, mostly in Xinjiang and Gansu in the northwest. Many also live just over the border of Xinjiang in the USSR.

POPULATION AND MINORITY NATIONALITIES/2

ETHNIC MINORITIES

There are some 56 ethnic groups in China. The Han, as 93 percent of the population, are the dominant race. But 60 percent of China's land area has a population dominated by minority peoples—ethnic groups other than the Han. These include Tibetans, Mongolians and the Turkic Uygurs in Xinjiang.

The minority population totalled 67 million in the 1982 census. Of the various groups, only 15 have a total of more than a million people each; 13 have more than 100,000; and 7 more than 50,000.

Many of the minority nationalities live in the border regions, and thus have affinities with the peoples of their neighbouring countries, including Korea, Mongolia, the Soviet Union and Burma. Their religious and cultural traditions are distinct from the ethical-political legacy of the Han; but there has always been a cross-cultural influence, which is still evident today.

DISTRIBUTION OF THE LARGEST MINORITY NATIONALITIES

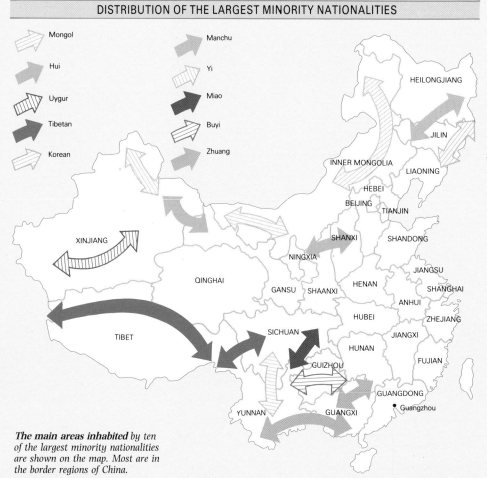

The main areas inhabited by ten of the largest minority nationalities are shown on the map. Most are in the border regions of China.

CHINA'S GROWING POPULATION

Reliable census figures show that since the Communists came to power in 1949 China's population has doubled. Tracing its rise and fall over a longer period is difficult, however, because census results in imperial China were notoriously unreliable.

Nonetheless the overall picture since the 18th century is clear. Between about 1700 and 1850, China's population trebled to something over 400 million. After that, rebellions, civil war, and decades of upheaval in the 20th century, kept the population growth rate down.

Since 1949 the trend has been going upward all the time. Government policies, encouraging late marriage and attempting to enforce birth control, have slowed but not reversed the rise.

Current estimates suggest that the population is likely to break the 1,200 million barrier early in the 21st century.

CONDITIONS FOR THE MINORITY GROUPS

With a few exceptions, most of the minority peoples live in remote, sparsely inhabited areas of China. Life for most is rural—often nomadic—and minority areas are generally less developed economically and culturally than the rest of China. Tibet and Ningxia—2 of the 5 Autonomous Regions created for the minority peoples—are by far the poorest areas in the country.

Many of the minority groups have clashed with the Han authorities at various times in their history. Disputes have arisen over religious freedom, economic control and cultural assimilation. Officialdom can sometimes be insensitive to the value of heritage and self-respect among the Tibetans and Mongols, for example. But however strained relations become between the Han and minority peoples, both sides realize that compromises

have to be made.

Since 1949 efforts have been made to modernize industry and agriculture in minority areas and improve living standards. And in the 1980s there is greater religious tolerance than at any time since the communist takeover.

Because minority peoples are generally allowed more children than the Han, the non-Han population is growing at a much faster rate. Between 1964 and 1982, national minority numbers increased by 69 percent; Han by 44 percent. However, since the Han majority is so large, it is unlikely that significant changes in the ethnic balance of China's population will result.

MINORITY LANGUAGES

All the peoples of China are encouraged to use northern Han Chinese called *putonghua* (common speech). In addition, however, 52 minority languages are recognized by the Chinese authorities and are very much alive in the relevant areas.

Some of the minority language groups—the Tibetans and Mongolians, for example—have ancient traditions and a published literature of world repute. Other ethnic minorities have only begun to transcribe their spoken languages into written form in the 20th century; southwestern groups, such as the Zhuang and Hani peoples, fall into this category.

Specialist publishers produce reading matter in the most widely spoken languages; these are also taught in local schools in addition to Han Chinese.

MINORITY NATIONALITY POPULATION

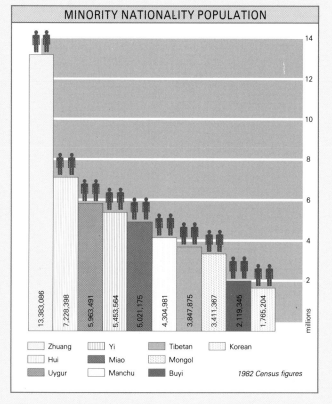

13,383,086 | 7,228,398 | 5,963,491 | 5,453,564 | 5,021,175 | 4,304,981 | 3,847,875 | 3,411,367 | 2,119,345 | 1,765,204

Zhuang	Yi	Tibetan	Korean
Hui	Miao	Mongol	
Uygur	Manchu	Buyi	*1982 Census figures*

The 55 minority nationalities in China account for only 7 percent of the population. Twenty of these nationality groups number fewer than 50,000. Figures for the largest groups are shown above.

Map legend:
Mongol, Hui, Uygur, Tibetan, Korean, Manchu, Yi, Miao, Buyi, Zhuang

Map labels: HEILONGJIANG, JILIN, INNER MONGOLIA, LIAONING, HEBEI, BEIJING, TIANJIN, SHANXI, SHANDONG, NINGXIA, JIANGSU, QINGHAI, GANSU, SHAANXI, HENAN, SHANGHAI, ANHUI, HUBEI, ZHEJIANG, XINJIANG, SICHUAN, JIANGXI, HUNAN, FUJIAN, TIBET, GUIZHOU, GUANGDONG, Guangzhou, YUNNAN, GUANGXI

THE ONE-CHILD POLICY

After the Cultural Revolution and Mao Zedong's death in 1976, the official approach to national family planning gradually tightened up. Demographers warned of impending disaster if, between 1975 and 2000, the population grew at the same rate as it did between 1950 and 1975.

In 1984 a policy was introduced restricting each couple—with the sole exception of some non-Han minorities—to just one child. In practice this has proved impossible to enforce. Many people simply defy pressure, pay their fines and continue to have more children.

It is only in the cities that the one-child family is the norm. Overcrowding and housing shortages are as persuasive as any government propaganda.

In the country, the population growth rate is much harder to control. Moreover, people are so desperate for sons, for economic as well as traditional reasons, that

cases of female infanticide have been reported.

The one-child family policy has attracted much criticism both inside and outside China. From the vantage point of the economic planner, it is the only solution to a problem that was allowed to drift untackled throughout the chaotic years of the 1960s and 1970s.

POPULATIONS OF MAJOR COUNTRIES	
China	1,060,000,000
India	745,012,000
USSR	275,000,000
USA	236,681,000
Indonesia	159,895,000
Brazil	132,580,000
Japan	120,018,000
Bangladesh	96,730,000
Pakistan	93,286,000
UK	56,682,000
	1986 figures

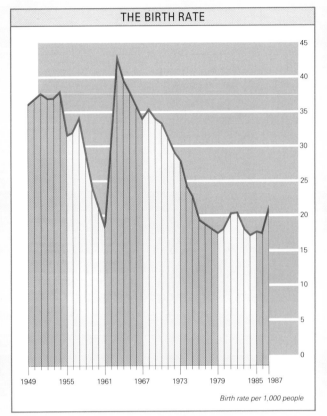

THE BIRTH RATE

Birth rate per 1,000 people

Political events have greatly affected China's birth rate. It fell to its lowest, for example, with the disastrous economic policies of the late 1950s and the famine of 1961, but soared again during the Cultural Revolution. Official policy since 1976 has been to keep the rate down and it has remained around 20 per thousand.

BIRTH CONTROL IN RURAL AREAS

Two policies central to the prosperity of China as a whole militate against each other in the countryside. Just as the planners and demographers were beginning to convince the politicians of the need for a national birth control policy, Deng Xiaoping introduced the agricultural reforms.

Economists were gratified with the increased output that resulted when families farmed their own patch of land. But peasants engaged in unmechanized agriculture want more labour. They are happy to pay the fines the government imposes on those who have larger families, knowing that a strong son will earn many thousand times that fine during a lifetime working on the land.

Press reports suggest that in some rural areas the birth rate has been creeping up to over 20 per thousand. Many of these extra births are beyond the norms approved by the state.

POPULATION DENSITY

Although China has such a huge population—more than a billion at the 1982 census—large areas of the country are uninhabited.

The majority of people live in the provinces along the eastern seaboard, that is, between Beijing and Guangzhou. The heaviest density of all is in Shanghai where there are some 1,967 persons per sq km (5,094 per sq mi). The most densely populated province is Jiangsu with 606 persons per sq km (1,570 per sq mi).

Much of China, however, is either rocky, mountainous or eroded terrain incapable of supporting any but the hardiest nomadic groups—if any population at all. Population density in Tibet, Qinghai and Xinjiang falls respectively to 2, 6 and 9 per sq km (5, 15 and 23 per sq mi).

Agronomists and meteorologists struggle to "green" the desert, but both

the climate and the terrain of most of inland China remain so inhospitable that relocation of city dwellers is not a practical answer to the population crisis.

The vast mineral resources in parts of the interior could, in theory, be exploited to revitalize the Chinese economy and create new centres of population, but communications in these regions are as yet too underdeveloped. Nor do the millions of citizens living in overcrowded conditions in the cities and villages of the east have any incentive to move to less populated rural inland areas.

The uneven distribution of China's population is likely to alter little in the next few decades.

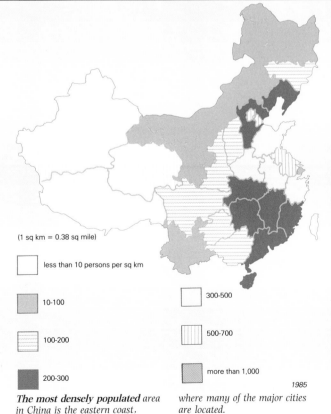

(1 sq km = 0.38 sq mile)

☐ less than 10 persons per sq km

☐ 10-100

☐ 100-200

■ 200-300

☐ 300-500

▥ 500-700

☐ more than 1,000

1985

The most densely populated area in China is the eastern coast, where many of the major cities are located.

POPULATION CONTROLS FOR MINORITY GROUPS

Those ethnic minorities with a population of under 10 million (which includes most of them) are exempt from the one-child policy. Couples are allowed to have 2 or even 3 children.

Paradoxically, it is the minority people who might accept birth control more willingly than the Han Chinese, since they are not driven by their traditional desire to produce sons in order to please the family ancestors.

But government leniency with ethnic minorities has a practical basis. Most of these groups form small communities of less than one million; and most live in remote, often strategically important, areas where the population is low at present. In these border regions an increase in the population would clearly be an advantage for China.

SEE ALSO PAGES 42–43, 52–53, 126–29

THE ROLE OF WOMEN

Contemporary Chinese society seems to be leap-frogging from the nineteenth to the twenty-first century, and the changing role of women in China reflects this rapid transformation. The symbols of women's status in old China as childbearers for their husbands' family lines—their confinement to home, bound feet, illiteracy and exclusion from the civil service and its examination systems—have gradually been superseded by images of women as workers, thinkers and leaders. Some traditions die hard, however, despite China's commitment to modern ways.

There are a good many parallels to be made between the experience of Chinese women and their sisters in the West. However, a fundamental difference is that, to a large extent, liberation has been thrust upon women in China by the government. For women in Western countries what liberation they have attained has grown more naturally from their own efforts.

Education is generally the first step toward social change. The early twentieth century saw the start of schooling for women in some Westernized areas of China. Girl students realized that they were entitled to use their educations for more serious ends than a more desirable marriage contract. Many joined demonstrations against weak and corrupt official-dom. The most daring bobbed their hair and prac-tised "free love"—like the modern women on the other side of the globe—in a self-conscious break with the traditional chaste and submissive conven-tions. The literature and films of the 1920s and 1930s are full of modern females, but in reality the majority of Chinese women were not affected by their sisters' rejection of the past.

Older women, peasants, the masses of illiterates who worked and served for pitifully low wages, were substantially untouched by the revolutionary ways of urban intellectuals. This remained true even when the revolution shifted its base from town to country. They still married the men of their parents' choice, serving first their mothers and later their mothers-in-law. And they continued to value themselves, and to be judged by others, solely in terms of their ability to produce sons.

Since 1949 the government has done much to improve women's status. Freedom of choice in marriage is officially upheld; child betrothals are forbidden; and women are still encouraged, in Chair-man Mao's phrase, "to hold up half the sky". But prejudices persist. The ruling Politburo does not have a proportionate number of female representatives. Few women run ministries, companies and farms. It is unlikely that there could be a female Premier of China before the end of this century.

As wage-earners today, Chinese women have gained an autonomy and an assurance unavailable to them in the past. Protected by new marriage and divorce laws, and with family size officially limited,

This woman lathe operator at work in the Luoyang tractor factory receives the same pay as her male colleagues. Although women are concentrated in certain industries, such as textiles, some have entered the traditionally male preserves of heavy industry.
Since many working women also have families, large factories provide child-care facilities such as crèches and kindergartens. Surveys reveal, however, that once home, women still bear the burden of the household chores.

they can enjoy better health and higher social standing than ever before. But challenges remain, not least of which are the conflicting burdens of household and workplace. Today they are also subject to the additional pressures of the materially oriented, image conscious 1980s. Women clearly need to make a great effort to do what is expected of them by their government, their leaders in various women's organizations and themselves.

While generalizing about women's roles, it must be remembered that China supports a great diversity of ways of life. A dichotomy is most apparent between

town and country. The cities are where independent single women live in greater numbers. In the rural areas, Confucian ways have not died out altogether. Traditional marriages are still the norm. Families save for years to pay for a magnificent wedding; dowries offered by the groom are enormous—and without one no family will part with the daughter it has nurtured at considerable cost since birth.

Because she joins her husband's family on marriage, a country wife may still suffer domination at the hands of that traditional "hate-figure" of Chinese mythology—the powerful mother-in-law. The latter

will be intent on exacting her due as it was once exacted from her. A city wife may suffer the more subtle pressure of the media, wondering whether her performance measures up. Both city and country wife will be cooking and keeping house with little as yet, by Western standards, in the way of modern conveniences, and the country woman will expect little domestic help from her husband.

But even if the modern Chinese woman must work extremely hard, at least for more than a generation she has been equal to any man in the eyes of the law. Her prospects do give grounds for optimism.

RELIGION TODAY

THE OFFICIAL LINE

In China today the authorities' attitude toward religious matters is informed by the Marxist view that religion is a product of class-divided societies. They believe that in socialist China religion will gradually wither away to be replaced by a secular value of selfless service to the people.

Continued adherence to traditional beliefs such as ancestor worship constitutes "feudal superstition" and undermines socialist principles. Folk religion is officially perceived as irrational, wasteful and too narrowly focused on family and local community.

In China's countryside, however, many peasants still prefer the supernatural to atheistic socialism. They attribute bumper harvests not to socialist reforms but to the munificence of the Earth God and their ancestors. Education and persuasion are seen as the appropriate methods for handling this backward thinking.

Official policies toward the organized and more "respectable" religions of Buddhism, Islam, Christianity and Taoism are relatively liberal. Freedom to believe in these religions is constitutionally guaranteed and the government allows new priests to be trained. Provided followers adhere to socialist principles and are loyal to China's socialist development such faiths are acceptable. To ban them would only cause many people to turn to "more primitive superstitions".

Relations between the state and the leaders of these religions are structured through specially created nationwide associations.

In the post-Mao era temples, monasteries, mosques and churches have been re-opened and many religious personages harshly treated during the Cultural Revolution have been rehabilitated.

A Buddhist monk at the Monastery of Divine Light in Chengdu.

CONFUCIANISM AND ANCESTOR WORSHIP

The first missionaries to China called its dominant way of thought Confucianism. But they disagreed about whether it amounted to a religion, and whether the respect paid to ancestors constituted religious ritual.

Confucius (*c.* 551–479 BC), though no enemy of religion, was chiefly concerned to transmit through his teaching all the surviving moral and cultural values of an idealized antiquity. These included hierarchically ordered family relationships: filial piety was to be shown toward parents in life and offerings made to the dead.

The imperial state promoted both the cult of Confucius and Confucian teachings. Until this century his name was among the first words a Chinese child learned to write. Many modernizers felt that it was only by discarding his legacy completely that China could break free from its past.

Now Confucius is officially regarded as a great historical figure of limited relevance to the present, although some Confucian virtues, such as respect for age and authority, seem to live on in new guises.

TAOISM

As an organized religion Taoism can be traced back only to the 2nd century AD. However, it draws on many ancient strands of Chinese thought, and even claims Lao-tzu, an alleged contemporary of Confucius, as its founder. Its diverse elements only came together gradually thereafter into a single religious tradition.

Tao, the Way, a term much used in ancient China, signifies in Taoism the one principle underlying all things in our world and beyond. Passing beyond the limitations of our world to an immortal state is a dominant theme in Taoism, and Taoist advocacy of meditational, alchemical and other paths to this goal has deeply influenced Chinese civilization.

In 1980 the government revived a Taoist Association to channel surviving support for Taoism away from active involvement in communal religion toward less controversial pursuits. These include the preservation of Taoist culture, such as music and literature.

The leaning pagoda is at the centre of the Baoguangsi or Monastery of Divine Light near Chengdu in Sichuan Province. The monastery was founded during the Tang dynasty (618–907).

BUDDHISM

Buddhism probably arrived in China via the trade routes from India almost 2,000 years ago. But the Buddha's message of the impermanence of this world, compared with the tranquil state of Nirvana beyond our deluded, selfish strivings, only found favour with all sections of Chinese society in the unsettled period following the 2nd century AD.

Even so, jealous Taoists and Confucians, outraged by its celibate clergy, which they saw as an affront to traditional family values, persisted in denouncing Buddhism as an alien creed. Although some emperors lavished their patronage on Buddhist sculpture and other art forms, most remained suspicious of its influence. They preferred to see monks meditating in isolation in their monasteries rather than preaching to crowds or indulging in popular pursuits such as fortune telling.

The influence of Buddhism has waned, but it remains the only major Chinese religion with international connections. It is attractive still to some 20th-century intellectuals.

World Buddhist opinion could not save Chinese Buddhists from persecution during the Cultural Revolution, but now, despite continuing difficulties in Tibet, there is a more liberal policy. The officially recognized Chinese Buddhist Association flourishes modestly—though it still warns its members against allowing fortune telling at monasteries.

ISLAM

A Muslim funeral for a member of the Hui minority nationality takes place at the Great Mosque in Xi'an, Shaanxi, in early 1988. The mosque was founded in 742, about 100 years after Islam reached China, but the present buildings date from the Ming dynasty (1368–1644), or possibly later.

Traders, mercenaries and sailors from Persia and the Arabian peninsula established Islam in China during the 7th century. It took root in the northwestern regions and the southeastern seaports of China. Intermarriage of Muslims with Han Chinese women, adoption and conversion created the Hui. One of China's largest national minorities, with some 7 million people, the Hui constitute approximately one-third of China's Muslim population.

In imperial times, Hui communities were focused on the "pure and true" temple (as the mosque is called in Chinese) and its prayer leader and teacher. Under communist rule the mosque continues to be a central feature of their social and religious life. The traditional Muslim prohibition of pork consumption is observed.

Hui restaurants—also described as "pure and true"—are found in many Chinese Muslim communities and along the trade routes formerly used by China's Islamic merchants.

From the 10th and 11th centuries onward the Uygur and other Turkic peoples of northwestern China were increasingly drawn to Islam and adherents to the faith are now to be found in a number of important ethnic minorities.

As a result, in socialist China Muslims have been characterized as minority peoples rather than a religious group. Except during the Cultural Revolution their religious practices have therefore been subject to less control by the state. For example, Muslims are allowed to celebrate the festivals of Id al Fitr, Qurban, and the Prophet's birth. Special

dining arrangements, ritual bathing facilities and acceptance of traditional burial practices are among other manifestations of the state's relatively tolerant attitude.

Nevertheless, the long-term official aim is to assimilate the Muslims and other minorities. It is with integration in mind that the government has translated the Koran into modern Chinese.

Relations between the authorities and Chinese Muslims are structured through the China Islam Association. The goal of this body, which was established by the government, is to develop Chinese Muslims' cultural education in a manner which is compatible with communist rule. The Association organizes goodwill missions to Islamic communities abroad as well as pilgrimages to Mecca.

CHRISTIANITY

Nestorian missionaries introduced Christianity into China during the 7th century. After making initial strides, however, the new religion gradually dwindled in importance. Subsequent missionary endeavours also enjoyed only limited success. Most Chinese considered Christianity to be a foreign faith incompatible with their cultural identity, and with their traditional religious concerns such as ancestor worship, and political loyalty to the emperor.

During the 19th century, however, the economic, political and military impact of the West on China was accompanied by substantial Protestant and Catholic evangelical efforts. Converts were made, often attracted not only by the spiritual elements of this Western religion but also by the missionaries' work in education and medicine. Others, such as the Taipings, were sufficiently influenced to want to radically remould Christianity into a more Chinese shape.

In the 1920s and 1930s converts to Protestantism took control of their church through the "three-self movement". Responsibility for evangelization, administration and finance passed from missionaries to the Chinese membership. At the same time, independent Protestant sects emerged and flourished. By 1949 Chinese Protestants numbered 700,000. Converts to Catholicism, however, totalled nearly 3 million.

The relative popularity of Catholicism rested on a variety of factors, including the Catholic missionaries' willingness to spread the gospel in the interior areas of China; their readiness to involve themselves in local political and legal matters in order to gain adherents; and the less rigorous demands made on prospective communicants.

Under socialist rule the organization and rituals of Christianity have been greatly simplified. Protestant

denominational and sectarian differences are not tolerated. A unified Protestant Church was created in 1951, the purpose of which is to structure relations with the state and to promote Christian belief.

The official policy toward the Catholic Church has been more severe; a Catholic National Patriotic Association was not set up until 1957. Loyalty to Rome and the notion of a universal church as well as close links with the Nationalist party have made Catholics less welcome in the eyes of China's socialist authorities. The Vatican's refusal to acknowledge the Chinese Catholics' independent administration through the Association has continued to bedevil relations between Rome and Catholics in China into the 1970s and 1980s.

By the late 1980s there were between 3 and 4 million Protestants in China. Some 1,600 churches have been opened for worship and in recent years more than a million copies of the Bible have been distributed, a new hymn book printed and theological journals and seminaries revived.

The Catholic Church has grown slowly under socialist rule; the estimated membership continues to be approximately 3 million. However there are signs that in the 1980s membership is expanding. For example, the Church of the Immaculate Conception in Beijing reports that some 300 new members join annually. In addition, a seminary at Shanghai has been re-opened and offers courses in the Catechism, pastoral theology, morality and the Holy Scriptures.

Although the political authorities in China believe that religion will gradually fade away, they recognize that many of the qualities of a good Christian also make a good socialist. If China's Christians support socialist reconstruction, the post-Mao leadership will allow them relative freedom to practise their religion.

LIFE IN THE COUNTRY

For the twenty years from 1958 to 1978, life in rural China was dominated by the communes, which controlled agricultural production as well as everything else. Peasants worked on the land in their community or village on a collective basis and had no individual responsibility for the distribution and marketing of crops.

In the far-reaching policy changes introduced in late 1978, the commune system was dismantled, and agricultural production was transferred back to the family unit. Land was divided up and contracted to each household among the 800 million people in rural areas; state quotas were allocated for the production of essential crops. Today, after these quotas and their own needs are satisfied, families are free to earn extra cash by selling surplus grain, vegetables, eggs, chickens or livestock. This new "free market" system has brought greater prosperity to some rural areas. Markets have proliferated in country towns, and a much greater variety and quantity of food is available in cities. Indeed, the most prosperous rural areas are usually those within easy reach of cities.

Peasants still do not own their land. But the contracts under the new "responsibility system" will run for at least ten to fifteen years, if not indefinitely. This is to encourage farmers to have confidence in the new agricultural policies and make long-term plans for land use.

These dramatic changes have put the economic focus of life back into the family unit, which is the social focus in China. Families in the rich agricultural regions of the south and east of China are building two- or three-storey mansions that reflect their improved standard of living. Some, who have exploited their proximity to big cities and specialized in, say, chicken farming or in a transportation business, have become "ten thousand yuan households". This approximately US $3,000 of income makes these successful peasants the Chinese equivalent of millionaires.

New purchasing power has increased the demand for consumer goods in the countryside. Washing machines are status symbols and are sometimes bought even though the owner has no electricity supply. In a sample survey conducted in 1985, twice as many rural households owned such items as sewing machines and radio sets as in 1978. Television is bringing an extraordinary range of new information and images to the rural population and is affecting consumer demand.

Such prosperity is by no means evenly spread across the country, for only about 10 percent of China's land is suitable for farming. Some provinces, such as Jiangsu and Sichuan, have fertile soil, good irrigation and a communications network to foster a burgeoning economy; but others, such as Gansu and Ningxia, have such inhospitable and unproductive land that people have little hope of doing any more than

Traditional houses are clustered closely together—a style typical of Chinese country villages. This one, surrounded by lush green fields, is in Guangxi, a relatively poor province in South China. The haystacks in front of the houses are built around central supporting poles.

scratching a living from it. According to government estimates, about 80 million people in the countryside have an income below the official poverty line of 200 yuan and 200 kg (440 lb) of grain per capita per year. Some state relief and welfare funds are available for hardship cases, but there is no free health care in rural areas. A family whose members cannot work because of illness can easily get into debt, both from the direct costs of medical expenses and the indirect burden of supporting non-productive individuals.

Prosperity levels vary even within a village. A

family's capacity to make money depends on the ages, and skills, as well as the number and sex, of its members. Most households consist of several generations and the bigger the family, the more hands there are to turn to work. Hence, the government has found it virtually impossible to implement its one-child family policy in rural areas and is attempting instead to enforce a maximum of two children per family.

Many families make extra cash from "sidelines", such as making handicraft items, raising animals,

growing herbs or mushrooms. These tasks are usually assigned to women, older people and children, while the strongest, most active family members are employed in the fields.

Even more change has come to the countryside since the mid-1980s, with the development of small-scale industry in country areas, which has been encouraged by the government. Where these industries do not flourish, men have started to leave their families to tend the land while they go and seek work in urban industry.

In the rural free markets (top) *peasants do a lively trade in livestock and vegetables. Pork is the most popular meat in China, and pigs the most widely kept livestock.*

Well-to-do peasants who have benefited from economic reforms are building new houses (above). *These "foreign houses", as they are known, feature styles and colours quite unlike those of traditional rural dwellings.*

LIFE IN THE COUNTRY/2

DINGXI—PROFILE OF A POOR RURAL AREA

Conditions in Dingxi district in Gansu Province, Northwest China, demonstrate some of the problems which may beset peasants in disadvantaged areas:

● Annual rainfall is low, down to 300 mm (11.8 in) in some years, only 13 percent of fields are irrigated.

● The area suffered severe drought in 1981–82.

● Winter temperatures can drop to −25°C (−13°F).

● There are twice as many sheep and goats as can be supported by current grazing practices.

● Fuel is in short supply. Dried animal manure is used for one-third of fuel needs; sod (the root systems of grass and shrubs) provides the rest.

● Erosion of topsoil has been accelerated by over-grazing and sod-cutting.

● The population is 10 percent larger than the land can support.

● Families have an area of only 0.5 ha (1.2 acres) on average to farm.

● Average annual income is less than 300 yuan.

● In a good year, a family's one annual crop of wheat provides only just enough for their own consumption.

● Some villages are not accessible by road.

● Peasants live in primitive mudbrick houses or in caves dug out of the loess soil.

Since the drought of 1981, Dingxi has received substantial grants from both the Chinese government and the World Bank. As a "test case" it will help establish whether such aid can improve conditions and generate future economic growth.

Funds are being spent largely on building irrigation systems, planting shrubs and grass on eroded hillsides and subsidizing coal supplies for fuel. It is hoped that the downward spiral of land degradation may be reversed by these measures.

OUTPUT OF CHINA'S PROVINCES

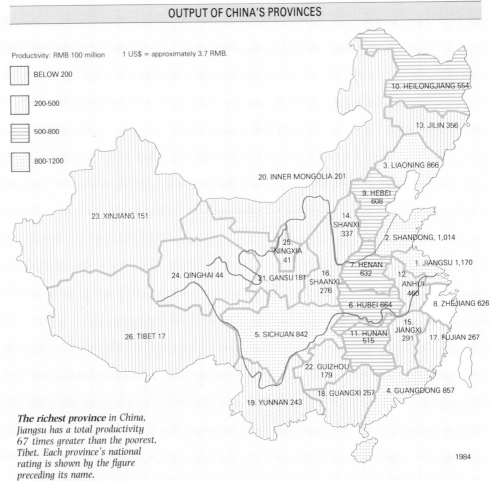

Productivity: RMB 100 million   1 US$ = approximately 3.7 RMB.

    BELOW 200

    200-500

    500-800

    800-1200

10. HEILONGJIANG 554
13. JILIN 356
3. LIAONING 866
20. INNER MONGOLIA 201
9. HEBEI 608
14. SHANXI 337
2. SHANDONG, 1,014
23. XINJIANG 151
25. NINGXIA 41
7. HENAN 632
1. JIANGSU 1,170
24. QINGHAI 44
31. GANSU 181
16. SHAANXI 276
12. ANHUI 460
8. ZHEJIANG 626
6. HUBEI 664
15. JIANGXI 291
17. FUJIAN 267
26. TIBET 17
5. SICHUAN 842
11. HUNAN 515
22. GUIZHOU 179
18. GUANGXI 257
4. GUANGDONG 857
19. YUNNAN 243

1984

The richest province in China, Jiangsu has a total productivity 67 times greater than the poorest, Tibet. Each province's national rating is shown by the figure preceding its name.

INCOME OF RURAL HOUSEHOLDS

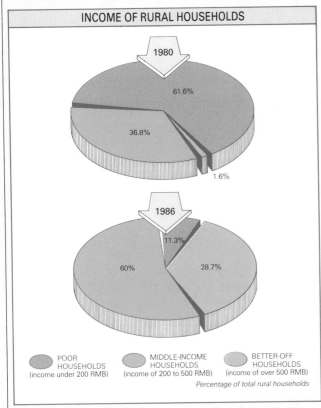

1980
61.6%
36.8%
1.6%

1986
11.3%
60%
28.7%

POOR HOUSEHOLDS (income under 200 RMB)

MIDDLE-INCOME HOUSEHOLDS (income of 200 to 500 RMB)

BETTER-OFF HOUSEHOLDS (income of over 500 RMB)

Percentage of total rural households

The proportion of middle-income households almost doubled between 1980 and 1986. Even allowing for an element of inflation, this sample survey shows a clear rise in living standards.

YUANHE—PROFILE OF A RICH RURAL AREA

Yuanhe village lies in the Yangtze River delta in southern Jiangsu, one of China's most prosperous regions. In 1985, due to the rapid development of rural industry run by towns and villages, Jiangsu Province overtook Shanghai as the biggest industrial producer.

Conditions here are very different from those in Dingxi.

● Population density is 700 per sq km (1,813 per sq mi)—among the highest in the world.

● The average per capita annual income is 1,034 yuan, 25 percent above the national average.

● In 1978 there were 400 people working in Yuanhe's fields. By 1986 only 19 of a total labour force of 730 were full-time farmers. Many of the rest are employed in new rural enterprises.

● 90 percent of village income is derived from industry.

● Specialized farmers can contract about 1.7 ha (4.2 acres) of land, much larger than the average plot.

● The grain harvest has increased by 5 percent each year since 1978.

● Extra payments of up to two-thirds of the basic price are made to farmers producing rice or wheat above their set quotas.

● The village runs a boatyard that manufactures river craft, a plant that produces oxygen for welding, and factories that produce furniture and confectionery.

● These rural factories hand over 30 to 40 percent of their pre-tax profits to the village economic committee to support agricultural subsidies, local investment and community services.

● Yuanhe has well-developed transport links, including a dense network of canals connecting it with the Yangtze River and Shanghai.

TRANSPORT

A water buffalo pulling a simple plough through a rice paddy or a donkey cart taking a family to market are common sights in the country. Tiny irregular fields do not lend themselves to mechanization, and well-tested ancient methods of cultivation often remain the most effective.

Bicycles are an important means of transportation in the country as they are in cities. With a rack or cart attached, they can be used to carry loads to market. Public bus services run from rural areas to market towns.

Some of the better-off rural residents, and many of the rural enterprises, are now able to afford their own vehicles. Trucks are the most practical means of carrying large loads and coping with the unsurfaced country roads. Of the 500,000 or so motor vehicles China produces annually, more than 60 percent are trucks.

COUNTRY/CITY CONTRASTS

In China as elsewhere, city people have traditionally looked down on country dwellers. But today, many urban people look with envy at the new prosperity of some nearby rural areas, where the inhabitants enjoy a standard of living and quality of housing that surpasses their own. The average housing space per person in rural areas is over 15 sq m (161 sq ft)—more than twice the average in urban areas.

While it is true that urban factory wages and teachers' salaries have not kept pace with the accelerating income of the most successful "suburban peasants", reports of a few rural entrepreneurs earning enormous sums have distorted the overall economic picture. In 1985 the average rural income of about 400 yuan was still less than half the average urban income of 821 yuan.

City dwellers also receive a range of welfare benefits from their work units, such as pensions and free medical clinics. Such benefits in the countryside depend mainly on pooled private funds. Country dwellers have to pay for medical treatment and schooling. This may be one reason why only 20 percent of rural women have completed their lower middle school education (up to age 15).

Country/city contrasts are at their greatest in the poorest, least developed areas of western China. There, for example, infant mortality is higher than 100 per 1,000. In Beijing it is only 11.6 per 1,000.

OWNERSHIP OF CONSUMER DURABLES

Bicycles 80.64

Sewing machines 43.21

Radios 54.19

Clocks 37.32

Wristwatches 126.32

TV sets 11.74

Goods possessed per 100 rural households (1985)

Rural families *still possess fewer consumer durables than city dwellers. This 1985 sample survey* *shows that only 11 percent own a TV set. This compares with 1 percent in 1980.*

HOUSEHOLD LIVING EXPENSES

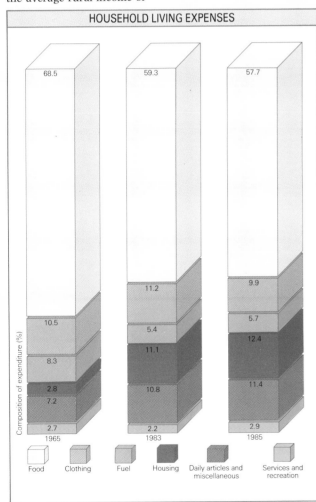

Composition of expenditure (%)

	1965	1983	1985
	68.5	59.3	57.7
	10.5	11.2	9.9
	8.3	5.4	5.7
	2.8	11.1	12.4
	7.2	10.8	11.4
	2.7	2.2	2.9

Food · Clothing · Fuel · Housing · Daily articles and miscellaneous · Services and recreation

Expenditure on housing *has risen considerably since the early 1980s, as shown in this sample survey.*

Better-off peasants are spending more on improving or even building houses.

THE FAMILY UNIT

Most rural families have 3 generations living under one roof. A typical household might comprise a couple, their son, his wife and child, and any other unmarried children. In a sample survey of rural households in 1985, the average household contained 5.12 permanent residents, living in an average of 5.11 rooms.

Since the 1970s, strict birth control policies have been in force to encourage couples to have only one child and thus reduce population growth. But in rural areas, peasant families want more children, particularly sons, to work the land and look after them in old age, and may have a larger family despite the fines and penalties they incur. 1986 saw the highest rate of second and third births for 4 years.

COUNTRY ADMINISTRATION

Each province of China is divided into prefectures and then into counties. Within the counties, the administrative structures in the countryside are towns, townships, which include surrounding rural areas, and villages. 1985 government statistics recorded 92,000 towns and townships and 820,000 villages.

SPECIALIZED HOUSEHOLDS

Under the new "responsibility system" of agriculture, some families have opted to specialize in a particular type of farming or sideline. These "specialized households" may engage in activities such as chicken farming, livestock raising, fish farming or even in making small handicraft items for sale.

Such specialization is becoming increasingly popular as a way of making a living. The per capita annual income of rural specialized households increased from 998 yuan in 1985 to 2,842 yuan in 1986.

However, some of these households have run into trouble by expanding too quickly, borrowing too much money or managing their affairs poorly. In a survey of 104 specialized households that were doing well in 1983, 53 had gone bankrupt, ceased production or were experiencing severe financial problems by 1986.

RURAL ENTERPRISES

A major change in country life since 1978–79 has been the introduction of rural enterprises—small-scale industries set up by villages and townships.

By 1987 there were 15 million such enterprises, employing 20 percent of the rural work force and creating 48.9 percent of the total rural income. They produce, for example, 29 percent of China's total coal output, 50 percent of its cement and 53 percent of its building materials.

The encouragement of rural enterprises is part of the government's policy for reducing the number of people dependent on agriculture so that China can prosper and develop as an industrialized nation. Critics of the scheme maintain that the small industries get in the way of larger enterprises by competing for scarce materials, and that they increase pollution.

SEE ALSO PAGES 38–53, 110–13, 154–57

LIFE IN THE CITY

There are now 324 cities in China, twenty-two with populations of a million or more. Although most are overcrowded, noisy and polluted, the cities still exert a strong pull on the predominantly rural population. For they offer a higher standard of living, better health care and education, a cultural life and popular entertainments, as well as a much wider range of goods and services.

Cities first boomed in China in the early years of the People's Republic, with the rapid development of heavy industry. Since 1949 the number of cities has more than doubled. The political importance of urban development has been backed by considerable financial advantages, making the city worker much better off than his rural counterpart. His place of work, whether factory or office, is referred to as a *danwei* or "work unit". The *danwei* provides its workers with a range of benefits including health clinics, subsidized food, day-care nurseries and, most important, housing. The biggest work units, such as large steel factories and universities, may even have their own schools.

Renting out accommodation to its workers is a major responsibility of the work unit. Almost all housing in Chinese cities is owned directly by the state or indirectly through state enterprises or work collectives. There is, as yet, very little private housing. In line with the government's low-wage and low-price system, rents have always been kept artificially low—between 1 and 5 percent of the average worker's wage. As a result, housing construction has failed in the past to keep pace with the growth in population, and lack of sufficient maintenance has inevitably led to the serious dilapidation of existing buildings as they age.

It is only since the economic reforms of 1978–79, that things have begun to change. More than 65 percent of housing construction since 1949 took place in the years between 1979 and 1986. Experimental policies announced in 1987 will allow rents to rise and encourage workers to buy their own homes; they will also stimulate further expansion in domestic building. Such policies will eventually undermine the role of the *danwei* as provider, and help create conditions for greater mobility of labour. (At present, for most people, leaving their jobs means leaving their home.)

Household registration, a system whereby people must register their place of residence and cannot change it without permission, has limited the migration of country people to the cities. China has thus avoided the phenomenon typical of developing countries in Africa and South America where shanty towns have sprung up in response to the city's lure of jobs and wealth. Policies that encourage the setting up of rural-based industries and the development of small towns are also aimed at keeping city populations at reasonable levels.

Some young peasants are inevitably, however,

drawn to the big cities and come to work as servants, nannies, street pedlars, and so on. For most, these are only temporary moves; the girls, for example, will usually go home to marry. As some established urban youth move onto the more glamorous and better-paid tourist industry, jobs also become available in factories. The country youth who fill these jobs are employed as contract workers with none of the usual *danwei* benefits. Basic accommodation is provided for the workers, but the job is intended to be short-term.

Problems of overcrowding are exacerbated, particularly in the major cities, by huge numbers of short-stay visitors. More than a million people visit Beijing, for example, every day. They come from all over the country to attend meetings, do business, see the sights or go shopping, and they place an enormous strain on an already overloaded and inadequate public transport system as well as on restaurants and hotels.

Street traders, bringing in fresh fruit and vegetables from the country or reselling scarce consumer goods, are among the new entrepreneurs. Privately run restaurants, even Western fast-food franchises, coffee shops, dance halls and fashionable clothes for sale in street markets all point to an expanding Western-influenced culture. Increasingly, private enterprise is offering new challenges to the state system—and contributing to the changing face of the Chinese city.

Japanese motorcycles are a new status symbol for the fashionable young and a sign of the changing face of Chinese cities. In 1985 there were some 27,000 motorcycles in Beijing alone, and numbers are fast increasing.

Young city dwellers now share an interest in chic clothes, imported electronics and Western music and ideas. But for every successful youngster with a motorcycle there are many more with poorly paid jobs or even no work at all who must forgo the trappings of the new youth culture.

Kerbside railings along Shanghai's Nanjing Road (above) prevent the bustling crowds from spilling onto the narrow street, itself congested with buses. Such crowds are an everyday feature of Shanghai life. Inside the buses it is just as packed. One visitor to Shanghai calculated that at peak hour every square metre of bus space is crammed with 11 passengers.

The overcrowding in Chinese cities is typified in this housing block—in the largest cities the average living space is less than 6 sq m (7 sq yd) per person. Every bit of space must be maximized; tiny balconies, for example, may be used for cooking and eating as well as hanging out washing. Because of the restricted space inside, people tend to gather out of doors to exchange gossip and relax.

LIFE IN THE CITY/2

TRANSPORT

City traffic is chaotic. Buses are twice as long as those in Western cities, so it only takes a few to cause a jam. And neither buses nor bicycles keep to their allotted lanes. Taxis and cars weave among them, and carts drawn by bicycles, horses or people add to the confusion.

Buses and bicycles are the main form of city transport. In rush hour, people defy the laws of mass and space as more and more crowd onto buses and still somehow find room to stand—there are only 3.9 buses per 10,000 people.

Bicycles are everywhere. Beijing is said to have more than 3 million, more than any other city in the world. At rush hour, hundreds stream across major crossroads, many with side cars and carts tacked onto them.

Most of the cars crowding the streets are either owned by work units or are being used as taxis. There are some 40,000 taxis in China's big cities and their number is increasing in order to meet the demands of tourism. Private cars are still rare.

POPULATION OF MAJOR CITIES

There are 52 cities in China with populations of more than 500,000, not counting that of counties under their administration. The greatest concentration of cities is in the Northeast.

Jixi 630,000
Qiqihar 970,000
Daqing 540,000
Harbin 2,250,000
Changchun 1,480,000
Jilin 910,000
Shenyang 3,250,000
Fushun 1,100,000
Fuxin 570,000
Benxi 700,000
Jinzhou 610,000
Anshan 1,110,000
Urumqi 940,000
Hohhot 570,000
Beijing 5,100,000
Dalian 1,380,000
Datong 700,000
Tangshan 940,000
Baotou 910,000
Qingdao 1,160,000
Tianjin 4,200,000
Jinan 1,160,000
Zibo 800,000
Shijiazhuang 930,000
Taiyuan 1,390,000
Handan 740,000
Xuzhou 730,000
Zhengzhou 1,010,000
Xining 500,000
Luoyang 650,000
Huainan 620,000
Nanjing 1,920,000
Lanzhou 1,060,000
Wuxi 730,000
Suzhou 630,000
Xi'an 1,730,000
Hefei 630,000
Shanghai 6,870,000
Hangzhou 1,020,000
Ningbo 550,000
Wuhan 2,960,000
Chengdu 1,590,000
Nanchang 910,000
Fuzhou 780,000
Chongqing 2,080,000
Changsha 960,000
Yichun 760,000
Guiyang 890,000
Liuzhou 520,000
Guangzhou 2,570,000
Kunming 1,080,000
Nanning 600,000

HOUSEHOLD LIVING EXPENSES

Composition of expenditure (%)

Food
Clothing
Fuel
House rent
Water and electricity
Articles for daily use
Articles for recreation, books, newspapers
Services (transport, postage, leisure etc)

1964
59.22
10.98
4.24
2.61
1.74
5.98
2.23
13

1984
56.66
14.79
1.94
1.39
0.97
11.14
9.56
6.62
8.07

1985
53.31
15.34
1.38
1.08
1.03
11.14
8.44
9.28

More than half the annual expenditure of the urban households in this sample survey is on food. This contrasts with only 18 percent in the USA and 14 percent in Great Britain.

DAILY ROUTINES IN THE CITY

The day begins early in Chinese cities. *Taijiquan* (tai chi) enthusiasts are often up by 5 o'clock to practise in the parks or at home in the quiet of the morning.

By 6 o'clock, the markets are selling vegetables brought in fresh from the country, and the streets are already bustling. Typically, the Chinese shop before going out to work, buying small quantities to ensure the freshness Chinese cooking demands. But with the rise in ownership of refrigerators—up from 0.22 percent in 1981 to nearly 10 percent in 1985 in a sample

urban survey—this is no longer always necessary and shopping may eventually become less of a burden.

Work starts at 8:00 am. Shops, other than food shops which open earlier, banks, schools and offices all open at this time. In some regions, such as the Northeast, work starts earlier in the summer, at about 7 or 7:30.

Traditionally most workers had a 2-hour break for lunch from 11:30. But in a bid for greater efficiency, this has been cut to 1 hour. Since many people like to go home for a rest as well as lunch this has not been popular.

School children have between 90 minutes and 2 hours for lunch. Young children finish school at about 3:00 pm; older ones at 4:00 to 4:30.

Most people finish work at about 5:00 pm (4:30 in summer). Factory workers may be on shifts, but power shortages mean that factories are often unable to operate a 24-hour day.

Few households possess many labour-saving devices so, once home from work, household chores are time-consuming for most families.

HOUSING CONDITIONS IN THE CITIES

Shortage of housing is the major problem in Chinese cities. And poor standards of construction and lack of upkeep and repair have resulted in low-quality housing stock which quickly becomes rundown.

The shortage affects young people particularly badly. Couples intending to marry can face a long wait for housing—up to 10 years in the worst instances. Since there is little private accommodation, most have no choice but to postpone their marriage until they are allocated housing by their work unit or to marry and move in with one or other set of parents.

Statistics in a sample survey on urban housing show that:
● Average living space is 6 sq m (64 sq ft) per person—less in the biggest cities.
● 42.5 percent of urban homes have indoor toilets.
● 69 percent of urban homes have use of a kitchen of some sort, usually shared with neighbours.
● The average urban household contains 3.82 people and has 2.2 rooms.
● 7.6 percent of urban homes have bathtubs, usually only with cold water.
● 96 percent of urban homes have electricity.

Government plans to improve the situation aim at providing a comfortable standard of housing for all city dwellers by the year 2000. This means expanding living space by at least 17 percent, as well as improving existing housing stock. The plan requires an investment of some 500 billion yuan.

OWNERSHIP OF CONSUMER DURABLES

Bicycles 163.72

Sewing machines 73.19

Wristwatches 286.68

Washing machines 52.83

Refrigerators 9.57

Sofas 135.72

Radios 80.80

Black and white TV sets 74.90

Colour TV sets 18.43

Tape recorders 48.41

Cameras 12.09

Goods possessed per 100 urban households (1985)

Ownership of washing machines and refrigerators may seem low by Western standards but this is compared with figures of 6.1 and 0.22 in 1981, only four years before this survey.

CRIME AND UNEMPLOYMENT

Although the crime rate is still low by comparison with many other countries, China is experiencing an increase. The rise is evident particularly in crimes of burglary and corruption, as values become more materialistic, and a growing differentiation in incomes fuels envy.

Unemployment in cities clearly contributes to the problem. According to official figures, in 1985 2.3 million were "waiting for work"; 1.9 million of these were young people. And China's strict moral code, reinforced by government policies on late marriage (to cut population growth), is thought by some outside observers to have contributed to the high number of sexual offences. (However, young female "delinquents" are often only guilty of having been discovered in a sexual relationship.)

Periodically the government shows its concern at the rising urban crime rate, with campaigns to "round-up" the so-called criminal elements. But policies recognizing the special needs of the young and the unemployed are going to be of increasing importance as the country modernizes at an ever quickening pace.

CITY ADMINISTRATION

China's three biggest cities—Beijing, Shanghai and Tianjin—are called "municipalities". With status equal to that of the provinces, they report directly to central government. All other cities come under the administration of the province they are in, at present, though more are to be granted municipality status.

Provincial and city governments operate as replicas of the national government, with the same ministries and civic organizations. There is a well-developed structure for transmitting central government directives to local government; the main role of local government is to carry out, rather than formulate policies. However, central government sometimes goes to great lengths to canvass local opinion which may influence overall policy.

Decentralization in the political and economic scene has given city governments greater financial responsibility. Municipalities can now keep a higher percentage of their gross product in order to encourage more investment and locally initiated projects.

LEISURE TIME

Most Chinese work a 6-day week. Although some factories stagger their workers' rest days, Sunday remains for most the one day the family can be together.

Shops are open, giving people a chance to decide together on major purchases. A typical Sunday off might include lunch in a restaurant, shopping and a visit to grandparents or a trip to the park.

As living standards rise demands on leisure facilities increase. But, although, for example, new privately owned restaurants are opening up, charging as much as 20 yuan a meal they are too expensive for many Chinese who may earn less than that in a week. Thus they fail to ease the pressure on the lower-priced state restaurants.

ENTERTAINMENT

Television is becoming more and more popular, taking over from more traditional leisure pursuits such as visits to the opera or the tea house. In a sample survey of urban households in 1985, 74 percent had black and white sets and 18 percent, colour. Programmes include documentaries, news features, sport, films and light entertainment.

Traditional opera has suffered declining audiences for years, despite the introduction of modern stories and new techniques in an effort to revive interest. Western-inspired spoken drama, as a performing art, only came to China in the early years of this century. Chinese dramatists have used the form to voice important issues.

Although some of China's new young film directors are winning awards abroad, their "art films" are often box office failures at home. More popular are films about love, action and melodrama which fill the cinemas but do not win international acclaim. Some popular films from the West also do well.

Live acrobatic and variety shows are highly popular, and tickets are hard to get. The local cultural bureau or the theatre management distribute some to important people, keep blocks for tourists, and people queue for the rest. Ticket touts often buy a number of seats which they then sell at inflated prices. In Beijing there may only be 4 to 8 shows on in any evening, compared with the much greater choice in most Western capitals.

SEE ALSO PAGES 38–55, 106–09, 162–65

EDUCATION

When Chinese children begin primary school at the age of six or seven they are faced with the daunting task of learning a complex writing system that employs thousands of separately composed "words" known as characters. Spoken Chinese is easily learned. The national language, a northern dialect known as *putonghua* (common speech), is taught in schools all over the country, even when local people speak a dialect of their own. But written Chinese takes far longer to learn than alphabetic languages such as English. Chinese children have no alternative other than to memorize and practise hundreds of distinct characters. They sit in disciplined rows, slowly and laboriously copying the characters until they learn to form each one correctly.

Reading and writing necessarily take up a large proportion of classroom time, but primary school pupils also study mathematics, general knowledge and political science. In some urban primary schools, they may start to learn English. Outside the classroom, children take a lively interest in sport: traditional martial arts and team games such as baseball

and basketball are all popular. Depending on the area, sports such as swimming, skiing and ice skating attract plenty of participants. Singing and dancing are also an important part of the primary curriculum. An abiding memory of many Western visitors to China is of confident enthusiastic children performing for their audience without a hint of self-consciousness.

From about thirteen to fifteen or sixteen years of age pupils attend lower middle school, after which only about 25 percent go on to upper middle school until they are eighteen. To the subjects studied in primary school are added history and geography, a foreign language—usually English—and the sciences of biology, physics and chemistry. In "vocational" middle schools, more practically oriented establishments, children may study subjects such as woodwork and agriculture.

In theory all children are supposed to attend school for at least nine years but in practice this is not always achieved, particularly in the remote, rural areas. The government's aim is that by the year 2000 every

Rows of children recite their lesson in unison, in this typical Chinese schoolroom. Learning by rote is a method still widely employed in schools in China. The class is large—numbers of 50 or 60 are normal—and there is little in the way of resources or additional teaching aids. The children wearing red neckties are members of a youth organization known as the Young Pioneers.

child should have at least nine years of schooling.

Competition for places in higher education is fierce. Only about 10 percent of upper middle school graduates succeed in the university entrance examinations. Students must attain an average of at least 90 percent in six subjects if they are to have any chance of winning a coveted college place. Of these subjects there is a common core of politics, Chinese language, mathematics and a foreign language. Candidates then choose to take either history and geography or science subjects. Every year there are press reports of illness and suicide among candidates who have succumbed to the enormous pressures involved.

Following the severe disruption of the system during the Cultural Revolution, it became clear in the 1980s that China needed to re-establish an efficient education system for two distinct reasons: first, to train scientists and to produce "leadership material" to take over the management of an ever more complex economy; second, to lift a large wedge of the working population out of a state of cultural and technological illiteracy. This persisted despite decades of efforts to make schooling accessible to all children in China.

Education is today the responsibility not of a ministry, but of a special State Commission. This is a measure of the importance the government gives this vital element in the move toward modernizing the economy. The Communist party is more ready than ever before to recognize the importance of intellectuals and their part in China's growth. But the problem of funding education remains. Many schools and universities operate in dilapidated buildings and are short of essential equipment. Research grants are few. But even if more money becomes available, there are simply not enough teachers—salaries are too low to attract candidates in sufficient numbers.

However, the 1980s have seen a significant increase in respect for education and a greater determination to modernize and improve the Chinese system for the future. But the solution of both economic and staffing problems is likely to be a long and costly process.

Under the watchful eye of her teacher, a pupil copies a character on the blackboard. In order to achieve the correct positioning and balance, she must follow the grid on which the model character is shown.

Learning written Chinese dominates the school timetable for younger children. Before moving on to middle school, they need to learn the meanings and master the strokes of several thousand characters.

MEDICINE AND HEALTH CARE

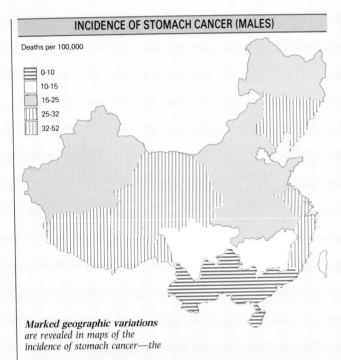

INCIDENCE OF STOMACH CANCER (MALES)

Deaths per 100,000

- 0-10
- 10-15
- 15-25
- 25-32
- 32-52

Marked geographic variations are revealed in maps of the incidence of stomach cancer—the

INCIDENCE OF STOMACH CANCER (FEMALES)

Deaths per 100,000

- 0-4
- 4-7.5
- 7.5-13
- 13-16
- 16-28

most common cancer in China. Distribution patterns suggest a link with environmental factors.

BAREFOOT DOCTORS

In the 1960s in an attempt to meet the desperate need for medical practitioners in the country districts, the government set up the "barefoot doctor" movement.

These "doctors" were farmers who worked as part-time medical auxiliaries. They were given sufficient training, combining modern and traditional Chinese medicine, to enable them to treat minor ailments, act in emergencies, teach rudimentary hygiene and lead campaigns of public sanitation. They were also taught to judge which cases needed more expert care by specialist physicians or in hospitals.

"Red Medical Workers" performed similar tasks in urban factories.

Up until the early 1980s there were some 1,000,000 barefoot doctors practising in rural China. There are now plans to improve and extend the training of those still working—few people now want to become barefoot doctors, since peasant earnings are higher and most people prefer the better-paid farm work.

HEALTH CARE IN CHINA

China's children are a wonderful advertisement for her advances in health care. Every morning in towns and cities, lines of rosy-cheeked, glossy-haired infants, each clutching the bright, padded jacket of the one in front, can be seen walking happily to kindergarten.

But 40 years ago as many as 6 out of every 10 children died before their first birthday. Because of poverty and malnutrition, those who did survive to adulthood fell easy victims to a variety of infectious and parasitic diseases. Syphilis, smallpox and typhoid fever ravaged the towns and cities; parasitic diseases such as schistosomiasis, hookworm,

kala-azar and trachoma were the scourge of the country. Cholera, plague and malaria epidemics were frequent, and tuberculosis was the major cause of death.

In the 1980s China's health-care system caters for over a billion people. The average life expectancy of 69 years compares well with that in developed countries, and outstrips most of the less developed. Many serious diseases have been controlled or eradicated, and nutrition has dramatically improved.

In planning their health-care system, the Chinese have sought to concentrate both on the availability of care and on the prevention of disease.

AVAILABILITY OF HEALTH CARE

Forty years ago most hospitals and doctors were concentrated in the eastern coastal provinces and in large cities such as Shanghai and Beijing. Today all of China's 2,000 rural counties have at least 1 hospital, and 60 percent of hospital beds are in rural areas.

A seriously ill patient in a remote village may have to go to a large city hospital many miles away, but most people can be treated at the local County Hospitals.

In response to growing prosperity in some rural areas, the government is encouraging a programme of private hospital facilities.

Most city hospitals have college- or university-trained

doctors. In the country the "rural" doctors have received a simpler training.

Patients must pay for medical treatment. In the country peasants used to share the costs of medical treatment, but this collective approach has largely declined in favour of individual payment. Some rural households now have medical insurance.

City dwellers are still relatively better served. Some work places have their own clinics or small hospitals and most have insurance funds that pay or contribute to the expenses if a worker is hospitalized.

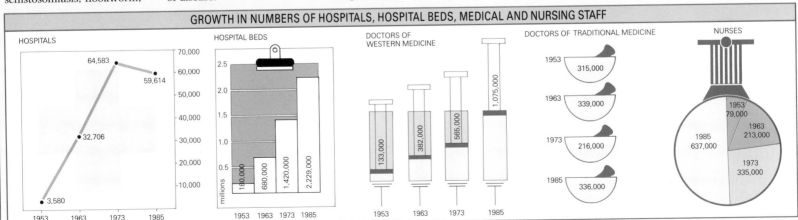

GROWTH IN NUMBERS OF HOSPITALS, HOSPITAL BEDS, MEDICAL AND NURSING STAFF

HOSPITALS

64,583
59,614
32,706
3,580

1953 1963 1973 1985

HOSPITAL BEDS

180,000
680,000
1,420,000
2,229,000

millions

1953 1963 1973 1985

DOCTORS OF WESTERN MEDICINE

133,000
382,000
565,000
1,075,000

1953 1963 1973 1985

DOCTORS OF TRADITIONAL MEDICINE

1953 315,000
1963 339,000
1973 216,000
1985 336,000

NURSES

1953 79,000
1963 213,000
1973 335,000
1985 637,000

Numbers of medical facilities and staff are steadily growing, but are still barely managing to keep pace with China's expanding population.

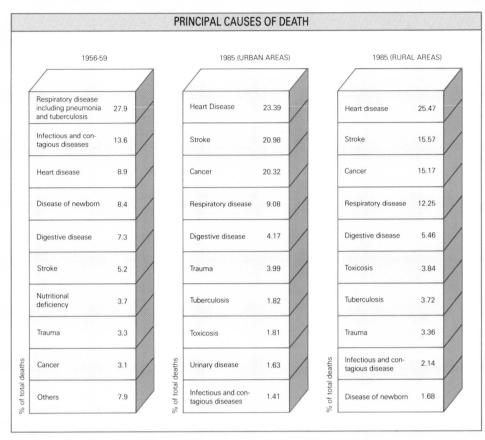

PRINCIPAL CAUSES OF DEATH

1956-59

	% of total deaths
Respiratory disease including pneumonia and tuberculosis	27.9
Infectious and contagious diseases	13.6
Heart disease	8.9
Disease of newborn	8.4
Digestive disease	7.3
Stroke	5.2
Nutritional deficiency	3.7
Trauma	3.3
Cancer	3.1
Others	7.9

1985 (URBAN AREAS)

	% of total deaths
Heart Disease	23.39
Stroke	20.98
Cancer	20.32
Respiratory disease	9.08
Digestive disease	4.17
Trauma	3.99
Tuberculosis	1.82
Toxicosis	1.81
Urinary disease	1.63
Infectious and contagious diseases	1.41

1985 (RURAL AREAS)

	% of total deaths
Heart disease	25.47
Stroke	15.57
Cancer	15.17
Respiratory disease	12.25
Digestive disease	5.46
Toxicosis	3.84
Tuberculosis	3.72
Trauma	3.36
Infectious and contagious disease	2.14
Disease of newborn	1.68

Comparison of causes of death in the 1950s with those in the 1980s (rural and urban) reveal the changing disease patterns, which have become more like those in the West. Infectious diseases are no longer a leading cause of death and disease of the newborn has been greatly reduced.

CHANGING PATTERNS OF DISEASE

The incidence of fatal infectious and parasitic diseases may have declined, but the longer-living population is now more likely to die from cancer, heart disease and strokes.

Cancer kills 11 percent of females and 8 percent of males. It is the leading cause of death in the 35 to 55 age group. Stomach cancer is the most common form, followed by cancers of the oesophagus, liver and lung. Cancer screening has been instituted in selected populations in an attempt to identify people at risk.

Probable causes of these cancers are the high nitrite content in food and water, contaminated air and water, and cigarette smoking. China is the world's largest producer of tobacco and Chinese men are heavy smokers.

Cigarette smoking is also a contributory factor in heart disease which, together with stroke, is the major cause of death in the industrial cities. It is estimated that some 7 percent of the total population suffers from high blood pressure—double that of the late 1960s.

Changing patterns of disease are also related to changes in diet. Chinese people consume more calories than in the past, as well as more salt and fats. These are contributory factors in hypertension and heart disease. The northern Chinese consume more salt than the southerners, and have, on average, higher blood pressure.

MOTHER AND CHILD HEALTH

The emphasis on prevention of disease is most evident in China's network of maternal and child health centres. The MCH workers care for expectant mothers and for China's 300 million children. MCH care is free, but small charges are made for vaccinations for those who normally pay at least some of their medical costs—for example, people in rural areas.

All mothers are visited by an MCH worker during their pregnancy, and delivery is usually in hospital. Government regulations set the minimum maternity leave at 56 days. After birth, babies are checked at 3, 6, and 9 months and at 1 year. They then receive annual check-ups. Mothers receive a post-natal check at which they are given advice on contraception.

In their first year children are immunized against common childhood diseases, such as measles, polio, diphtheria, whooping cough and smallpox. But there is still some incidence of rickets and serious gastrointestinal infection, particularly in rural areas.

Infant mortality rates, though vastly improved, vary considerably over the country as a whole. In Beijing only 1 child in 100 dies in its first year but in some of the poorest regions of western China, such as Xinjiang, the figure is still as high as 1 in 10.

TRADITIONAL MEDICINE

China's system of traditional medicine is more than 2,000 years old and still thriving. The government takes active steps to promote its survival, and there are at present 440,000 traditional doctors and pharmacists in China. New training schools are planned.

The basic tenet of Chinese traditional medicine is that man and the environment form an organic balanced whole, and disturbance of this balance causes illness. Treatment includes drugs, acupuncture, moxibustion, massage and *qigong*—a form of breathing therapy.

More than 90 percent of the traditional medicines come from plants, compared to about 35 percent in the United States; others are of mineral or animal origin. Deer antlers are one example. The powdered horn is used to aid blood circulation and improve kidney function and is also sometimes employed in the treatment of impotence and sterility.

Despite the widespread use of Western medicine, traditional treatments still have their place. For instance, some clinical studies in China have shown that traditional medicines used to treat pneumonia and dysentery in children were more successful than antibiotics.

Traditional methods are also used in combination with Western medicine. Acupuncture is used as an analgesic, for example, during certain types of surgery.

ACUPUNCTURE

In China acupuncture is usually an adjunct to drug therapy. It has become fashionable in the West in greatly simplified form. Acupuncture, like other therapies, manipulates *qi*, energy, which includes inborn vitality as well as matter and energy extracted by the body from air and food.

Qi must circulate freely through the body to keep it alive and growing. If the circulation is blocked or upset, a needle, inserted at certain spots on its path, can adjust the flow or release blockages.

Modern Western physicians explain the effectiveness of acupuncture as being partly due to the fact that needling-spots often coincide with nerve trunks and junctions, so that stimuli compete with and block pain signals. Needling also stimulates the body to make substances that control pain, and increases the body's immune response.

MEDICAL ACHIEVEMENTS

High-technology medicine is limited but Chinese doctors have developed some world-famous techniques. They are particularly skilled in micro-surgery, which involves working with tiny blood vessels.

The first triumph came in 1966 when Chinese microsurgeons succeeded in sewing back a finger severed by machinery. Since then they have perfected this technique and even grafted big toes onto hands that have lost fingers. Another success has been the transplanting of tissue from the groin to the face in order to repair flesh ravaged by cancer, burns or other accidents.

A particularly notable achievement of Chinese microsurgery was the reconstruction of a man's penis which had been badly damaged in a factory accident. The man later went on to father a child.

SEE ALSO PAGES 98–101, 106–13, 180–81

SPORT AND LEISURE

After years of non-participation in international sport, China has emerged since 1980 as a potential giant. At the Los Angeles Olympics in 1984 its athletes won fifteen gold medals. China's entry onto the world stage will be complete in 1990 when Beijing hosts the Asian Games. The Chinese hope that this will be a prelude to the staging of the Olympics in the year 2000 and the Football World Cup in 2002. Sport has long thrived as a leisure activity. It is estimated that over 300 million Chinese take part in some kind of sport.

Traditionally, though, sport in China is less competitive, concentrating rather on forms of exercise which combine ritual movements with mental training and contemplation. Typical are the Chinese martial arts or *wushu*, of which there are many varieties, some performed bare-handed, others using weapons. The most famous is *kung fu*, one form of which was developed by the monks of the Shaolin monastery in Henan.

Most popular is a branch of *wushu* called *taijiquan*, known and practised in the West as tai chi. The graceful stylized movements are practised daily by millions of Chinese and there are more than a hundred coaching centres in Beijing alone. *Qigong*, a system of therapeutic deep breathing exercises, is becoming increasingly popular, and it is estimated that over twenty million Chinese practise it.

The People's Republic has always encouraged people to take part in daily exercise routines in schools and factories. Every morning city streets and parks are alive with joggers and *taijiquan* enthusiasts taking their exercise in the open air before they go to work.

Some of the minority nationalities have their own traditional sports. In Inner Mongolia the vast grasslands are ideal for horsemanship and archery competitions. Wrestling is a tradition among Mongolians and in minority groups in Yunnan. Since 1982 China has held a national event for the traditional sports of minority peoples. Athletes representing all fifty-five minorities come together from all parts of the country to participate in this annual competition.

Western-style sports were mostly introduced into China by missionary organizations from the mid-nineteenth century onward. Now there are eleven physical education institutes around the country, and promising sportsmen and women are recruited by local teams. Once every four years the provincial teams meet in the All-China Games.

With the opening up of China since 1976, national champions have been able to compete with the world. The women's volleyball team are international champions, and Chinese marksmen, badminton players, divers and gymnasts rank among the best in the world.

Table tennis, however, is probably the sport for which the Chinese are most famous. There are more than four million tournament players in China and,

China's women's volleyball team are international champions and took the gold medal in the 1984 Olympic Games. The sport is generally popular in China with both men and women, and "courts" can be easily improvised—players need only a piece of rope and a patch of ground to enjoy an energetic contest.

except for the period of the Cultural Revolution, the Chinese have dominated the world scene since 1959. As from the 1988 Games, table tennis has been included in the Olympics.

Other less strenuous games are also popular, particularly the card, dice and board games, such as Chinese chess, which have a long history in China. On summer evenings people play cards and chess on street corners. Bridge, too, is thriving—Deng Xiaoping himself is an excellent and enthusiastic player. Snooker has recently become popular and *aficionados* have taken to constructing their own small snooker tables. Snooker tournaments, some of them even featuring top players from Great Britain, have re-

Games of Chinese chess are a common sight on city street corners. Squares are drawn out on the pavement with chalk or simply scratched in the dirt.

The gentle rhythmic movements of taijiquan are performed regularly by millions of Chinese (below). Most go out in the early morning to exercise in groups in parks or even by the roadside. There are two important principles in taijiquan: relaxation and serenity. The body must stay relaxed so that movements are gentle and unforced, and the mind must be serene so that attention is focused on the exercise. Thus taijiquan trains both the body and mind.

cently been staged in Beijing and Shanghai.

Sports facilities are improving to keep pace with increasing interest and sports and recreational centres are being built in many towns and cities. With the tourist in mind, golf courses have opened near Beijing and in Guangdong Province; there is also an annual Hong Kong to Beijing motor rally.

On a less positive note, gambling, long a passion of the Chinese, is on the increase. This is despite the party's efforts to stamp it out with the banning of traditional gambling games such as mahjong. And China experienced its first major outbreak of football hooliganism in 1985 when China was eliminated from the World Cup by Hong Kong.

FOOD AND REGIONAL COOKERY

REGIONAL CUISINES

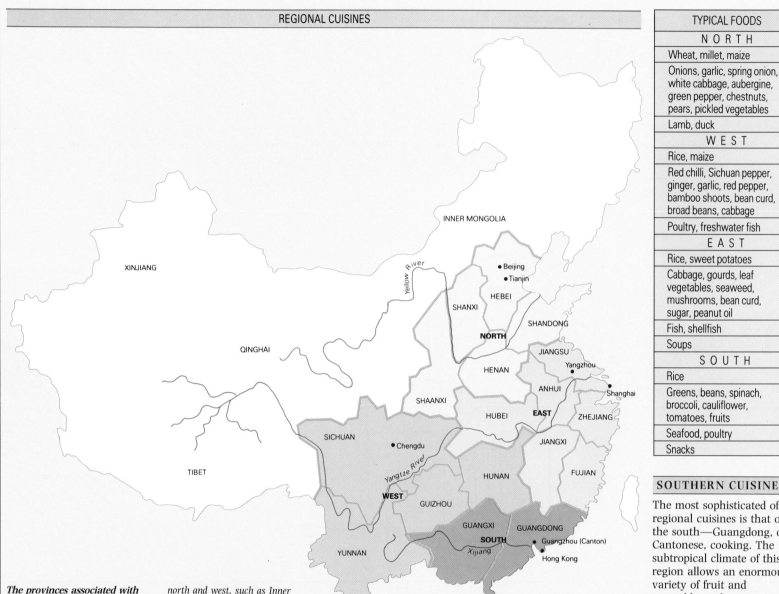

TYPICAL FOODS
N O R T H
Wheat, millet, maize
Onions, garlic, spring onion, white cabbage, aubergine, green pepper, chestnuts, pears, pickled vegetables
Lamb, duck
W E S T
Rice, maize
Red chilli, Sichuan pepper, ginger, garlic, red pepper, bamboo shoots, bean curd, broad beans, cabbage
Poultry, freshwater fish
E A S T
Rice, sweet potatoes
Cabbage, gourds, leaf vegetables, seaweed, mushrooms, bean curd, sugar, peanut oil
Fish, shellfish
Soups
S O U T H
Rice
Greens, beans, spinach, broccoli, cauliflower, tomatoes, fruits
Seafood, poultry
Snacks

The provinces associated with the four main types of traditional Chinese cuisine are shown on the map. Within each there are many local variations. Areas to the north and west, such as Inner Mongolia and Tibet, which are inhabited largely by minority nationalities, have their own cookery styles.

SOUTHERN CUISINE

The most sophisticated of the regional cuisines is that of the south—Guangdong, or Cantonese, cooking. The subtropical climate of this region allows an enormous variety of fruit and vegetables to be grown, and this has given rise to a varied and lively cuisine.

Delicacy, lightness and a seemingly limitless range of ingredients are its hallmarks, and stir-frying and blanching are popular cooking methods. Vegetables are lightly cooked so that they remain crunchy.

Seafood is particularly popular—steamed fish is a deceptively simple example of Guangdong cooking at its best. The fish, the fresher the better, is topped with a little fresh ginger and spring onion, and then steamed until perfectly cooked; it is basted occasionally with a light stock while steaming.

Dim sum, tasty snacks such as light dumplings and spring rolls, are also typical of this region.

A FAMILY MEAL

On a normal working day an average Chinese family might eat the following: *for breakfast*: porridge, dough sticks, soy milk and pickled vegetables; *for lunch*: noodles in broth; *for supper*: rice, vegetables, shrimps or meat, and eggs.

The family food bill can account for around 50 percent of the monthly income—much housing is subsidized and rents are low compared to those in the West. In the United Kingdom only 14 percent is spent on food and in the United States 18 percent.

REGIONAL CUISINES

China probably has a greater variety of food, and ways of preparing it, than any other country in the world. Within China, too, different regional styles of cookery have developed in response to the varying resources, terrain and climate of particular areas.

The great divide in food— as in language, taste and outlook—is between north and south; that is, roughly speaking, north and south of the Yangtze River.

To the river's north lie fields of sorghum, millet, wheat and maize, which are the staples of the northern diet; to its south are market gardens producing a huge variety of vegetables, and rice paddies—rice is the mainstay of the southern diet. Because so many more foods can be grown in its gentler climate, the south has the richer cuisine.

The four main regional cuisines are southern, eastern, western and northern. There are, of course, subdivisions of these, as well as many mixtures and similarities of styles. A recipe peculiar to one region may be found in another part of the country, but with minor variations and perhaps a different name.

The most elaborate examples of a particular style are found in banquet food and in the grandest restaurants. In simpler restaurants and at home people eat a modified version. In home cooking less protein and more grain and vegetables are eaten than in restaurant meals.

Regions of China that are largely populated by minority nationalities, such as Tibetans and Mongols, have their own cuisines.

EASTERN CUISINE

The cooking of the eastern region is perhaps the least known outside China. Each town or area may have its own specialities, but in general this cuisine emphasizes the flavour of fresh, carefully chosen ingredients. Some of the best dishes are those prepared with local freshwater eel, turtle and crab.

Stews are popular, particularly when prepared by the "red cooking" method in which food is stewed gently with stock and soy sauce. Sugar is used more generously than in other cuisines to flavour sauces.

WESTERN CUISINE

Lavish use of red chilli, garlic and fagara (Sichuan pepper) distinguishes the food of Sichuan and Hunan—which is spicy and richly flavoured. Traditional wisdom holds that the use of spices helps rid the body of excessive moisture and counteracts the effects of the region's humid climate.

One famous dish is Mrs Pockmark's Bean curd, named for the woman who created it. This hot, spicy stew is made with minced pork, bean curd, dried red pepper flakes and Sichuan pepper.

Chicken in hot sauce and crispy spiced fish are other typical dishes.

NORTHERN CUISINE

The cooking of the north—of which Beijing/Peking cuisine is a subdivision—is less spicy than that of Sichuan but uses a great deal of garlic and spring onion. It is a robust cuisine in which food is generally more simply prepared than in the south. Slow-cooked, braised and simmered dishes are a particular feature of northern food.

Influenced by Moslem and Mongolian tastes, northern cuisine is renowned for its mutton and lamb dishes. Typical is sauteed lamb with spring onion. Seafood, including sea slugs, is also popular.

At home, wheat, not rice, is the staple food because it is the main grain crop of the region. It is the basis of the many noodle and dumpling dishes. Vegetables are more thoroughly cooked than they are in the south. Some varieties, such as cabbage, are pickled to preserve them for the long winter.

THE CONSUMPTION OF MAJOR FOODS

	1978	1980	1985
Grain	195.5 kg	213.8 kg	254.4 kg
Vegetable oil	1.6 kg	2.3 kg	5.1 kg
Pork	7.7 kg	11.2 kg	14.0 kg
Poultry	0.44 kg	0.80 kg	1.56 kg
Eggs	1.97 kg	2.27 kg	4.98 kg
Aquatic products (fish, shellfish, seaweed, etc)	3.50 kg	3.41 kg	4.89 kg

1 kg = 2.2 lb

Per capita consumption

The economic reforms of 1978 have made more grain and protein foods available. Grain—and vegetables—remain the dietary staples but protein consumption has doubled.

THE IMPORTANCE OF GRAIN

A Chinese family meal usually has 2 components: one is of grain, such as rice, noodles, or steamed bread, while the other is of vegetables plus a small amount of protein food such as meat, fish or eggs.

Between 80 and 90 percent of the calories supplied by the average Chinese diet comes from grains. Ensuring sufficient supplies of grain for China's huge population has thus been a central preoccupation of the country's rulers and governments down the ages.

Although grain output has risen since the establishment of the People's Republic in 1949, so too has the number of people to be fed on that grain. Because of government policies on grain rationing, and its distribution around the country, purchase actually declined between 1957 and 1978.

New agricultural policies introduced in 1978 reversed this trend and reduced the extent of state control over food production and marketing. Since then the Chinese diet has both improved and changed. In 1987 people were not only eating more grain but also twice as much meat, poultry and eggs as in 1978.

YIN AND YANG

In the West people think of a balanced diet as one containing certain amounts and ratios of carbohydrates, proteins, fats, fibre, vitamins, and so on. For the Chinese, planning a healthy diet means taking into account personal and climatic characteristics, as well as striving to achieve a balance of yin and yang, the 2 opposing but complementary forces of nature.

The Chinese regard food as yin or yang—that is, having "cooling" or "warming" properties. Cooling foods are often low in calories and pale in colour; examples are crab, celery, buckwheat, frog's legs, green tea, oranges, cucumber, and bean curd.

"Warming" foods are often high in calories or spicy in nature and are thought of as "stimulating" or even "irritating"; examples are apricots, ginger, sugar, wine, black tea and chilli. Meat, too, is yang.

Cooking can alter the qualities of foods. Roasting and stir-frying will render a food "warm", while making a dish salty or sour will "cool" it.

It is no accident that a typical Chinese meal is made up of dishes offering contrasting but complementary ingredients, flavours and textures.

EATING FOR HARMONY

The Chinese believe that what people eat and drink is of fundamental importance, not only to their physical well-being but also to their mental health and harmony. Whatever is consumed affects every organ of the body.

Thus they combine an impressively varied cuisine with a rich tradition of health food and folk dietetics. An 11th-century Chinese writer summed up this wisdom: "Nutritional therapy should be resorted to first and drugs prescribed only after proper feeding has failed."

In Chinese cookery the correct combination of this food with that, or the beneficial effects of this particular food on that particular ailment, is a complex science in itself.

Traditional Chinese thinking relates different tastes to specific organs of the body: sweetness to the spleen, sourness to the liver, hotness to the lungs, bitterness to the heart, and saltiness to the kidneys. If any of these flavours is excessive in the diet, the related organs will not function properly.

FAST FOOD

Takeaway snacks and processed food are becoming more common in cities, where there is a growing demand for labour-saving meals. Food processing now ranks second among China's light industries.

Western fast food franchises have been introduced in Beijing. The largest fast food restaurant in the world, a branch of the Kentucky Fried Chicken chain, opened in the city in 1987.

CUSTOMS AND FESTIVALS

For all his revolutionary zeal, it is unlikely that even Mao Zedong expected to sweep away two thousand years of Chinese customs at a stroke. While change can be superimposed on a government or economy, the traditional rituals of a people are so deeply ingrained they cannot be suppressed. In 1949 the Communists struck a balance of sorts between old and new by adapting existing festivals and introducing modern holidays.

The private behaviour of the population was, and is, more elusive of state control, particularly in remote rural areas where the authorities have a problem monitoring everybody's activities. Traditional attitudes to life's major events—birth, marriage and death—still persist. Thus the party proposes and the peasant disposes.

The government advocates birth control and tends to feature attractive little girls in posters promoting

Stilt dancers traditionally perform at Spring Festival celebrations for the Lunar New Year in northern China. Although such festivals were abolished during the Cultural Revolution they have been revived in the 1980s and are particularly popular in country areas.
  The Spring Festival is the most important holiday of the year. It is a time when families take days off work to gather together for feasting and special entertainments.

its one-child policy. In the country to remain single is seen as an aberration; people believe that the spirits of their ancestors demand male progeny as reassurance that the family line will continue. The birth of a baby boy calls for a great celebration. Daughters remain unheralded, because most will marry and leave their family.

Marriage in modern China should be the union of two people making a free choice. In fact, many traditionally-minded parents still insist on checking horoscopes and take matchmakers' advice before negotiating the contract that will effectively make their daughter another family's valuable property.

Wedding celebrations perpetuate customs that long predate the revolution. Wealth and well-being are synonymous to most Chinese. Foods such as fish (*yu*—homonym for riches) and chicken (*ji*—homonym for good luck) are essential. The bride-

groom's family demonstrates the importance of "show" by providing a lavish banquet. And it is their duty as hosts to ensure that provisions at the wedding feast are so plentiful the guests could never consume them all.

Any decision-making over life's major choices in which the factors include time, date, location or people may occasion recourse to astrologers, geomancers or fortune-tellers. The pseudo-science of geomancy or *fengshui* (wind and water) is having a resurgence. Houses should be sited, some Chinese still believe, facing south. They should be in places calculated to harmonize with the natural patterns of the earth: ideally with mountains behind and water in front. Outraged officials had the first rail tracks ever laid in China ripped up because they were distressed at the harm caused to *fengshui* by tracks criss-crossing the veins of the earth.

With the loosening of state control over life in the countryside since the economic reforms of the 1980s, many customs and practices surrounding death and mourning have reappeared. Fortune-tellers are consulted to choose an auspicious day for a funeral; geomancers pronounce on a suitable place for burial; and professional musicians and mourners accompany the corpse on its way to the grave. Burial grounds are eating up agricultural land at a rate unimaginable under the stridently anti-feudal, anti-religious policies of the Maoist period. Urban dead, however, are almost always cremated—since space is at a premium in Chinese cities.

These customs have been revived predominantly in rural areas, but the need to honour traditional beliefs and values, such as the respect and worship of ancestors, is evident throughout the whole of Chinese society.

White is the colour of mourning in China. Here, white-robed relatives accompany the deceased to his burial place. The huge coffin contains not only the corpse, dressed in special burial clothes, but also a number of items that he may find useful in the next life, such as blankets, tea, his pipe and tobacco. The wreath of paper flowers on top of the coffin will eventually be left on a bamboo tripod erected over the grave.

Although this coffin is being carried by boat, lorries are the usual form of transport.

CUSTOMS AND FESTIVALS/2

FESTIVALS AND HOLIDAYS

Certain important days in the Chinese calendar—such traditional celebrations as the Spring and Mid-Autumn Festivals—are linked to the farming seasons. They fall on different dates each year, according to the phases of the moon.

The lunar calendar is still observed for fixing dates of festivals, although the Gregorian 365-day calendar has been in official use in China since 1911. A lunar month is the interval between new moons (29 or 30 days). Years of 12 moons (354 or 355 days) and 13 moons (383 or 384 days) are interspersed to make the long-term average of 365.24 days.

As in the past, festivals give expression to the communal wish for such blessings as a good harvest, prosperity, longevity, and good fortune in general. Some also serve as days of remembrance.

Often celebrated with glorious pageants, these festivals provide a valuable outlet for the creative talents of the Chinese and allow them to express pride in their heritage. They are also a boon to the country's burgeoning tourist industry.

Additional modern holidays with a socialist theme—such as Labour Day and National Day—were introduced by the government in 1949. These occur on fixed dates.

Christmas and Easter are not widely observed in China, but some Christians in the big cities celebrate them.

SPRING FESTIVAL

The Lunar New Year, when this festival is held, is undoubtedly the most important date in the Chinese calendar. Its celebration is comparable in scale to that of Christmas in the West. The first lunar month begins on the day of the first new moon after the sun enters Aquarius on January 21. The last date on which the New Year can fall is February 20.

For the workers, it is the only substantial break in the year. In the cities, it is held over the first three days of the first lunar month; in the country, it goes on longer if work schedules permit. Relatives are visited on the first day, friends on the second or third.

It is the time when family members living apart come together and exchange gifts. The main event is a family feast, often featuring a large fish, served whole to symbolize family unity. Many couples get married at Spring Festival time, for it is thought to be an auspicious season for weddings.

In pre-1949 China, there were certain rituals attached to the Spring Festival. Traces of these still survive, notably in the countryside. As the holiday approaches, people settle their debts and clean out their houses, since it is unlucky to enter the New Year with any dust of the past clinging to you. They also decorate their front doors with red paper posters bearing New Year greetings and messages of good will.

The kitchen god, Tsao Wang, customarily had honey smeared on his mouth to ensure all his reports to the heavenly Jade Emperor were sweet. This happens less frequently today since people now have pictures of the kitchen god instead of statuettes.

Food has to be prepared in advance for the family feast on New Year's day, because working in the first few days of the New Year is considered unlucky. And no knives or scissors can be used on these days in case they cut through good fortune.

TRADITIONAL FESTIVALS

JANUARY/FEBRUARY
● **Spring Festival**
Chinese Lunar New Year on the day of the first new moon after January 21

FEBRUARY
● **Lantern Festival**
15 days after Spring Festival

4/5 APRIL
● **Grave-sweeping Festival**
Fixed date based on solar agricultural calendar. This celebration is also known to Chinese as the Festival of Clear Brightness.

MAY/JUNE
● **Dragon Boat Festival**
5th day of the 5th lunar month

SEPTEMBER
● **Mid-Autumn Festival**
15th day of the 8th lunar month (also known as the Moon Festival)

JANUARY/FEBRUARY
● **Offerings to the Kitchen or Hearth God**
23rd or 24th day of the 12th lunar month (preparation for Spring Festival)

MODERN HOLIDAYS

1 January	Solar New Year
8 March	Women's Day
1 May	Labour Day*
1 June	Children's Day
1 August	Army Day
1 October	National Day* – commemorates the founding of the People's Republic in 1949

(* Public holidays)

Throngs of masked revellers *celebrate the Spring Festival in Shandong Province.*

GRAVE-SWEEPING FESTIVAL

This celebration, which is known as the Festival of Clear Brightness, links the old and new China.

Traditionally, families visit the graves of their ancestors, sweep and tidy them, and bring flowers and sweetmeats as offerings for the spirits. This is done to reassure the ancestors that their descendants care for their well-being. (The spirits of the dead are thought to fear neglect above all else.) The Chinese believe that ancestral spirits remain a presence in the family, that they deserve love and care as living elders do, and like them must be informed and consulted about family events.

Under the Communists, this ceremony has been adapted as a day of remembrance. The nation mourns the millions who died in the civil and revolutionary wars of the 1930s and 40s. In town squares all over China, wreaths of white flowers are laid on the monuments to the heroes of the revolution.

This particular festival is also associated with kite-flying, although the Chinese now fly their brightly coloured and intricately made kites throughout the year.

DRAGON BOAT FESTIVAL

The 4th-century BC court poet, Qu Yuan, is remembered in this festival, which the south of China celebrates more than the north. Qu lived in the southern state of Chu during the Warring States period. He drowned himself in despair when he was dismissed by the king (or, according to another version of the legend, when his homeland was conquered). The people threw rice into the lake, hoping the fish would eat it and leave the body of the drowned poet untouched.

The legend lives on in a treat called *zongzi*, made and eaten around festival time. It consists of sticky southern rice, sweetened and wrapped in reed-leaf parcels.

The dragon boat races now being revived in south China have their origins in Qu Yuan's story as well; they are thought to symbolize the grieving people rowing out to search for the poet after he had drowned himself.

The ceremony might even predate Qu Yuan's time, harking back to primitive beliefs in river dragons, which the Chinese credited with the control of clouds and rain. Since this festival takes place during the summer rainy season, farmers traditionally made offerings to the Dragon King, hoping that rain would come at the right time to ensure a good harvest.

MID-AUTUMN FESTIVAL

According to Chinese tradition, the moon is yin (female) and the sun is yang (male). This celebration of the harvest—also known as the Moon Festival—is very much a woman's occasion.

The story behind the festival, as told to children, is of the Divine Archer. Thousands of years ago, a talented archer named Hou Yi was given the pill of immortality. His wife, Chang E, ate the pill and flew off to the moon, where she turned into a toad. She wards off the arrows her husband shoots at her from his palace in the sun, given to him as a reward for fighting false suns.

The old custom of sitting outside to view the beauty of the full harvest moon, while making it offerings of round fruit (pomegranates were popular because their seeds symbolize money), moon cakes and spirit money, has generally disappeared from mainland China. It is more often observed in overseas Chinese communities and in Japan.

All over China, however, people still make or buy moon cakes—round, pielike confections. There are regional varieties of sticky sweet fillings and of the moulded shapes decorating the pastry top.

THE CHINESE ZODIAC

The Chinese calendar is associated with a repeating 12-year cycle, each year linked to a particular animal.

Every Chinese person knows which year he or she belongs to and can tell you the strengths and weaknesses of people according to the animal sign of the year of their birth.

In addition, the year itself is thought to be influenced by the animal of the moment; for example, tiger years are exciting; dragon years, demanding.

The animal zodiac is much consulted when marriages are arranged. Modern thinkers may dismiss horoscopes and see them simply as remnants of the superstitious past, but many Chinese still believe firmly in fate, and in the need to reconcile astrological influences when choosing a husband or wife.

THE ZODIAC CYCLE

Rat	1900	1912	1924	1936	1948	1960	1972	1984	1996
Ox	1901	1913	1925	1937	1949	1961	1973	1985	1997
Tiger	1902	1914	1926	1938	1950	1962	1974	1986	1998
Rabbit	1903	1915	1927	1939	1951	1963	1975	1987	1999
Dragon	1904	1916	1928	1940	1952	1964	1976	1988	2000
Snake	1905	1917	1929	1941	1953	1965	1977	1989	2001
Horse	1906	1918	1930	1942	1954	1966	1978	1990	2002
Sheep	1907	1919	1931	1943	1955	1967	1979	1991	2003
Monkey	1908	1920	1932	1944	1956	1968	1980	1992	2004
Rooster	1909	1921	1933	1945	1957	1969	1981	1993	2005
Dog	1910	1922	1934	1946	1958	1970	1982	1994	2006
Pig	1911	1923	1935	1947	1959	1971	1983	1995	2007

Rat

Ox

Tiger

Rabbit

Dragon

Snake

Horse

Sheep

Monkey

Rooster

Dog

Pig

A particular animal sign is associated with each year in the 12-year zodiac cycle. The sign of a year is thought to affect both the year itself and the life and personality of those born during it.

THE CHINESE LANGUAGE

A resident of Beijing visiting Guangzhou (Canton) in the south would find the language spoken there virtually unintelligible. The dialects of Beijing and Guangzhou are both Chinese but are as different as, for example, Portuguese and Rumanian, which share a common Romance ancestry but have developed quite separately.

The Chinese language is usually classified as a branch of the Sino-Tibetan family, which also includes Tibetan, one of the languages of Burma, and other languages of Southeast Asia. Two major features of Chinese are the distinction between the written and spoken language, and, partly as a result of this, the diversity of dialects.

There are seven major dialect groups, each with its own sub-groups. Northerners speak the dialect known as mandarin by Westerners; there are four variants of the dialect. South of the Yangtze, the major dialect groups are Wu, Xiang, Gan, Hakka, Min and Yue (of which Cantonese is a sub-group spoken in the south of Guangdong Province). All these groups are referred to as dialects even though by linguists' standards they are distinct languages.

The term "mandarin", no longer used in China, was first used by the Portuguese in the sixteenth century to describe the dialect of Beijing, spoken by officials. (It comes from the verb "mandar" meaning to govern.) These officials were sent off to administer different provinces in China, but were sometimes forced to use interpreters since they could not understand the local dialects. In 1955, in an attempt to overcome such difficulties, the Chinese government proclaimed a "national language" based on the Beijing pronunciation of the northern dialect. This was called *putonghua*, literally "common speech", and is the Chinese taught in schools and learned by most foreigners. In this age of telephones, radio, cinema and television, a national spoken language is essential.

In the past, officials who could not understand local dialects were helped by the fact that, although spoken dialects differ, the written language is understood by all who can read. Characters on a page convey the same meaning to northerner and southerner alike, although when spoken aloud the words sound quite different.

This distinction has come about because of the extraordinary development and unusual complexity of the written Chinese language. First based on pictures (pictographs) of natural objects, Chinese continued to develop into the depiction of more complex ideas (ideographs), still as "pictures". Most other scripts eventually moved toward an alphabet reflecting the sound of the spoken language. But, although Chinese characters may contain a hint of the pronunciation, this is by no means reliable. Thus, the spoken and written systems have developed separately: the spoken dialects have diverged for reasons of geographical distance; the writing system

A calligrapher holds the brush almost upright, and does not allow his arm to rest on the table, as he writes the character shou, meaning longevity or long life.

Traditional auspicious themes displayed on posters on the wall include an illustration of the god of longevity—a white-haired old man with a bulging head.

has increased in complexity and is understood by educated, literate speakers of all dialects.

The earliest known written characters to survive date from the eleventh century BC. They are already quite complex and ideographs appear among the pictographs.

The complexity of the written language gradually increased in two ways. In the first, groups of two or more pictures were assembled to create a new meaning; for example, a picture of the sun with one of the moon meant "bright"; a picture of a woman beside that of a child meant "good"; a picture of a roof over one of a pig meant "home", and so on. In the second method, unusual characters were used for abstract ideas with the same pronunciation. In these "phonetic loans", the picture of an ear of corn was used for the verb "to come", which has the same

是我国的一项基本国策

...NING—A BASIS NATIONAL POLICY OF CHINA

pronunciation. The picture of a cauldron was used to convey "his, hers, its", pronounced in the same way. The distinct and different meaning of the phonetic loan was clear from the context.

From the seventh to the second century BC when China was split into separate kingdoms, each developed slightly different writing styles. But after the unification of China in 221 BC, the Qin writing style was imposed throughout the country. This was slightly modified and modernized during the Han dynasty (206 BC to AD 220) into the style still used today. A modern Chinese scholar would find the characters of the Han period reasonably easy to understand.

Now there are some fifty thousand different characters in the biggest dictionary. While a scholar might recognize up to ten thousand or so, ordinary people need a knowledge of only two to three thousand to attain the basic level of literacy necessary to read newspapers and popular magazines.

A huge poster in both English and Chinese advocates the one-child family policy. Its illustration also subtly hints that the ideal healthy family might include a daughter, rather than the son all peasants desire to carry on the family line.

On the pavement below, passersby are absorbed in reading newspapers pinned up on boards. Daily papers are often displayed in this way outside newspaper offices in China.

THE CHINESE LANGUAGE/2

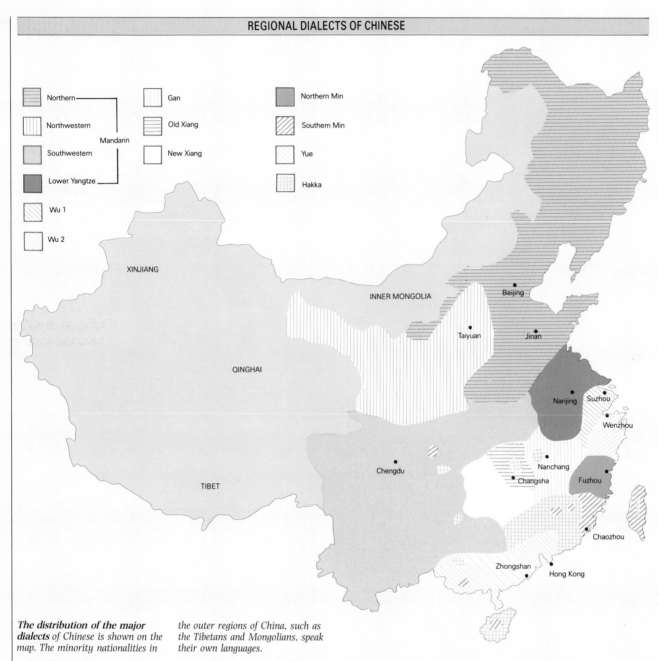

REGIONAL DIALECTS OF CHINESE

Legend:
- Northern — Mandarin
- Northwestern — Mandarin
- Southwestern — Mandarin
- Lower Yangtze — Mandarin
- Wu 1
- Wu 2
- Gan
- Old Xiang
- New Xiang
- Northern Min
- Southern Min
- Yue
- Hakka

Map labels: XINJIANG, QINGHAI, TIBET, INNER MONGOLIA, Beijing, Taiyuan, Jinan, Nanjing, Suzhou, Wenzhou, Nanchang, Changsha, Chengdu, Fuzhou, Chaozhou, Zhongshan, Hong Kong

PERCENTAGE OF POPULATION SPEAKING DIALECTS	
Mandarin	70 PERCENT
Wu	8.4 PERCENT
Xiang	5 PERCENT
Gan	2.4 PERCENT
Hakka	4 PERCENT
Min	1.5 PERCENT
Yue	5 PERCENT

LANGUAGE DEVELOPMENT

FISH		PROTECT
	Shang	
	Zhou	
	Qin	
	Han	
	Han – 20th Century	
	Simplified (post 1956)	

The distribution of the major dialects of Chinese is shown on the map. The minority nationalities in the outer regions of China, such as the Tibetans and Mongolians, speak their own languages.

The progression from the simple pictures of 3,000 years ago to modern characters is shown above.

REGIONAL DIALECTS

Though some 80 percent of the population are said to speak modern standard Chinese, pronunciation varies considerably from place to place. People speaking different dialects are virtually unintelligible to one another.

The spoken language has evolved differently in north and south. Northern Chinese has developed with a limited number of sounds (about 420 distinctly pronounced syllables). There are 4 different tones or pitches to the voice which help distinguish words which would otherwise sound the same. The southern dialects, which include Cantonese, are thought to be an older form of the language which have evolved less than northern forms.

Cantonese, for example, has more tones and many more possible endings to syllables.

Apart from the dialects of Chinese itself, minority peoples, such as the Yi people of Sichuan and Yunnan, the Miao of Yunnan and the Manchu of the northeast, have their own distinctive languages.

SYSTEMS OF ROMANIZATION

Westerners have adopted various ways of writing Chinese in roman letters. The best known among English speakers is the Wade-Giles system, created in 1867 by the first Professor of Chinese at Cambridge University, in England, Thomas Wade, and his successor, Herbert Giles.

In 1955 the Chinese introduced their own system, pinyin, and in 1977 this became the international standard for place names.

Pinyin spelling differs somewhat from Wade-Giles and has thus caused confusion among non-Chinese speakers. But its aim is to eliminate the greater confusion caused by different countries each employing its own system.

In fact, Beijing (pronounced Bayjing) is how the *Bei* (northern) *jing* (capital) has always been known to its inhabitants. The spelling "Peking" comes from the 17th-century French romanization system where "k" is used for the sound "j".

"ORACLE BONES"

The earliest writing so far discovered in China is that on the "oracle bones" of the Shang dynasty (c. 1480 to 1122 BC).

These "bones", usually the shoulder blades of oxen or the shells of turtle, were used by the diviners when consulting the spirits. They heated the bones or shells and the resulting cracks were interpreted as the "answers" to questions put to the other world. Both questions and answers were then etched with sharp metal instruments onto the bones or shells.

CHINESE CHARACTERS

Most Chinese characters are divided, often arbitrarily, into a radical part, generally connected with meaning, and a phonetic part that 2,000 years ago usually gave some idea of the sound. The most common system used 214 radicals.

Although in modern Chinese the meaning of some of them is no longer clear, others have a strong element of meaning. For example, radical 38 means "woman", and is supposedly derived from a picture of a woman sitting cross-legged: its inclusion nearly always

indicates that the character relates to women. Thus the woman radical with the graph for "child" means "happiness"; the radical for woman with the graph for "broom" means "wife".

The remainder of the character is the phonetic but, particularly in the more evolved northern dialects, the sound links may not be very strong. For example, when the phonetic which on its own is pronounced *ke*, meaning "can/be able to", is joined by the "water" radical in the character meaning "river", it is pronounced *he*.

BUILDING WORDS FROM CHARACTERS

1 tree = tree

woman (ancient graph)

woman + eyebrow = flattery

2 trees = grove/ woodland

woman

3 women = treachery

3 trees = forest

woman + child = good

Irregular teeth (complex character, 25 strokes)

Chinese characters are "built" in different ways. The same character can be used more than once ("tree" examples, above) or combined with others to make different words ("woman" examples, above).

CALLIGRAPHY

The art of calligraphy is held in as high esteem as the art of painting and has a special place in Chinese culture.

The materials used, the brush and ink-stick and paper or silk, are the same as those used in painting and the two arts are virtually inseparable.

A piece of calligraphy is valued for itself, but a

painting is enhanced by calligraphy which becomes a part of it, such as the colophon of the artist, recording and perhaps dedicating the painting, as well as further colophons and seals added by collectors who have owned and appreciated the work. Such calligraphic inscriptions increase the painting's value.

PAPER AND PRINTING

The world's earliest extant printed "book" is a copy of the Buddhist *Diamond Sutra* printed in China in AD 868, some 600 years before the art of printing reached Europe.

The woodblock carver's skill, evident in the fine frontispiece illustration and beautifully carved text, suggests that the *Diamond Sutra* was a product of a mature craft. Earlier cruder examples of single sheets of printing have been found elsewhere

in the Far East.

The invention of paper in China, traditionally ascribed to AD 104, but now thought to be earlier, was an essential precursor of the invention of printing. Until the 19th century, Chinese printing was primarily by woodblock, with 2 complete pages of characters carved into each block, a method that suited the non-alphabetic Chinese language.

Experiments with

movable type in the 11th century, predating the use of movable type in Europe by some 400 years, were rarely repeated. The font (the complete set of type) required for such printing in Chinese would have had to comprise millions of pieces. Modern printing presses in China, though, do use movable metal type.

The Arabs took the secret of paper making to Europe from China in the 8th century.

LEARNING THE ART OF CALLIGRAPHY

Traditional calligraphic wisdom has it that all the movements of the brush necessary for good calligraphy are found in the 8 strokes of the character *yong*, meaning eternity.

The character yong, meaning eternity, contains the eight basic strokes of calligraphy.

Wang Xizhi, a great calligrapher of the 4th century, is said to have spent 15 years practising that single character because of its completeness. But it is recognized that to become a calligrapher means mastering many strokes and many styles embodied in classic models of writing.

When learning to write, Chinese children have to copy characters exactly. They learn to execute strokes in the logical order, so that as their writing speeds up the flow of the pen continues to follow a recognizable pattern and characters are still legible. A character is incorrect if strokes have not been executed in the right order.

The correct grip of the brush in calligraphy is demonstrated in this Chinese illustration.

LITERARY CLASSICS

One of the great early classics is the *Shi jing* or *Book of Songs*. A collection of folk songs (some with overtones of political protest) and ritual hymns, it dates from the 11th to 6th centuries BC. Other classics include works on philosophy and historical records.

Poetry was the first of the major literary genres to develop its traditional form; in the Han dynasty (206 BC– AD 220) poetry expressing the sorrow of separation and exile, was written in 5-character lines and was already allusive and indirect

in both its language and its imagery.

The great poets were those of the Tang dynasty (618– 907), Li Bai (Li Po in Wade-Giles romanization), Du Fu (Tu Fu) and Bai Juyi (Po Chu-i).

Short stories were already popular in the Tang dynasty, telling of young lovers kept apart by parents or fate, of earnest young men striving for advancement by studying for bureaucratic examinations and the alluring fox fairies who assumed human form and distracted the students.

Longer fictional works appeared later, with the 16th-century stories of bandit heroes such as San guo zhi (*Romance of the Three Kingdoms*) and Shui hu zhuan (*Water Margin*).

The greatest of the romantic novels is *Hong lou meng*, *Dream of the Red Chamber/Story of the Stone*. Written by Cao Xueqin and published posthumously in 1791, this novel has elements of allegory, satire and mystery and tells of the splendours and gradual decline of a great family and its retainers.

SEE ALSO PAGES 114–5, 98–101

ARCHAEOLOGICAL DISCOVERIES

Of the excavations undertaken in China before the establishment of the People's Republic in 1949, a number were carried out by foreign archaeologists, most in less than ideal conditions. However, since the revolution—and particularly following Chairman Mao Zedong's exhortation to "let the past serve the present"—archaeology in China has had government support. Systematic, controlled excavations are now carried out by teams of archaeologists (usually organized at provincial level) using all the modern techniques available. Discoveries from these digs are regularly published in various Chinese journals devoted to the subject.

Great progress has also been made in recent years in the preservation of archaeological finds; specialist groups have been set up to develop a wide range of conservation techniques, including those for silk, paper, lacquer and bronze. There is an expanding exchange of information on archaeology and art history with other countries and the People's Republic has held a number of international conferences on aspects of Chinese archaeology.

Recent finds have provided further evidence that the ancient Chinese, besides inventing gunpowder, paper, the compass and cross-bow mechanisms, were pioneers in such fields as bronze casting and ceramics. Of all the significant discoveries by Chinese archaeologists, the one that has most captured the imagination of the Western public, as well as that of the Chinese themselves, was that made at Xi'an in 1974 of the vast terracotta army guarding the tomb of the first emperor, Qin Shi Huangdi.

The sites uncovered in archaeological excavations fall into three main categories: habitation (including religious buildings), industrial (such as kiln sites and foundaries), and burial. A good many of these have been found by accident. So great is the wealth of remains left by thousands of years of Chinese civilization that preparing the ground for almost any new construction—from a well to a hospital building—is likely to bring new treasures to light.

The earlier habitation sites yield the material of the greatest anthropological interest. The best-known find is doubtless that in 1929 of Peking Man (*Sinanthropus pekinensis*). Whole skulls and long bones of the Pleistocene age of human evolution were found in limestone caves at Zhoukoudian (about 48 km [30 mi] southeast of Beijing). These remains were lost during World War II, but more were discovered in 1959 and 1966.

Less well known, but arguably even more important, was the discovery in 1963–64 of an even earlier type, Lantian Man (*Sinanthropus lantienensis*). Excavated from the iron-rich clay just over 48 km (30 mi) from Xi'an, Lantian Man has been assigned to the stage of evolution immediately prior to that of Peking Man in the Middle Pleistocene period some 600,000 years ago. Tools found near the bones were somewhat less advanced than those of Peking Man.

Silent sentinels in their thousands, the soldiers of the spectacular terracotta army are revealed in the positions they have held for the past 2,000 years. Now a vast hangar protects the pit near Xi'an where they were discovered. The lifesize soldiers, horses and chariots were made to guard the tomb of the first emperor, Qin Shi Huangdi, who died in 210 BC and is buried a mile or so away.

Although some of the figures have undergone careful restoration, they remain in their original strict formations, those on the flanks facing outward in defensive positions.

This lively detail is from the fine murals decorating the 8th-century tomb of the Princess Yongtai near Xi'an (left). It shows court ladies wearing flowing robes in the Central Asian style that was fashionable at the Tang court of the time. Although they are in procession, the ladies are naturalistically grouped and appear to be engaged in conversation.

Burial sites have often proved the richest source of superb examples of Chinese craftsmanship; indeed, the tombs themselves can be highly complex constructions. The tombs belonging to the ruling classes of the Han (206 BC–AD 220) and Tang (618–907) dynasties have produced some of the most impressive finds of recent years, including the "flying horse" excavated from an Eastern Han tomb at Wuwei in Gansu in 1969. Complete jade funerary suits, made for members of the royal house in the hope of protecting the body from decay, were excavated from a Western Han tomb at Mancheng in Hebei in 1968, and the tomb of Tang-dynasty Princess Yongtai was found to contain more than 800 pottery figures, as well as beautiful murals in the antechamber.

In times of great prosperity the tombs of the wealthy became more elaborate and the deceased would be committed to the afterworld with all the splendid trappings of earthly existence. When the practice of entombing servants and childless concubines with their deceased masters was abandoned before the Han, they were represented instead by straw, wooden and ceramic figurines. In Tang times models of people and animals (as well as other funerary goods, such as vessels) were arrayed outside the tomb until the cortège had entered; they were then installed in the niches lining the walls of the ramp leading into single or multiple tomb chambers, as well as in the chambers themselves.

In later dynasties, tombs, particularly those built for members of the ruling house, were increasingly ornate, as can be seen in the royal Ming tombs which, from the early fifteenth to the mid-seventeenth century, were built to the north of Beijing. Some of the animal and human figures lining the "Spirit Way" (along which the body of the deceased passed on its way to its final resting place) have been preserved, as have some of the gates, stone tablets and buildings above ground used for the preparation and dedication of offerings. Some of the tomb chambers, too, have been excavated; with their ingeniously constructed stone doors (complete with stone locks) and their high-vaulted ceilings they attest the great skill of Ming-dynasty masons.

ARCHAEOLOGICAL DISCOVERIES/2

THE YELLOW EARTH

The geological feature of most significance to the archaeologist in China is the "yellow earth"—the alkaline loessic clay soil that covers much of the northwestern region of the country.

This powder-fine loess was originally blown south from the Gobi Desert region, and is particularly deep, up to 30 m (100 ft), in Gansu and Shaanxi Provinces. There, in places, its exceptional texture has contributed to an extraordinary phenomenon: soil replicas of ancient artefacts. In these the shape of the object remains as a "ghost" left in the soil after the wood it was made of has decayed.

The archaeologist is alerted to their existence by a change in soil colour and texture. Although extremely fragile, such "ghosts" made of soil and decayed organic material have been excavated intact.

Outstanding examples of this phenomenon are to be found at the Shang- and Zhou-dynasty burial sites, where chariots have been excavated as soil impressions. At the royal Shang tomb at Xibeigang (12th–11th century BC), wooden burial chamber canopies have remained as soil "ghosts", complete with impressions of intricate carving and flakes of the original red lacquer decoration. The wood from which they were made has disintegrated.

● Archaeological site

TREASURES OF XI'AN

Xi'an in Shaanxi Province is one of China's richest archaeological areas since it was the seat of government during several periods of China's history. Its many treasures include:

● **The terracotta army**
The loess also provided the fine clay used to construct the spectacular, lifesize ceramic figures of horses and soldiers belonging to China's first emperor, Qin Shi Huangdi, who died in 210 BC. They were discovered in 1974 by members of the local commune who were digging a well to the east of the emperor's burial mound.

Three pits were found. Pit 1 has been fully excavated and is completely protected by a huge, hangar-like building covering an area of 16,000 sq m (19,000 sq yd). The site has proved so popular with tourists that pit 2 is being opened up in order to relieve the congestion at pit 1.

Archaeologists calculate that there are probably more than 7,000 warriors, some 600 horses, about 100 wooden war chariots, and a large quantity of weaponry—bows, cross-bows, halberds, lances, daggers, battle-axes, swords and knives.

Most of the figures have been made in several pieces that were luted together (joined using clay) before firing, except for the head, which was slotted into the neck cavity. The figures are now mostly the buff colour of the original clay, but when they were interred they were brightly painted to

One of the superb bronze chariots found near Qin Shi Huangdi's tomb at Xi'an is examined, after its restoration, by archaeologists and technicians. Not only is the casting remarkably sophisticated, but the ratio of copper to tin used for the various parts of the chariot is marvellously precise. Each chariot, which is half lifesize, is composed of 3,462 separate parts.

enhance the intricate facial and clothing details.

Tests on the remaining particles of paint reveal that the pigment was mixed with gelatine before being applied.

● **The emperor's chariots**
In 1980, 20 m (66 ft) west of Qin Shi Huangdi's tomb, 2 magnificent bronze imperial chariots were excavated, of about half size. Each had a driver and 4 horses with trappings of gold and silver. The bronze was realistically painted, and silk decked the inside of the covered chariot. The actual tomb of the emperor has yet to be excavated.

● **The Banpo village**
Banpo is a Neolithic village site of the 5th–4th millennium BC. The site was excavated in the 1950s, and is covered to protect it from the elements.

Archaeologists estimate that the village housed 200 to 300 people who had reached an advanced stage of development in farming. They were associated with the painted pottery culture named for another village, Yangshao, where such pottery was first discovered. The Banpo people appear to have cultivated millet and kept domestic animals, such as goats, dogs and pigs.

Excavations have unearthed prepared floors, hearths and post-holes, which indicate the range of dwellings built. The site was broadly divided into 3 areas: habitation, pottery making and burial, although young children were buried in the habitation area.

The Yangshao culture is notable for its pottery painted in earth colours. This fine ware was made by the coiling method, and many of the large vessels found still bear the imprint of the mats on which they were placed to facilitate turning. These impressions give a detailed indication of the weaving skills of the people of this culture.

XINJIANG

Some of the most interesting archaeological sites in China are shown on this map. Shaanxi, Henan and Hunan are particularly rich in archaeological remains.

THE MAWANGDUI TOMBS

In 1971 a new hospital was to be built east of Changsha in Hunan Province, in an area already known to be rich in archaeological remains. Archaeologists were therefore allowed to excavate the site before building began. They discovered a tomb of the Western Han period (206 BC–AD 24) with an extremely unusual construction.

The burial chamber was

MAJOR ARCHAEOLOGICAL SITES

THE ROYAL TANG TOMBS

Fine mural paintings, and vast numbers of earthenware figures, came to light near Xi'an during the excavation of 3 tombs belonging to the Tang imperial family, all of which date from the early 8th century.

The tomb of Princess Yongtai was excavated in 1964; those of the princes Zhang Huai and Yi De in the early 1970s. Together they contain some 800 sq m (950 sq yd) of mural paintings.

The 19-year-old Princess Yongtai was reburied here in 706, after the death of her grandmother, Empress Wu Zi Tian, who is generally held to have been responsible for the young princess's death. On the walls of the antechamber of her tomb are paintings of court ladies (probably Yongtai's attendants), carrying fans, cups, boxes, back-scratchers and bundles of silk. Wearing flowing robes in the Central Asian style, the elegant ladies appear to be conversing.

In contrast, Prince Zhang Huai's tomb affords lively depictions of polo players. This game, a Persian import, was much in fashion among both men and women at the court in Tang times.

THE MOGAO CAVES AT DUNHUANG

Tang-dynasty murals of a rather different type from those in the royal tombs were found at the Mogao caves at Dunhuang in Gansu Province.

Far from the royal court, painting style in this border region shows some Western influence. Since the paintings are in Buddhist shrines they tend to be more often religious than secular.

Many of the hundreds of paintings on the cave walls depict the Buddha in his many forms, bodhisattvas and attendants in paradise. Some also show scenes from the life of the Buddha and from his previous incarnations. These include depictions of more everyday themes, including architecture and agriculture, and also reveal the beginnings of the landscape painting tradition.

Buddhist shrines had been established in these caves as early as 366, and continued to exist there until the Yuan dynasty of the 14th century.

The caves were discovered before the revolution, but it was only in 1951 that the Dunhuang Research Institute was set up to conserve and study them for their remarkable murals and the statuary and other items they still contained.

It has been a major task for the Institute to protect these caves from both the visitors and the elements—particularly the destructive sand storms that bear down on the region from the Gobi Desert.

In order to preserve the murals it has been necessary to reinforce the cave walls themselves, and a number of the interconnecting passageways have had to be rebuilt.

encased in a layer of charcoal, 38–48 cm (15–19 in) thick, which was topped with a layer of white clay, 90–120 cm (3–4 ft) thick. These acted as a filter so that almost no oxygen or bacteria penetrated the chamber. Liquid had, however, entered the tomb, and in these conditions its contents—the deceased, as well as silks, lacquerwares and other funerary objects—were all in a remarkable state of preservation.

The body in tomb number 1 is thought to be that of the wife of Li Cang, first Marquis of Dai. She died at about 50 years of age, probably of a heart attack. Her body, dressed in silk, was wrapped in 20 quilts. It was in a special preserving liquor of a complex chemical make-up and encased in 3 lacquered wooden coffins.

After more than 2,000 years, her skin was still elastic, her joints moved, and her hair was firmly rooted. Pathologists were able to conduct an autopsy which revealed not only that her left coronary artery was constricted, that she had suffered arteriosclerosis and gallstones, but also that she had been eating melon seeds shortly before her death.

Laid over the innermost coffin was a silk banner painted with characters from Chinese mythology, as well as a likeness of the lady herself, attended by her servants and leaning on a stick. This is one of the earliest extant painted portraits.

This drawing of a detail from the painted silk banner in the Mawangdui tomb shows the tomb's occupant leaning on a stick.

MAWANGDUI BANNER

SEE ALSO PAGES 134–37, 138–41, 142–45

PAINTING AND CERAMICS

The two most highly esteemed visual arts in China have traditionally been calligraphy and painting—the pursuits of the gentleman-scholar. The decorative arts have never been held in such high regard, and almost without exception those who produced them have been viewed, at best, as craftsmen, and only rarely as true artists.

The majority of Chinese paintings, murals apart, are done on paper or silk—both materials that were first developed in China. The second-century BC Mawangdui banner (page 133) is a complex painting on silk using a number of colours. Indeed it seems likely that it was during the highly creative Han period (206 BC–AD 220) that painting began to flourish as a specific art rather than merely as applied decoration on an item of lacquer or ceramic ware.

A number of factors distinguish Chinese painting from that of the West. These range from more tangible aspects such as composition, choice of subject and materials to less tangible matters of attitude, purpose and the nature of appreciation.

Many Chinese paintings use little or no colour, but are executed in ink. The main constituent of this ink is carbon, produced by burning various organic materials—principally wood and oils. Traditionally, the carbon was mixed with a type of glue, then heated and pounded. By mixing the ink with different quantities of water the artist could obtain a wide range of shades.

As a rule the media used in old Chinese painting did not include oil paints as they are now known (although oil paints of a kind were used to decorate lacquerware). Instead, colours were made of ground pigments mixed with water and a little glue. Until the late nineteenth century when aniline dyes were introduced, every colour of the Chinese painter's palette was derived from either vegetable or mineral sources. The dominant hues were red, brown, blue, green and yellow, in addition to black and white.

The symbolism used by the Chinese in both their decorative and fine art often eludes the Western eye. Plants, fruits, creatures—all can be subjects or elements chosen for their traditional associations as much as for their inherent beauty.

The lotus, for instance, not only has Buddhist connotations, but also represents summer and purity; it is one of the "flowers of the four seasons". The others are peony for spring, as well as riches and honours; the chrysanthemum for autumn and longevity; and the prunus (blossoms of plum, apricot or almond), for winter and beauty. Another much depicted group of plants is the trio of bamboo, prunus and pine. Called the "three friends of winter", together they symbolize China's religions (Buddhism, Taoism and Confucianism).

Truly abstract themes, even in the decorative arts, have been extremely rare. The most popular subjects in both painting and ceramic decoration have been landscapes, figure painting, animals and birds, and

flower compositions (the last two frequently being combined in "bird and flower paintings").

One of the most conspicuous differences between Chinese and Western paintings is the manner in which they are displayed. Chinese paintings are not traditionally framed; they are mounted in the form of hanging scrolls and hand scrolls, album paintings or fan paintings. This naturally influences their composition. Paintings executed as hand scrolls, for instance, are designed to be unrolled and examined a little at a time, not viewed all at once.

While the painter worked on flat material, be it paper or silk, the ceramic artist usually worked on a surface curved in one or more plane. It is much to the credit of the ceramic decorator that the viewer is often not aware of the curvatures of his "canvas"—so skilfully has he compensated for them.

In the production of ceramics Chinese potters combined an early mastery of complex techniques with the good fortune of having quantities of near-perfect raw materials at hand. The geology of China provides a range of mineral deposits suited to the making of ceramic wares and these have been fully exploited by Chinese craftsmen. The two most important components in the making of ceramics in China are kaolinic clays and the mineral known as "porcelain stone". As a rule, the wares of the north contain a higher proportion of clay, while those of the south have a higher proportion of porcelain stone.

High-quality earthenwares were being made as early as the Neolithic period. Stonewares were developed in the Bronze Age, when glazing first seems to occur. It was, however, in the eighth century during the Tang dynasty that there appeared a white, high-fired, translucent material—the porcelain that has become synonymous with the name China in the eyes of the world.

In this charming detail from a 4th-century scroll painting on silk by Gu Kaishi, an attendant is dressing an elegant lady's hair. The latter is gazing at her reflection in a round bronze mirror, polished on one side. Lacquered toilet boxes, containing cosmetics, combs and hair pins, lie in readiness at her feet.

The scroll painting is called Admonitions of the Instructress to the Court Ladies *and is intended as an illustrated guide to court life. It contains a series of scenes, many with an accompanying text, advising ladies on appropriate behaviour.*

This exquisite porcelain flask, about 29 cm (11½ in) tall, dates from the Qing-dynasty Yong Zheng reign (1723–35). It is a particularly fine example of bird and flower painting in overglaze famille rose *enamels. As is usual in such decorative schemes, the birds are painted on a smaller scale than the flowers to allow for a more harmonious and integrated composition.*

Famille rose *describes a group of porcelains from this period all of which are decorated with a particular palette of overglaze enamels which includes a rose pink derived from colloidal gold.*

The other side of the flask is decorated with a similar design in paler tones.

PAINTING AND CERAMICS/2

LANDSCAPE PAINTING

The Chinese term for landscape is *shanshui* (mountain and water), and it is the most highly regarded subject for paintings. Its origins may be traced to the cloud and wave-like landscapes painted as a background to mythical creatures on late Bronze Age lacquer objects.

Landscape painting is praised in an essay by Zong Bing (AD 375–443), but there is little extant material from this period; it appears to have been only in the Tang dynasty (618–907) that landscape developed as a major theme. Of the various Tang styles, the "blue and green" of the 8th century was one which inspired numerous succeeding generations of artists.

Man's relationship with the landscape is shown at its two extremes in paintings of the Northern and Southern Song periods. In the style associated with Northern Song (960–1126), nature is predominant. Human participation may be implied in the title of Xu Daoning's 11th-century *Fishing in a Mountain Stream*, but monumental mountains in the background dwarf the tiny fishermen and their boats in the foreground.

In contrast, the painters of the Southern Song (1126–1279) showed man as a more important element in their work. The landscapes are less awe-inspiring and man appears more in harmony with his surroundings. The figure of a scholar is often the focal point. In the late-12th-century *Walking on a Mountain Path in Spring*, non-essential elements of landscape have been omitted, and large areas of unpainted silk convey a feeling of space.

The principles of these painting schools, and the styles of the masters of the succeeding Yuan dynasty (Zhao Mengfu, Huang Gongwang, Wu Zhen and Ni Zan), have been a source of inspiration to landscape painters up to the present.

Nature dwarfs the human element in this 11th-century landscape, which is typical of the period. Part of a hand scroll on silk painted by Xu Daoning, it is entitled Fishing in a Mountain Stream. Yet the fishermen are completely dominated by dramatic mountain scenery.

MULTIPLE MEANINGS

Puns and rebuses (the representation of a name or word by pictures suggesting its syllables) are popular themes in Chinese art.

Bats, pronounced *fu*, can stand for happiness, also pronounced *fu*. Five bats signify the "five blessings" of longevity, riches, peace, virtue and a good end to life. Fish, pronounced *yu*, is symbolic of abundance, which is also pronounced *yu*.

An artist could also use subtle allusion to express controversial feelings in a seemingly uncontroversial way. The artist Zheng Sixiao exploited this possibility in his painting of an orchid made in 1306, which tacitly states his loyalty to the Song dynasty ousted in 1279 by the Mongol conquest of China.

The orchid, identified with the high principles of a gentleman, is depicted simply in ink on paper; it is a single, modest bloom—a suitable symbol of the unassertive artist.

However, when Zheng was asked why he had not painted earth or roots, he explained that the earth had been stolen by the barbarian invaders—the Mongols.

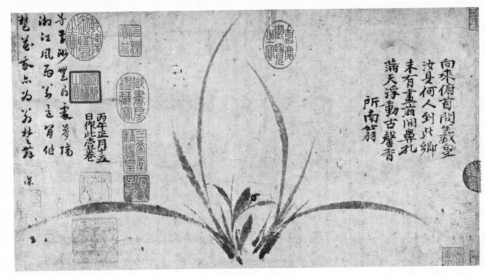

This is much more than a simple ink painting of a graceful orchid. It dates from the year 1306, during the Mongol rule of China. The artist, Zheng Sixiao, painted it without roots or earth—a subtle yet powerful political allusion to the theft of his own land by Mongol invaders.

CERAMIC BURIAL WARES

Many of the surviving ceramics of the Han and Tang dynasties were made specifically for burial with the dead. These included vessels and models of other items the deceased might require in the afterlife.

During the Han dynasty a lead glaze was used on some burial wares that was toxic and rendered the objects unsuitable for general use. A number of these green, lead-glazed vessels were made in imitation of more costly bronze.

The Han ceramic models were usually of items that might be useful in the afterlife, such as cooking stoves, wells, pig-pens, granaries and farm animals. There were also models of buildings, including 3-storeyed examples which are at least 1 m (3 ft) high.

The Tang-dynasty funerary wares were, however, more colourful, and for the most part were models of human or animal figures. In the early 8th century, the period of the Tang's most ostentatious burials, a bright lead-glazed type known as *sancai* (three-colour) was popular. Examples were excavated from the tomb of the Princess Yongtai in the early 1960s.

The most popular animals were horses and camels. Human figures included beautifully gowned ladies, falconers, grooms, and a number of representations of foreigners— Armenians, Persians, Arabs and Southeast Asians.

KILN SITES

Some of the traditional centres for ceramics and locations of kilns are shown above. Many are still famous for ceramics today.

("yao" is the Chinese for kiln)

CLASSIC SONG CERAMICS

Some of the most subtly beautiful ceramic ware was produced during the classic period of Chinese ceramics, the Song dynasty. Imperial taste dictated style and at this time favoured pieces that owed their aesthetic appeal to the elegance of their shape and the loveliness of their subtle monochrome glaze.

The Ding wares of northern China had soft, ivory-coloured glazes; the Longquan celadons of Zhejiang Province farther south had a jade-like appearance; while the Guan wares even had a deliberate crackle in their blue-grey glaze in imitation of the fissures in jade.

The Emperor Hui Zong had published a 30-volume illustrated catalogue of his archaic bronzes in the early 12th century, and jade collections were also catalogued. In the Southern Song period (1126–1279) these catalogues inspired ceramic craftsmen with an interest in ancient vessels produced in these other media—an interest that was reflected in glazes that imitated jade, and shapes based on ancient bronze or jade models.

DECORATIVE THEMES

From the mid-15th century on as the blue and white style gradually became acceptable to Han Chinese taste, its decorative themes began to echo those of the fine arts, and of the wood-block illustrations in printed books. (Many of the scenes depicted are episodes from drama and novels popular at the time.)

With the development of fine overglaze enamel painting in the Qing dynasty, the links between painting and ceramic decoration became even closer. Bird and flower painting on the finest porcelain was of an extremely high standard.

In the 18th century, the painting on these fine porcelain wares (like that in the fine arts) began to show the influence of European Jesuit painters who were resident at the Chinese court. This was particularly evident in figure painting, with the use of light and shade on faces and drapery.

WESTERN PERSPECTIVES ON CHINESE ART

Two styles of Chinese painting familiar in the West are those of the artist Qi Baishi (1863–1956), whose depictions of animals, insects and plants have found considerable favour among Europeans; and the Chan (or Zen) Buddhist painters of the Northern and Southern Song periods.

Chan painters were distinguished by their ability to capture the spirit of their subject in a few lines, aiming for the essence, rather than necessarily a precise likeness, and it was this that earned them admiration in the West. The anonymous, 13th-century *Patriarch and Tiger* (from the pair of scrolls, *Two Patriarchs Harmonizing their Minds*) is a fine example of this style of economic brushwork.

BLUE AND WHITE WARES

Compared to their tradition of elegant restraint, the Han Chinese found the highly decorated blue and white wares, produced in considerable quantities mainly for export during the Mongol Yuan dynasty, "very vulgar".

A few pieces with underglaze blue decoration had been produced since Tang times, but it was not until the Yuan (1271–1368) that large quantities of these blue and white wares were made to satisfy the tastes of the Near Eastern market— and the Mongol rulers' desire for profit.

Evidence for the outlet for these blue and white porcelains comes from the two finest collections of 14th-century material to survive—one is housed in the Topkapi Seray, Istanbul; the other is to be found in the Collection of the Ardebil Shrine in Iran.

CONTINUING TRADITIONS

China's unbroken 7,000-year ceramic tradition continues to the present day. Jingdezhen in Jiangxi Province is still the main centre for the production of porcelain, as it has been since Yuan times. The dark stonewares made of so-called "purple sand" are still being made at Yixing (the teapots are particularly famous and much beloved by tea connoisseurs); and Cizhou wares, in the style of their Song predecessors, remain in production in the north.

Indeed at many traditional centres in China, ceramics are being produced in the style of ancient wares, using the same raw materials, and many of the same centuries-old techniques. Many, such as the modern Ding wares and northern black wares, bear comparison with their ancient counterparts. Experiments with new glazes, colouring oxides and decorative styles continue at many modern kilns with a view to both domestic and export markets.

Simple yet graphic brushwork was the hallmark of the Chan (or Zen) Buddhist painters of the 12th and 13th centuries. This painting known as The Patriarch and the Tiger exemplifies the technique.

METALWORK, JADE AND SCULPTURE

The Chinese distinguished themselves among Bronze Age cultures by producing cast bronze of unequalled quality. Ritual vessels of the Shang and Zhou dynasties (approximately fifteenth to fifth centuries BC) are among the most impressive technological as well as artistic achievements in early Chinese history.

In addition to the *cire perdue* (lost wax) process of bronze casting used in the West, Chinese craftsmen evolved a complex piece-mould method. Ceramic piece-moulds appear to have been made around a model of clay or wood which gave only a general shape, while the intricate decoration was tooled directly on the mould pieces. *Cire perdue* was easier, and allowed for the casting of more complex shapes, but the piece-mould method required more skill and could produce crisper, more intricate surface designs.

The sections of the piece-mould needed to fit together tightly. Usually a core had to be made, and spacers of either metal or ceramic placed between the core and the sections of the mould to ensure the walls of the vessels would be of even thickness. The joins in the moulds and the pins required to keep the inner core and outer mould apart inevitably left their marks on the vessel. In some instances this was turned to decorative advantage by giving the piece large flanges running down the sides.

A rich find of vessels of this type was made in the royal Shang tomb discovered at Yinxu, Hebei Province, in 1976. It was identified as that of Fu Hao, consort of King Wuding (1324–1266 BC). Among the 1,500 or so funerary items with which her relatively small tomb was packed were 440 magnificent bronzes, which included bells, tools, mirrors, weapons and chariot fitments, in addition to twenty different types of ritual vessels.

Although the Bronze Age metalwork, mainly comprising weaponry and the ritual vessels associated with burial and religious practices, is considered the high point of Chinese artistry in bronze, some excellent small sculptural pieces, particularly in gilt bronze, were also produced. Among the most interesting are the Buddha figures made in response to the spread of Buddhism in the Wei period (fifth century). Many of these figures are portrayed standing on a lotus or seated on a "lotus throne", their hands in mystic ritual gestures or *mudrás*.

The sculptural material most highly valued by the Chinese for carving smaller figures and vessels has always been jade. Their word for it, *yu*, refers not only to the mineral aggregates nephrite and jadeite (the only two minerals internationally accepted as jade), but also means "precious", "pure" and "noble", as well as "stone worthy of carving".

All early jade carvings are of nephrite, one of the most highly prized being the white variety of the colour and texture called "mutton fat". The main sources of the various colours of nephrite were in Khotan and Yarkand in what is today the Autonomous Region of Xinjiang in the extreme Northwest.

This water buffalo is a masterpiece of jade carving. At 43 cm (17 in) long it is also unusually large for a jade object. The crouched posture was probably chosen to make best use of a big stone. Jade is difficult to date but this piece is thought to be either from the Yuan dynasty (1271–1368) or early Ming dynasty (1368–1644).

This delightful bronze elephant is in fact a zun or lidded wine vessel; the smaller elephant on its back serves as the lid handle. The vessel dates from the Shang dynasty (c. 1480–1122 BC).

The middle fingers of the colossal Buddha near Leshan (far left) are 8.3 m (27 ft) long—an indication of the immense scale of this statue. It is the largest of its kind in China and measures 71 m (233 ft) in height and 28 m (92 ft) across at the shoulders.
Begun in 713 the Buddha took 90 years to complete. It is carved into the cliffs of Phoenix Perch Peak which towers above the confluence of three rivers. Tradition has it that the figure was made in the hope that it would encourage the Buddha himself to calm the turbulent waters at this spot where many had met their deaths by drowning.

Jadeite, which also comes in a variety of colours (most notably the bright green now synonymous with the name of the stone), was first imported into China from Burma in the eighteenth century.

Because of its crystalline structure—long needle-like crystals felted together in nephrite, and short interlocking crystals in jadeite—jade is exceptionally difficult and time-consuming to work. Lapidaries could not carve either nephrite or jadeite in the usual manner, but had literally to wear them away using tools often made of bamboo and coated with an abrasive material even harder than jade, such as almandine garnets, powdered quartz or crushed corundum. (Carborundum, which became available only this century, greatly facilitated the working of jade.) Certainly even as late as the 1930s, Chinese lapidaries employed techniques and tools virtually identical to those in use for centuries.

Before the introduction of Buddhism in the Han dynasty, possibly between 50 BC and AD 50, large-scale three-dimensional sculpture does not appear to have been undertaken in China. Early examples reflect the influence of the Indo-Hellenic styles.

Colossal figures, when they were produced, were no doubt influenced by examples such as the gigantic Buddha at Bamiyan in Afghanistan.

Among the best known of the early Chinese colossal Buddhas is the one seated outside cave twenty at Yungang, Shanxi Province. It was begun in 460 and is nearly 14 m (45 ft) high from its base to the top of the protuberance (one of thirty-two marks identifying a Buddha) on the top of its head. Another is the eighth-century Buddha at Leshan.

Three-dimensional figure sculptures may be seen at several cave temple complexes which have survived to the present day. In addition to Yungang, there are caves at Longmen in Henan Province; Maiji in Gansu; Tianlong in Shanxi; Dazu in Sichuan and, notably, Dunhuang in Gansu. Low-relief sculpture was executed on stelae and also on the walls of the caves. One of the finest examples is the relief from the Binyang cave at Longmen (early sixth century) showing female donors—the empress and ladies of the court who had paid for the carvings. This naturalistic group achieves an illusion of depth by the careful placement of the figures.

METALWORK, JADE AND SCULPTURE/2

RITUAL BRONZES

Ritual bronze vessels may be divided between those made to cook or hold food; those made to heat or hold wine; and those made for pouring or containing water.

Of the cooking vessels, one of the most interesting is the *xian* (a type of steamer). It has pouched hollow legs and a constricted waist. Inside, at the waist, is a hinged, perforated tray on which the food was placed to steam. An example from the 11th century BC has survived in such good order that the hinge (for lifting one side of the tray when cleaning the *xian*) still moves.

Some of the Shang- and Zhou-period vessels (15th to 5th century BC) were almost sculptural in concept. A number of surviving *zun* (lidded wine vessels) were made in the shape of various birds and animals— elephants and owls are particularly favoured.

The depiction of humans on bronzes is relatively rare. There are, however, some spectacular exceptions, such as a quadrangular vessel with 4 legs discovered in Hunan. This has a broad human face cast on each side. Moulds for making masks of human faces were found at Anyang, while the bronze masks themselves were unearthed in Sichuan.

METAL MIRRORS

Bronze and precious metals were also used to make mirrors. These were usually round and without handles (like the one in the scroll painting on p. 134), polished on one side and highly decorated on the other. Most had a knob from which hung a silk tassel.

Bronze mirrors of the Han period (206 BC–AD 220) bore intricately cast geometric and naturalistic designs.

Many of the silver mirrors of the Tang period (618–907) were irregularly shaped (as flowers), or square, and were often embellished with gold or silver, sometimes set in lacquer. They are among the best examples of the skill and fluency of Tang silver- and goldsmiths.

THE LI XIULI HOARD

During the Tang dynasty Chinese work in gold and silver reached a peak. Outstanding examples of Tang craftsmanship can be seen among the pieces excavated at Hejiacun, near Xi'an, in Shaanxi Province.

In 1970 more than 1,000 items of gold, silver and precious stones, as well as medicines, were found hidden in two pottery containers and a silver urn at the site of a mansion that had belonged to Li Xiuli, Prince of Bin, who died in 741. There were also many coins of Sassanian, Byzantine and Japanese origin as well as Chinese.

Many of the gold and silver items in this hoard show the influence of Sassanian (3rd-7th century Persian) gold and silver

work, but are nevertheless undoubtedly Chinese in origin.

The treasures include a particularly beautiful gold bowl on a high foot. Its sides are shaped by repoussé petals. The petals and the spaces between them are embellished with birds, flowers and deer, traced against a "pearl-matting" background of tiny circles. Beaded relief work edges the footrim.

Another exceptionally fine piece from this hoard is a hanging censer, made of two elaborately pierced and traced hemispheres. Inside, an unpierced hemisphere (to hold the aromatic woods for burning) was mounted like a gyroscope so that it would remain horizontal during use and not spill its contents.

JEWELLERY AND ADORNMENTS

Precious metals were used to make jewellery and other personal adornments, from crowns to belt hooks. Since the Bronze Age, jade and gold has been a favourite combination. In later periods jade of the colour known as "spinach green" was particularly appreciated in jewellery.

In 1956 archaeologists excavating the tomb of the Wanli Emperor (1573–1619), one of the Ming tombs to the north of Beijing, found more than 3,000 items in the underground chambers, including the emperor's magnificent gold crown. It is made of gold thread, worked as a kind of

fine net. Two relief dragons worked in the same way decorate the raised back of the crown.

Also found were 4 even more elaborate "phoenix coronets". Each of these has 6 gold dragons among clouds, leaning down to open-winged phoenixes, precious jewels and pearls. The clouds, phoenixes, and some flowers are embellished with an inlay of kingfisher feathers.

As many as 2,160 jade plaques went into making this burial suit found at the tomb of Prince Liu Sheng and his wife Princess Dou Wan in Hebei. It dates from about 100 BC.

FUNERARY JADE

One of the properties attributed to jade in ancient China was that of preventing bodily decay. Nephrite cicadas were often placed on the tongue of the deceased, while various jade shapes, such as pigs, were used to plug other orifices.

In Han times this tradition was carried even further by the very wealthy when funeral palls—and even entire suits—were sometimes

made from plaques of jade. The plaques had holes drilled at each corner so that they could be wired together. The imperial family merited gold wire; for those of lesser rank silver or copper was used.

Two superb examples of these suits were excavated at Mancheng, Hebei Province, in 1968. They belonged to the Han-dynasty Prince Liu Sheng and his wife, Princess Dou Wan.

BRONZE VESSELS

Xian (steamer)

Zun (lidded wine vessel)

The intricacy of early Chinese bronze vessels is evident from these typical examples.

A JADE BURIAL SUIT

Jade burial suits were made up of various sections each composed of many jade plaques. How these sections fitted together is clear from the pattern above. The suits were made to encase the entire body, since jade was believed to prevent decay. Those excavated, however, contained only dust.

LARGE-SCALE STONE SCULPTURE

Most surviving large-scale stone sculptures in China are of Buddhist subjects, but there are also a number of secular subjects to be found among funerary sculptures.

The best known of these are the splendid animals and officials lining the Spirit Way (processional route) to the royal Ming tombs north of Beijing; and the superb horses, lions and human figures from the Spirit Way of the emperor Gaozong (d. 683), near Xianyang, Shaanxi.

The most famous sculpted horses, however, are those in a set of 8 low reliefs, each over 1.5 m (5 ft) high, commissioned by the emperor Taizong in 637 to grace his mausoleum outside Xi'an. They depict his favourite battle chargers, and are believed to be based on designs by the great Tang-dynasty artist, Yen Liben. There were originally 8 in the set but only 6 remain in China; the other 2 are in a museum in Philadelphia.

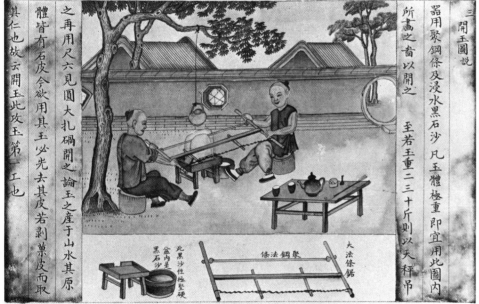

Using a saw made of bamboo and wire, the workmen in this turn-of-the-century drawing are cutting into a large jade rock. Jade is an extremely difficult stone to work and has to be literally worn away by cutting tools primed with an even harder material such as almandine garnets.

This splendid stone horse is one of the 18 pairs of stone statues lining the Spirit Way, the approach to the Ming imperial tombs near Beijing. The statues include representations of lions, camels, elephants and unicorns.

THE LAPIDARY'S ART

Jade has been used over the centuries to make vessels of various kinds—either simple designs intended to highlight the beauty of the stone itself, or elaborately carved as *tours de force* of the lapidary's art.

The latter sometimes incorporate flourishes such as intricate pierced work or chain links, emphasizing the skill and patience of craftsmen who had to wear away their material, rather than carve it.

A few large jade items are known to have been made. Some Buddha figures exist, and a massive wine bowl from the Mongol Yuan period (1271–1368) was found in the Round Fort, Beijing. This bowl is in black jade and measures an impressive 1.4 m (4½ ft) across at the brim.

However, some of the most charming jade objects are quite small and often demonstrate the ingenuity of the lapidary in exploiting the natural features of a given stone—either to the extent that he has used the colours within the stone to provide the markings on an animal, for instance, or in the way that he has seen within the shape of a jade pebble the form of, say, a recumbent camel. (Because jade was so expensive a raw material and had to be brought considerable distances, there was a great incentive for the lapidary to waste as little as possible.)

Many small jade pieces fit nicely into the palm of the hand, and indeed one of the joys the Chinese take in jade is holding it, for well-polished jade has a most pleasing tactile quality.

BUDDHIST SCULPTURES

Large-scale sculptures were also executed in materials other than stone. Many were carved from wood, but dry lacquer, ceramics and even iron were also used.

Particularly fine wooden examples of bodhisattvas, usually polychromed, survive from the Song, Yuan and Ming periods. (A bodhisattva was a mortal on the point of Buddhahood who chose to guide his fellow men on earth toward a similar enlightenment.)

Many surviving examples of such statues portray the bodhisattva Guanyin, often in the reclining position known as Maharajalila ("royal ease"), with one leg flexed upward and the other flexed and horizontal; in another similar position the second leg is pendant.

Bodhisattvas were usually depicted as male or genderless in the Indian tradition, but in China Guanyin gradually came to be equated in the minds of ordinary people with Chinese goddesses and eventually took on many of their feminine traits.

SILK AND LACQUER

There were two products with which China was especially associated in the ancient world—silk and lacquer. As early as the Neolithic period, the Chinese had appreciated and utilized the remarkable properties of these materials.

Silk and lacquer share various characteristics which made them ideal for export along the famous Silk Road across Central Asia. For instance, both are light in weight, reasonably durable and have always been luxury items that could be sold for high prices. (These factors are no less valid today; silk centres such as Wuxi and Suzhou, and the lacquer workshops in Beijing, Yangzhou and parts of Sichuan Province continue to produce goods that are exported around the world.)

Even before the Silk Road was established, silk was leaving China as gifts for rulers of other countries. Fragments of silk have been found at a number of archaeological sites beyond China's borders. Ancient textiles are not often excavated in good condition, but there are several notable exceptions with regard to Chinese silk. From the so-called "frozen tombs" at Pazyryk in the USSR's Altay region, a burial site dating from the fourth century BC yielded embroidered tribute silks of quite complex weaves, as well as a piece of the coarser wild silk, tussore. The latter was decorated with embroidered birds and flowers, and had been used to cover a saddle-cloth.

Other well-preserved silks were found at the archaeological site at Mawangdui (see pages 132 to 133). The unusually constructed tomb contained a variety of silk cloths, some of which had been block-printed, painted or embroidered, as well as pile-looped brocades and patterned gauzes. There were complete articles of silk clothing, as well as a painted banner with silk tassels.

The passion for silk in other parts of the world was to have a profound effect on China's history and economy. So closely were the Chinese linked with the cloth that in classical times, the Greeks and Romans referred to them as *Seres* ("the silk people"). In the first century AD, the Roman scholar Pliny noted (not without a certain asperity) that silk imported by the empire from China "enables the Roman matron to flaunt transparent raiment in public."

Lacquer, like silk, is an exceptional material that seems to have been first developed by the Chinese. It is used to give a hard, smooth, protective coating to materials such as wood and is made from the sap of the lacquer tree (*Rhus verniciflua*, also known as *Toxicodendron verniciflua*). The tree is indigenous to China and, according to ancient texts, it was once found over all but the most northerly areas. It was particularly abundant south of the Yellow River, from the western borders to the eastern coastal regions, but today grows only in southern China.

Evidence of the use of lacquer has been discovered at Neolithic sites such as one at Hemudu, near modern Hangzhou, where a black lacquer bowl from

Three people are needed to iron this newly woven length of silk. It is wound round a pole at each end, and two ladies hold it taut while a third presses it with a bronze iron. The iron has a hinged handle and is filled with hot coals.
   This detail is from a hand scroll painting (left), itself on silk, by Emperor Hui Zong who reigned from 1101 to 1126. It is a copy of an original painting by 8th-century artist, Zhang Xuan.

This exquisitely carved red lacquer box dates from the early 15th century. The lid is decorated with a landscape, a popular motif for such boxes at this time, and sky, water and land are each denoted by a different background pattern. The landscape is divided horizontally by the usual device of a fence and a double-roofed pavilion. The scene is carved in such minute detail that even the leaves on the different types of tree are precisely depicted.

the fourth millennium BC was excavated. In Shang times, lacquer was used to decorate and protect vessels, such as bowls—fragments of bowls were found in 1973 at a site in Taixicun in the province of Hebei—as well as the structural wooden beams found at sites such as Gaocheng in Henan Province.

Lacquer has a number of properties that make it much like a natural plastic. It is ideal for coating other materials, particularly organic ones, since it is resistant to heat, water, acid and termites. When properly applied, it is strong and takes on a beautiful glossy sheen. Although it is naturally a dull grey, it can be coloured using a number of pigments. The

Two mandarin ducks—symbols of conjugal happiness—swim on a lotus pond in this detail from a ke si (cut silk) tapestry. Mandarins, said to mate for life, were a popular motif.

The tapestry dates from the 15th to 16th centuries, during the Ming dynasty. It is a highly decorative creation, employing the solid blocks of colour characteristic of the ke si of this period.

most popular colours for lacquer in antiquity, red (from cinnabar) and black (from iron sulphate), are still the two most commonly used today.

The disadvantages of lacquer are that, in its raw state, it can cause disfiguring skin reactions in the craftsmen using it; also, its main component, urushiol, will polymerize and harden only if it is exposed to air and high relative humidity. This means that the lacquer must be applied one thin layer at a time, giving each time to harden. Thus lacquerware is time-consuming to produce.

Despite these drawbacks, lacquer's many positive qualities made it suitable for a number of uses. These ranged from the decoration and protection of wooden coffins, vessels and architectural features, as well as the decoration and strengthening of leather armour and shields, to providing a base on metal into which gold or mother-of-pearl inlay could be applied. In modern times lacquer provides an ideal surface for laboratory workbenches.

Lacquerware is exceptionally durable, as is demonstrated by the small carved red lacquer jar found in the cargo of a Yuan-dynasty vessel sunk off the Korean coast. The jar had survived intact in 21 m (70 ft) of water from the 1330s to 1975, when the wreck was discovered.

SILK AND LACQUER/2

SERICULTURE

The rearing of silkworms and the production of silk (sericulture) has been practised in China since as long ago as the Neolithic period (c.7000 to 1600 BC). Silkworm cocoons have been discovered at a Neolithic site in Shanxi Province. Silk weaving was well advanced by the Shang dynasty, judging from the silk fragments that have been excavated from a Shang site at Taixicun in Hebei. The silk had been used to wrap bronze vessels.

Silk production in China is based primarily on the larvae of the moth, *Bombyx mori*, traditionally reared on basketwork trays, as they still are today. The larvae, or worms, are fed on hand-picked leaves of the white mulberry (*Morus alba*) until they spin cocoons—on average 30 days after hatching.

The cocoons are made of filaments excreted from two glands on either side of the worm's body, and joined by a natural gum called sericin.

Before the moths can emerge, the cocoons are plunged into boiling water. This softens the sericin and allows the ends of the silk fibre to be caught and drawn off on a reel. The fibre of a cocoon is in one continuous length, and with skill and care can often be reeled off unbroken.

The average length of a fibre is roughly 500 m (1,640 ft). They are extremely fine, and between 6 and 30 filaments (depending on the weight required) must be combined to make a usable thread.

Normally, silk need not be spun in the way that wool is; but if, for instance, the filament lengths are short, because a cocoon is damaged, these can be spun to form a different type of thread. When woven, silk can be used to produce fabrics with a wide range of appearances, but nearly all are characterized by their luxurious texture and lustrous sheen. Silk also has a softness that modern scientists have tried to imitate in manmade fibres.

KE SI

A form of silk weaving for which the Chinese are famous is *ke si* or cut silk. This is a type of silk tapestry that sometimes incorporates woven pictures; such is the fineness of the weave that at first sight they may be mistaken for paintings. The technique appeared in China at least as early as the Song dynasty (960–1279), although the term *ke si* does not seem to have been used before the 12th century.

Ke si utilizes undyed warp threads and coloured wefts.

The weft colours appear only where required, not necessarily continuing from selvage to selvage. The term "cut silk" refers to vertical slits that occur between adjacent areas of colour parallel to the warp. To avoid long slits, which might weaken the finished fabric, long vertical lines were usually avoided in designs for *ke si*. The richness of these tapestries was also sometimes enhanced by the use of metallic threads in addition to the silk.

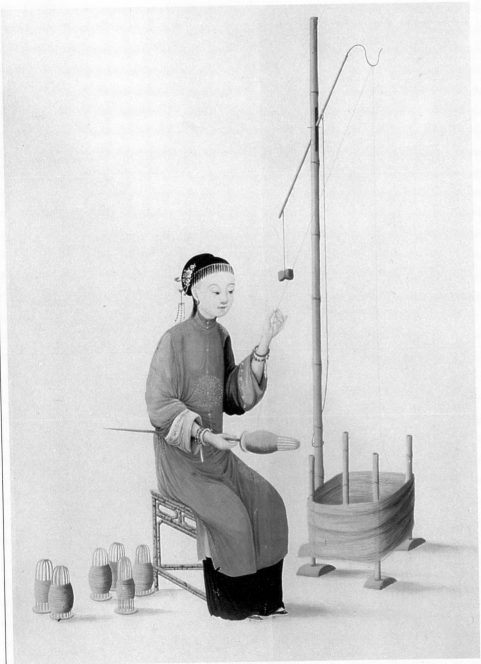

Between six and thirty filaments unravelled from silkworm cocoons are needed to make silk thread. This does not need to be spun but the filaments must be twisted together. The silk worker depicted in this late 18th-century watercolour is transferring silk thread to bobbins.

This ke si, *or cut silk, dragon robe* with horsehoof cuffs dates from about 1800. It incorporates the traditional features of dragons, 12 imperial symbols and a stylized wave pattern around the hem.

A detail from a richly embroidered robe of the late 18th century shows a crane in a circle of flowers. The crane was a symbol of longevity and a popular motif in painting as well as embroidery.

USES OF LACQUER

Lacquer's unusual properties make it both utilitarian and ornamental, as the ancient Chinese clearly appreciated.

In the early periods lacquer appears to have been used in 3 main ways: to provide protection for organic materials such as wood and leather; to add decoration, and to provide strength.

The earliest archaeological evidence of lacquer shows it being used mainly on wood to provide colour (most often red or black), and as a protective coating to carved wood—whether architectural beams or vessels.

It had also been used to harden as well as decorate the leather shields excavated from sites of the Warring States period (453–221 BC) in the Changsha area.

DECORATION OF LACQUER

In making ornamental pieces, lacquer was applied over a base—most often of wood, but also of metal, cloth, bamboo, leather or ceramic. A lightweight product called dry lacquer was made by saturating cloth with lacquer, shaping it around a form and adding further coats to build up the strength before the form was removed. This was used both for vessels and for statuary.

Some of the many types of lacquer decoration include:

● Painted lacquer

One of the earliest decorative uses of lacquer was in designs of contrasting colours, the most usual combination being red and black. Other colours such as brown, yellow, white and green were also used, but the palette was restricted by the limited number of colours that combined successfully with lacquer.

A particularly famous piece is a lacquer basket excavated from the Han Commandery at Lolang in Korea, which realistically depicts 94 seated figures around its borders.

Although often eclipsed by its more ostentatious rivals, painted lacquerware continued to be made in succeeding dynasties.

● Carved lacquer

The earliest carved lacquer appears on the armour found at Fort Miran, which revealed layers of different colours; this technique of carving curvilinear designs in cuts of "v"- or "u"-shaped profiles was further developed in the carved marbled wares of the Song and Yuan dynasties. It was, however, in the Yuan dynasty (1271–1368) that the familiar carved lacquers seem to have first appeared.

Carved lacquer pieces were highly prized not least because of the time and effort that went into producing them. A coat of lacquer would be no more than 0.05 mm (0.002 in) thick, and a good piece for carving might require up to 200 layers, with drying and polishing between each.

The carving was often done to several depths, most notably on pieces decorated with landscape scenes. The lacquerer would put in a thin layer of contrasting colour to show the carver the depth for a particular part of the design, lest he ruin months of work by taking his knife too deep.

In the Yuan and early Ming periods, the most popular motifs were floral scrolls and figures in landscapes with pavilions. The latter became subject to certain conventions, employing stylized designs for the depiction of sky, water and land.

In the Qing period, the range of decorative designs used on lacquer objects broadened considerably, as did the choice of colours for subsidiary parts of the design, though red and black continued to predominate.

● Inlaid lacquer

Inlays of shell and bone have been found on lacquered objects of the Shang period, while silver foil inlays—either depicting animals or of quatrefoil shape—appear on Han-dynasty toilet boxes.

In the Tang dynasty, inlays of mother-of-pearl were used to decorate a range of objects including musical instruments; gold and silver foil, often with finely incised detail, was inlaid into a lacquer layer on the back of mirrors. Mother-of-pearl inlay saw a revival of popularity in the Yuan dynasty which it has enjoyed ever since.

DRAGON ROBES AND OTHER OFFICIAL ATTIRE

Styles of dress at the Chinese court varied during its long history. Foreign influences, for example, can be seen in clothing favoured by several dynasties, not least the Tang (618–907) when for a while Central Asian dress was fashionable among the courtiers.

Some of the most elaborate official robes were made during the last dynasty, the Qing (1644–1911). These garments also incorporated a number of elements possibly imported into China—this time by the ruling Manchus. Some of the elements reflect the former nomadic lifestyle of the Manchus, taking into account the practical demands of horse riding and hunting. Tight-fitting sleeves, for instance, ending in embroidered "horsehoof" cuffs, replaced the wide, flowing sleeves of Han Chinese robes.

As the Qing dynasty progressed, so court apparel became codified. This culminated in the publication in 1759 of the *Huang chao li qi shi*, which was an illustrated guide to ritual paraphernalia. Types of garment were described in detail and, in some instances,

precise indications of appropriate colour and decoration for particular occasions were given. Not only were types of garment specified, but also, in some cases, how they were to be decorated and what colour they should be for particular occasions. White has traditionally been the colour of mourning in China; red is regarded as an auspicious colour suited to ceremonies such as weddings. Yellow was the colour particularly associated with the emperor.

The most famous of the Qing court robes were the so-called dragon robes. These were worn when conducting official business, although not on state occasions. They were usually worn by men, although there were roughly equivalent garments for women.

Dragon robes were most often made with a blue background; around the hem and sleeves was a design of stylized waves from which arose mountains and, among clouds, the dragons that give the garments their name. The use of the five-clawed dragon was officially restricted to members of the imperial family, but by the

19th century this rule was no longer strictly observed.

Some official court robes worn by the emperor were also decorated with 12 symbols which were the insignia of the imperial family. These 12, which include such devices as constellations, axes and cups, appear on robes dating from both the Ming and Qing dynasties. While they obviously derive from ancient sources, these are not known and it is impossible to interpret their meaning with any certainty.

Specific symbols were also used as badges of rank by Chinese officials. These were usually worn as embroidered squares applied to the front and back of the dragon robes. The front square was made in 2 halves to accommodate the opening of the robe.

ARCHITECTURE AND GARDENS

What most distinguishes traditional Chinese from Western architecture is the extent to which, from the earliest archaeological discoveries onward, all buildings, great and small, relate to one another. The continuity of style, form and construction is expressed from the city plan, through the palace and temple complex, to the simple domestic courtyard. Buildings incorporate similar materials and methods and differ in scale rather than in essence. Although there are regional variations, patterns are consistent within regions.

Architectural historians have faced a difficult task because for thousands of years the Chinese have used timber as their primary building material. Thus few buildings have survived intact for more than a millennium. Information about earlier constructions is gleaned from such diverse sources as paintings and stone carvings. Of particular value are the pottery tomb models—notably those from the Han dynasty—representing contemporary houses, gates and towers in miniature.

Ideally, in the Chinese city, all buildings were square or rectangular in plan, with entrances oriented toward the south, and elements perfectly balanced on either side of this defined north-south axis. The main hall of a building was on the north side of a courtyard whose square walls and gate would be echoed on a larger scale by the city's own rectangular perimeter walls. Xi'an in Shaanxi Province is a prime example. However, in southern cities, such as Nanjing in Jiangsu Province, hilly and watery terrain often made this rectangular ideal impracticable.

Smaller dwellings would have a single courtyard; grander ones a courtyard complex, providing separate areas for kitchen, storage, animal pens, and so on. Within the sheltering walls, gardens were situated at the rear for privacy. Again, although Chinese gardens might vary in scale or display regional differences, they have marked unifying features. Whereas in a Western garden the emphasis is on plants, in China the use of water, ornamental buildings such as pavilions, rocks—even calligraphic inscriptions on stones and walls—are of equal importance.

The materials from which houses were built, from about the Han dynasty (206 BC–AD 220) onward, were timber, tamped earth, bricks, stone and decoratively stamped ceramic tiles. The basic structure, whatever the size, was a timber frame with wooden pillars to support the tiled roof. The walls built up around the wooden frame were not load-bearing. Projecting eaves, which sheltered the walls from rain, were supported by wooden brackets.

These brackets were of particular significance, and altered through the ages in their decorative complexity as well as in their structural function. They began in the Han dynasty as simple U or rounded W forms and gradually became more ornate. Stunning examples surviving from the Tang period are intricate

"forests" of beautiful joinery. In the Qing and Ming dynasties brackets were often highly coloured and reduced in size to form more of a decorative frieze below the roof (as can be seen on Beijing's Imperial Palace, built during the Ming dynasty).

Roofs were another important area for decoration. Tiles moulded with dragons, lions' faces grinning or snarling, or other good luck motifs might adorn the eaves and the line of the roof ridge made a decorative contribution in its own right. As seen most typically in the south, an exaggerated upturn of the eaves often accompanied a concave curve in the roof ridge. The curve is said by some to emulate the soft curves of the lush vegetation in southern gardens.

The modern trend in Chinese architecture is to reduce regional variation. The nineteenth century saw the arrival of Western-style buildings in the great commercial cities of Shanghai and Tianjin. In the 1950s the growth in city population created pressure for economic housing, and quantity became more important than quality.

The dawning of the age of prefabricated concrete set architects searching for a new "national style", exemplified by Beijing Railway Station, the History Museum and the Great Hall of the People of the late 1950s. By contrast, the handsome Fragrant Hills Hotel in Xiangshan, completed in 1983, uses echoes of China's past. Designed by Chinese-born American architect I. M. Pei, it incorporates the appealing forms and colours of traditional southern gardens.

In a typical southern garden in Suzhou (above) the elegant pavilions are in a muted monochrome that sets off lush green vegetation to best advantage. The absence of colour is characteristic of buildings in southern gardens, where plants remain luxuriant year-round. The effect relies on the harmonious fusion of all elements rather than on the emphasizing of individual features.

The dramatically upturned eaves of the grey-roofed pavilion give it a light, graceful appearance and echo the soft curves of surrounding foliage.

A tranquil lake and carefully sited pavilions are almost more important than plants in this northern garden (right). The garden is part of park in a hot springs area in Xi'an.

The lakeside pavilions are solid structures, with slightly upturned eaves and touches of colour on pillars and tiles to brighten the scene in winter when foliage dies. Such pavilions provide shade in summer and some shelter in winter for visitors who wish to sit and enjoy the air and the scenery. The pavilion on the right is in the form of a mock boat with a dragon prow—a popular device in garden architecture.

ARCHITECTURE AND GARDENS/2

TRADITIONAL HOUSES

In general, ordinary domestic houses showed greater variation in regional style than grand temples and palaces.

For example, in northern houses (notably those in Inner Mongolia and north of Beijing), the courtyard was a relatively large open space. making the most of the slanting rays of winter sun to warm the low grey buildings around it. A vine or tree was grown to provide some shade from the midsummer sun.

Southern houses featured an internal courtyard, almost covered by a roof to keep out both the monsoon rains and intense summer sun. The narrow opening in the roof (often above a water-filled stone tank containing live carp) allowed some light and air into the courtyard. It was called a "heaven well"—a reference perhaps to the Taoist tale of a frog in a well who thought he knew all about the world, just from the tiny patch of sky he could see above him.

● BEIJING STYLE
Traditional houses in the capital were single-storey, grey brick buildings set around a courtyard. Roofs were double-pitched and grey-tiled, while woodwork was painted dark red. Above the low front wall were two rows of windows, traditionally made of pretty, geometric lattice-work, and pasted over with fine white paper rather than glazed. This feature can still be seen in rural areas today.

● XI'AN STYLE
Northwest of Beijing, around Xi'an, houses were constructed with timber frames, and their yellow walls built up by pounding earth between the wooden struts. Buildings were often two-storey and single-pitched, with a sharp angle at the ridge and a steep pitch into the courtyard.

Window frames and doors were painted black, bordered with a thin red line.

● SUZHOU STYLE
Just south of the Yangtze, the house-garden complexes of Suzhou are famed for their beauty. Pretty buildings of dark, carved hardwood and whitewashed walls had elaborately carved lattice windows.

Circular openings or moon-gates frame the view of a tiny garden which makes the most of the restricted space in the city. Such gardens usually contained water and rocks as well as plants.

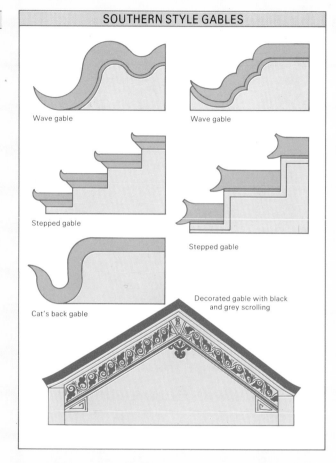

SOUTHERN STYLE GABLES

Wave gable

Wave gable

Stepped gable

Stepped gable

Cat's back gable

Decorated gable with black and grey scrolling

Decorative gables in many forms are seen on houses throughout southern China. Some examples are shown above. More than one type of gable may be employed in a large building complex.

● SOUTHERN STYLE
Farther south, where it is hotter, the houses had larger, enclosed courtyards, dark and cool, with tiny openings in the roof above for light and air.

Southern houses were often decorated under the eaves with cartouches enclosing painted scenes, and with black and grey scrolling on the whitewashed walls. This type of decoration, common in the provinces of Hunan and Anhui, is also seen on houses in western Yunnan, near the Burmese border.

Different gable-wall forms were seen across southern China. The stepped gable was found from coastal Ningbo through into Yunnan, as were varieties of curved gable. The Chinese give these names such as "wave gable" and "cat's back", the latter being in the form of a cat's arched back with an upright tail.

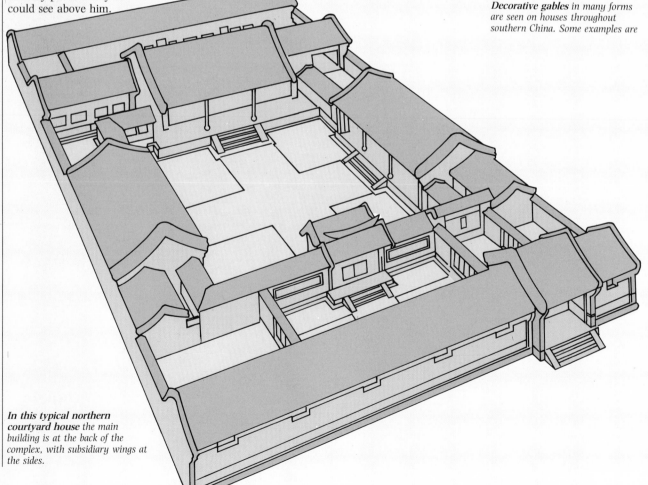

In this typical northern courtyard house the main building is at the back of the complex, with subsidiary wings at the sides.

Cave dwellings on the loess plateau of northern China are *tunnelled into cliffs or lead off courtyards dug down into the soil.*

● CAVE HOUSES

Where timber had long been exhausted, in the Xi'an area and throughout the loess or yellow-earth regions of northern and northwestern China, cave houses were built. These were either tunnelled out in rows along a cliff, or else the courtyard was cut down into the ground, with tunnelled rooms cut out on three sides and steps down on the fourth. The front of the tunnelled rooms was finished with a large wood and paper window.

Like most houses in the rural north, cave houses were furnished with a brick platform (or bed) called a *kang*, which is heated from beneath by a small stove.

● MODERN RURAL HOUSING

While distinctive local styles were once characteristic of Chinese housing, economic developments since the late 1970s have led to a revolution in rural architecture. Peasants, who at least in some areas are richer as a result of economic reforms, are building new houses that bear no relation to traditional forms.

The major influence is the recent architecture of Hong Kong's New Territories. Here flat-roofed "Mediterranean-style" villas, with concrete openwork panels for external decoration, and Western-style bathrooms and kitchens are popular.

These buildings are colloquially known as "*yang fang*" (foreign houses) and are causing some concern to Chinese architectural historians, who fear that they herald the disappearance of the traditional styles and regional distinctions.

GARDENS

Traditional gardens in China range from imperial enclosures in the north, which are large enough to hunt in, to the compact private courtyards of the south. The latter were designed as havens of peace and beauty in the heart of crowded cities.

● IMPERIAL ENCLOSURES

The grand imperial gardens surviving in the north incorporated lakes, dozens of buildings, and hunting parks stocked with deer. Brilliant colours were used to paint ornamental buildings and walkways, offsetting the grey tones of northern winters.

Preserved examples of the style are to be found at the Summer Palaces of Beijing— the Yiheyuan ("Garden where peace is cultivated"), and the 18th-century Yuanmingyuan ("Garden of perfect brightness").

● SUZHOU GARDENS

The city of Suzhou in Jiangsu Province is famous for its dozens of enclosures—half house, half garden—which are now open to visitors.

Most combine the following elements:
● Water, in the form of a pool or stream, part covered by water lilies, but sufficiently exposed to allow the reflection of clouds and wind-whipped ripples to give life to the composition.
● Buildings, both domestic and decorative.
● Rocks, preferably gnarled and water-worn crags from nearby Lake Tai at Wuxi. These are grouped to form miniature mountain ranges.
● Plants, including trees, creepers (such as wisteria), roses, peonies, and lilies. Bamboos are grown against whitewashed walls where their brush-stroke-like leaves resemble natural calligraphy.
● Space-enhancing devices, such as walkways, pierced walls to give the passerby a picture-gallery effect, and moon-gates to frame a view.
● Poetry and calligraphy, in the form of carved inscriptions, to adorn pavilions and stones.

GEOMANCY

Known in China as *fengshui* (literally "wind and water"), geomancy is the traditional practice of siting houses, public buildings and even graves to harmonize with the earth's vital energy and thus ensure good fortune for the occupier. Bad siting incurs the risk of bringing evil to the inhabitants.

Despite the government's disapproval, geomancy is still practised, particularly in the south of China. And it is very much alive in Hong Kong, where skyscrapers can only be built after consulting a geomancer, and office furniture may be repositioned according to his instructions if business is not booming.

Geomancy dates back thousands of years and its precepts were first written down during the Han dynasty (206 BC–AD 220) in books with such intriguing titles as *The Mysteries of the Blue Bag* (blue bag meaning the universe).

Armed with special *fengshui* compasses and handbooks, geomancers study a proposed site carefully before determining the position of a grave, house or building to be erected there.

Five main factors have to be considered when choosing a site: its topography; the type of ground; the surrounding landscape; any nearby rivers, streams or other water sources, and finally, the direction in which the site faces. All these contribute to the site's *qi* or energy.

Geomancy also had its practical aspects. Buildings would be sited in the shelter of hills, for example, and near water supplies. The planting of trees as windbreaks was often recommended.

Moreover the aesthetic elements in geomancy have greatly enhanced the Chinese landscape, with the often breathtakingly beautiful integration of houses, pagodas, temples and other monuments into their natural setting.

BUILDING MAGIC

Protection for a house and its inhabitants from evil spirits and such dangers as fire was sought with the aid of building magic. The practice still survives but is less common than in the past. The two most important aspects of this magic were protective decoration and the relations between owner and builder.

● PROTECTIVE DECORATION

Vulnerable areas, such as the roof ridge and the edge of the eaves, were adorned with tiles bearing good-luck characters, and protective designs such as the lion face.

Dragon-like heads at both ends of the roof ridge were thought to protect against fire. (Dragons were said to live in clouds and rivers and thus were associated with water in China.)

A "spirit wall" was built just inside the main gate, since it was believed that evil spirits could only fly in straight lines and would be unable to negotiate this barrier into the courtyard.

● OWNER-BUILDER RELATIONS

If, during the building of a house, the owner was mean, skimping on the meat meals he owed to his workers, they might wall up broken bowls or chopsticks to cause noises at night.

In extreme cases, a builder might build a fragment of clay and a broken saw into a wall. This would betoken the death of the householder, remarriage of his wife (a family disgrace) and the dispersal of his family.

To counteract misfortunes, the houseowner could wall up an ink-stick or a cinnamon leaf to ensure descendants of the scholarly class, while a piece of wood and a length of string would ensure that no one would hang himself in the house.

SEE ALSO PAGES 74–77, 164–65

NATURAL RESOURCES

In common with most large countries China, taken as a whole, is rich in natural resources—that is, in the variety of naturally occurring phenomena that man may draw upon.

But resources are not, usually, simply "there for the taking". They must be identified and surveyed, and they require capitalization—sometimes on a huge scale—for access as well as extraction. The process of extraction may also present problems of pollution and threaten the environment. Moreover, although China as a nation may be considered rich in resources (and, in some, such as arable land, coal, and hydroelectric potential, exceptionally rich), this abundance is still not in proportion to the country's immense population.

Natural resources may be unrelated to one another, like water and coal; or negatively related, like forest and farmland—forest may have to be cut down to provide farmland. A resource such as coal may occur either where another resource (such as farmland) is strong, as in the northeast; or where the other is weak, as in the central north (Inner Mongolia, Gansu). Regions such as Henan are rich in many kinds of resource; others, such as Tibet, are, as far as is known, poor.

China's land resources can be divided into seven categories primarily in terms of present use. The seven, shown on the map, fall into two main groups: wild environments and arable or part-arable areas. The first four categories indicated in the map key represent a variety of wild environments. Forest is essentially a residual category. Most of eastern China was originally forested, but forest now remains only in peripheral, inaccessible areas, including some in the southeast, which are classified as arable with forest.

The other three classifications in the wild environment group cover the Central Asian part of China: high mountains with prairie and forest; desert and high elevation cold prairie. Deserts in China are either rock surfaces or sand seas; their summers are hot, but winters extremely cold.

All four wild environment categories combined support only about 5 percent of the Chinese population—mainly the nomadic peoples of Central Asian origin. Herding of animals and overland trade are their traditional occupations, although, as can be seen on the map, there are important arable pockets, where agriculture is being increasingly encouraged by the Chinese government.

Chinese civilization, the nomadic tradition apart, has been firmly based on agriculture since Neolithic times. The other three categories which are shown as arable or part-arable represent the results of a long-term process, whereby the climatically most favoured and most accessible parts of the wild environment were adapted for cultivation.

This process is oldest, and has most transformed the environment, in the North China Plain (Hebei,

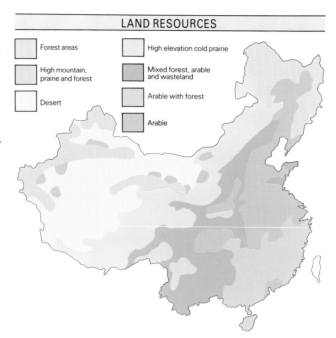

LAND RESOURCES

- Forest areas
- High mountain, prairie and forest
- Desert
- High elevation cold prairie
- Mixed forest, arable and wasteland
- Arable with forest
- Arable

The first four categories on the map are wild environments. The remaining three are areas that have been cultivated and changed to varying degrees and are now arable or part-arable.

China's hydroelectric potential is immense—greater, perhaps, than that of any other country in the world. But the huge cost of harnessing this energy has prevented its full exploitation. This picture of a dam being constructed at Longyangxia in Qinghai Province gives an indication of the scale and complexity of such operations.

Henan, Shandong) and its outlier to the west, in southern Shaanxi and Shanxi.

Continuous colonization, from before the first century AD onward, extended this original agricultural zone south to the Yangtze River and into Sichuan. Over the past century a comparable development has extended it into the northeast. But most of the southeastern corner of China is still represented as arable with forest. In this geographically diverse area of interlocking mountain chains, plains and basins, agriculture is usually restricted to level land suitable for paddy rice.

The arable regions of the east are bordered inland by a vast belt, lying northeast to southwest, of mixed forest, arable and wasteland. Conditions in the belt vary considerably, but the causes of limitation of agriculture in the region as a whole are a blend of topographical, climatic and other natural factors related to the environment; on the southern section there are precipitous mountains with patches of forest, denuded hillsides and isolation; in the northern sections, dry plateau country with ramifying gulleys.

Mountains comprise a significant "negative" feature of Chinese land resource. About half the country's area is mountainous, with characteristic problems of isolation and backwardness.

China's great size itself has a negative aspect. Where natural resource is relatively plentiful, as in the eastern half of the country, size may be regarded as an asset; but where it is sparsely distributed, as in the western half, the vast distance between the widely scattered settled areas becomes a burden, particularly for transportation by land.

Farmland is China's most valuable resource. In this part of Guizhou Province in southern China every available inch is planted with crops, and terracing extends the cultivated areas onto the hillsides. Flanking this productive arable land are wild environments—forest and high mountains.

NATURAL RESOURCES/2

FARMLAND

Moisture, warmth and soil determine the quality and extent of this, China's most important resource.

● MOISTURE
The map shows the distribution of natural surplus and deficiency in water supply (precipitation as compared to evaporation and transpiration). It shows, for example, that some areas have 400 mm (16 in) less than they need and other areas 400 mm (16 in) more. Broadly, northern China is dry, as is the west. Southern China is wet.

● WARMTH
The number of frost-free days in the year is shown on the map. This indicates the length of summer in each part of China, and, predictably, suggests a much stronger foundation for agriculture in the southeast of the country than in the north and west. (Maps for summer and winter isotherms are on pp. 36 and 37.)

● SOILS
The soils of western China are of mountain and desert types, while those of the east are of forest and prairie types.

In eastern China, the soils of the subtropical south are generally moist, poor in lime, but rich in iron and manganese compounds, sticky and water-retentive— hence suited to paddy rice.

Those of the north are generally dry, often rich in lime, fertile, but not water-retentive—much more suitable for "dry" crops such as wheat, millet and potatoes than for rice.

RAINFALL

Figures in millimetres of rainfall equivalent (25 mm = 1 in) per year

- –400
- 0 to –400
- 0 to +400
- +400

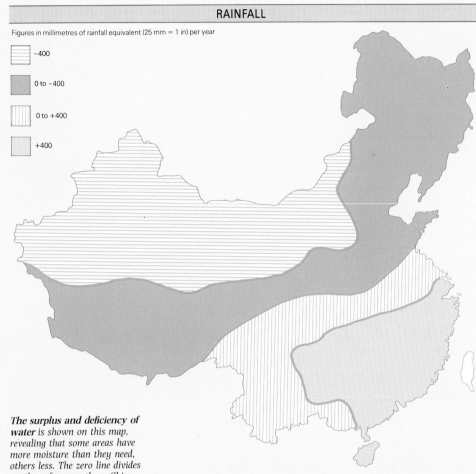

The surplus and deficiency of water is shown on this map, revealing that some areas have more moisture than they need, others less. The zero line divides northern from southern China.

FROST-FREE DAYS

Number of frost-free days per year

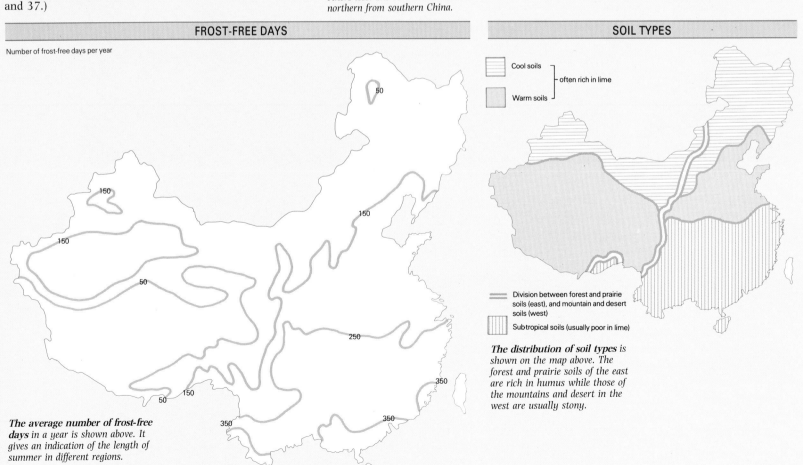

The average number of frost-free days in a year is shown above. It gives an indication of the length of summer in different regions.

SOIL TYPES

- Cool soils ⎤
- ⎥ often rich in lime
- Warm soils ⎦

— Division between forest and prairie soils (east), and mountain and desert soils (west)

‖ Subtropical soils (usually poor in lime)

The distribution of soil types is shown on the map above. The forest and prairie soils of the east are rich in humus while those of the mountains and desert in the west are usually stony.

FORESTS

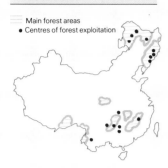

☰ Main forest areas
● Centres of forest exploitation

Large areas of forest have been cleared to provide fuel and agricultural land. Only 11 percent of China's land is now forested.

Eastern China was originally forested, but after more than 2,000 years of settlement by generally dense populations, little of the original cover remains.

Forests now occupy mainly inaccessible mountain regions at the fringes of the country in south and north, together with pockets of difficult mountainous environments in the southeast and centre. Timber resources in southern China include bamboo (used for scaffolding, among many other functions), as well as hardwood; softwoods are more typical in the forested areas of the northeast of the country.

China's timber resources have come under mounting pressure during the 20th century, due to improved transportation, mechanical handling and the increasing demand for fuel. Also, some forests have been cleared for agriculture or plantation crops. The total forested area has thus been reduced and reafforestation programmes have not always been successful because of management problems and physical difficulties.

Forest now accounts for around 11 percent of China's total area. Official policy proposes a rapid increase in this figure, but it will be difficult to manage in the face of environmental constraints (such as inaccessibility and drought) and alternative preoccupations (such as cost and the need for farmland and firewood) in the rural community.

WATER RESOURCES

In general, southern China has a natural surplus of water, while northern and western China are deficient (see farmland map opposite). Both experience appreciable differences between summer, when water is relatively abundant (particularly in the south), and winter, when water is relatively scarce (sometimes extremely so in the north and west).

Serious drought can occur in northern China, even in summer; while in the south, summer floods are not uncommon. Crop irrigation in the south is usually by diverted streams; in the north, usually from wells.

Urban water supplies call for investment in storage and distribution systems, as well as adequate amounts of water. Although there has been heavy investment in the necessary installations, supplies are still often inadequate—seriously so in some cities of the north, where there are shortages and periodic rationing.

Abundance of rainfall in the south leads to good flow in most rivers, and hence the widespread use of water transport. In the north (and still more so in the inland west), natural flow in rivers is often scanty and always unreliable, so that water transport is far less common.

MINERAL ORES

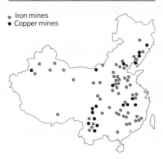

● Iron mines
● Copper mines

Extraction of mineral ores is concentrated in the east, but it is likely that there are sources yet to be discovered in the west.

In assessing whether or not metallic ores and other non-hydrocarbon minerals are a potentially valuable natural resource, various related geological and physiographic factors are taken into account. The most significant are the chemical characteristics of the different rocks and the extent to which those rocks that contain useful minerals in an exploitable form are obtainable.

Many minerals, such as iron, occur naturally in more than one chemical form, and in more than one kind of rock formation. In China these factors produce a widespread distribution of minerals in mountains in both north and south, where older crystalline rocks are exposed.

Although a great deal of scientific prospecting has taken place in China during the 20th century (mostly since 1949), it is likely that ore-bodies remain to be discovered in various remote parts of the country—in particular, the west, the southwest and the northeast.

At the other end of the scale, in "old" China (which is the densely populated southeastern third of the country) there has been extensive mining of ores (mainly iron and copper) for more than 2,000 years.

Small local mining enterprises are probably still operating in many of these ancient sites, mostly owned and run by villages or towns. However, in principle, all Chinese minerals are owned by the state.

ENERGY

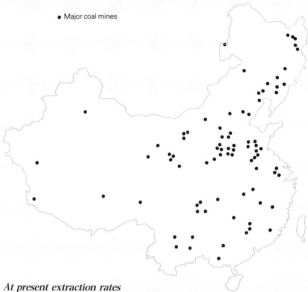

● Major coal mines

At present extraction rates China's coal deposits are expected to last for well over 100 years.

● COAL
China contributes about 18 percent of world coal output, and ranks with the United States and the USSR among the top producers.

China's coal reserves are concentrated in the north of the country, in northern Shanxi, Shaanxi and Gansu. In these provinces, huge deposits remain untouched because of their isolation. Shanxi, however, produces about 24 percent of China's total output, much of it from open-cast mining. About half of Shanxi's output is from local mines operated by villages and towns.

Large deposits in the southwest are exploited only to a limited degree, again due to isolation and the enormous investment required to set up extraction processes and transport.

● Major hydroelectric installations
● Oil wells
● Natural gas sources

Only a part of China's oil, gas and hydroelectric potential has so far been exploited.

● OIL AND GAS
China produces about 4 percent of world oil output, some 134 million tonnes in 1987. About half this oil output comes from northeastern China and most of the rest from the shores of the Bohai Gulf in Hebei or Shandong. There are also plans to develop what are thought to be rich offshore reserves in both the East and South China Seas.

At an official level there is conflict between the internal needs of industry and transport, and the profits to be won from exports, most of which go to Japan.

● HYDROELECTRIC POWER
China probably possesses the world's greatest potential resources of hydroelectric power, but is unable to exploit them fully at present. This is due to the inaccessible locations of the resource and to the huge capital investment required. One major site that is under construction is the Gezhouba project on the upper reaches of the Yangtze.

Water power is exploited and administered on two main levels: local installations in the mountainous southeast; and substantial, state-financed projects on the upper reaches of major rivers such as the Yangtze and Yellow River.

SEE ALSO PAGES 36–37, 154–57, 164–65

AGRICULTURE

In China some 7 percent of the world's cultivated land supports more than 20 percent of the world's human population in almost all its needs for food and clothing. Two key factors that make this remarkable achievement possible are the availability of a huge labour force and the high quality of much of the cultivable land.

There is as yet little mechanization in Chinese agriculture, but a vast supply of workers is available for labour-intensive tasks such as sowing and gathering crops. Plentiful labour also assists the common practice of growing more than one crop in the year. Double cropping has evolved over several centuries during which the rural population has quadrupled or more.

Labour-intensive agricultural methods are now at odds with official policy, however. It is generally acknowledged that up to one-third of the agricultural labour force is superfluous, and that with continual modernization and high-earning, better-motivated workers, this proportion is going to increase. The state would like to see these "excess" farm workers take non-agricultural employment in future. The new jobs might be in local industry in villages or country towns, in processing locally produced crops, or in rural services such as commerce and transport (still much in need of development). There may also be jobs in nearby cities.

About 50 percent of the agricultural land in China, mainly that in the subtropical south, is of excellent quality. Much of the rest is fertile lowland which can produce good crops provided it is not affected by drought or flood.

In a country as large in China natural conditions vary greatly from region to region with consequent variations in agricultural development. Major differences are those in rainfall and the duration and intensity of cold in winter (see pages 36 to 37). All parts of China are dry in winter; in summer, the subtropical south gets abundant rain, but in the north rainfall is barely enough to support crops and may be inadequate. The length of the winter determines whether or not the land can produce more than one crop in the year.

Farming in China is no longer collective. Villages, which own the land, allocate it to individual families who sign contracts promising agreed outputs. The state is eager to increase the commercial aspect of farming, both in food crops and in the rearing of such livestock as pigs and chickens. Some official opinion would like to see bigger farms. Commercialization has been most successful where reliable markets are close by—that is, in the immediate (30 km/20 mi or less) vicinity of cities. In these areas some peasants already enjoy incomes above those of city dwellers. But in many their land is also under threat from urban growth; since 1957 about 10 percent of China's arable land has been lost to industry, housing, roads, airfields and reservoirs.

The main form of direct state intervention in agriculture is the contract system intended to guarantee the supply of grain to the cities. State procurement agents negotiate with local units for supplies at standard prices, with "bonuses" such as fertilizer. The grain is then produced by households who accept these arrangements.

Grain farming is rarely highly profitable, although both yields and output have risen with the increasing use of modern agricultural methods. Commercial outputs such as pigs and poultry, industrial crops such as sugar and cotton, and vegetable and mushroom farming in the most fertile areas (or where there are urban markets) are the most reliable routes to prosperity on the land.

Modern inputs to agriculture are of growing importance, notably where two harvests are habitually taken in one year, sometimes of the same crop. Traditional coarse organic fertilizers are increasingly supplemented by artificial mixtures; chemical pesticides and herbicides are used; new "green revolution" varieties more widely introduced. Some problems with the chemical pollution of water and soil have been reported as a result of these measures, but the use of modern agricultural techniques is a clear trend for the future.

Harvesting cabbages, in Guangdong Province (above), is backbreaking work. It is also highly labour intensive—each cabbage has to be uprooted by hand, then upturned and left in a neat row along with thousands of others to be picked up later.
Vegetable growing is a thriving business in the fertile, low-lying province of Guangdong. In this mild southern climate crops can be grown throughout the year and high yields find a huge ready market in nearby Hong Kong as well as locally.

Thousands upon thousands of maize cobs are stacked in serried rows, making golden walls of grain (right). Maize is the third most important grain crop in China, after rice and wheat, and every bit of the plant is used. The kernels from the cobs are eaten whole or ground into maize flour from which a heavy steamed bread is baked. Husks, dry cobs and other parts unfit for human consumption are fed to pigs.

AGRICULTURE/2

AGRICULTURAL REGIONS

The 6 regions shown in the map together cover the whole country. They are:
- **Central Asian China**
Herding region with agriculture locally.
- **Northeast and North**
One crop annually.
- **North China Plain**
Three crops in two years.
- **Southeast**
Two rice crops annually.
- **Centre-East**
Two crops annually—rice (summer) and wheat (winter).
- **Southwest**
Mountainous area. One or two crops, such as rice, annually.

All but Central Asian China, where herding of animals is the dominant activity, are agricultural regions, but the proportion of land area used for farming differs greatly from region to region.

Northeast and North, Southeast and Southwest all have major mountain chains with large forests, which reduce the available cultivable land.

Even in the North China Plain, a major agricultural region, farmland takes up only 40 percent of the total area, and in the Southeast about 16 percent.

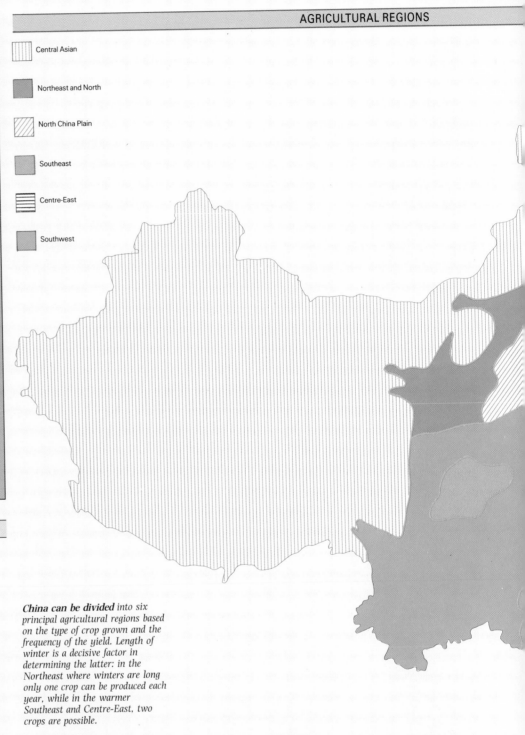

AGRICULTURAL REGIONS

- Central Asian
- Northeast and North
- North China Plain
- Southeast
- Centre-East
- Southwest

China can be divided into six principal agricultural regions based on the type of crop grown and the frequency of the yield. Length of winter is a decisive factor in determining the latter: in the Northeast where winters are long only one crop can be produced each year, while in the warmer Southeast and Centre-East, two crops are possible.

CENTRAL ASIAN CHINA

Almost half China's area is part of the vast Central Asian region of mountain ranges with desert plateaus and basins, which extends as far as Iran. Summers are hot, winters extremely cold; and water is always scarce.

The indigenous populations, such as Mongolians and Uygurs, are nomadic, and have their own languages and social structures. Their traditional livelihood is herding—horses, goats, asses and camels—rather than agriculture.

While the emphasis remains on the nomadic, herding way of life, agriculture has been increasingly developed. The main food crops are wheat and maize; other important crops are cotton and fruits such as melons, grapes and apricots.

THE NORTHEAST AND NORTH

Harsh winters generally restrict crop growing to the summer in Northeast and North China. Spring wheat, maize and millet are the standard grain crops, together with potatoes and soy beans—the latter are an important food in China.

Commercial crops are sugar beet, stone fruits, such as apricots and peaches, and apples. The northern part of the region is an important source of state supplies of commodity grain.

The southwest part of this region lies on the loess plateau. This is an area of soft, loose soil—fertile once stabilized—and is subject to periods of drought. Having been settled and cultivated for centuries, the naturally fragile environment is under heavy human pressure.

THE NORTH CHINA PLAIN

As the homeland of Chinese civilization, the North China Plain has been intensively cultivated for more than 3,000 years; little or nothing of the original forest environment still survives.

Winters are short and sunny, but cold; summers are hot, but rainfall is not reliable. Irrigation from wells and diverted rivers is now widely available.

Agriculture is centred on food crops for the local population, which, without taking the cities (such as Beijing) into account, is now around 250 million.

The main grain crops are wheat in winter, and millet, maize, sweet potatoes and soy beans in summer. The main commercial crops are cotton, tobacco, orchard fruits and peanuts.

The most common cultivation systems produce 3 crops in 2 years—for example, summer millet, followed by winter wheat (sown in October and harvested in May), followed by cotton.

Favoured areas of the plain may grow 2 crops in a year, but these cannot include cotton which needs a long growing season.

THE SOUTHEAST

The topography of the Southeast region is one of complex mountain chains interspersed with valleys, basins and plains. Rice growing, which requires level land for the sake of water control, is confined to the lowland areas, but other crops—particularly tea plantations and orchards—have replaced forest on the hillsides; some have also been terraced for rice growing.

Rice is the staple food crop of the Southeast and the growing of 2 crops annually is common. The first is sown in March, transplanted in May and harvested in July; the second is sown in June,

transplanted in August and harvested in November. Abundant supplies of workers are needed for this labour-intensive cultivation and the land must be kept well fertilized.

Winter crops, typically winter wheat or even sweet potatoes, are sometimes alternated with summer rice.

Commercial crops include cotton, silk (from silkworms fed on mulberry leaves), sugar cane, peanuts, oranges and lychees. Fishing and the keeping of pigs and poultry are also sources of income. A number of provinces in this region, such as Hunan and Guangdong, supply surplus grain to the state.

THE SOUTHWEST

Southwest China is isolated by its extremely rugged topography—high mountain chains, deep valleys and gorges which are peripheral to the main mountain ranges of Tibet such as the Himalayas.

Less than 10 percent of the land is cultivated. In spite of its proximity to the tropics, high elevations keep summer temperatures moderate—producing the climate often described by Chinese writers as "perpetual spring".

The variable character of agriculture in the Southwest is due to differences in physical conditions, local population density and accessibility of commercial outlets, in a region where isolation tends to restrict both trade and rural modernization.

Rice is the usual crop on level land; on the hillsides maize, millet and sweet potatoes are grown. Winter wheat may alternate with summer rice, giving 2 crops in the year where conditions permit or there may be 3 crops in 2 years.

Tobacco and tea are the major commercial crops in the Southwest. Forestry, too, is important, and there are some rubber plantations.

THE CENTRE-EAST

Agriculture in this densely populated and highly urbanized area, upstream from the mouth of the Yangtze, is both intensely commercialized and quite exceptionally developed. Rural areas are densely populated and there is an abundance of local urban markets.

Staple food production is based on alternating a

summer rice crop (June–October) with a winter wheat crop (October–May). Some localities, however, grow 2 rice crops, as in the Southeast.

Commercial crops include oilseed rape (a winter crop in southern China, harvested in late spring like wheat), cotton and peanuts. Tea, silk and a variety of orchard fruits is produced on

permanent plantations.

In spite of its population density, the rural Centre-East is an area of food surplus. As the local commercial economy develops, encouraged by the present political climate, families are involved increasingly in the direct supply of pork, eggs, fish, vegetables and fruit to the free markets in the large urban centres.

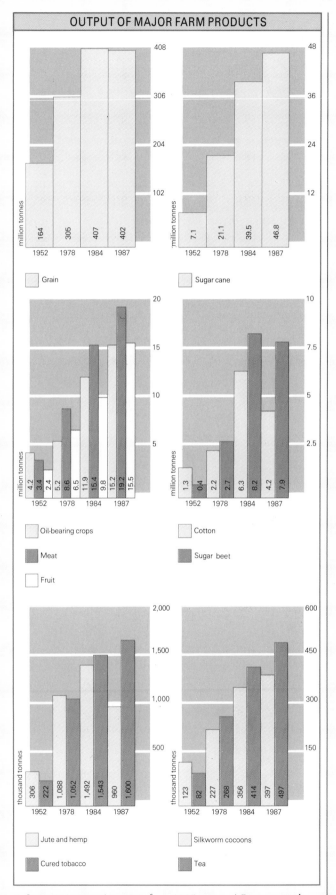

OUTPUT OF MAJOR FARM PRODUCTS

Grain (million tonnes): 1952: 164; 1978: 305; 1984: 407; 1987: 402

Sugar cane (million tonnes): 1952: 7.1; 1978: 21.1; 1984: 39.5; 1987: 46.8

Oil-bearing crops / Meat / Fruit (million tonnes): 1952: 4.2, 3.4, 2.4; 1978: 5.2, 8.6, 6.5; 1984: 11.9, 15.4, 9.8; 1987: 15.2, 19.2, 15.5

Cotton / Sugar beet (million tonnes): 1952: 1.3, 0.4; 1978: 2.2, 2.7; 1984: 6.3, 8.2; 1987: 4.2, 7.9

Jute and hemp / Cured tobacco (thousand tonnes): 1952: 306, 222; 1978: 1,088, 1,052; 1984: 1,492, 1,543; 1987: 960, 1,600

Silkworm cocoons / Tea (thousand tonnes): 1952: 123, 82; 1978: 227, 268; 1984: 356, 414; 1987: 397, 497

A dramatic increase in output of most major agricultural products followed the economic and rural reforms of 1978. Total output in 1987 was up 4.7 percent on the previous year. In 1987, too, grain neared its 1984 record level after reduced outputs in 1985 and 1986.

SEE ALSO PAGES 150–3

LIGHT INDUSTRY

Following the formation of the People's Republic in 1949, the economic emphasis in China was on the building up of heavy industry. It then took some ten years of intensive investment for the output of heavy industry, low prior to 1949, to equal that of light industry. But with the reforms announced in 1978, the pattern began to change again. The emphasis gradually shifted back from heavy to light industry, in particular to sectors such as food, textiles and machine building.

One innovative effect of the new policies was the starting up of "rural industries". Since 1978 people in rural areas, some 70 to 80 percent of the population, have been free to start collectives—enterprises under collective ownership and run by townships and villages—making light industrial products to sell to the state. Any surplus above their planned state targets can be sold on the open market. In 1984 "urban reforms" were announced that allowed city dwellers, too, to start collectives.

As a result of these reforms the value of light industrial output doubled in the period 1978 to 1985, with an average annual growth rate of some 13 percent. In fact, in the first half of 1985 the growth rate in light industry was so great—at some 23 percent—that it could not be sustained by the rest of the economy. Supplies of electricity and basic materials could not keep pace with demands made by the burgeoning light industry, and production had to slow down again.

Since the early 1980s there has been a further development of private enterprise and free market trade in both rural and urban areas. In 1985 private enterprise accounted for some 16 percent of total retail sales volume, collectives for about 37 percent, state-owned enterprise for 40 percent and sales by peasants for about 7 percent. In 1987 official surveys indicated that over nine million households and about thirteen million people were engaged in private commerce, catering and service trades.

Overall the total value of retail sales increased more than threefold between 1978 and 1986 (inflation has remained low). In 1988 consumption levels in rural areas, though, were still lower than those in urban areas. Thus, with only 20 percent of the population, urban areas absorb some 45 percent of the total retail volume.

However, problems remain on the domestic market. In the late 1980s growth in output of manufactured goods lagged behind increased purchasing power and demand. There was a shortage of some marketable goods such as high-quality electrical and electronic goods. Conversely, there was a surplus of low-quality goods, particularly of certain domestic electrical appliances and outmoded garments. In 1986 there was a nationwide "glut" of wristwatches: twice as many were produced as were bought.

The expansion of light industry has helped China

Foreign imports are seen as status symbols and a Japanese manufacturer of electrical goods dominates this advertisement hoarding in Beijing. Although Chinese production of such consumer goods as television sets and cassette recorders has soared since the late 1970s, many people still prefer imports, particularly from Japan. With import duty, they cost more than the home-produced versions, but they are generally of more modern design and superior quality.

improve its trade with the rest of the world. Since the economic reforms of 1978 it has nearly doubled its share of world trade from 0.75 percent to some 1.40 percent in 1986. This increase has been achieved by switching the bulk of its exports from raw materials and minerals to semi-manufactured (such as silk and cotton fabrics) and manufactured light industrial products. The latter now account for about 64 percent of total Chinese exports, compared with only 46 percent in 1978.

Traditionally Chinese export products have been

textiles such as cotton, silk, carpets and embroidery, basketwork, ceramics, porcelain, and fireworks and firecrackers. (The Chinese invented gunpowder and fireworks as early as the ninth century.) Textiles and clothing are now more important than ever. They already earn one-quarter of the country's foreign exchange and exports are increasing every year. Such luxury items as mink and pearls are also important exports. China produces 90 percent of the world total of freshwater pearls, and her South Seas or Hepu pearl is regarded as better than other cultured pearls and is

far more expensive. China's mink exports account for 10 percent of world volume.

Light industry has been given priority over heavy industry in plans for China's future development. This is partly in order to meet domestic demand, and partly to increase foreign currency earnings from the export of these products. But the problem remains—and will do for some time to come—of the imbalance between supply and demand, and the inability of the manufacturers to adapt rapidly enough to meet the growth of China's purchasing power.

In a silk factory at Hangzhou in *Zhejiang Province, women workers operating reeling machines process one of China's most famous exports. Ninety percent of the raw silk on the world market comes from China and the product is an important foreign exchange earner.*

Hangzhou has been a major centre for silk production since as long ago as the 7th century and is often referred to as "silk city".

LIGHT INDUSTRY/2

LIGHT INDUSTRIAL OUTPUT

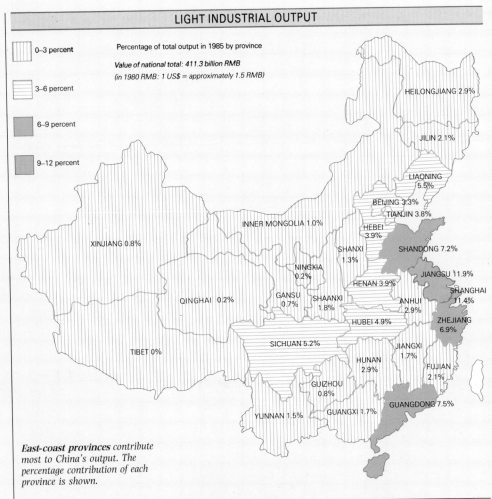

0–3 percent

3–6 percent

6–9 percent

9–12 percent

Percentage of total output in 1985 by province

Value of national total: 411.3 billion RMB

(in 1980 RMB: 1 US$ = approximately 1.5 RMB)

HEILONGJIANG 2.9%

JILIN 2.1%

LIAONING 5.5%

BEIJING 3.3%

TIANJIN 3.8%

INNER MONGOLIA 1.0%

HEBEI 3.9%

XINJIANG 0.8%

SHANXI 1.3%

SHANDONG 7.2%

NINGXIA 0.2%

JIANGSU 11.9%

HENAN 3.9%

SHANGHAI 11.4%

QINGHAI 0.2%

GANSU 0.7%

SHAANXI 1.8%

ANHUI 2.9%

ZHEJIANG 6.9%

HUBEI 4.9%

TIBET 0%

SICHUAN 5.2%

JIANGXI 1.7%

HUNAN 2.9%

FUJIAN 2.1%

GUIZHOU 0.8%

GUANGDONG 7.5%

YUNNAN 1.5%

GUANGXI 1.7%

East-coast provinces contribute most to China's output. The percentage contribution of each province is shown.

Every province in China has some light industry but output varies greatly. Five provinces—Jiangsu, Guangdong, Shandong, Zhejiang, and Liaoning—and the municipality of Shanghai account for more than 50 percent of total light industrial output although they have only some 28 percent of China's total population.

Some branches of light industry are concentrated in particular areas. Shanghai municipality, for example, is noted for the production of textiles and clothing, sewing machines (32 percent of the country's total), bicycles, radios and TV sets.

Jiangsu produces 35 percent of total salt output, 35 percent of radios and 15 percent of China's textile and clothing output.

Guangdong produces 38 percent of total sugar output, as well as many household appliances, such as refrigerators, washing machines and cameras.

TYPES OF LIGHT INDUSTRY

Food and textiles are the main industries, accounting respectively for 23 percent and 31 percent of light industrial output.

In the food industry leading sections are food processing and edible oils, slaughtering and meat processing, and tobacco (classified as "food"). In textiles, cotton is the most important product, with synthetics, wool and silk accounting for smaller, roughly equal shares of the output.

Next in importance is machine building (14 percent of the total), including such consumer goods as bicycles, TV sets, washing machines, cassette recorders and electrical and electronic appliances.

The chemical industry accounts for 9 percent of light industrial output, with pharmaceuticals being the largest branch.

Clothing and leather make

up nearly 7 percent. Cultural, educational and "art" articles (including printing) account for a further 5 percent of light industry, and the paper making industry 2 percent.

THE FOOD INDUSTRY

Output of canned food, sugar, other food products and tobacco (included in the food industry) more than doubled in the years between 1980 and 1986.

Canned food is an important export item. For example, China now leads the world in the export of canned mushrooms which are produced by many regions. A producer of both cane and beet sugar, China ranks sixth in the world in

sugar production. But the supply of sugar does not meet domestic demand and in 1987 it was rationed in several provinces.

In the years 1981 to 1985 the output of alcoholic drinks grew faster than it had ever done before. Soft drink output multiplied nearly 4 times in the same period (partly as a result of joint ventures with foreign firms such as the Coca-Cola company).

COMPONENTS OF LIGHT INDUSTRY

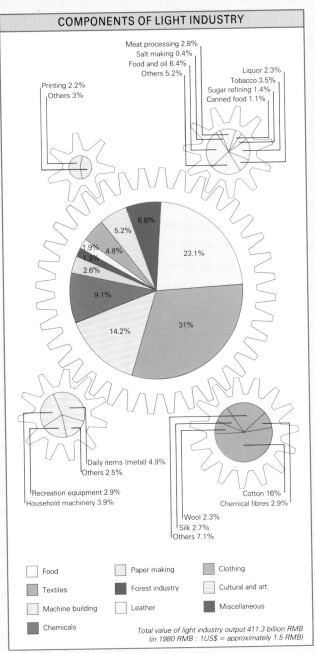

Meat processing 2.8%
Salt making 0.4%
Food and oil 6.4%
Others 5.2%

Liquor 2.3%
Tobacco 3.5%
Sugar refining 1.4%
Canned food 1.1%

Printing 2.2%
Others 3%

6.8%

5.2%

23.1%

1.9%

4.8%

1.3%

2.6%

31%

9.1%

14.2%

Daily items (metal) 4.9%
Others 2.5%

Recreation equipment 2.9%
Household machinery 3.9%

Cotton 16%
Chemical fibres 2.9%

Wool 2.3%
Silk 2.7%
Others 7.1%

Food

Textiles

Machine building

Chemicals

Paper making

Forest industry

Leather

Clothing

Cultural and art

Miscellaneous

Total value of light industry output 411.3 billion RMB (in 1980 RMB : 1US$ = approximately 1.5 RMB)

The food and textile industries together account for more than half of China's light industrial output.

The relative proportions of all the major sectors of light industry are shown above.

TEXTILES AND CLOTHING

In 1986 textiles and clothing became China's largest export item, accounting for a quarter of foreign currency earnings. China has a long history of producing textiles—cotton yarn and cloth, silk, linen and ramie as well as wool and synthetic fibres.

Silk is the textile for which it is most famed. More than half the world's silk is made in China and 90 percent of the raw silk on the world market is Chinese.

However, despite growth in the textile trade China's clothing exports still lag behind those of Hong Kong, Korea and Taiwan. China exports less of its textile product as clothing—25 percent, compared with 85 percent for Hong Kong, and the average unit price of its clothing exports is much lower. (In 1985 US $35.4 per dozen, compared with US $62 for Hong Kong.) The poor design and quality of some of the clothing compounds the problem.

In an effort to improve the textile industry's performance, a number of export-oriented enterprises are being expanded in coastal areas. Equipped with modern technology and with the emphasis on high-grade clothing and textiles, these enterprises should help to increase China's share of the world market.

MACHINE BUILDING

Output of many consumer durables, products of the machine building industry, has risen sharply since 1978.

In the period 1978 to 1985, for example, output of bicycles and wristwatches multiplied 4 times, of refrigerators 50 times, and of cassette recorders more than 80 times. In 1978 only a few thousand colour TV sets and a few hundred washing machines were manufactured so the increase in their output is even larger; production increased more than 1,000 times and 22,000 times respectively.

Since 1981 a computer industry—another rapidly expanding branch of machine building—has been established in China. According to official estimates, China will require 30 to 35 million micro-computers annually through the years 1988 to 1998 to meet its needs.

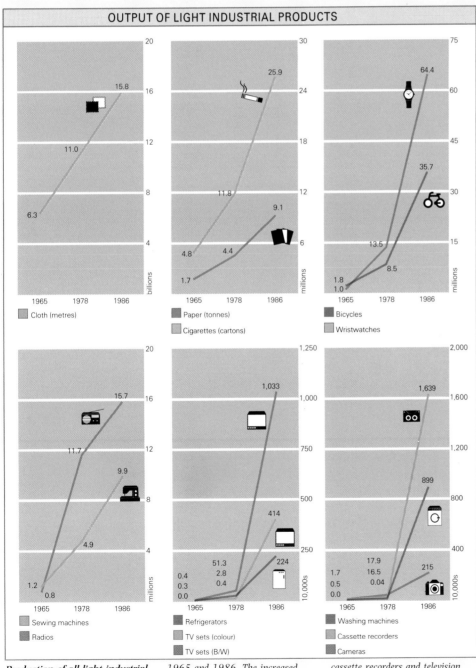

Production of all light industrial items rose dramatically between 1965 and 1986. The increased output of washing machines, cassette recorders and television sets has been particularly startling.

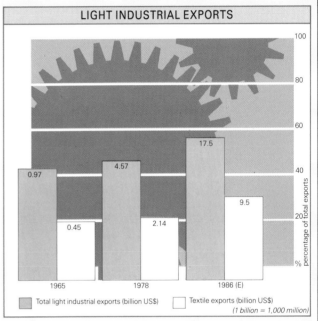

An increasing share of China's exports has been taken by light industrial products, particularly textiles. Estimated figures show that textiles made up 30 percent of total exports in 1986.

SUPPLY AND DEMAND OF CONSUMER DURABLES

The increase in supply of items such as TV sets, cassette recorders and washing machines has been in response to consumer demand. The strength of this demand was shown during 1985 when import controls were temporarily relaxed, resulting in a flood of imported goods, particularly from Japan.

This episode also served to highlight the fact that many consumers preferred imports because of their better quality and design.

The increased production of popular consumer durables, such as TV sets, radios and wristwatches, combined with a flood of imports, has led to market saturation. The result is a more quality-conscious market. Consumers are more inclined to pick and choose from the range available than to rush for whatever they can get.

China's policy is to protect its domestic industries. Electronics producers, for example, are encouraged to use domestic-made components wherever possible, provided these are of a sufficiently high quality. But to compete effectively with foreign imports, light industry needs to anticipate consumer demand with the appropriate high-quality products.

SEE ALSO PAGES 162–65

HEAVY INDUSTRY

Oil, steel, coal, electricity and machinery manufacture form the backbone of China's heavy industry. But outmoded technology and unmotivated workers have kept productivity low, and inadequate transportation, combined with entrenched bureaucracy and management, aggravate the problem.

China's heavy industry is based on a mixture of technologies, dating from the early 1900s to the mid-1980s. The first steps toward the modernization and expansion of the original industrial plants were made in the 1930s in Northeast China by the Japanese who occupied the area at that time. Further expansion took place in the 1950s with the assistance of the USSR. A period of stagnation followed, but after the Cultural Revolution, purchases from the West injected some modern technology into the industrial system and led to increased output.

When Deng Xiaoping came to power in 1978, he and his colleagues set out to reform the structure and technology of heavy industry. Some modern Western plant, such as that of the Baoshan steel complex near Shanghai, was swiftly ordered, mainly from Japan. Foreign exchange problems two years later put an end to such large-scale purchases, but since the early 1980s industries have been allowed to make selective imports to update existing factories. This policy has been reasonably beneficial, but foreign engineers have had problems in training unskilled Chinese workers to use the sophisticated imported technology.

China's size and topography, which make the movement of raw materials expensive and often difficult, create further problems for industry. The traditional heavy industrial centres are in Northeast China and Shanghai, with a few other key locations such as Wuhan in Hubei Province, and they must supply other manufacturers throughout China. Transporting high-grade steel from Anshan in Northeast China to the isolated Guiyang optical instruments factory hundreds of miles south in Guizhou, for example, is both slow and costly.

Raw materials are supposed to be obtained by government officials on behalf of the factory. These officials may have to negotiate through a pyramid of other officials in the appropriate ministry—none of whom has a direct interest in solving the factory's problems. Hence big factories often prefer to run their own subsidiaries to provide their fuel or other essentials, which adds to the proliferation of small and uneconomic plants.

Since 1984 the government has been trying to reform this unsatisfactory industrial structure. Factories have been encouraged to deal with suppliers or with one another "horizontally", that is, directly, instead of through intermediaries working up one ministerial hierarchy and down another. Since 1985 some basic commodities have been legally available outside the state marketing system, at a market price. Coal mines and steel plants, for instance, are allowed

to sell to other customers once they have fulfilled their state contracts.

Factory managers have also been given more freedom in running their enterprises. By 1988 most were operating according to new rules under which they borrow funds from the bank rather than being given a state grant, and pay taxes on profits instead of remitting their takings to the state. Many now guarantee a certain contribution to state revenues in return for increased decision-making powers under the new "contract responsibility system".

New approaches, such as allowing people to lease factories from the state, are being tried in an effort to change hidebound functionaries into entrepreneurs. Within factories, many managers now operate an internal "responsibility system" in which workshops are given quotas to produce. If quotas are exceeded workers receive a bonus, but if production falls short, they must pay a penalty.

Early 1988 saw another key change. A law separating the management of state-owned enterprises from the ownership was passed by the National People's Congress. This enterprise law frees managers from party control and gives them much greater powers to hire and fire, find their own suppliers and fix their own prices. It will make companies far more independent and free to decide for themselves what to produce and how to sell it.

The controversial bankruptcy law, under which loss-making businesses can be closed or merged with profitable ones, is due to be promulgated shortly after the enterprise law. These measures could be the decade's most important contribution to increasing China's industrial productivity.

China's biggest iron and steel works, at Anshan in Liaoning Province, employs about 200,000 workers. It was founded by the Japanese in 1918 during their occupation of Northeast China, and was modernized in the 1950s as part of a drive to expand heavy industry.

Present annual capacity is some seven million tonnes, but plans to import foreign technology to modernize the plant should both increase output and, more importantly, improve its quality. Although China ranks fourth in the world for steel production it is also one of the world's largest importers, being unable to produce enough high-grade steel for its own needs.

More than 100,000 workers are employed at the Shengli oilfield in Shandong. It covers an area of 47,000 sq km (18,200 sq mi) of northern China and is the second largest field in the country. In output it may soon rival China's biggest oilfield at Daqing which is now past its prime. Shengli's 1990 target is 50 million tonnes—one-third of the projected target for China as a whole by this date.

HEAVY INDUSTRY/2

STEEL

In 1987 China produced 55 million tonnes of steel, making it the world's fourth largest producer. Its target for 1990 is 60 million tonnes.

Quantity, therefore, is not a problem. But the steel industry suffers from the overall poor quality of its output and lack of special steels, largely because the technology of most of its plants is at least 30 years old. As a result, China is also one of the world's largest importers of steel: in 1987 it bought 15 million tonnes.

Ironically, in June 1987 the country had 30 million tonnes of steel unsold, either because of faults in manufacture or because of distribution difficulties. Moreover, some factories hoard steel because it is often hard to obtain when needed. As part of the overall economic reform, the government has tentatively initiated "free markets" in steel in an attempt to move these stocks.

China's one modern integrated steel complex, bought from Japan and West Germany, is at Baoshan, near Shanghai. The first stage was finished in 1985 and the second is due for completion in 1990, when production will be 3 million tonnes a year. With its sophisticated equipment and use of mainly imported, high-quality Australian ore, this plant has brought China's steel industry into the 1980s.

Other steel plants are antiquated. The biggest, Anshan in Liaoning, dates from 1918, though much equipment has been added since then, mostly in the 1950s. In recent years most major plants have installed some items of imported equipment and this has begun to update the industry.

HEAVY INDUSTRIAL OUTPUT

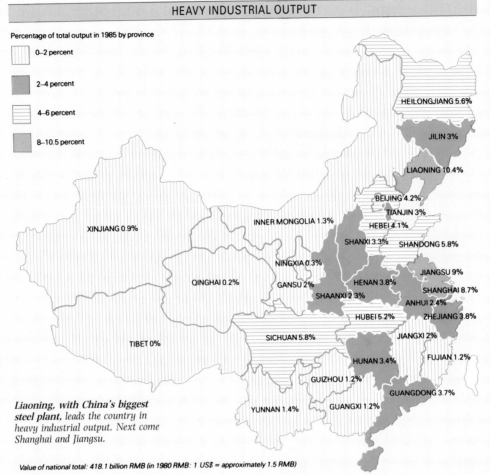

Percentage of total output in 1985 by province

- 0–2 percent
- 2–4 percent
- 4–6 percent
- 8–10.5 percent

HEILONGJIANG 5.6%
JILIN 3%
LIAONING 10.4%
BEIJING 4.2%
TIANJIN 3%
HEBEI 4.1%
INNER MONGOLIA 1.3%
XINJIANG 0.9%
SHANXI 3.3%
SHANDONG 5.8%
NINGXIA 0.3%
JIANGSU 9%
QINGHAI 0.2%
GANSU 2%
HENAN 3.8%
SHANGHAI 8.7%
SHAANXI 2.3%
ANHUI 2.4%
HUBEI 5.2%
ZHEJIANG 3.8%
TIBET 0%
SICHUAN 5.8%
JIANGXI 2%
FUJIAN 1.2%
HUNAN 3.4%
GUIZHOU 1.2%
GUANGDONG 3.7%
YUNNAN 1.4%
GUANGXI 1.2%

Liaoning, with China's biggest steel plant, leads the country in heavy industrial output. Next come Shanghai and Jiangsu.

Value of national total: 418.1 billion RMB (in 1980 RMB: 1 US$ = approximately 1.5 RMB)

COAL

More than 70 percent of China's energy is provided by coal, and this percentage is not expected to change significantly in the forseeable future. Production in 1987 was 900 million tonnes and is expected to reach 1.2 billion by the year 2000.

But the black smoke pouring from the chimneys in a way now rarely seen in the developed world, and the consequent pollution, is a symptom of the inefficient use of fuel. Three-quarters of the available energy is wasted: industrial boilers, which use about half the nation's coal, send some 85 percent up the smokestack.

Only about half of China's coal output comes from large, reasonably well-equipped mines. Small pits owned by local governments or collectives produce the rest. Many are just pick-and-shovel operations (notorious for their high accident rate), which have benefited from the relaxation of government controls over all industrial and economic activity.

AUTOMOTIVE INDUSTRY

In 1987 there were more than 3.4 million vehicles on the road in China, but about two-thirds dated from before 1980 and were built to 1950s designs. In response to growing demand for road transport, the country is speeding up vehicle modernization—for example, setting up joint ventures and buying new technology to equip factories.

Joint ventures with foreign motor manufacturers that have already been set up include Shanghai Santana (Volkswagen), Guangzhou Peugeot, Tianjin Daihatsu and Beijing Jeep (American Motor Corporation).

There was no significant passenger car industry in China until these factories went into production. In 1984–85, 100,000 vehicles were bought from Japan's Toyota company alone, and this heavy foreign expenditure pushed the government into setting up its own industry. In 1987 more than 400,000 motor vehicles were manufactured in China, an increase of 39 percent on 1986 figures.

Truck production, centred on Changchun in the northeast and Wuhan in the Yangtze valley, has always been important. But until 1987 only the 1950s "Liberation" lorry was produced. Each year Changchun also made a few hundred "Red Flags"—the prestigious curtained black sedans.

In 1987, in an attempt to leap the decades, the Changchun works bought machinery and technical help from the Chrysler Corporation. With this they aim to produce up to 300,000 engines a year for new designs of 2- and 3-ton trucks and a passenger car. This, the first car designed in China since the Red Flag, is expected to resemble the Toyota Crown.

OIL

After reaching a plateau of around 100 million tonnes per year in the early 1980s, China's oil production began to grow again in 1984. By 1987 it had touched 134 million tonnes. The rise probably resulted from successful explorations onshore after several unproductive years spent with foreign oilmen searching offshore for commercially exploitable sources.

Rich undersea reserves were confirmed in 1987 west of Hainan Island in the south, in the mouth of the Pearl River near Guangzhou, and in Liaodong Bay off China's northeast coast. However, extraction problems have discouraged the foreign companies who do not see the reserves as economic, given the falling price of oil on the international market. The Chinese are now working on their own at developing offshore wells in the East China Sea.

Onshore, about half of the country's oil comes from the field of Daqing in Heilongjiang. Discovered in the 1960s, the field is probably past its peak. Western technology introduced in the 1980s keeps output up by enhanced recovery techniques, but the costs are high. Most of the rest of China's current oil production comes from fields lying in a belt from south of Daqing to northern Jiangsu Province. The Shengli oilfield in Shandong is now the second largest in the country.

Small amounts of oil are produced in the far west of the country where there may be huge reserves. But, so far, exploration has been hampered by the difficult conditions of the mountainous and desert terrain and by lack of transport.

ELECTRICITY

Dim lighting and factories brought to a standstill by lack of power are a fact of life in China. Although the country's installed generating capacity grew from less than 70,000 megawatts in 1980 to 100,000 megawatts in 1987, the gaps in supply are still alarming. More than 20 percent of industrial capacity lay idle in 1987 because of power cuts. Power output in that year had increased by 10 percent on 1986 to 490 billion kilowatt/hours but with factory expansion and increased demand from urban consumers, this was still not enough to meet the need.

By the end of 1987 total generating capacity was 100,000 megawatts; the 1990 target is 120,000 megawatts. By 1988 about 70 percent was coal-fired and 30 percent hydro-powered, with the possibility of some 5 percent being nuclear by the end of the century.

Major problems are caused by the fact that coal reserves are mainly in northern China and hydroelectric power sources largely in the mountainous southwest, both far from the densely populated and industrial east. The dilemma, therefore, is whether to build minemouth plants, in order to cut out coal transport costs, or city power stations to avoid the expense of long transmission lines.

OUTPUT OF MAJOR HEAVY INDUSTRIAL PRODUCTS

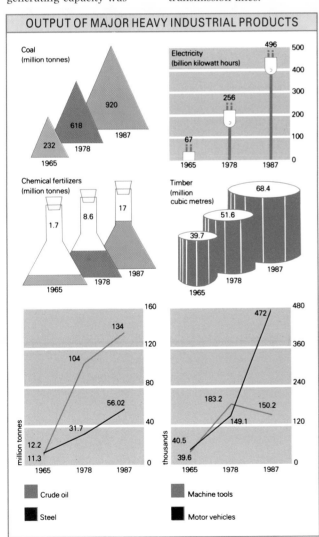

The production of coal, oil, steel and other major industrial items has increased substantially since the reforms of the late 1970s but is still not enough to fulfil the country's needs.

NUCLEAR POWER

Since the late 1970s China has been developing a nuclear power industry, but is unlikely to have a plant in operation before the end of the 1980s. First will be the 300-megawatt installation at Qinshan, near Shanghai, which is scheduled for completion in 1989.

Next, in 1992, will come the 1,800-MW Daya Bay plant, near Hong Kong. The nuclear element will be imported from France and the turbines from Britain.

The Qinshan and Daya Bay plants will provide a crucial boost to China's electricity generating capability. Eastern and southern parts of the country, many miles from coal or hydroelectric resources, have long been starved of power.

But China's ability to build a safe nuclear plant has been seriously questioned, especially since the USSR's Chernobyl disaster of 1986. Anxiety was heightened in 1987 when it was found that half the metal reinforcing rods for Daya Bay's foundations had been omitted.

Other nuclear plants at Sunan near Shanghai, and in Fujian Province, have been tentatively planned.

However, the cost of these, combined with environmental and safety problems, has made the nuclear programme a political "football". Plans announced in 1985 to build 10 nuclear power plants before the year 2000 have now been dropped.

COMPONENTS OF HEAVY INDUSTRY

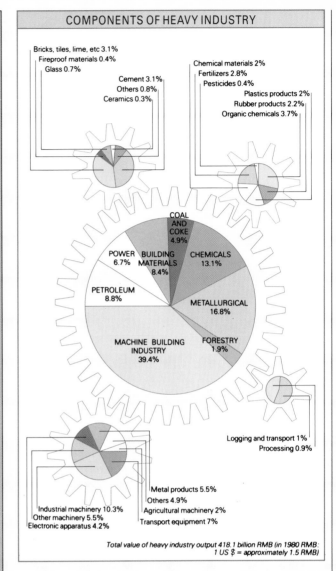

Total value of heavy industry output 418.1 billion RMB (in 1980 RMB: 1 US $ = approximately 1.5 RMB)

Machine building is the most important branch of heavy industry. It includes the manufacture of trucks, cars and industrial machinery, and accounts for more than a third of output.

THE SPACE INDUSTRY

World attention was focused on China's space industry in 1986, when it stepped into the breach left by disasters to the US shuttle, *Challenger*, and the French rocket, *Ariane*. The Chinese signed several contracts to launch satellites belonging to Western companies.

The space industry began in the 1950s, probably with aid from the USSR. Research, and the construction of a test base and launch pad, were followed in the 1970s by trial launches of satellites. The first, during the Cultural Revolution period, transmitted the anthem "The East is Red" as it spun around the globe.

Over the period 1970–87 there were about 21 launches, with several failures. There are 2 launch sites. One is at Jiuquan, a military test site in the desert in Gansu Province. The other, Xichang in Sichuan Province, is about 50 km (30 mi) from a military base where equipment is stored between launches.

Launchings are first tracked by the base and after the first 300 km (200 mi) or so by the Space Centre at Xi'an in Shaanxi Province.

In 1984 the Chinese successfully used their Long March 3 rocket to put their first telecommunications satellite into orbit.

SEE ALSO PAGES 150–53, 158–61

DEVELOPMENTS IN TRADE

The "Open Door" policy of promoting foreign economic relations has been one of the principal policies of the Chinese government in the late 1980s. This contrasts sharply with most of China's pre-revolutionary and post-revolutionary history.

Gone is the insular imperial China, typified by Emperor Qianlong's famous response in 1793 to British trading overtures: "We possess all things. I set no value on objects strange or ingenious, and I have no use for your country's manufactures." In its place is an outward-looking Beijing where there is at least one international trade exhibition, and sometimes two, taking place at any given time.

The Treaty Ports China opened so reluctantly in the mid- to late-nineteenth century are now the setting for lively negotiations. Shanghai and Guangzhou (Canton) are key exhibition venues, and it is in such trade fair surroundings that the informal introductions can be made which later blossom into business agreements. The ports have evolved as centres for the new development of foreign trade and investment.

The avoidance of economic dependence on Europe, America and Japan was originally a major tenet of Chinese Communist Party policy. But after 1949 a combination of Soviet help and Western opposition forced China to rely on the USSR, which became its main trading partner. After a decade of growing ideological divergence, China broke with the Soviet Union in 1960, and became isolated, both politically and economically. "Self-reliance" was seen as not only necessary but desirable; the value of trade and foreign technology were played down, so that the importance of such commerce in the economy was reduced significantly.

While this self-reliance helped China to develop its own capabilities, the country began to lag in international technological development. When in the early 1970s, China opted for increased involvement in the world economy, it began large-scale imports of foreign equipment and plant—for example in the chemical industry—and expanded exports.

The next change of direction came after the death of Mao in 1976 with the adoption of the Four Modernizations plan. Initially, this stressed the growth of China's oil exports to pay for imports of heavy industrial plant. By 1978 it was evident that oil production would not be adequate to realize such ambitious targets, while the further expansion of heavy industry exacerbated existing bottlenecks in the economy.

In the face of these problems, China's Open Door policy encourages both trade and foreign investment as part of its comprehensive economic reform. Both exports and imports are expected to be some 15 percent of national income by the early 1990s, having risen from under 5 percent in the early 1970s. Clearly China is entering into the world economy on a much larger scale than ever before.

However, relative to its population, China's involvement is still low compared with other countries. The contrast between the People's Republic and Taiwan whose population is only about one-fiftieth of that of mainland China is marked; in the mid-1980s Taiwan's trade with the rest of the world was roughly equal to that of the People's Republic of China.

Another part of the government's economic reforms is a break with the previous system of making foreign trade operate through state trading corporations. There have been two main changes: one, the decentralization of authority to local governments; the other, a growing independence for some enterprises who now conduct their own trade negotiations. Making the transition has been difficult, if desirable. Limiting the power of previous systems of administrative control was partly responsible for the huge trade deficits in the mid-1980s. However, a rapid growth in exports and other foreign exchange earners, such as tourism, has done much to alleviate this problem.

An expanding modern city of towering skyscrapers, Shenzhen (right) is the most advanced of the four Special Economic Zones, set up to attract foreign investment. In these zones, all centred on cities on China's south coast, foreign investors are granted preferential treatment. This includes cheap land and utilities, and greater management freedom than elsewhere in China.

A backlog of container cargo awaits shipment on the dockside at Shanghai, China's largest port (left). Although its annual handling capacity exceeds 90 million tonnes, Shanghai's facilities, like those of all ports in China, are overloaded. Expansion and modernization are urgently needed to cope with ever-increasing demands.

DEVELOPMENTS IN TRADE/2

SPECIAL ECONOMIC ZONES AND COASTAL CITIES

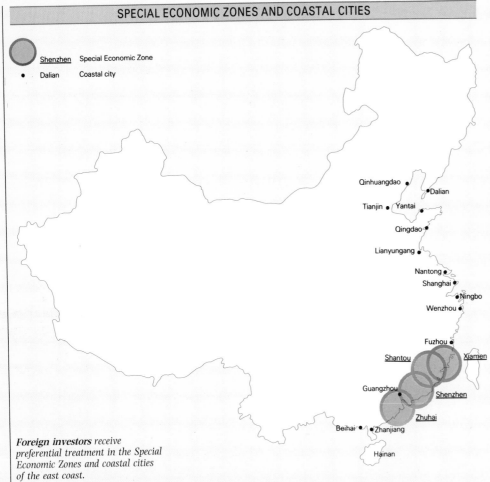

Shenzhen — Special Economic Zone

Dalian — Coastal city

Foreign investors receive *preferential treatment in the Special Economic Zones and coastal cities of the east coast.*

EXPORTS

China's exports increased rapidly during the 1970s, and even more so in the 1980s. By the mid-1980s, they were more than 10 times their 1970 level.

Following the severe trade deficit in 1985, exports grew quickly. This was partly due to the devaluation of the yuan against the US dollar.

In 1985 primary products accounted for 51 percent of commodity exports. These included:

● 25 percent oil exports
● 14 percent food products
● 10 percent non-food agricultural and animal products

Major items of the 49 percent of exported manufactures were:

● 12 percent textiles
● 8 percent garments
● 5 percent chemical and related products

In 1986 China's export revenues declined with world oil prices. Toward the end of the decade, however, the importance of manufactured goods (such as electronic items) was increasing relative to primary products.

Earnings from tourism and overseas labour contracts have also helped to offset a negative trade balance.

TRADING PARTNERS

Having suffered from its dependence on the Soviet Union for trade in the 1950s, China has since the 1970s sought to diversify its partners and, in the late 1980s, is increasing its trade with most areas of the world.

China's trade is now centred on certain of its near neighbours and the more advanced industrial nations, rather than Third World or other socialist countries. In 1985 China's main trading partners were:

● Japan (30 percent)
● Europe (21 percent)
● Hong Kong (17 percent)
● USA (11 percent)
● USSR (3 percent)

SPECIAL ECONOMIC ZONES

In 1980, in an attempt to encourage more foreign investment, China created 4 Special Economic Zones. The zones, all in southeastern China, are around Shenzhen, Zhuhai, Shantou and Xiamen.

Within these zones foreign investors receive preferential treatment, including:

● Low corporate tax rates
● Reduced—or zero—taxes for several years after establishing certain new businesses
● Cheap land and utilities
● Reduced formalities and greater management freedom, compared with the rest of China

Fourteen coastal cities and Hainan Island were also given similar, but less extensive, incentives.

The economic performance of the zones, which were officially aimed at exploiting foreign capital, technology and management in export-oriented industries, proved disappointing at first. Much of the investment was in the service sector, and the level of imported technology was often low.

In the late 1980s, however, exports increased substantially, as a result of greater emphasis on export-oriented industry.

Politically, the zones are seen as playing a part in persuading Hong Kong, Macao, and ultimately Taiwan, that reunification with China will not entail either a fall in living standards or unacceptable social change.

Early 1988 saw plans for the creation of further "open areas" in the coastal region. The State Council also recommended that Hainan Island be made a province and that it should become China's largest Special Economic Zone. It is hoped that Hainan will compete with Taiwan and Hong Kong.

MAJOR TRADING PARTNERS

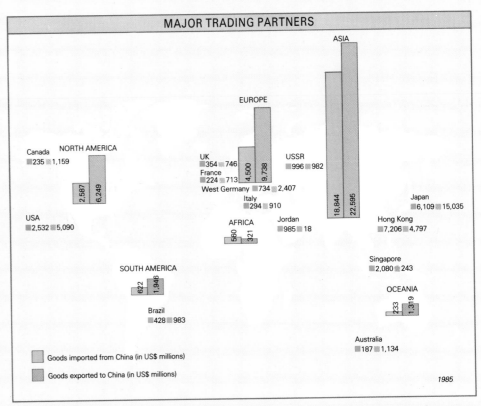

NORTH AMERICA
Canada ■235 ■1,159
USA ■2,532 ■5,090

EUROPE
UK ■354 ■746
France ■224 ■713
West Germany ■734 ■2,407
Italy ■294 ■910

AFRICA ■560 ■321

SOUTH AMERICA
Brazil ■428 ■983

ASIA
USSR ■996 ■982
Jordan ■985 ■18
Japan ■6,109 ■15,035
Hong Kong ■7,206 ■4,797
Singapore ■2,080 ■243

OCEANIA
Australia ■187 ■1,134

■ Goods imported from China (in US$ millions)
■ Goods exported to China (in US$ millions)

1985

China now trades with most areas of the world, although Asian countries are its major partners. In 1985 30 percent of China's total trade was conducted with Japan. Imports exceed exports with most trading partners since demand for Chinese goods is still limited.

IMPORTS

China has sought to achieve a trade balance between exports and imports, with both rising roughly in tandem. Given current exchange rates, there is more demand for imports than for Chinese goods abroad. Hence, in practice, imports are limited by the growth of exports.

In 1985 only 13 percent of China's imports were primary products, of which foodstuffs accounted for 4 percent and industrial raw materials, such as wood and yarn, 8 percent.

The other 87 percent of imports were manufactured goods. Major items were:
- 17 percent iron and steel
- 12 percent industrial machinery
- 11 percent chemical and related products
- 8 percent vehicles
- 7 percent electronic equipment

Textile products, fertilizers and non-ferrous metals each accounted for 4 percent.

In the mid-1980s, imports shot up for two main reasons: first, because of the lack of control over purchasing arising from decentralization; second, in response to increased purchasing power.

This performance contrasted sharply with past policies which had tended to stress the import of raw materials and industrial equipment rather than of manufactured goods.

Government concern grew at the indiscriminate importing of foreign goods—especially when there were locally produced equivalents. Another growing problem was the importing of machinery that required continuing imports of other products to keep it running (for example, imported television assembly lines needing components from abroad).

The government has now limited imports by administrative action, despite the fact that this contravenes its reform policies of allowing enterprises greater freedom.

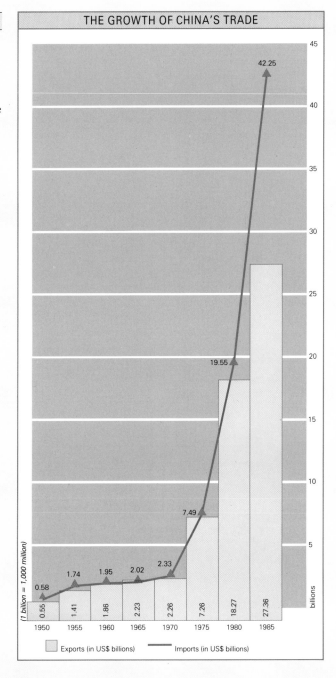

THE GROWTH OF CHINA'S TRADE

The volume of both exports and imports has increased dramatically since the 1950s. In 1985 imports far exceeded exports, but China hopes to achieve a more balanced trade in future.

TRADE DEFICITS

China has a trade deficit with such advanced industrial countries as Japan and the USA. While not large in world terms, China would prefer more balanced trade. However, demand for machinery and equipment to modernize the economy—as well as for vehicles and some consumer goods—outstrips demand for Chinese manufactured goods (which are often of poor quality).

Also the potential for growth in primary product exports is limited.

It has been easier to keep a balanced trade with other socialist economies, such as those of Eastern Europe, through bilateral agreements because of the level of state involvement. Typically, agreements on the volume of trade are made in advance and are "guaranteed" by state planning bodies.

THE HONG KONG CONNECTION

In anticipation of the 1997 changeover of authority in Hong Kong, China has been strengthening its economic links with what will be its first Special Administrative Region. Direct and indirect Chinese investment in Hong Kong is increasing, as are direct trading links.

Hong Kong companies have similarly expanded their contacts with China, by direct investment and by contracts with Chinese enterprises involved in the electronics, food and hotel industries. In 1987 Hong Kong and Macao firms were contracting processing and assembly work to around 10,000 factories, employing almost 1 million workers in Guangdong Province.

Such trends should help ease the transition as Hong Kong is reunited with China, although political and economic uncertainty remain.

FOREIGN INVESTMENT

China has made a start in attracting the foreign investment necessary for modernization. Companies can either create joint ventures with Chinese partners, or set up wholly-owned subsidiaries.

Joint ventures can be of 2 types—equity and contractual. China tries to encourage equity joint ventures, in which a new company is formed with both Chinese and foreign shareholdings.

Contractual joint ventures are preferred by most foreign investors who feel they are more flexible and less risky than equity ventures. Contractual ventures simply need a contract specifying contributions and benefits.

By the end of 1986 China had 6,532 enterprises with foreign investment:
- Equity joint ventures (46 percent)
- Contractual joint ventures (51 percent)
- Wholly owned foreign firms (2 percent)

Between 1979 and September 1987, direct foreign investment totalling US $21 billion was agreed, although less than half this sum (US $7.6 billion) had actually been invested. China has also set up 277 enterprises abroad (including Hong Kong and Macao), many of them joint ventures with foreign partners. China's total investment in such ventures was US $275 million at the end of 1986.

While most joint ventures claim to be operating well, there have been problems. Typical are complaints of the weak infrastructure, administrative bureaucracy, constraints on foreign exchange and the poor-quality labour force.

There are also conflicts over objectives. While China wants to increase exports and absorb advanced technology, some foreign investors are primarily seeking entry to the vast potential of the country's domestic market.

NEGOTIATING WITH CHINA

Westerners can find it difficult to negotiate with Chinese enterprises and government bodies. Some of their problems arise from cultural differences:
- The importance to the Chinese of not losing "face".
- The greater respect in China for age and hierarchy.
- The Chinese emphasis on trusting and continuing personal relationships rather than on legal contracts.

- Differing management methods.

Other problems arise from the Chinese political system. There is still a high degree of government control (despite significant decentralization of authority), over major investment projects. So, those negotiating on the Chinese side may not wield the same level of power as those in the foreign team.

SEE ALSO PAGES 158–61, 162–65

AN EXPANDING ECONOMY

Only some 10 percent of China's land is capable of being cultivated. On this small proportion of its total landmass it must today support more than one billion people, a fifth of the world's population. This number is increasing rapidly and may threaten future development. The basic dilemma facing China's economic leaders is how to raise the standard of living to acceptable modern levels within these constraints.

The government embarked on economic reforms after Chairman Mao's death in 1976, when China's economy was at a virtual standstill. These began in 1979 with paying farmers and workers more, and progressed in 1984 to liberalizing the industrial system so that managers could, for instance, fire lazy workers or sell some of their output on the free market instead of always to the state. By 1986 it had raised the national income from the 1978 average of 301 yuan to 779 yuan—a 95 percent rise at constant prices, according to the Chinese. By 1987, however, the reforms themselves were causing problems.

In the early 1980s food production soared above the mid-1970s figures. Free markets—markets in which produce could be bought and sold freely—proliferated. But by 1987 grain output, which fell sharply in 1985, had still not regained its 1984 peak of 407 million tonnes. Farmers were turning away from the production of grain to more profitable sidelines, such as vegetable growing.

Less grain meant less animal feed was available, and pig keeping declined. In December 1987 pork—by far the most important meat for most Chinese—had to be rationed in Beijing and other major cities for the first time in many years. Aware of the discontent caused in Eastern European countries by frequent food shortages, China's leaders opted for rationing as the lesser of two evils.

On the credit side, the rural reforms have begun to reduce the unemployment problem in the countryside. Rural industry expanded enormously through the 1980s, and by 1987 was already employing nearly a quarter of the rural work force. This growth has successfully boosted rural standards of living—at least in some areas—and has helped to curb migration to the towns.

The expansion of urban industry has proved more difficult. Up to 1978 all factories were run by the state, and all remitted their (usually meagre) profits to the state. Then a few experimental pilot schemes were introduced. Small groups, usually of young people, and sometimes even individuals were allowed to set up independent businesses—restaurants or repair shops, for example—and share the profits among themselves. In some state-run enterprises, such innovations as the payment of taxes and the retention of profits were introduced. In 1984 this new system was applied nationwide.

Since then China has had a constant problem with inflation, officially reported at around 10 percent a

A Chinese millionaire and his wife pose beside their proudest possession—a new car. Since so few people in China can afford to own one, a private car is an obvious symbol of wealth.

The Chinese definition of a millionaire is someone with an annual income of more than 10,000 yuan (approximately US $3,000). The successful couple in the picture are making five times that amount from the beancurd business they started in 1980.

year, but in reality probably nearer 20 percent. The wage rises, bonus payments and rapid expansion of businesses that followed the 1984 reforms threw vast quantities of money into the economy. At the same time waste and inefficiency have grown, often through the duplication of effort: for example, in 1985 dozens of competing Chinese enterprises purchased foreign production lines to manufacture colour televisions.

The expansion has been mainly in industries with a rapid turnover and high profit margins, rather than in the less profitable heavy industry or in infrastructure. The government now faces the problem of how to finance new roads, rail and other communications

Discriminating shoppers in an urban free market are a sign of the changes in China's economy since the late 1970s. In these markets, where produce brought in from the country is bought and sold relatively free of state control, consumers have a far greater choice than before. Increased demand has led to increased production, and vegetable growing has become a highly profitable sideline for farmers.

networks, all of which are badly needed but commercially unattractive to foreign or Chinese investors.

The results of trade reforms have also been mixed. In the late 1970s many Chinese recognized that Mao's "self-reliance" policy had meant that the Chinese had missed out on advances in technology taking place elsewhere. The new leadership, anxious to catch up, threw open the doors to foreign investors and businessmen in order to attract technical knowledge as well as finance. But by 1988 only about one-third of the joint foreign-Chinese investment ventures were actually making money; another third were in real difficulties. Foreign partners have been discouraged by the rapidly fluctuating cycles of boom

and freeze in China that have made it almost impossible to build up steady business. Moreover, China has run up large deficits in the boom periods.

So although trade and output figures for the 1980s show encouraging growth, this is only one side of the story. There are severe strains in the economy, of which inflation is a symptom.

China has made all the easy gains the reforms first offered. What now remains is hard work and the challenge of tuning the reforms correctly and modernizing the management of China's economy. Unless the government can achieve this, both the reformist leadership and the reforms themselves may be at risk.

AN EXPANDING ECONOMY/2

BANKING AND FINANCE

China's banking system is undergoing a major revolution. Until 1978 it was completely monolithic; the banks merely transmitted grants from government to state enterprises and acted as a channel for the settlement of transactions.

In the countryside there was barely even a money-based economy; since there were no free markets where produce could be bought and sold, there was little need for banks.

By the mid-1980s the situation had changed, and the People's Bank had assumed a central banking role. Two new banks, the Industrial and Commercial Bank and the Agricultural Bank, have begun to handle business with the public.

New pressures on the banks have arisen as managers, made financially independent by economic reform, seek to expand their businesses by borrowing large sums.

China's bankers have not previously been trained to assess the creditworthiness of a project. Nor do they have the status to be sufficiently firm with plant management in refusing or reclaiming loans.

Managers, however, accustomed to having the state to bail them out, pay scant attention to rising interest rates. In 1987 bank officials claimed that capital investment outside the state budget, financed with bank loans, was almost equal to the credit provided inside it. This was a key factor in the rising inflation rate that year.

In late 1987 the People's Bank planned stringent checks on credit for the future. These included lending quotas, larger reserve requirements for the retail banks, and higher interest rates. It clearly recognized the need to get the control of lending back into the hands of Beijing.

The 1988 enterprise law aims to make managers of state firms the masters of their factories. Like this manager of a joint foreign-Chinese venture, they will be responsible for profits and losses.

INFLATION

In the late 1980s inflation became a serious problem in China. With the introduction of economic reforms earlier in the decade, wages and bonuses soared, while productivity remained stagnant. Erratic agricultural production meant that particular foods sometimes suddenly disappeared from the markets, and prices rocketed.

The huge expansion of industry, mainly financed by borrowing from the banks, fuelled rising demand for construction and for raw materials such as cement and steel. This borrowing poured money into the economy.

In each of the 3 years from 1985 to 1987 money in circulation rose by 30 percent. "China's money-printing presses have been running red-hot, night and day, for months", observed one economic analyst in late 1987.

Another important factor in the rising rate of inflation has been the rapid growth of the money economy in the countryside. At the end of the 1970s, money was hardly used in rural areas. But with the spread of free markets, money started changing hands and cash circulation boomed.

In addition, farmers themselves began to earn more when, in 1979, the state raised the price of grain paid to the growers. At the same time, the state subsidized the urban price to keep it low for town dwellers, thus indirectly injecting more cash into the economy.

Official Chinese figures for annual inflation did not exceed 10 percent for the years 1979–87, but some foreign financial analysts believe it was, in fact, much higher. Occasional figures recorded in particular cities—such as the huge jump in vegetable prices, of 65 percent over the previous year, which occurred in Shenzhen in August 1987—tend to confirm their opinions.

COMPOSITION OF NATIONAL INCOME

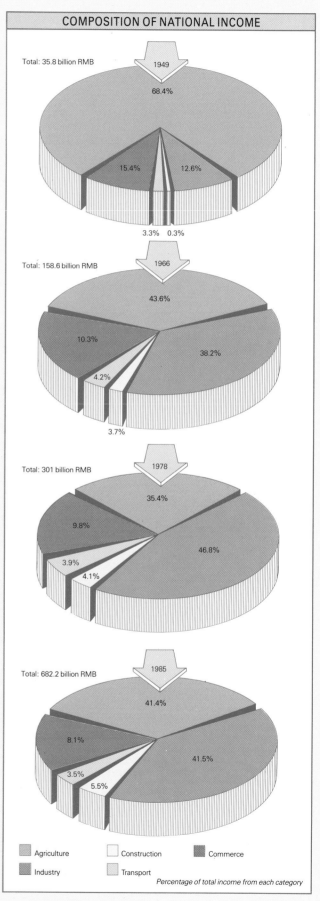

Total: 35.8 billion RMB — 1949
68.4%
15.4%   12.6%
3.3%   0.3%

Total: 158.6 billion RMB — 1966
43.6%
10.3%
38.2%
4.2%
3.7%

Total: 301 billion RMB — 1978
35.4%
9.8%
46.8%
3.9%
4.1%

Total: 682.2 billion RMB — 1985
41.4%
8.1%
41.5%
3.5%
5.5%

Agriculture   Construction   Commerce
Industry   Transport
Percentage of total income from each category

Industry now rivals agriculture in its contribution to the national income. While the percentage contributed by agriculture has declined, that of industry has tripled since 1949.

CURRENCY

Renminbi, (RMB), literally the "people's money", is the currency in China. Each yuan subdivides into 10 *jiao* or *mao* which in turn divide into 10 *fen*. Notes in common use are mostly of small value, but in 1987 China began to issue higher-denomination currency, starting with a 50 yuan note, worth approximately US $13.

This move was a sign of the growing amount of money in circulation in China. It also reflected rising costs and the ever-increasing monetarization of what was in the countryside virtually a subsistence economy. The new notes were designed to ease the growing problem of carrying around large bundles of small-denomination notes.

RMB is not a convertible currency, but appears to be informally linked to the US dollar. In July 1986 it was officially devalued from RMB 3.2 to RMB 3.7 to the dollar, and held to this value even when the dollar sank against other major currencies in late 1987.

STOCKS AND BONDS

The trading of stocks and bonds, which seems the essence of capitalism, has reached communist China. By the end of 1987 some 27 cities had been allowed to open financial markets where enterprises could sell "shares", as they are often referred to by the Chinese, although most, in fact, were bonds. (A bond is a written promise to repay a loan made to the enterprise. It carries an interest rate, but, unlike a proper "share", no part-ownership in the issuing enterprise.) Currently bonds and shares are mostly sold by the organization concerned direct to the public. Secondary markets, where members of the public can sell shares to one another, are promised for the near future.

Experimental schemes began in the mid-1980s, with large enterprises such as the Tianjin Bicycle Factory selling 2-year bonds. Collectively run rural enterprises raised funds in the same way. Provinces also started issuing bonds for large but uncommercial schemes such as the construction of new roads.

By the end of 1987 the People's Bank was planning wide-ranging issues of bonds by local authorities. This seemed a workable alternative to Beijing handing out grants for the financing of infrastructure, which it no longer wanted to do.

Signs are that the issuing of real shares, carrying a genuine stake in the enterprise, will soon be allowed.

THE GROSS NATIONAL PRODUCT

788 billion RMB   983 billion RMB   1,092 billion RMB

In 1988 1 US$ = approximately 3.7 RMB   *(1 billion = 1,000 million)*

In 1987 China's gross national product ranked 7th *in the world. This was its record GNP, but since* *it amounted only to about 1,030 yuan (US $280 a head), China is still rated a poor country.*

LABOUR

One of Deng Xiaoping's key reforms has begun to put an end to the "iron ricebowl", the system of jobs-for-life, in operation since the Communists took over China in 1949.

Under the new regulations, from 1986 onward all new workers are hired under contract so that they can, if necessary, be fired. The aim is to end the laziness and inefficiency endemic in China since the Cultural Revolution. By the end of 1987, 6 percent of workers in state-run enterprises, and around 20 percent in collectives were on contract.

The rights of parents to pass on their jobs to their children have been phased out. And a new flexibility in labour is tentatively emerging. Under the old system it was almost impossible to change jobs, but it has been recognized that this often meant wasting talent and experience.

UNIVERSITY GRADUATES

In 1987 the government began to consider the vexed question of how to deploy university graduates. Under the old system, they were simply allotted jobs, often quite unsuited to their training.

A new plan, in which about 70 percent of students would have to pay their own tuition fees but could then choose their employment, was under consideration in early 1988. The remaining subsidized 30 percent would be allocated to the less popular jobs.

This policy also aims to bring the supply of students with appropriate training into line with demand. The plan is to eliminate the surplus of students with qualifications in history and basic science in favour of more with English, computer science, accounting and agriculture which are seen as being subjects of more direct practical use.

BANKRUPTCY—NEW PROPOSALS

Chinese officials began debating bankruptcy proposals in the mid-1980s in the hope of finding a way of closing down some of the country's many loss-making enterprises.

Bankruptcy had hitherto been regarded as a capitalist concept. It had not figured in socialist societies because, in theory, no enterprise that is owned by the people can be bankrupt. In addition, the Chinese did not think it right that workers should lose their jobs and all that goes with them: housing, medical care, and so on, for what are often the mistakes of the management.

On its side the government was unwilling to exacerbate existing urban discontent at rising prices, by the major job losses attendant on bankrupting enterprises. And in fact it was sometimes impossible for enterprises to stay solvent since prices and shortages of raw materials were completely outside their control. Because of these factors an enterprise could be reasonably efficient and still make a loss.

So, although a bankruptcy law was drawn up in 1986 and passed for trial implementation, by the end of 1987 only 2 businesses in China had actually gone bankrupt—a factory and a shop. Others had been given a warning that they might be closed, which seemed to inspire subsequent efficiency.

Officials have begun to look at an alternative system in which loss-making enterprises would be leased to a successful manager with another business. For example, a food company has taken over an ailing enamelware plant and turned it over to making cakes. As yet, however, it is arguable as to how successful such a system could be.

TRANSPORT AND COMMUNICATIONS

Given China's huge and mountainous landmass and population of more than a billion, it is not surprising that its transport network is hard-pressed to cope with the volume of freight and passengers needing to be moved from place to place. Economic policies since 1949 have contributed to the problem: first priority in investment was given to heavy industry, and transport failed to keep pace with the growing demands made on it.

The uneven spread of China's natural resources increases the burden on the transport system. Oil and wood from the northeast, coal from the north and minerals from the west must be carried hundreds or thousands of miles to industries in the east and south. At harvest times grain and other foodstuffs are transported north from the milder, more fertile south. China's road network is still underdeveloped and congested and the waterway network, though important, is concentrated in the centre of the country, so the burden of transporting goods and passengers falls largely on the railways.

The old-fashioned steam locomotives in daily use may thrill the Western tourist, but more than four-fifths of the network is single-track, much of it poor quality, and as a result speeds are low. New electrified lines are under construction and many more are planned in an effort to modernize the system.

Despite the pressure on the rail network freight transport is not always organized in the most economical way. Coal, for instance, accounts for around 40 percent of rail tonnage, yet most of it is not screened to eliminate rocks and impurities before transportation. Many factories are sited with little reference to transport needs and costs. And the nationally fixed price of the product to the consumer often does not reflect the cost of carriage, resulting in excessive movement of goods.

To reduce pressure on the rail network the government now discourages freight transport by train over short distances. Pricing reform (relating prices more to production costs), and relocation of enterprises, are also expected to improve the situation.

Passenger traffic takes second place to freight and trains are generally extremely crowded. There are always long queues for tickets, which go on sale three or four days before departure and quickly sell out. A ticket for passage on a train to be boarded in a given city cannot be bought elsewhere. On most trains there are three categories of accommodation: hard seat (simple benches); hard sleeper (tiers of berths in an open carriage); and soft sleeper (four berths in a separate compartment). Soft sleeper passengers (mostly officials and foreigners) enjoy comfortable compartments with frilly curtains, lacy pillows and even bonsai plants. On short journeys there are usually soft and hard seat categories available.

The Chinese of the 1980s are more mobile than ever before. Not only have their incomes risen as a result of economic reforms since 1978, but they are

no longer obliged to obtain their employer's written authority to travel. As a result increasing numbers are travelling for pleasure and becoming tourists in their own country.

A few Chinese—5,000 out of nearly 10 million people in Beijing in 1987—can afford private cars, mostly small and of poor quality. The wealthy "suburban peasants" who make a living out of selling produce to the cities are increasingly able to buy vehicles which help them in their business. Well-to-do urban youths may disport themselves on Japanese motorcycles. More numerous are those who have access to a car or truck owned by their work unit. However, even those who own vehicles cannot always use them as much as they would like; there

*A **great locomotive** trails clouds of smoke as it shunts through the maze of lines at Harbin, capital of the northeastern province of Heilongjiang. This region boasts the densest network of railways in the country.*

China is the only country in the world still making steam engines: in 1987 some 900 locomotives were manufactured.

are often fuel shortages and, as yet, there are few filling stations.

For the majority of people, though, private motorized transport remains a dream. In the countryside, horse-drawn carts, hand tractors and collectively owned trucks still carry the bulk of goods, and bicycles carry most people. Towns are connected by extensive networks of bus services. In cities, buses and bicycles are the main forms of transport.

With the economic reforms begun in 1978 spending on the whole transport infrastructure has been increased in an attempt to remove what is recognized as an impediment to economic development. New rail links have been built to carry coal from Shanxi and Shaanxi Provinces to the coast, and other extensive rail and road projects are underway in eastern China. Urban expressways are being built in many of the largest cities. Beijing has a peripheral underground railway system and one is under construction in Shanghai. Air transport is growing fastest of all. In 1987 there were 277 internal and external air routes, 99 more than in 1980, and a number of private airline companies had begun to operate.

Despite the lack of adequate fuel resources and the shortage of suitable land (much of China is mountainous or otherwise unsuitable for the construction of roads or railways), efforts are being made to modernize transport. Mobility is becoming more and more a part of Chinese life.

A ferry, laden with passengers and freight, makes its way into Shanghai harbour. Water transport between the coastal cities and along the many canals and rivers, particularly the great Yangtze, is still important in China. In 1987 more than 40 percent of freight was carried by boat.

Tractors are used as much for transporting people and goods as for agricultural work. They are tough and durable and thus ideal for negotiating the rough, unmade roads common in rural China.

TRANSPORT AND COMMUNICATIONS/2

RAILWAYS

Nearly two-thirds of China's freight is carried by rail, some 947 billion tonnes/km in 1987. This is despite the fact that the network (at only 52,000 km/32,300 mi) is small for so large a country. Even the tiny UK has a network of more than 37,000 km (23,000 mi).

Almost a quarter of the rail system is still concentrated in the northeast, and a further third in eastern China, leaving the western regions poorly served. Yet since 1949, the network has more than doubled in length, extending to Urumqi in Xinjiang, the far west of China, in 1963, and to Golmud in Qinghai in 1979. The Ministry of Railways' 1986 plans aimed for the completion of another 1,726 km (1,072 mi) before 1990.

More than 80 percent of the existing rail network is single track and steam locomotives are still in use. Speeds are low because track is in poor condition; signalling is outmoded and marshalling facilities have reached saturation point. The high proportion of mountainous terrain in China also creates problems for the railways, making routes circuitous and requiring major engineering. For example, the stretch of line between Chengdu and Kunming, a distance of 1,100 km (700 mi), passes through 427 tunnels.

However, improvements are in hand. Lines are being electrified, double tracking is being provided on the busiest routes and new lines are under construction.

But there is much criticism of safety standards on China's rail system. In the first month of 1988 at least 140 people were killed in serious rail accidents. Party leaders have spoken out against transport officials, blaming inadequate regulations and poor management.

The chart shows the distance, by rail, between some of the major tourist cities.

THE RAILWAY NETWORK

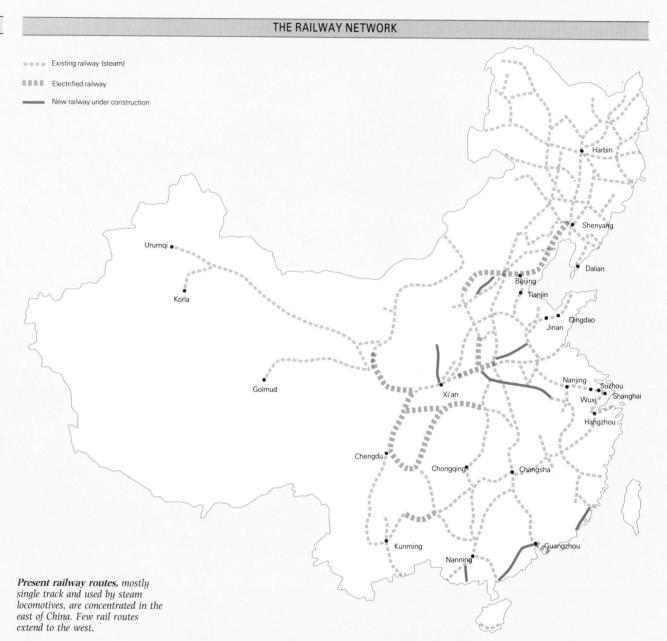

- - - Existing railway (steam)
▪▪▪▪ Electrified railway
—— New railway under construction

Present railway routes, mostly single track and used by steam locomotives, are concentrated in the east of China. Few rail routes extend to the west.

DISTANCES BETWEEN MAJOR CITIES

Shortest distance between cities by rail in kilometres

1 kilometre = 0.62 miles

	Beijing	Shanghai	Tianjin	Guangzhou	Nanning	Changsha	Nanjing	Wuxi	Suzhou	Hangzhou	Jinan	Qingdao	Xi'an	Kunming	Chengdu	Chongqing	Dalian	Shenyang	Harbin
Beijing	Beijing
Shanghai	1462	Shanghai
Tianjin	137	1325	Tianjin
Guangzhou	2313	1811	2450	Guangzhou
Nanning	2565	2063	2702	1334	Nanning
Changsha	1587	1187	1724	726	978	Changsha
Nanjing	1157	305	1020	2116	2368	1492	Nanjing
Wuxi	1334	128	1197	1939	2191	1315	177	Wuxi
Suzhou	1376	86	1239	1897	2149	1273	219	42	Suzhou
Hangzhou	1651	189	1514	1622	1874	998	494	317	275	Hangzhou
Jinan	494	968	357	2284	2536	1558	663	840	882	1157	Jinan
Qingdao	887	1361	750	2677	2929	1951	1056	1233	1275	1550	393	Qingdao
Xi'an	1165	1511	1302	2129	2381	1403	1206	1383	1425	1700	1177	1570	Xi'an
Kunming	3179	2677	3316	2216	1501	1592	2982	2805	2763	2488	3119	3512	1942	Kunming
Chengdu	2048	2353	2185	2544	1829	1920	2048	2225	2267	2542	2019	2412	842	1100	Chengdu
Chongqing	2552	2501	2689	2040	1325	1416	2552	2729	2771	2312	2523	2916	1346	1102	504	Chongqing
Dalian	1238	2426	1101	3551	3803	2825	2121	2298	2340	2615	1458	1851	2403	4417	3286	3790	Dalian
Shenyang	841	2029	704	3154	3406	2428	1724	1901	1943	2218	1061	1454	2006	4020	2889	3393	397	Shenyang
Harbin	1388	2576	1251	3701	3953	2975	2271	2448	2490	2763	1608	2001	2553	4567	3436	3940	944	547	Harbin

ROADS AND TRAFFIC

China's road network extends to approximately 960,000 km (600,000 mi), of which two-thirds are in rural areas. There are only 250 km (155 mi) of first-class highway—motorway with segregated lanes and limited access.

This is but a small fraction of the road density (length of road network related to size of country) in Western industrialized countries. In the USA, for example there are almost 5 million km (3 million mi) of road network.

Most of the roads are unsurfaced (fewer than 20 percent are asphalted),

INLAND WATERWAYS

Because water transport was cheaper than other means before modern times, canals played an important role in China's transport system for centuries. Of the major artificial waterways, the earliest and best-known is the Grand Canal, started in the 4th century BC and completed in the 1200s, to carry grain north to Beijing.

The canal is being renovated to expand transport capacity in this part of eastern China.

A large proportion of China's 109,000 km (67,730 mi) of navigable rivers and canals are in Jiangsu and Zhejiang in the centre of the country. They provide useful access to the centres of light industry and rich agricultural areas surrounding Shanghai.

Another important network consists of the Yangtze River (Chang Jiang) and its tributaries. The Yangtze is navigable for nearly 3,000 km (1,864 mi), as far as Yibin in Sichuan, and is a principal artery for east-west traffic. Seagoing ships can reach as far inland as Chongqing in Sichuan, making China's interior accessible to the outside world.

Most of the vessels on inland waterways are small motorized boats, barges and sampans; only a few sailing junks remain.

PIPELINES

China's 12,000 km (7,460 mi) pipeline network carries oil, oil products and natural gas.

The country's biggest oilfield, Daqing in the northeastern province of Heilongjiang, is linked to the ports of Qinhuangdao and Dalian by pipeline. The system also connects the oilfields near Tianjin and Shandong with refineries and chemical plants in Beijing and Nanjing. This removes some freight traffic from the overloaded railways.

AIR TRAVEL

In the late 1980s the air network is the fastest growing transport system in China, but standards are still poor and seats hard to obtain. Only a small proportion of goods and passengers travel by air. Air travel is important, though, for the burgeoning tourist industry, for the delivery of some perishable goods and for urgent official journeys.

The most extensive air network is in Xinjiang, China's largest province, where distances between towns are large and road conditions particularly poor. Airports are being expanded to accommodate international flights, and former military airfields are being turned over to civilian use.

FREIGHT AND PASSENGER TRANSPORT

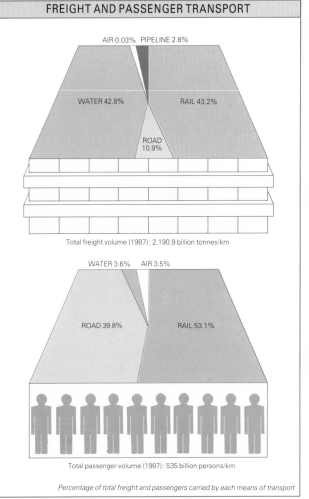

AIR 0.03%   PIPELINE 2.8%

WATER 42.8%   RAIL 43.2%

ROAD 10.9%

Total freight volume (1987): 2,190.9 billion tonnes/km

WATER 3.6%   AIR 3.5%

ROAD 39.8%   RAIL 53.1%

Total passenger volume (1987): 535 billion persons/km

Percentage of total freight and passengers carried by each means of transport

Rail is the most important means of transport. *But the volume of freight and passengers* *going by air, although still small, rose 37.5 and 27.4 percent respectively in 1986–88.*

PORTS

Because inland transport has been so congested, coastal shipping is an essential part of goods movement.

Coal, for example, is now shipped from ports such as Qinhuangdao on the Bohai Gulf, and the new port at Shijiusuo in Shandong. It is transported south along the coast to the big industrial centres of Shanghai and to the provinces of Jiangsu, Zhejiang and Guangdong. This relieves north-south rail routes.

Trade with Japan, China's largest trading partner, is an important part of the activity of the east coast ports. Shanghai, the country's biggest port, handles more than 90 million tonnes of cargo a year—around one-third of China's total.

The long-standing problem of congestion is gradually being overcome as new port facilities are opened, with wharves specialized for handling containers, grain, coal, timber and ores. And lighters (flat-bottomed craft used for loading or unloading boats anchored some distance from the wharves) are being used to save quayside space and expand handling capacity.

unusable during the rainy season, or too narrow to take heavy traffic.

Traffic is further restricted by slow-moving tractors, animal-drawn vehicles, and even, on occasion, by farmers winnowing their grain on the road. For these reasons, little long-distance passenger or freight traffic goes by road.

However, considerable efforts are now being made to improve the system. New high-quality freeways are being built across the country, from Shanghai to Xinjiang, and from Beijing to Guangzhou. Shorter urban

expressways are being built around major cities.

Some of these projects have been funded by the World Bank or by foreign interests.

City roads are rapidly becoming more congested as bus and taxi services proliferate; traffic is now a serious source of pollution and the accident rate, particularly for cyclists and pedestrians, is high. While private motoring is on the increase, it is still restricted, not only by cost, but also by the lack of a countrywide network of filling stations and petrol shortages.

COMMUNICATIONS

● **Postal Service**

China's first modern postal service was set up by the Maritime Customs administration in the late 19th century when that organization was under foreign control. It has always been one of the country's most efficient means of communication, and a large subsidy makes it the cheapest.

The basic price of a stamp for sending an inland letter has been kept the same since shortly after the 1949 revolution. More than 53,000 post offices throughout the country handle more than 5 billion letters every year.

● **Telephones**

In 1987 there were approximately 10 million telephones in China, only 2 million of them in the rural areas where 80 percent of the people live. That is less than 1 telephone per 100 people, compared with 85 per 100 people in Sweden and 80 in the USA.

Private users are extremely rare, and connection costs may represent several months' wages. Officials in the middle and upper ranks are entitled to telephones at home. In 1987 some 250,000 organizations and individuals were officially reckoned to be on

waiting lists for telephones.

Coastal cities have been given priority in communications because of their importance in trade and business. Since 1984 many have been equipped with automatic exchanges, optical fibre cables, and microwave or satellite links. Major projects are underway, using foreign technology, to expand the number of direct-dial lines in service.

The number of telephones continues to grow faster than the number of lines. Even in the cities, it may take hours to put through a long-distance call.

THE ARMY AND DEFENCE

Traditionally, soldiering was not admired in China. The general attitude was summed up in the saying: "You don't use good iron to make nails". Protected by natural boundaries such as the Himalayas and the Gobi Desert, China remained largely at peace from the time of the Mongol invasion in the thirteenth century until the intrusion of European traders and the Opium Wars in the nineteenth.

Communist China's founding father, Mao Zedong, brought a new approach to military thinking, which had stagnated in this prolonged period of peaceful isolation. Although in the internal disorders of the nineteenth and twentieth centuries, "armies" had emerged, most of the rank-and-file were untrained in practical warfare skills, and sometimes little more than peasant or bandit rabbles. Mao taught his People's Liberation Army a code of discipline and honour which, even after 1949, put it centre-stage in political life and earned it the fear and respect of millions. Until Mao's death in 1976 the army played a key role in maintaining power, especially during the Cultural Revolution (1966–76) when it eventually moved into the power vacuum created by bureaucratic upheaval and began to run the country.

Mao's major contribution to military thinking was his doctrine of guerrilla war. This doctrine recommended rural-based forces which could target an enemy unit, destroy it and disappear back into the countryside. While this method was successful against Chiang Kai-shek in the 1930s and 1940s, it was not appropriate for the kind of wars China might be faced with thereafter. When, in the late 1970s, China began to open up, under Deng Xiaoping, the military realized that post-World War II advances in technology had passed them by. They would have been quite unable to counter, say, a Soviet invasion, even one based only on conventional weapons. China, despite its ability to make atomic bombs, still relied on a military strategy based on Mao's guerrilla tactics.

In the 1980s Deng Xiaoping effected a major shift in military strategy, recruitment and weaponry. He and the top military personnel realized that, contrary to Mao's belief, war with the USSR was not inevitable, nor even likely. Hence they could safely prune China's armed forces, then numbering around four million, retire many older officers, and train and arm the remainder more effectively. Obsolescent arms factories were turned over to making such non-military goods as motor cycles and steel pipes, and the profits invested in new military technology.

As a result of these measures China has reduced its forces to three million (including naval and airforce personnel). Another important indication of changing attitudes, and the switch to a more technological age, is the withdrawal of the army from the political arena. The Politburo announced after the 1987 13th Party Congress contained only two military leaders.

In the 1977 11th Politburo there had been ten.

But the army's acquiescence in its loss of political power may depend too much on its regard for Deng Xiaoping's ability as leader. The country's top military post, chairman of the party's Military Affairs Commission, was retained by Deng at the 1987 Congress, despite his having earlier expressed a wish to retire. This suggests that neither he nor the army trusts other potential candidates for the post. But, at least, the speed with which younger men are being trained and promoted means that by the early 1990s the military modernization programme will probably be irreversible. By then the army should be committed to its new professional role with no regrets for its political one.

Defence comes behind both agriculture and industry in China's priorities. Its share of the national

Peaked caps and a new-style uniform are one part of the army's drive to modernize and improve its image. They are worn here by young recruits to the prestigious Shijiazhuang Military Academy in northern China.

Ranks were abolished in the Chinese army in the 1960s. However, at the spring 1988 National People's Congress it emerged that the ranking system is likely to be restored. After 25 years this would be extremely difficult to implement and it remains a highly controversial issue.

A new all-female armed unit undergoes rigorous commando-style training. Most of the women come from cities and their average age is 20. The unit was formed in 1987 in Sichuan expressly for the task of guarding the frontier at the province's main airport.

budget fell from about 20 percent in 1979 to 8 percent in 1987, although the amount disbursed, about 20 billion yuan, has hardly changed. Western experts believe there is an emerging consensus for using this money to equip elite units, and to purchase selected items of technological equipment, such as avionics, from abroad. Such units would provide the Chinese with a flexible rapid deployment force to deal with possible surprise attacks.

It was China's weapons exports, rather than imports, which captured world attention in 1987. Alleged sales of its Silkworm missiles to Iran infuriated the United States and other concerned nations. China has in fact become an exporter of arms on a massive scale—the bulk of them low-technology items such as tanks and rifles—reportedly earning more than US $5 billion in the years 1983 to 1986.

MODERN SCIENCE AND TECHNOLOGY

SCIENCE AFTER 1949

At the time of the establishment of the People's Republic in 1949, organized scientific activity in China had barely survived the war with Japan and the civil war that followed.

The first step taken by the new government to remedy the situation was the founding of the Chinese Academy of Sciences (CAS) in November 1949. This combined the existing Central Academy of Sciences and the Beiping Academy of Sciences, which between them operated 21 research institutes.

All scientific activity thenceforth was to be directed by the government, which was convinced of the need to strengthen science and technology for the service of the national economy and for defence.

Basic research in the scientific academies had been largely restricted to geology and plant and animal taxonomy. New plans were introduced to update the range of scientific disciplines by embracing, for example, nuclear physics, and the chemistry and engineering of rocket propulsion.

Research institutes for Archaeology, History, the study of Marxism, and Linguistics were also included under the Academy of Sciences. These have since been grouped under a separate Academy of Social Sciences, established in 1977, which includes institutes of Economics, Philosophy, World Religions and Journalism.

SCIENTIFIC PERSONNEL

In 1949 the total number of research and technical personnel in China was no more than 50,000. Of these, only about 500 were engaged in full-time scientific research.

Help in planning a strategy for developing a strong scientific and technological base, and in the supply of manpower, was provided by the Soviet Union. Soviet "experts" were sent to China, and Chinese scientific and technical staff went to the USSR for training. This assistance, together with the skills of a growing group of Western-educated Chinese scientists and engineers, and the rapid expansion of higher education, contributed to an increase in scientific expertise and trained manpower.

By 1959, only 10 years after the Chinese Academy of Sciences was established, it had grown to include 86 research institutes and more than 10,000 scientific and technical personnel. Highly trained scientists and technologists worked in research units attached to government ministries, ranging from agriculture, health and mining to defence, and every local authority had its scientific advisers.

Scientists subject all items of equipment to rigorous checks before a satellite is launched. China has put considerable emphasis on this area of research and since 1970 has launched 21 satellites.

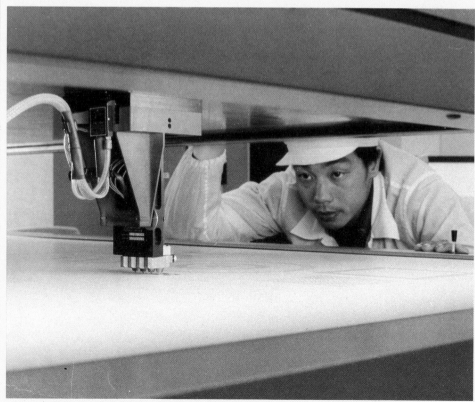

As China enters the computer age microelectronic technology is becoming increasingly important.

In this Wuxi factory an electronic, computer-aided drafting machine automatically draws an integrated circuit diagram. Highly trained personnel are needed to supervise such operations.

ACHIEVEMENTS OF THE CHINESE ACADEMY OF SCIENCES (CAS)

The stable environment the CAS created led to modest successes. Achievements were mainly directed toward immediate benefits for the nation: the improvement of agriculture in order that the country would have sufficient food, and the improvement of the health of the whole population.

Better crop varieties, more efficient irrigation and drainage systems, and the wider application of pesticides were introduced. Community health education programmes and the greater availability of clinics brought down infant mortality rates and reduced the number of people suffering from tuberculosis and venereal and parasitic diseases.

Geological advice and data were vital to the developing nation for siting railways, roads and bridges, and for identifying sources of raw materials such as metals and oil. Special teams of geologists were formed to provide this information.

In 1956 the long-term plan identified the following areas for special attention: computing technology, semiconductor research, automation, electronics, nuclear science and jet propulsion. Political upheavals meant that many plans had to be modified, but two milestones marked the entry of China into the modern age: their first atom bomb was exploded in 1964, and bovine insulin (the mainstay of treatment for juvenile diabetics) was synthesized for the first time in 1965.

A continuing upward curve of scientific achievements would have followed had political events not intervened. The most damaging of these was the Cultural Revolution of 1966–76.

THE CULTURAL REVOLUTION PERIOD

During the Cultural Revolution years there was what amounted to a persecution of "intellectuals". This term included scientists and technologists, and for 10 years very few research projects were continued.

Among approved projects were those relating to defence. In June 1967 a hydrogen bomb was exploded. In the 1970s the first successful test launching and retrieval of various satellites took place.

Many researchers, some diverted from other branches of science, were set to work on traditional Chinese medicine. Acupuncture and the examination of the active principles of plant drugs were favoured topics. Even so, surgical procedure continued unabated. In hospitals at this time doctors were perfecting the techniques of microsurgery, in which China now leads the world.

SCIENCE IN THE 1980s

Despite successes in some fields, by the 1970s China was being left behind in the new technological age. After the chaos of the Cultural Revolution, the government set about restoring the status of science and technology in the context of economic reconstruction. Science and technology are now officially recognized as essential factors in the development of a strong and prosperous nation but research must be oriented toward its ultimate application.

The State Science and Technology Commission published a document in September 1986 which emphasizes how science and technology can modernize, and ultimately enrich, China.

The document sets out current strategy, which is twofold. First, Chinese scientists should concentrate on 7 areas of high-technology projects in an effort to close the gap between China and the developed nations. These are:
- Biotechnology
- Space exploration
- Information technology
- Industrial automation
- Lasers
- Generation of energy
- New materials (for example, superconductors)

Second, rural areas (with 80 percent of China's population) must be helped, by means of appropriate technology, to set up new industries. These will utilize surplus manpower released from traditional agricultural labour as working methods gradually change.

A Long March rocket lifts off from the launching pad. Fifteen of China's 21 satellites have been carried by these rockets, first used in 1970. Work is now in progress on an improved version of Long March III. Since 1985 China has been offering satellite launching services to other countries.

INTO THE 21ST CENTURY

Research scientists are aware that a utilitarian view of science could well displace research that is still looking for a practical application. They have convinced the government to fulfil its promise to build an electron-positron collider and a heavy ion accelerator to explore the fundamental nature of matter.

Leading scientists have also played a part in convincing administrators of the need for better treatment of scientific personnel—allowing them increased job mobility as well as freedom to travel abroad to make new contacts and attend conferences.

The "Open Door" policy of the government since 1978 has manifested itself in a series of new "Open Laboratories". These are better equipped, are able to attract short-term staff from other organizations or from abroad, and have the freedom to pursue fundamental as well as the more directly utilitarian aspects of scientific research.

From a total of only 50,000 people engaged in scientific work in 1949 China has built up a science and technology work force which numbers 7.8 million in the late 1980s. Of that, some 336,000 are professional staff; the remainder are technical and other support personnel.

Evidence from recent advances in fields as diverse as space science, biotechnology and superconductor research show China poised to make its own, unique contribution to scientific advance as the next century approaches—a far cry from the situation as it entered this century.

SEE ALSO PAGES 74–77, 164–65

THE VISITOR'S CHINA

GROWTH OF TOURISM

In 1978, when China first began to open its doors wide to the world and welcome visitors, some 1,800,000 tourists visited the country, more than during the whole of the previous 30 years.

Since then tourism has developed rapidly. In 1986 nearly 23 million people visited China. The vast majority of these were Chinese from Hong Kong, Macao and Taiwan, but there were nearly 1.5 million other visitors.

However, the rate of increase of foreign visitors has not been as great as expected, and is falling short of projections for an annual total of 5 million by 1990. The government now realizes that tourist facilities must be improved if a further decline in numbers is to be prevented.

AMENITIES FOR TOURISTS

The difficulties that tourists face in China are a shortage of accommodation, particularly at the most popular sites; inadequate transportation systems, and a shortage of good interpreters, guides and other tourist services.

More than 900 hotels in China with some 140,000 rooms are still not enough to meet demand in the late 1980s. A hundred new hotels are under construction in an attempt to ease the accommodation shortage.

Plans are also underway to improve the management of transport services. The Civil Aviation Administration now has 99 more air routes than in 1980, and in 1987 brought 25 more passenger aircraft into service.

Four specialist tourism colleges, and many departments in other higher education institutions, are training workers for the new industry. Improvement in the training and competence of hotel staff, guides and other travel personnel is thought to be a key factor in the expansion of China's tourist industry.

MAJOR TOURIST ATTRACTIONS

From the Great Wall in the north to the tropical forests of Xishuangbanna in the south, China offers a wealth of attractions. The chart below lists sightseeing highlights.

BEIJING Tiananmen Square, Imperial Palace. Temple of Heaven. Summer Palace. Ming Tombs. Great Wall.
CHANGSHA Museum (Mawangdui mummy).
CHENGDE Kangxi's Summer Palace.
CHENGDU Du Fu's Thatched Cottage. 256 BC Water Conservation Project.
CHONGQING Yangtze River cruise.
DATONG Yungang Caves.
DAZU Buddhist caves and carvings.
DUNHUANG Mogao Caves.
MOUNT EMEI Sacred mountain. Temples.
FUZHOU Hualin Temple. Yongquan Temple. One Thousand Buddha Pagoda.
GUANGZHOU Shamian Isle. Guangxiao Temple. Zhenhai Tower. Dr Sun Yat-sen Memorial Hall. Ancestral Temple of Foshan.
GUILIN Karst peaks. Li River.
HANGZHOU West Lake. Pagoda of Six Harmonies.
HARBIN Ice sculptures (in winter).
HOHHOT Mongolian grasslands.
MOUNT HUA Sacred mountain.
MOUNT HUANG Scenic landscape.

JINAN Baotu Spring Park. Black Tiger Spring Park.
KAIFENG Tieta Pagoda. Xiangguo Monastery.
KUNMING Dian Chi Lake. Stone Forest.
LANZHOU End of Great Wall. White Pagoda Mountain.
LESHAN Giant Buddha.
LHASA Potala Palace.
MOUNT LU Scenic resort. Caves. Botanical garden.
LUOYANG Longmen Grottoes.
NANJING Dr Sun Yat-sen Mausoleum. Tomb of the Ming Emperor. Yangtze River Bridge.
NANNING South Lake. Botanical garden.
NINGBO Tianfeng Pagoda. Tianyige Library. Putuo (Buddhist island).
QINGDAO Beach resort. Pier.
QUFU Birthplace of Confucius. Temple and Tomb of Confucius.
SHANGHAI Yuyuan Garden. Temple of the Jade Buddha. The Bund (waterfront). Nanjing Road.
SHANHAIGUAN Start of Great Wall.

SHAOXING Shen Family Gardens. Birthplace of Lu Xun (China's great modern writer).
SHENYANG Imperial Palace Museum. North Imperial Tomb.
SUZHOU Tiger Hill. West Garden. Parks and gardens.
MOUNT TAI Sacred Mountain. Temple. Granite steps to summit.
TAIYUAN Jin Temple. Xuanzhong Temple.
TIANJIN Old foreign concession areas.
TURPAN Sugong Mosque. Gaochang Ancient City.
URUMQI Lake of Heaven.
WUHAN East Lake. Yangtze Bridge.
WUXI Lake Taihu. Grand Canal.
XIAMEN Gulangyu Island.
XI'AN Big Goose Pagoda. Banpo Museum. Tomb of Emperor Qin Shi Huang (terracotta army).
XISHUANGBANNA Tropical forests.
YANGTZE RIVER GORGES
YANGZHOU The Slim West Lake. Daming Temple.
ZHENGZHOU Shaolin Temple.
ZHENJIANG Jinshan Temple.

TOURIST AGENCIES

Tourism in China is state controlled. The travel industry officially began to take shape in 1954 with the founding of the China International Travel Service (CITS).

In 1964 the National Tourism Administration was set up to oversee all tourism matters. But the fact that this occurred only two years before the Cultural Revolution (when the numbers of tourists dwindled to a mere handful) meant that it had little opportunity to exercise its powers. It is thus still a relatively inexperienced organization.

A related agency responsible for handling visitors from abroad is the China Travel Service (CTS) whose customers are overseas Chinese, and Chinese residents of Hong Kong, Macao and Taiwan. China does not regard the latter three as foreign territories and visitors from these places—known as *tongbao* or compatriots—usually receive such special privileges as lower airfares and reduced hotel tariffs. Compatriots travelling on Chinese trains pay the regular fare; foreigners are usually charged at least 70 percent more.

A third agency, the China Youth Travel Service, caters for students or young visitors on cultural exchanges.

NEW DIRECTIONS IN TOURISM

As part of the overall reform of the Chinese economy since the late 1970s, the government has started to decentralize and deregulate the tourist industry. Since late 1985, regional branches of CITS have begun to deal directly with foreign tour operators and earn foreign currency, instead of waiting to be assigned tour groups by head office. Many have started competing with one another for business.

Large numbers of new tour operators, some state-owned, some private or run by collectives, have sprung up. Some are modest enterprises catering only to local Chinese tourists; others are ambitious enough to offer nationwide services and to have their own guides and interpreters as well as their own fleets of taxis.

SPECIAL-INTEREST TOURS

Since the mid-1980s provincial tourist bureaus have organized special-interest tours to attract overseas visitors. Examples include tours focusing on bird-watching, steam locomotives, folk customs, Chinese cooking and bicycle riding. There are also study tours on Chinese literature and arts, and special tours for honeymooners.

Other plans for the expansion of the tourist industry include the provision of 14 golf courses. The largest of these, the 18-hole Beijing International Golf Club set in the hills near the Ming tombs, opened in July 1986. Financed by a number of Japanese firms, it caters mostly for Japanese businessmen, known for their passion for golf. China now receives more visitors from Japan than from any other country—more than 470,000 in 1985.

MONEY

Instead of the Renminbi (literally "people's money"), the money used by the Chinese, tourists are issued with *waihuijuan* or foreign currency certificates (FECs) against their own currencies. Introduced in 1980, these were designed to be used by visitors only for payments at hotels, the so-called Friendship Stores and other places or services used by tourists.

Like Renminbi banknotes, FECs are denominated in yuan. (One yuan is equivalent to approximately 30 US cents.) A yuan is worth 10 *jiao*, and one *jiao* is worth 10 *fen*. To complicate matters the yuan is colloquially referred to as *kuai*, while the *jiao* is called *mao*.

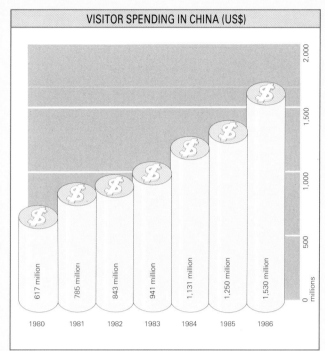

VISITOR SPENDING IN CHINA (US$)

1980	617 million
1981	785 million
1982	843 million
1983	941 million
1984	1,131 million
1985	1,250 million
1986	1,530 million

Revenue from tourism more than doubled between 1980 and 1986, but prices have remained reasonable. In 1987 a double room of medium standard in a Beijing hotel cost about US $22.

VISITOR ARRIVALS IN CHINA

Foreign visitors

Year	Number
1979	362,000
1980	529,000
1981	675,000
1982	765,000
1983	873,000
1984	1,134,000
1985	1,370,000

Overseas Chinese and Chinese from Hong Kong/Macao/Taiwan

Year	Number
1979	3,842,000
1980	5,173,000
1981	7,092,000
1982	7,160,000
1983	8,604,000
1984	11,765,000
1985	16,464,000

Japanese and Americans are the largest groups of foreign visitors to China, accounting for 34 and 17 percent of the total. But Chinese visitors continue to vastly outnumber the foreigners.

HOTELS

Striking evidence of China's new "Open Door" policy is provided by the presence of international-style hotels run by foreign chains. By 1990 there will be 25 such hotels in Beijing and Shanghai alone.

With their Western-style restaurants serving international cuisine, rooftop bars, discos, health clubs— and prices to match—these hotels are a startling departure from traditional Chinese hostelries. But a number of Chinese hotels have now copied their features.

Chinese hotels range from European-style, colonial "hangovers" of pre-revolution days to fifties buildings of functional massiveness. In the past not all were allowed to accept foreign customers. But rules have now relaxed in order to help ease the acute shortage of accommodation created by the tourist boom.

However, standards in some hotels are poor. In 1987 the Beijing Tourism Bureau listed only 97 of the capital's 218 hotels as suitable for use by foreign tourists.

WHAT TO SEE IN CHINA

Much of China is still as remote, strange and exciting for tourists as it must have seemed to Europeans when they heard Marco Polo's account of his travels there more than 5 centuries ago.

Visitors often find themselves torn between the country's physical and its cultural attractions. Of the many scenic wonders, Mount Tai in Shandong Province and Mount Hua in Shaanxi are among the most popular. These mountains were considered sacred in ancient China, and have been the site of many pilgrimages. Now tourists as well as believers come to admire their beauty.

Despite their fame, these peaks are by no means the highest in China. Mount Tai is only 1,500 m (4,950 ft) above sea level. Visitors can climb a stone staircase of about 7,000 steps to its peak to be rewarded with breathtaking views.

Oddly shaped rocks have always had an appeal for the Chinese, and the striking karst limestone pinnacles rising straight from the plain near Guilin and in Yunnan's Stone Forest have long been among the most popular tourist sites.

Some of China's most spectacular cliffs can be seen on boat trips down the gorges of the Yangtze River (Chang Jiang) in Central China. Here the rugged grandeur of the scenery is spiced with the excitement of negotiating the rapids.

Among lakes, the most famous is undoubtedly Hangzhou's West Lake in Zhejiang Province, the subject of many poems and a great favourite with honeymooners.

China abounds in ancient cultural relics, monuments, monasteries, pagodas, mosques, lamaseries, tombs and ancient stone carvings. Among the most remarkable of these are the Forbidden City in Beijing; the Great Wall; the terracotta soldiers of the buried army in Xi'an; the Buddhist carvings of Dazu and the Yungang Caves; the home and tombs of Confucius' family in Qufu; and the Dunhuang cave murals and statues.

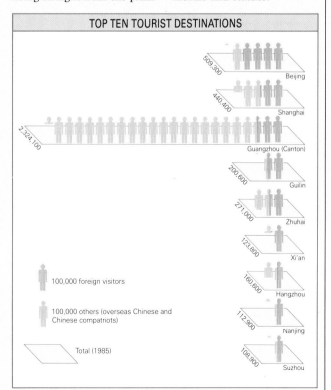

TOP TEN TOURIST DESTINATIONS

City	Number
Beijing	509,300
Shanghai	440,400
Guangzhou (Canton)	2,324,100
Guilin	200,600
Zhuhai	271,000
Xi'an	123,800
Hangzhou	160,600
Nanjing	112,900
Suzhou	108,900

100,000 foreign visitors

100,000 others (overseas Chinese and Chinese compatriots)

Total (1985)

Of the ten most visited cities in 1985, Guangzhou had by far the highest proportion of Chinese tourists—many on short trips from Hong Kong and elsewhere to visit relations and sightsee.

SEE ALSO PAGES 38–55, 62–65, 122–25

HONG KONG

CROSSROADS OF THE WORLD

Hong Kong's strategic location in Asia—for trade, international air travel, finance, manufacturing and tourism—has made it a unique global crossroads.

When mainland China was, from choice, inward-looking and insular, Hong Kong had long since been a city that flourished in its dedication to international trade.

Hong Kong's outstanding physical advantage—the sheltered deepwater harbour, with a 6,000-ha (14,800-acre) anchorage—and the compactness of its communications network—seaport, airport and rail terminus all within a 5-km (3-mi) radius—makes it supremely efficient in the trans-shipment of both goods and passengers.

THE CROWN COLONY

In 1840, during the first Opium War, the British were forced by the Chinese to leave their borrowed quarters in Portuguese Macao. They took ship, crossed the mouth of the Pearl River, and anchored in the harbour between the island of Hong Kong and the Kowloon peninsula.

The move convinced them of the harbour's great value. In 1842, at the war's end, the British stipulated cession of the island as one of the spoils of victory.

In 1860, as a result of a second war, they secured the whole harbour by obtaining the cession of Kowloon. Finally in 1898, a large area of land north of the Kowloon peninsula was leased from China for 99 years. These New Territories (as they came to be known), together with Hong Kong and Kowloon, were administered by Britain as the Crown Colony of Hong Kong. Briefly, during World War II, the Colony fell into Japanese hands; but since 1945, the British have firmly retained their hold. In 1976, the title Colony was replaced by that of Territory.

POPULATION

Both Hong Kong island and the Kowloon peninsula were virtually uninhabited when they came under British rule. And in 1898 the New Territories had a settled population of fewer than 100,000. From these small beginnings, Hong Kong grew at a rapid pace.

By 1941 there were well over 1,000,000 inhabitants. Despite a fall during the Japanese occupation, the post-war flood of people into the Territory soon sent the total soaring—to over 3,000,000 by 1961, and about 5,400,000 in 1986. Immigrants from China, both legal and illegal, and refugees from Vietnam, have continued to come to Hong Kong, swelling the figures.

The population density of Hong Kong is one of the highest in Asia. It averages as many as 165,000 people per sq km (427,000 per sq mi) in certain districts.

96 percent of the population are ethnic Chinese. The remaining 4 percent consists of a mixture of Americans, British, Indians, Japanese, Philippinos, Portuguese and many other nationalities.

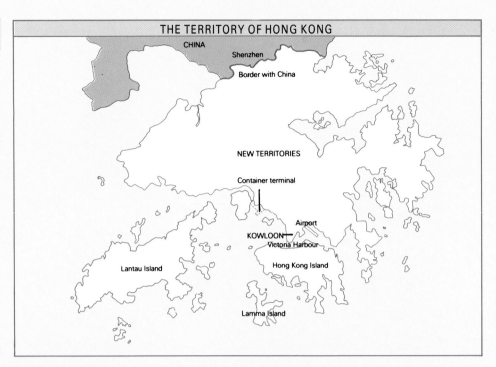

THE TERRITORY OF HONG KONG

The administrative region known as Hong Kong includes not only the island which gives the Territory its name, but also the adjoining mainland areas of Kowloon and New Territories and *many smaller islands. The total area of Hong Kong is more than 1,000 sq km (nearly 400 sq mi).*

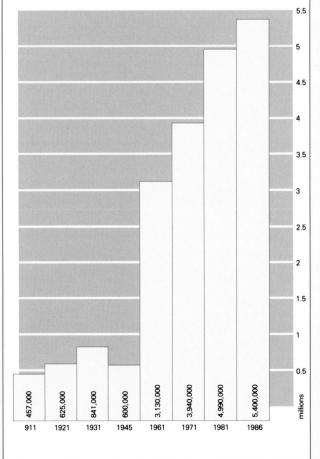

POPULATION GROWTH IN HONG KONG

Year	Population
1911	457,000
1921	625,000
1931	841,000
1945	600,000
1961	3,130,000
1971	3,940,000
1981	4,990,000
1986	5,400,000

Hong Kong's population has soared since World War II. It is now ten times greater than when it first came under British rule. In the 1980s nearly a quarter of its residents are aged 15–24.

TRADE AND INDUSTRY

Originally, the quality and position of its harbour accounted for Hong Kong's growth. Conveniently situated for the entire East Asian area, it was a natural centre for the trans-shipment of goods.

The Korean War of 1950–53, and the subsequent United Nations embargo on trade with China, brought a sudden halt to this trade. To survive, Hong Kong transformed itself from warehouse to factory. It made use of the vast new resource of refugee labour, which had come as a result of the Chinese civil war of 1945–49. Wedding this cheap manpower to Chinese refugee capital produced, almost overnight, a manufacturing industry which competed fiercely on world markets.

Some 90 percent of output is exported, and the harbour has therefore remained a key element in the economy. It is used by more than 11,000 ocean-going vessels each year, loading or discharging more than 37,000,000 tonnes of foreign and domestic cargo.

Containerization was an early priority, and a large-scale building programme has been maintained.

By early 1988 Hong Kong had overtaken first New York and then Rotterdam to become the busiest container port in the world.

Hong Kong International Airport (Kai Tak) also benefits from the Territory's geographical position, if not from its difficult topography. (The harbour city, ringed with mountains, has never had flat land to spare.) With its single runway built out into the water on reclaimed land, Kai Tak manages to be one of the world's busiest airports.

More than 350,000 tonnes of air cargo move through its computerized air freight system each year. This includes, in terms of value, some 25 percent of all Hong Kong's exports.

HONG KONG'S DOMESTIC EXPORTS

Percentage of total domestic exports 1986

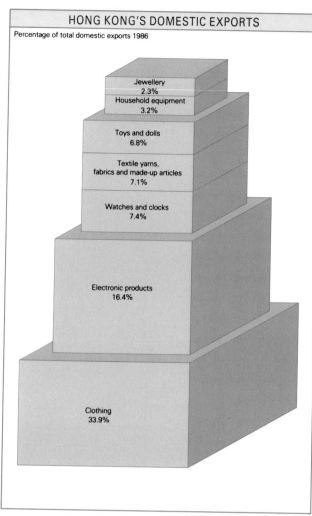

Jewellery 2.3%
Household equipment 3.2%
Toys and dolls 6.8%
Textile yarns, fabrics and made-up articles 7.1%
Watches and clocks 7.4%
Electronic products 16.4%
Clothing 33.9%

Textiles account for some 40 percent of Hong Kong's domestic exports. In 1986 the total value of these was about US $18 billion.

Re-exports—goods imported by Hong Kong and exported again— were worth a further US $16 billion.

HONG KONG'S MAJOR MARKETS

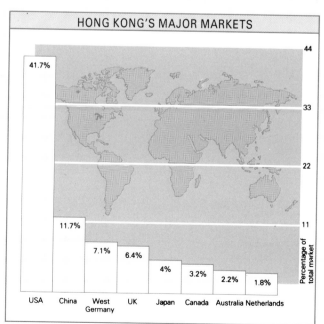

41.7%	11.7%	7.1%	6.4%	4%	3.2%	2.2%	1.8%
USA	China	West Germany	UK	Japan	Canada	Australia	Netherlands

Percentage of total market: 44, 33, 22, 11

Western countries are the biggest buyers of Hong Kong's products. In 1986, for example, the USA, UK

and West Germany alone accounted for more than half of the total market.

THE GOVERNMENT ROLE IN THE ECONOMY

Industry, finance, commerce and tourism are the 4 pillars of the Territory's economy; and free enterprise its apparent hallmark. But the hand of the government is highly evident in the current infrastructure.

A major item of government expenditure is the public housing in which 49 percent of the population lives. Other large-scale government-backed engineering development schemes include roads, airports, tunnels, waterworks, under- and overground railways and site

preparations. Taken together, public capital works consume about 25 percent of Hong Kong's budget.

The cost of education is shared with the private sector, but government participation has become greater over the years. Children receive 9 years' free and compulsory education up to the age of 15.

The government has set up semi-autonomous bodies to promote tourism and trade. The duty-free policy on all goods bar liquor, tobacco, hydro-carbon oils, cosmetics, methylalcohol,

and non-alcoholic beverages has made Hong Kong a jet-set shopper's paradise. Its range of products includes items—often electronic goods—making their first appearance on world markets.

The mixture of government and free enterprise has been beneficial. Hong Kong has low income tax and a low rate of unemployment.

Altogether, the Territory of Hong Kong has prospered and its people now enjoy one of the highest standards of living in Asia.

THE JOINT DECLARATION

In 1997, Britain's lease on the New Territories runs out. In 1982, with just 15 years' lease to run, Britain and China embarked on long negotiations on Hong Kong's future, resulting in the Sino-British Joint Declaration, which was signed in December 1984 and ratified in May 1985.

When the New Territories, as well as Hong Kong and Kowloon, return to Chinese sovereignty, Britain's role will come to an end, but China has pledged that the Territory will retain a high

degree of autonomy. With the status of Special Administrative Region, Hong Kong can maintain its capitalist system and lifestyle for 50 years after 1997.

The Joint Declaration has been hailed by many as a triumph of reason, a model exercise in diplomacy, an agreement which is acceptable to both sides and yet does not sacrifice the interests of the people of Hong Kong whose future is at stake. This judgment is not unfair, but in the end, it will be the people of Hong

Kong who will make a success or failure of the historic accord.

In 1987 it was clear that many Hong Kong citizens, with either the skills or the money to make them attractive immigrants, were acquiring foreign passports, notably for Canada. The brain and finance drain this portends could be disastrous for Hong Kong—and for China.

INTERNATIONAL FINANCIAL ROLE

Hong Kong's geographical position has also contributed to its becoming a major international financial centre. This, and the fact that it offers a free money and foreign exchange market.

Banks, pension funds, insurance companies and money brokers abound. In recent years, the Stock Exchange, and the Gold and Silver Exchanges, have all been extremely active.

MACAO

The peninsula and two small islands which comprise Macao have been in Portuguese hands for 430 years. The population, which probably numbers about 500,000, includes some 10,000 people of Portuguese descent, but the majority, at least 97 percent, are Chinese.

With no deepwater harbour and no airport, Macao depends heavily on tourism, much of it generated by the casinos which operate legally there. Its own market is so small that 90 percent of Macao's production is exported.

In 1987 the Portuguese

and Chinese governments reached agreement on Macao's future in much the same terms as the Sino-British Joint Declaration. The handover to Chinese rule is set for December 20, 1999.

Guangzhou

Zhuhai
Macao

SEE ALSO PAGES 82–85

CHINA'S FUTURE

REGIONAL DIVISIONS IN FUTURE STRATEGIES

Eastern Coastal

Central

Western

Economic policies for the future divide China into three main regions. Each of the three will have its own strategies and targets.

THE REFORM PROGRAMME

Continued—and more radical—economic reforms are necessary if China's ambitious economic goals for the 21st century are to be attained.

Some, such as the trend away from state enterprise to allow more private ownership, will be contentious. An inevitable result of such changes will be growing inequality between both individuals and regions. But the extent of that inequality will still be less marked than in most Third World countries.

In this changing economy middle-level government and Communist party officials will lose influence in favour of managers and professionals. Thus, while most people will ultimately benefit from reforms, many who wield power will not, and may oppose the programme as a whole.

If, however, the present direction of reform is effective and not blocked by political opposition, China will move away from a state-controlled, planned economy, in which decisions are made primarily by government, toward a market system, with many decisions made by competing economic units. This will still be a socialist not a capitalist economy—state and other forms of public and cooperative ownership will predominate.

REGIONAL DIFFERENCES

In the run-up to the 21st century, differences in prosperity between the various regions of China are likely to become more marked. Current economic strategies divide the country into three main areas: Eastern Coastal, Central and Western.

● EASTERN COASTAL REGION
While the prosperity of all regions should improve, this area will probably develop fastest and benefit most from current policies. It will have most contact with the rest of the world, expanding its exports and developing more sophisticated industries and services. However, it will also face serious problems of overcrowding, particularly in urban areas.

● CENTRAL REGION
The centre will be further developed as a base for the supply of energy, minerals and raw materials. It will also become increasingly important for the cultivation of grain and cash crops.

● WESTERN REGION
This region will focus on agriculture, including livestock and forestry, together with the exploitation of some energy and mineral resources. There are plans for improvements in transport links, both within the region and with other parts of the country.

The gap in prosperity between Eastern and Western China is likely to widen. In 1986 output per person in the Eastern region was 80 percent higher than in the Western, and there are no signs of that region catching up.

ECONOMIC GOALS

China's current priority is economic development. Her leaders have proposed a set of goals for economic growth to be attained by the middle of the 21st century. By then, they hope that China will be at least close to economic parity with the developed countries of the world.

There are 3 main stages to these goals:

● By 2000 to have reached a per capita gross national product of US $800 (in 1980 dollars), compared with the 1987 GNP of around US $300.

● By 2020 to have attained the level of "an intermediately developed country".

● By 2050 (approximately the 100th anniversary of the founding of the People's Republic of China) to have "come close to the level of economically developed countries".

Achieving these targets will require a consistent and fairly high economic growth rate of 5 to 7 percent a year. While ambitious, these goals are not impossible.

POLITICAL CHANGE

In the 1980s a new generation of political leaders emerged. The older generation had died or retired by the late 1980s, although some, notably Deng Xiaoping, retained significant power and influence in the background.

From the late 1980s onward there will be an increasing majority of Chinese who do not remember a pre-revolutionary past. And, since many of the leaders will have been raised since the 1949 revolution, current achievements rather than the once-essential revolutionary credentials will be the yardstick for political advancement.

There will be pressure for greater openness and democracy in government. Rising levels of education and political awareness will lead intellectuals and others to demand more freedom to contribute to, and criticize, government and party policies.

Within the Communist party, some argue that an increase in democracy is necessary to avoid a repetition of events such as the Cultural Revolution. They believe that a limited choice of candidates in elections will increase popular support for political leaders. But many others in the Communist party react against such challenges to their authority and privileges.

China's political leaders would like to maintain overall party control while allowing some reform and democratization of the political system. They are likely to seek this through greater separation of the Communist party and government organizations; at present they are virtually synonymous.

There may also be moves toward contested elections (more than one candidate per vacancy) and greater freedom of expression. However these changes will be kept within a single party system.

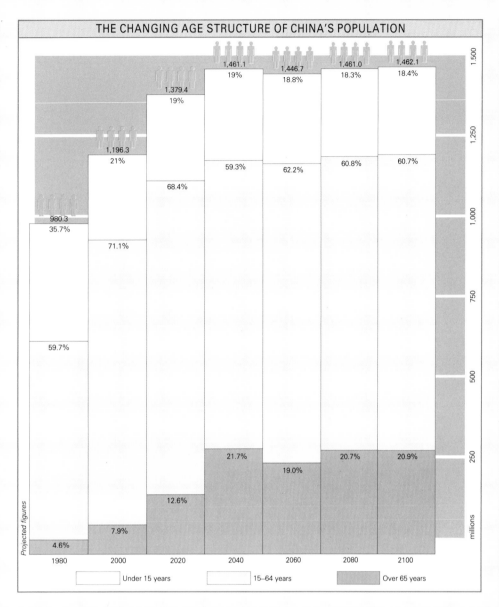

THE CHANGING AGE STRUCTURE OF CHINA'S POPULATION

Projected figures

Legend: Under 15 years | 15–64 years | Over 65 years

Projected population figures for the 21st century indicate not only growth but a marked change in age distribution. Here the percentage of each age group is shown as a proportion of the total population (indicated in millions at the head of each column). The figures suggest that by 2100 the proportion of over-65s will quadruple, while that of the under-15 age group will be almost halved.

SOCIAL CHANGE

As it moves into the 21st century China faces major social change.

Most of its population will have been raised since the revolution, and many in the relative prosperity of the years since the 1970s. Their expectations of prosperity will rise with the changing economy but may not be satisfied. The opening up of China to the world will fuel these rising expectations as the Chinese people become more aware of living conditions in other countries and in areas such as Hong Kong and Taiwan. Meeting these expectations will be a major economic challenge; failing to meet them could lead to dissatisfaction and perhaps significant social upheaval.

The one-child family policy in operation since 1984 means that China's population will contain an increasing proportion of over-60s—creating immense social and economic pressures.

Until about 2020, the creation of sufficient jobs will be a major concern; but subsequently the problem will focus rather on how to support a greatly increased retired population.

Because a significant proportion of the population will have been brought up as only children there are fears that this could also have a major psychological impact. Some anticipate that these only children may be more individualistic, and less willing to work collectively, and may thus undermine the communist ideal.

THE MAPS OF CHINA: INDEX

The following index includes all place names on the maps of China (pages 14–35). The page number is followed by the map grid reference for each entry.

INDEX

ACKNOWLEDGMENTS

PICTURE CREDITS

l= left; r= right; t= top; c= centre; b= bottom

3 Jacky Yip/China Photo Library; 4*l* Gamma/Frank Spooner Pictures; 4*cl* Hiroji Kubota/Magnum Photos; 4*cr* Zefa Picture Library; 4*r* Hiroji Kubota/Magnum Photos; 7 Georg Gerster/ The John Hillelson Agency; 38/39 G & P Corrigan; 40/41 Peter Carmichael/Aspect Picture Library; 42/43 Shostal Associates; 44/45 Peter Carmichael/Aspect Picture Library; 46/47 Georg Gerster/The John Hillelson Agency; 48/49 Heather Angel; 50/51 Leo Meier/Weldon Trannies; 52/53 Jacky Yip/China Photo Library; 54/55 Kurt Scholz/Shostal Associates; 56/57 Dr C. Grey-Wilson; 58*t* Kenneth W. Fink/ Ardea; 58*b* Hiroji Kubota/Magnum/The John Hillelson Agency; 59 Keith & Liz Laidler/Ardea; 60 Martin Williams; 61 Paul van Riel/Robert Harding Picture Library; 62 G & P Corrigan; 62/63 Manley Features-Tucson/Shostal Associates; 63 Gamma/Frank Spooner Pictures; 65 G & P Corrigan; 66/ 67 E.T. Archive; 67 Robert Harding Picture Library; 69 The Mansell Collection; 70 Freer Gallery of Art, Smithsonian Institution/E.T. Archive; 71 Bibliotheque Nationale, Paris/E.T. Archive; 73 The MacQuitty Collection; 74*t* Derek Bayes/ Aspect Picture Library; 74*b* BBC Michael Holford; 75 by permission of the Syndics of Cambridge University Library; 76 from Joseph Needham in *Science and Civilisation in China* vol IV part II, Cambridge University Press 1965; 77*l* from a paper by A.W. Sleeswyk and N. Sivin in *Chinese Science* vol VI November 1983; 77*tr* reconstruction of tower by John Christiansen from Joseph Needham in *Science and Civilisation in China* vol IV Part II, Cambridge University Press 1965; 77*br* from Joseph Needham in *Science and Civilisation in China* vol IV Part II, Cambridge University Press 1965; 78/79 Tom Nebbia/Aspect Picture Library; 79 J.M. Charles/Rapho; 81 The Needham Research Institute; 82/83 E.T. Archive; 83 Mary Evans Picture Library; 85/86 The Mansell Collection; 87*l* The Mansell Collection; 87*r* Victoria & Albert Museum; 88 Popperfoto; 90*t* Adam Woolfitt/Susan Griggs Agency; 90*b* Marc Riboud/Magnum/The John Hillelson Agency; 90/91 Rene Burri/Magnum/The John Hillelson Agency; 92 Xinhua News Agency; 94/95 Paolo Koch/Vision International; 97 Wang Jingde/Xinhua News Agency; 98 Hiroji Kubota/ Magnum Photos; 99*tl* Paul Conklin/Colorific!; 99*tr* Peter Carmichael/Aspect Picture Library; 99*bl* Eve Arnold/The John Hillelson Agency; 99*br* Sarah Errington/Hutchison Library; 102/103 Peter Carmichael/Aspect Picture Library; 104 Sally & Richard Greenhill; 105 Michael Palmer; 106/107 Adam Woolfitt/Susan Griggs Agency; 107*t* Chris Fairclough Colour Library; 107*b* Sally & Richard Greenhill; 110 Sally & Richard Greenhill; 110/111 J.M. Charles/Rapho; 111 Alain le Garsmeur/Impact Photos; 114/115 Leo Meier/Weldon Trannies; 115 Shostal Associates; 118/119 Michael K. Nichols/Magnum/The John Hillelson Agency; 119*t* Sarah Errington/Hutchison Library; 119*b* Michael K. Nichols/ Magnum/The John Hillelson Agency; 122 G & P Corrigan/ Robert Harding Picture Library; 122/123 Wang/Sygma/The John Hillelson Agency; 124 Li Jin/Xinhua News Agency/ SACU; 126 J.M. Charles/Rapho; 126/127 Sally & Richard Greenhill; 130 Robert Harding Picture Library; 130/131 Laurie Lewis/Frank Spooner Pictures; 134 British Museum; 135 Percival David Foundation; 136*t* The Nelson-Atkins Museum of Art, Kansas City, Missouri (Nelson Fund); 136*b* Osaka Municipal Museum of Fine Arts; 137 Tokyo National Museum; 138/139 G & P Corrigan/Robert Harding Picture Library; 139*l* Freer Gallery of Art, Smithsonian Institution, Washington D.C.; 139*r* Fitzwilliam Museum/Michael Holford; 140 Derrick Withy/Times Newspapers; 141*l* The Metropolitan Museum of Art, Gift of Heber R. Bishop, 1902; 141*r* G & P Corrigan; 142*t* Museum of Fine Arts, Boston/BPCC/Aldus Archive; 142*b* Victoria & Albert Museum; 143 Victoria & Albert Museum/E.T. Archive; 144*l* Victoria & Albert Museum/Michael Holford; 144*r* Victoria & Albert Museum; 145 Michael Holford; 146/147 Zefa Picture Library; 149 G & P Corrigan; 150 Hiroji Kubota/Magnum Photos; 150/151 Paul Slattery; 154/155 Jacky Yip/China Photo Library; 158 Georg Gerster/The John Hillelson Agency; 158/159 Alain le Garsmeur/Impact Photos; 162 Sally & Richard Greenhill; 163 Hiroji Kubota/Magnum Photos; 166 Peter Carmichael/Aspect Picture Library; 166/167 Peter Charlesworth/Colorific!; 170/ 171 Sally & Richard Greenhill; 172 Financial Times; 174/ 175 Hiroji Kubota/Magnum/The John Hillelson Agency; 175*t* Robert Harding Picture Library; 175*b* Alain le Garsmeur/ Impact Photos; 178/179 Alain le Garsmeur/Impact Photos; 179 Gamma/Frank Spooner Pictures; 180*t* Zou Yi/SACU; 180*b* Zheng Zhensun/SACU; 181 Yang Wumin/Xinhua News Agency

The Publishers would like to thank the following people for their invaluable help in the making of this book: Mrs J. A. Beadle for the index; Bryan Ford for advice on statistics; Maggi McCormick for Americanizing the text; Amos Gelb and Louise Bostock for research; Roy Perrott for his contribution to the original plan of the book.

ROMANIZATION OF CHINESE NAMES

Some readers may be more familiar with the old (Wade-Giles) style of romanization than the modern Pinyin. The following list includes some of the most frequently used names in which the romanization differs in the two systems.

WADE-GILES	PINYIN
Mao Tse-tung	Mao Zedong

Provinces and Autonomous Regions

Anhwei	Anhui
Chekiang	Zhejiang
Fukien	Fujian
Heilungkiang	Heilongjiang
Honan	Henan
Hopeh	Hebei
Hupeh	Hubei
Kansu	Gansu
Kiangsi	Jiangxi
Kiangsu	Jiangsu
Kirin	Jilin
Kwangsi	Guangxi
Kwangtung	Guangdong
Kweichow	Guizhou
Ningsia	Ningxia
Shansi	Shanxi
Shantung	Shandong
Shensi	Shaanxi
Sinkiang	Xinjiang
Szechuan	Sichuan
Tsinghai	Qinghai

Towns and Cities

Amoy	Xiamen
Canton	Guangzhou
Chungking	Chongqing
Dairen	Dalian
Foochow	Fuzhou
Hangchow	Hangzhou
Hsining	Xining
Kweilin	Guilin
Nanking	Nanjing
Peking	Beijing
Shamchun	Shenzhen
Sian	Xi'an
Soochow	Suzhou
Tientsin	Tianjin
Tsingtao	Qingdao